CASANOVA

Luxuria

by MATT FRACTION & GABRIEL BÁ
Lettering by SEAN KONOT

IMAGE COMICS, INC.
Erik Larsen Publisher
Todd McFarlane President
Marc Silvestri CEO
Jim Valentino Vice-President
Eric Stephenson Executive Director
Mark Haven Britt Director of Marketing
Thao Le Accounts Manager
Rosemary Cao Accounting Assistant
Traci Hui Administrative Assistant
Joe Keatinge Traffic Manager
Allen Hui Production Manager
Jonathan Chan Production Artist
Drew Gill Production Artist
Chris Giarrusso Production Artist

www.imagecomics.com

CASANOVA: LUXURIA. First Printing. Published by Image Comics, Inc. Office of publication: 1942 University Avenue, Suite 305, Berkeley, California 94704. Originally published in single-magazine form as CASANOVA #1-7. PRINTED IN CANADA.

W.A.S.T.E and E.M.P.I.R.E. logos by Ben Radatz
Original issue design and book design by Laurenn McCubbin

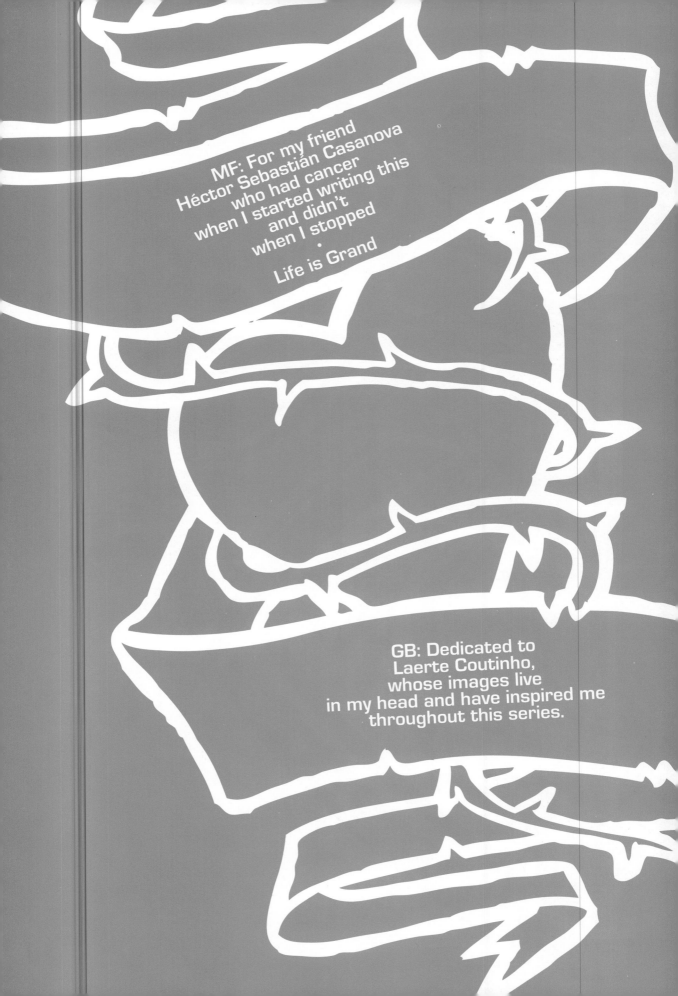

MF: For my friend
Héctor Sebastián Casanova
who had cancer
when I started writing this
and didn't
when I stopped
·
Life is Grand

GB: Dedicated to
Laerte Coutinho,
whose images live
in my head and have inspired me
throughout this series.

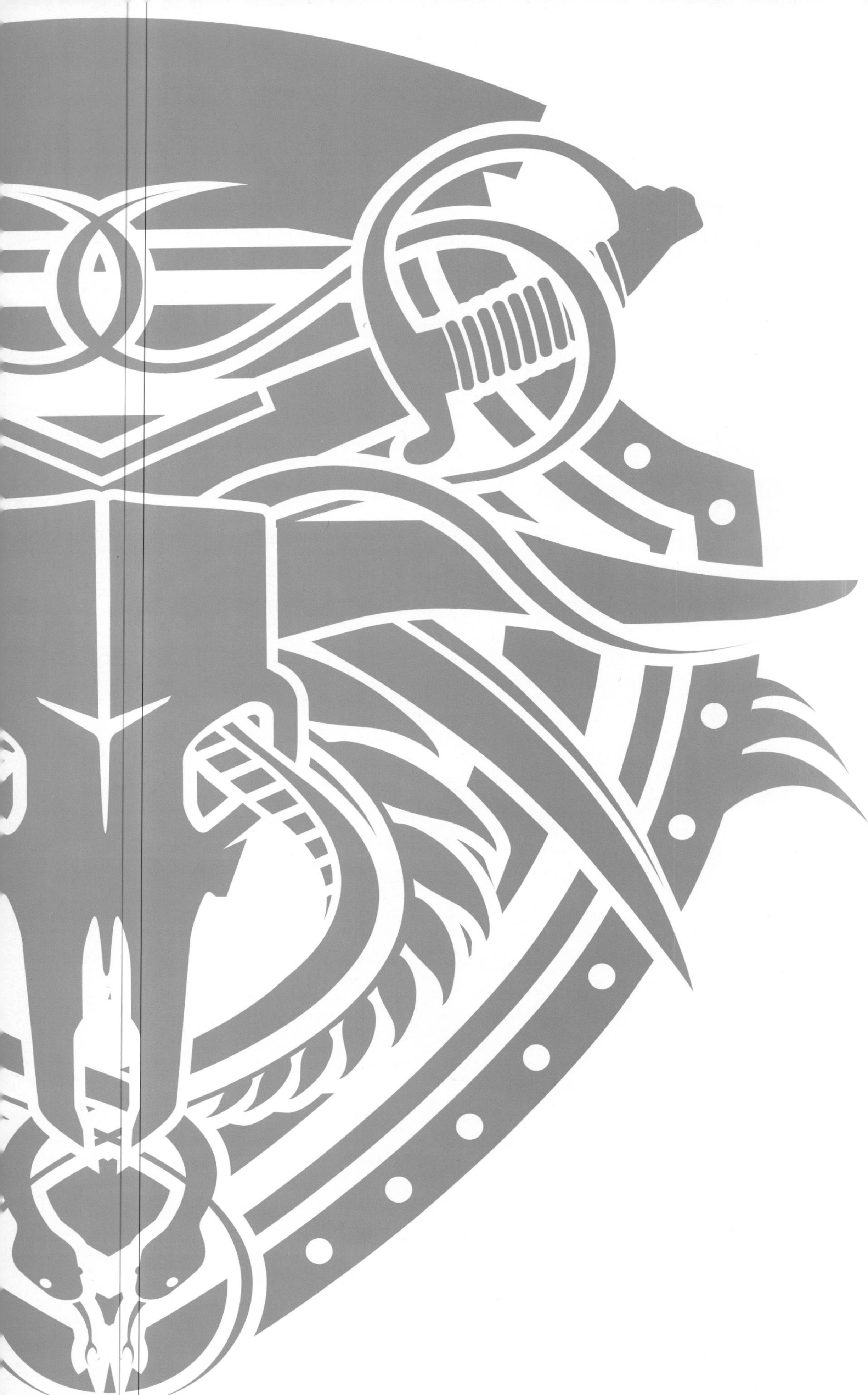

"Quantum mechanics
forbids a single history."

Thomas Hertog

"...My parents... don't worry in the
least about their own insignificance;
they don't give a damn about it...
While I... I feel only
boredom and anger."

Ivan Turgenev
FATHERS AND SONS (1862)

"Boys, Girls, Men, Women!
The World Is On FIRE
Serve the LORD
and You Can Have These Prizes!"

Ad on the back cover of
WEIRD SCIENCE-FANTASY #24,
June 1954

Chapter One
Execution Days

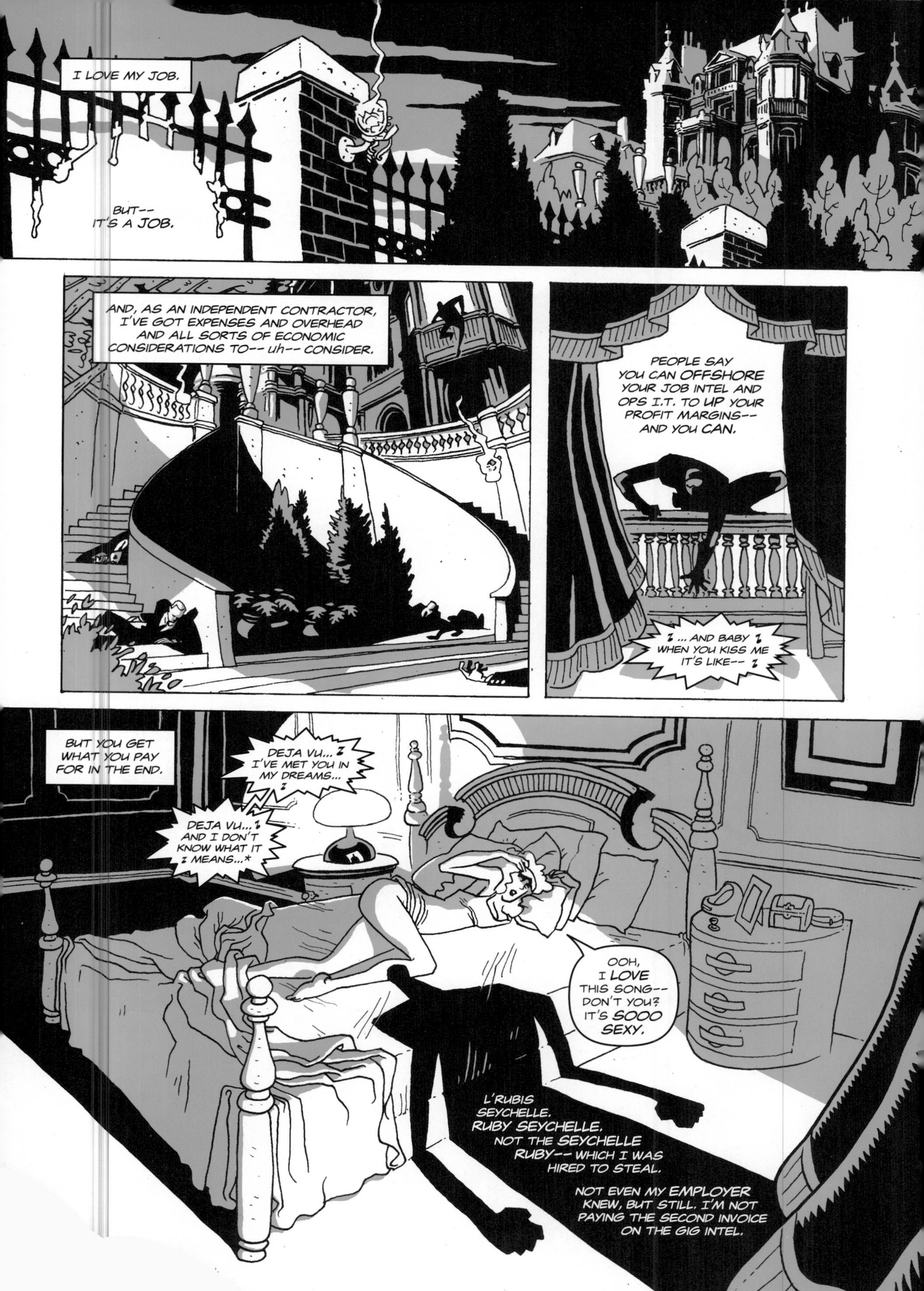
I LOVE MY JOB.
BUT-- IT'S A JOB.
AND, AS AN INDEPENDENT CONTRACTOR, I'VE GOT EXPENSES AND OVERHEAD AND ALL SORTS OF ECONOMIC CONSIDERATIONS TO-- uh-- CONSIDER.
PEOPLE SAY YOU CAN OFFSHORE YOUR JOB INTEL AND OPS I.T. TO UP YOUR PROFIT MARGINS-- AND YOU CAN.
♪ ...AND BABY ♪ WHEN YOU KISS ME IT'S LIKE-- ♪
BUT YOU GET WHAT YOU PAY FOR IN THE END.
DEJA VU... ♪ I'VE MET YOU IN MY DREAMS... ♪
DEJA VU... ♪ AND I DON'T KNOW WHAT IT ♪ MEANS...*
OOH, I LOVE THIS SONG-- DON'T YOU? IT'S SOOO SEXY.
L'RUBIS SEYCHELLE. RUBY SEYCHELLE. NOT THE SEYCHELLE RUBY-- WHICH I WAS HIRED TO STEAL.
NOT EVEN MY EMPLOYER KNEW, BUT STILL. I'M NOT PAYING THE SECOND INVOICE ON THE GIG INTEL.

*"DEJA VU," BY TEEN AGE MUSIC INTERNATIONAL, 'I.M.A.T.A.M.I.' SOMA RECORDS.

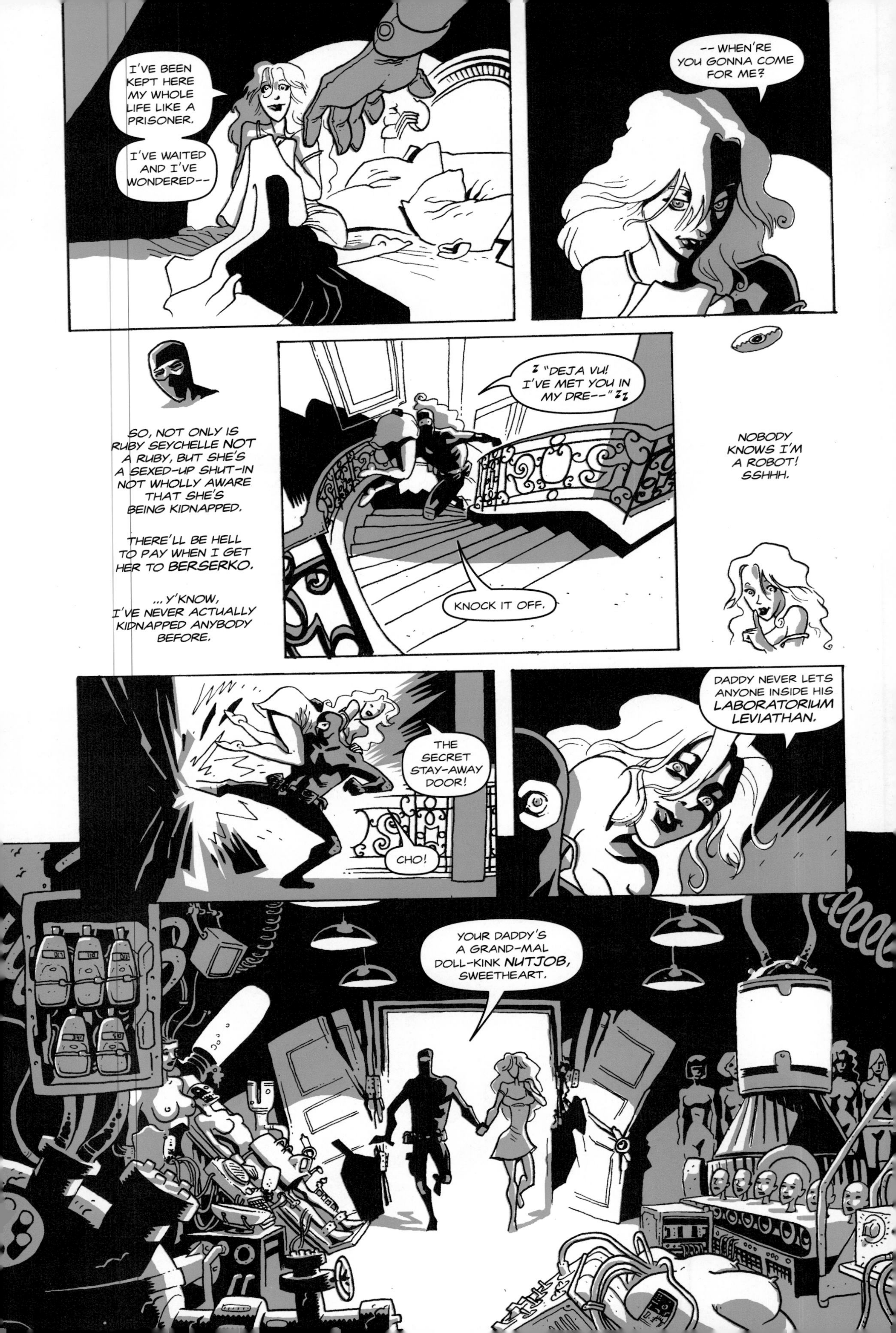
I'VE BEEN KEPT HERE MY WHOLE LIFE LIKE A PRISONER.
I'VE WAITED AND I'VE WONDERED--
--WHEN'RE YOU GONNA COME FOR ME?
SO, NOT ONLY IS RUBY SEYCHELLE NOT A RUBY, BUT SHE'S A SEXED-UP SHUT-IN NOT WHOLLY AWARE THAT SHE'S BEING KIDNAPPED.
THERE'LL BE HELL TO PAY WHEN I GET HER TO BERSERKO.
...Y'KNOW, I'VE NEVER ACTUALLY KIDNAPPED ANYBODY BEFORE.
"DEJA VU! I'VE MET YOU IN MY DRE--"
KNOCK IT OFF.
NOBODY KNOWS I'M A ROBOT! SSHHH.
THE SECRET STAY-AWAY DOOR!
CHO!
DADDY NEVER LETS ANYONE INSIDE HIS LABORATORIUM LEVIATHAN.
YOUR DADDY'S A GRAND-MAL DOLL-KINK NUTJOB, SWEETHEART.

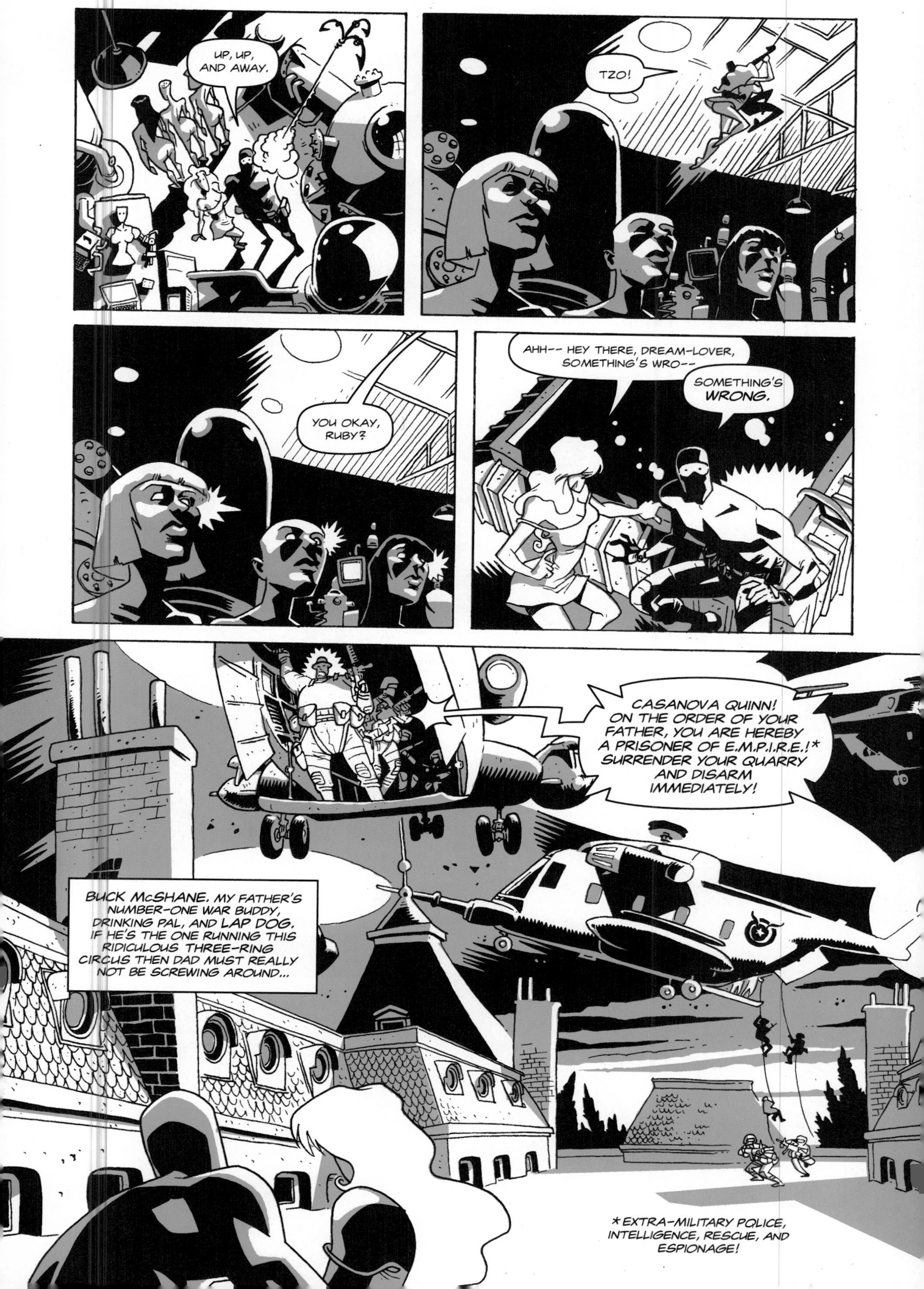
UP, UP, AND AWAY.
TZO!
YOU OKAY, RUBY?
AHH-- HEY THERE, DREAM-LOVER, SOMETHING'S WRO--
SOMETHING'S WRONG.
CASANOVA QUINN! ON THE ORDER OF YOUR FATHER, YOU ARE HEREBY A PRISONER OF E.M.P.I.R.E.!* SURRENDER YOUR QUARRY AND DISARM IMMEDIATELY!
BUCK McSHANE. MY FATHER'S NUMBER-ONE WAR BUDDY, DRINKING PAL, AND LAP DOG. IF HE'S THE ONE RUNNING THIS RIDICULOUS THREE-RING CIRCUS THEN DAD MUST REALLY NOT BE SCREWING AROUND...
*EXTRA-MILITARY POLICE, INTELLIGENCE, RESCUE, AND ESPIONAGE!

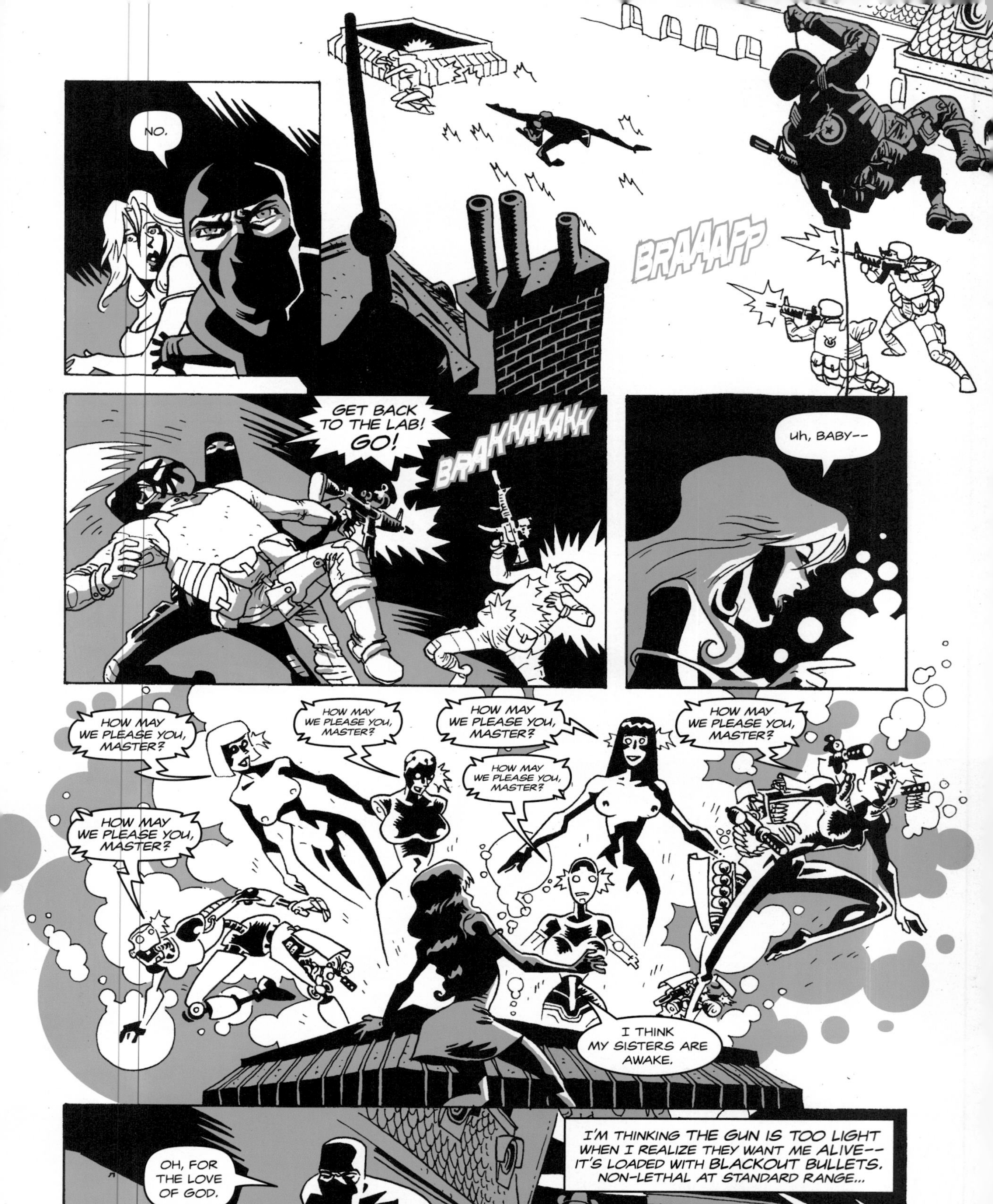
NO.
BRAAAPP
GET BACK TO THE LAB! GO!
BRAKKAKAKK
uh, BABY--
HOW MAY WE PLEASE YOU, MASTER?
HOW MAY WE PLEASE YOU, MASTER?
HOW MAY WE PLEASE YOU, MASTER?
HOW MAY WE PLEASE YOU, MASTER?
HOW MAY WE PLEASE YOU, MASTER?
HOW MAY WE PLEASE YOU, MASTER?
I THINK MY SISTERS ARE AWAKE.
OH, FOR THE LOVE OF GOD.
I'M THINKING THE GUN IS TOO LIGHT WHEN I REALIZE THEY WANT ME ALIVE-- IT'S LOADED WITH BLACKOUT BULLETS. NON-LETHAL AT STANDARD RANGE...
BRAKKAKAKK
BRAAAPP

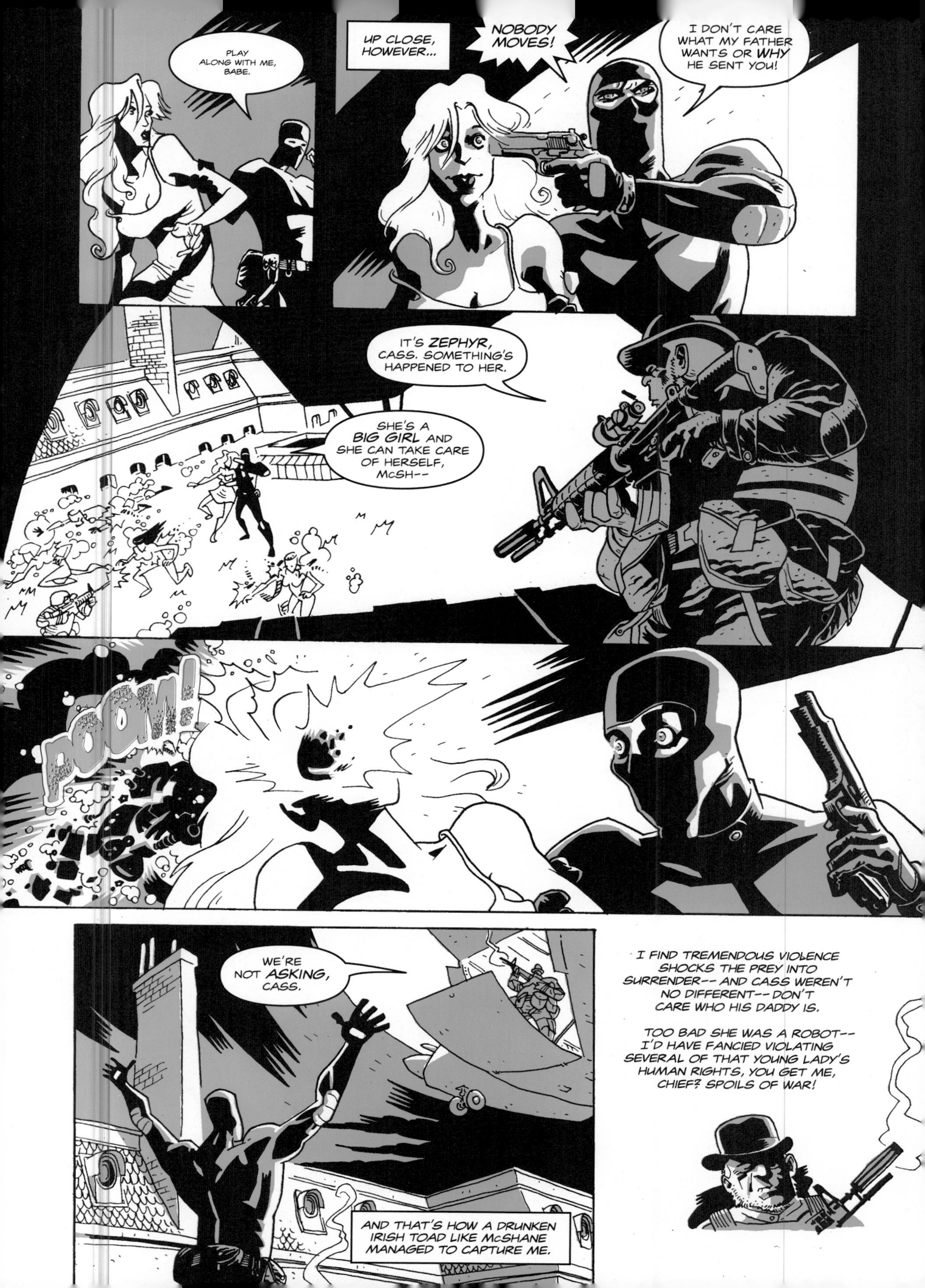

PLAY ALONG WITH ME, BABE.
UP CLOSE, HOWEVER...
NOBODY MOVES!
I DON'T CARE WHAT MY FATHER WANTS OR WHY HE SENT YOU!
IT'S ZEPHYR, CASS. SOMETHING'S HAPPENED TO HER.
SHE'S A BIG GIRL AND SHE CAN TAKE CARE OF HERSELF, McSH--
POOM!
WE'RE NOT ASKING, CASS.
AND THAT'S HOW A DRUNKEN IRISH TOAD LIKE McSHANE MANAGED TO CAPTURE ME.
I FIND TREMENDOUS VIOLENCE SHOCKS THE PREY INTO SURRENDER-- AND CASS WEREN'T NO DIFFERENT-- DON'T CARE WHO HIS DADDY IS.
TOO BAD SHE WAS A ROBOT-- I'D HAVE FANCIED VIOLATING SEVERAL OF THAT YOUNG LADY'S HUMAN RIGHTS, YOU GET ME, CHIEF? SPOILS OF WAR!

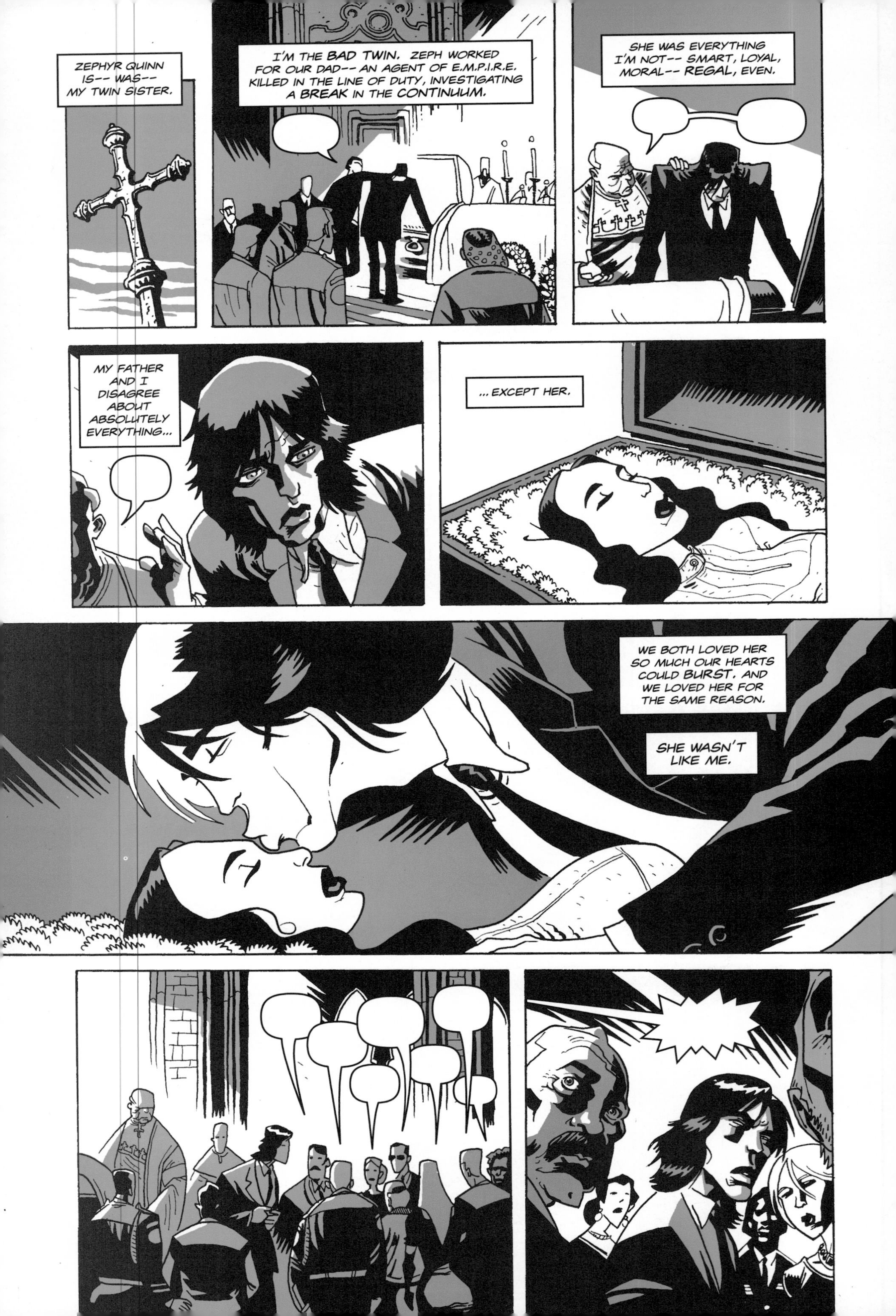
ZEPHYR QUINN IS-- WAS-- MY TWIN SISTER.
I'M THE BAD TWIN. ZEPH WORKED FOR OUR DAD-- AN AGENT OF E.M.P.I.R.E. KILLED IN THE LINE OF DUTY, INVESTIGATING A BREAK IN THE CONTINUUM.
SHE WAS EVERYTHING I'M NOT-- SMART, LOYAL, MORAL-- REGAL, EVEN.
MY FATHER AND I DISAGREE ABOUT ABSOLUTELY EVERYTHING...
...EXCEPT HER.
WE BOTH LOVED HER SO MUCH OUR HEARTS COULD BURST. AND WE LOVED HER FOR THE SAME REASON.
SHE WASN'T LIKE ME.

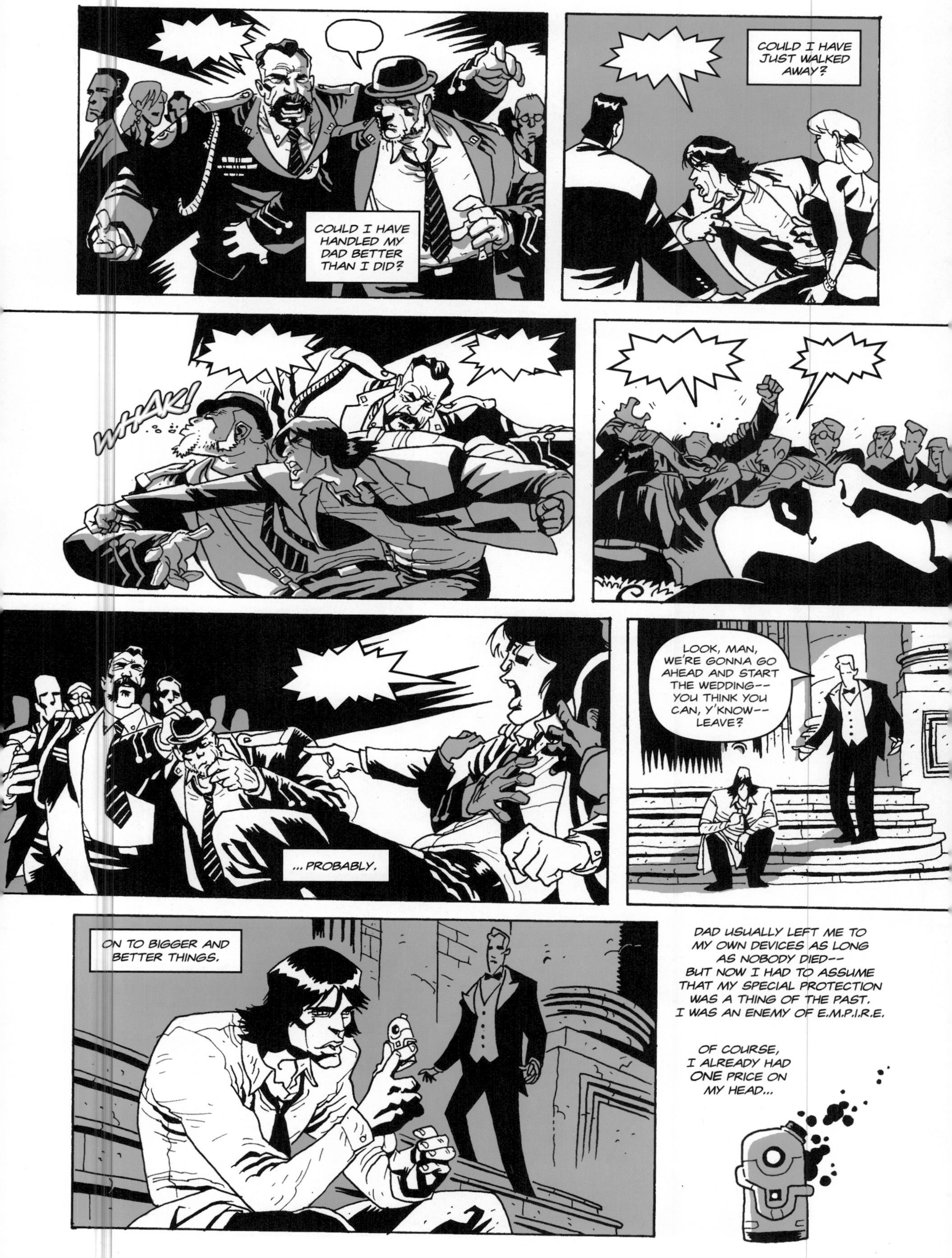
COULD I HAVE HANDLED MY DAD BETTER THAN I DID?
COULD I HAVE JUST WALKED AWAY?
WHAK!
...PROBABLY.
LOOK, MAN, WE'RE GONNA GO AHEAD AND START THE WEDDING-- YOU THINK YOU CAN, Y'KNOW-- LEAVE?
ON TO BIGGER AND BETTER THINGS.
DAD USUALLY LEFT ME TO MY OWN DEVICES AS LONG AS NOBODY DIED-- BUT NOW I HAD TO ASSUME THAT MY SPECIAL PROTECTION WAS A THING OF THE PAST. I WAS AN ENEMY OF E.M.P.I.R.E.
OF COURSE, I ALREADY HAD ONE PRICE ON MY HEAD...

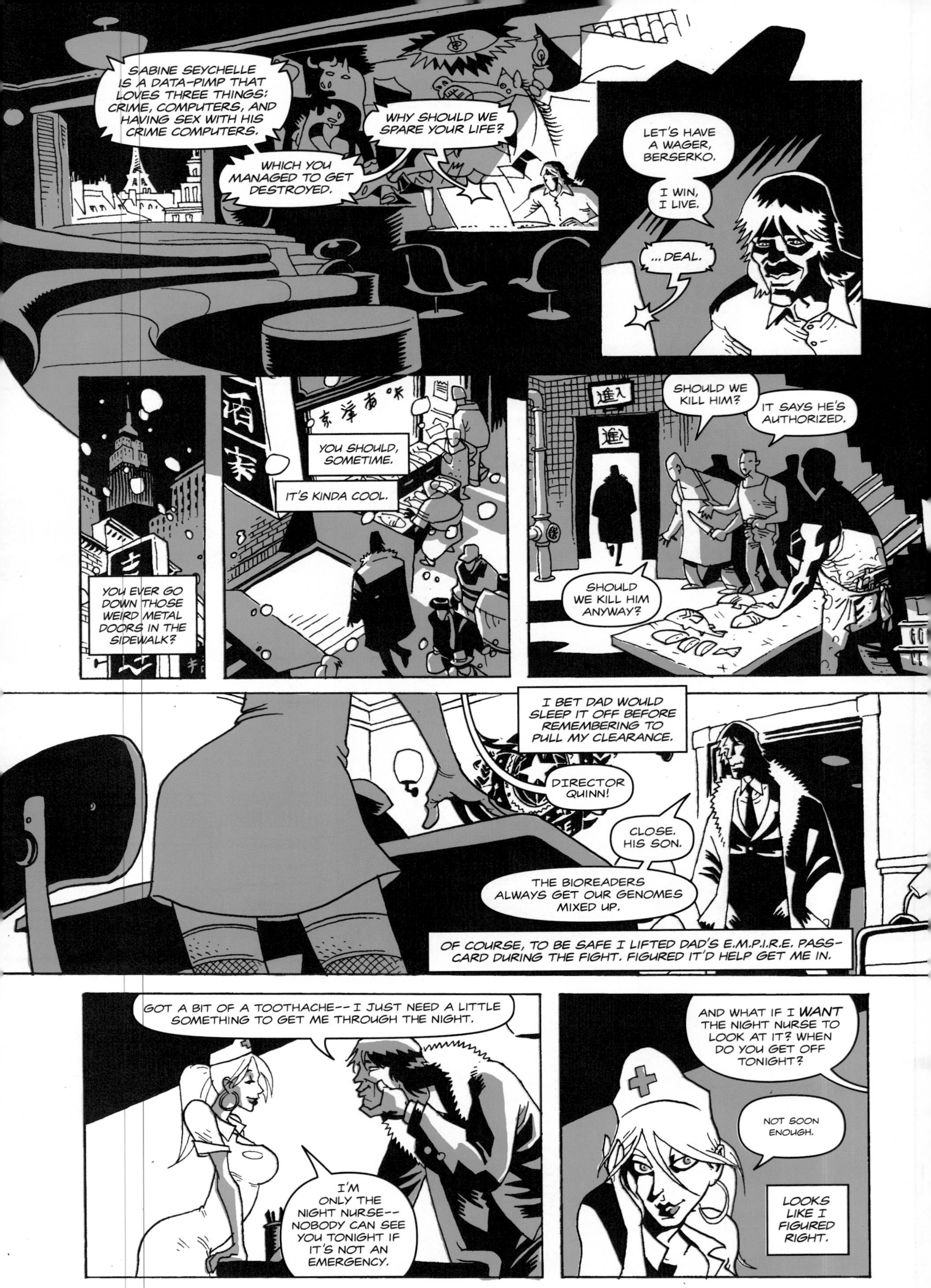

SABINE SEYCHELLE IS A DATA-PIMP THAT LOVES THREE THINGS: CRIME, COMPUTERS, AND HAVING SEX WITH HIS CRIME COMPUTERS.
WHICH YOU MANAGED TO GET DESTROYED.
WHY SHOULD WE SPARE YOUR LIFE?
LET'S HAVE A WAGER, BERSERKO.
I WIN, I LIVE.
...DEAL.
YOU EVER GO DOWN THOSE WEIRD METAL DOORS IN THE SIDEWALK?
YOU SHOULD, SOMETIME.
IT'S KINDA COOL.
SHOULD WE KILL HIM?
IT SAYS HE'S AUTHORIZED.
SHOULD WE KILL HIM ANYWAY?
I BET DAD WOULD SLEEP IT OFF BEFORE REMEMBERING TO PULL MY CLEARANCE.
DIRECTOR QUINN!
CLOSE. HIS SON.
THE BIOREADERS ALWAYS GET OUR GENOMES MIXED UP.
OF COURSE, TO BE SAFE I LIFTED DAD'S E.M.P.I.R.E. PASS-CARD DURING THE FIGHT. FIGURED IT'D HELP GET ME IN.
GOT A BIT OF A TOOTHACHE-- I JUST NEED A LITTLE SOMETHING TO GET ME THROUGH THE NIGHT.
I'M ONLY THE NIGHT NURSE-- NOBODY CAN SEE YOU TONIGHT IF IT'S NOT AN EMERGENCY.
AND WHAT IF I WANT THE NIGHT NURSE TO LOOK AT IT? WHEN DO YOU GET OFF TONIGHT?
NOT SOON ENOUGH.
LOOKS LIKE I FIGURED RIGHT.

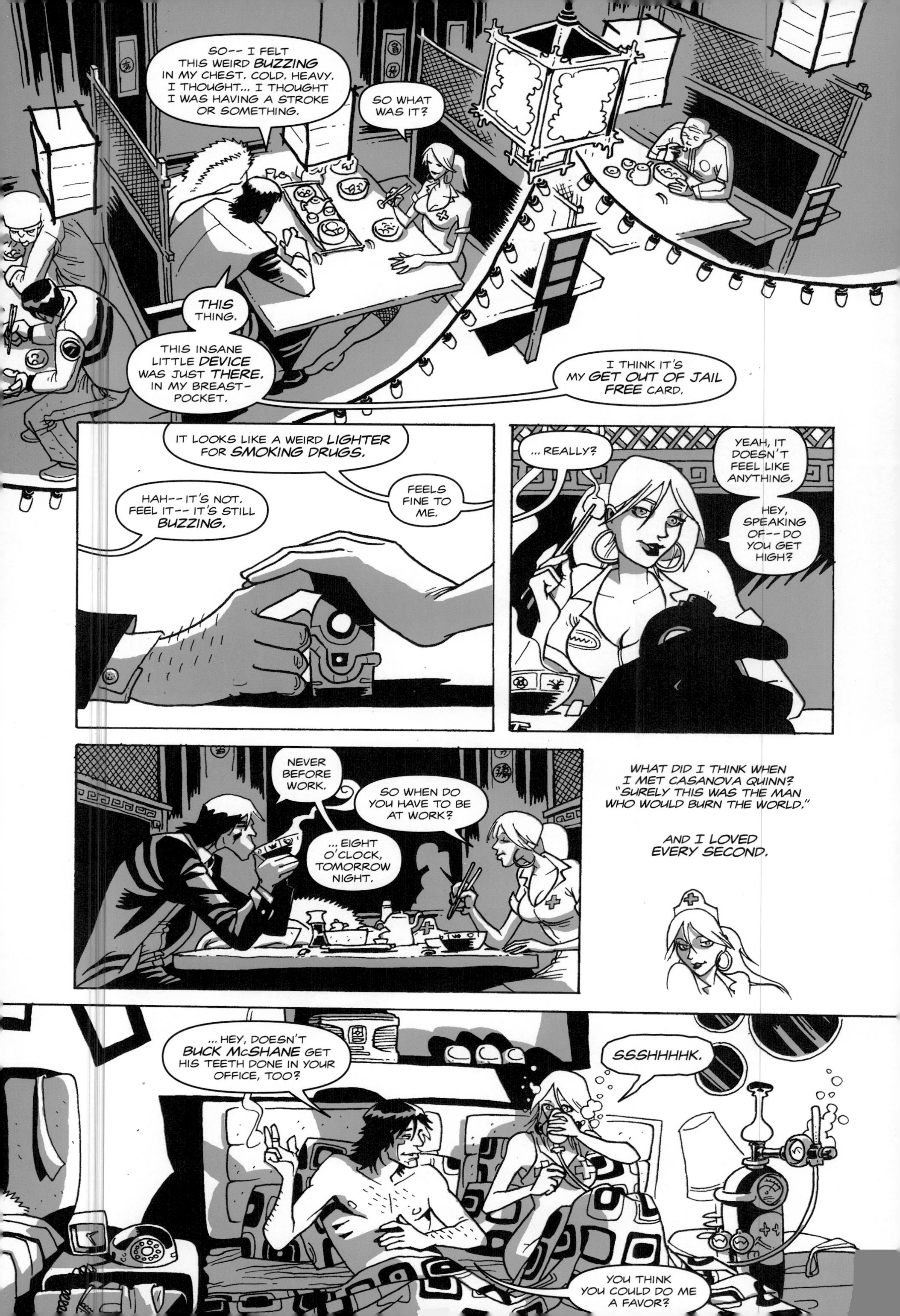
SO-- I FELT THIS WEIRD BUZZING IN MY CHEST. COLD. HEAVY. I THOUGHT... I THOUGHT I WAS HAVING A STROKE OR SOMETHING.
SO WHAT WAS IT?
THIS THING.
THIS INSANE LITTLE DEVICE WAS JUST THERE. IN MY BREAST-POCKET.
I THINK IT'S MY GET OUT OF JAIL FREE CARD.
IT LOOKS LIKE A WEIRD LIGHTER FOR SMOKING DRUGS.
HAH-- IT'S NOT. FEEL IT-- IT'S STILL BUZZING.
FEELS FINE TO ME.
...REALLY?
YEAH, IT DOESN'T FEEL LIKE ANYTHING.
HEY, SPEAKING OF--DO YOU GET HIGH?
NEVER BEFORE WORK.
SO WHEN DO YOU HAVE TO BE AT WORK?
...EIGHT O'CLOCK, TOMORROW NIGHT.
WHAT DID I THINK WHEN I MET CASANOVA QUINN? "SURELY THIS WAS THE MAN WHO WOULD BURN THE WORLD."
AND I LOVED EVERY SECOND.
...HEY, DOESN'T BUCK McSHANE GET HIS TEETH DONE IN YOUR OFFICE, TOO?
SSSHHHHK.
YOU THINK YOU COULD DO ME A FAVOR?

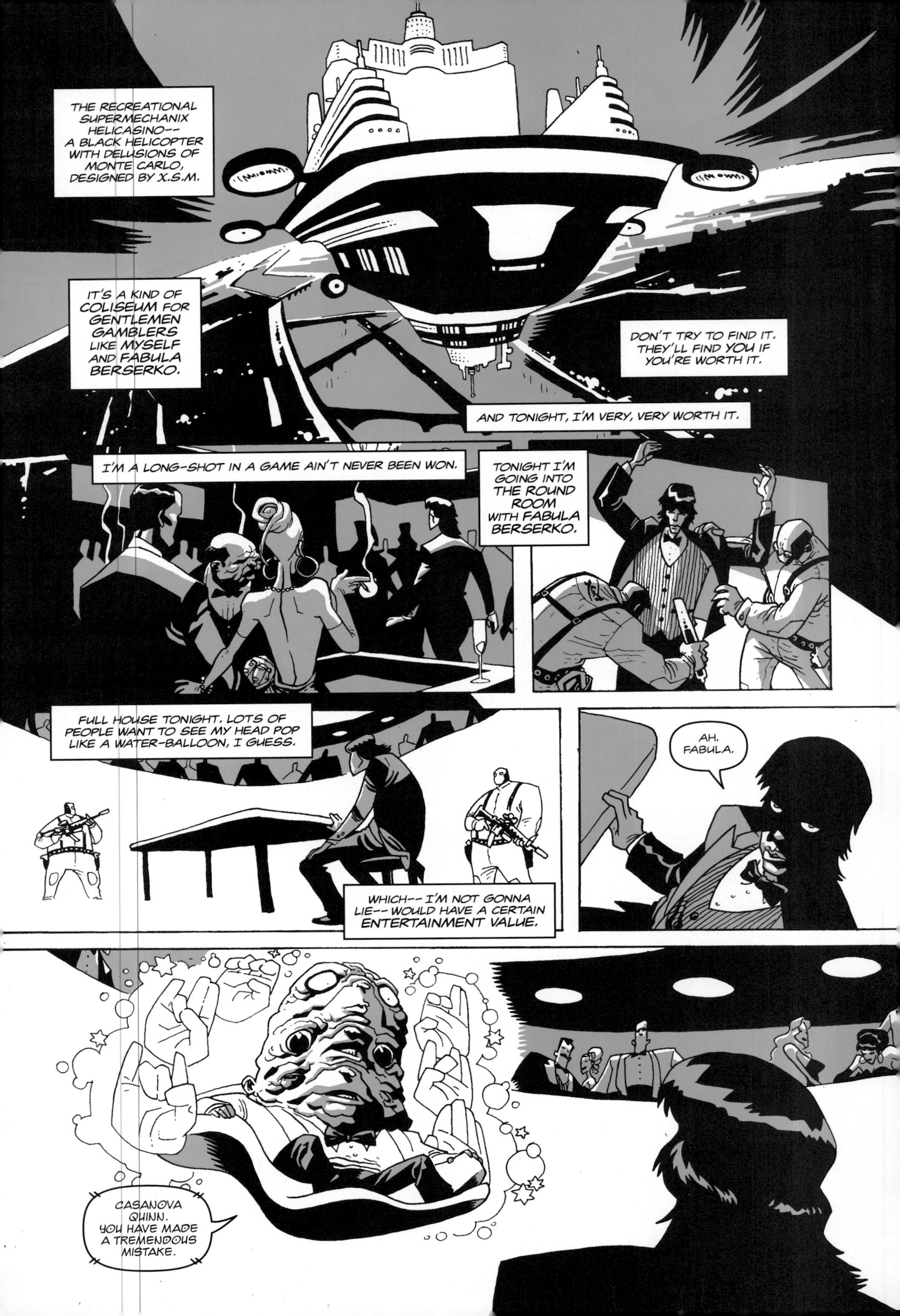
THE RECREATIONAL SUPERMECHANIX HELICASINO-- A BLACK HELICOPTER WITH DELUSIONS OF MONTE CARLO, DESIGNED BY X.S.M.
IT'S A KIND OF COLISEUM FOR GENTLEMEN GAMBLERS LIKE MYSELF AND FABULA BERSERKO.
DON'T TRY TO FIND IT. THEY'LL FIND YOU IF YOU'RE WORTH IT.
AND TONIGHT, I'M VERY, VERY WORTH IT.
I'M A LONG-SHOT IN A GAME AIN'T NEVER BEEN WON.
TONIGHT I'M GOING INTO THE ROUND ROOM WITH FABULA BERSERKO.
FULL HOUSE TONIGHT. LOTS OF PEOPLE WANT TO SEE MY HEAD POP LIKE A WATER-BALLOON, I GUESS.
WHICH-- I'M NOT GONNA LIE-- WOULD HAVE A CERTAIN ENTERTAINMENT VALUE.
AH. FABULA.
CASANOVA QUINN. YOU HAVE MADE A TREMENDOUS MISTAKE.

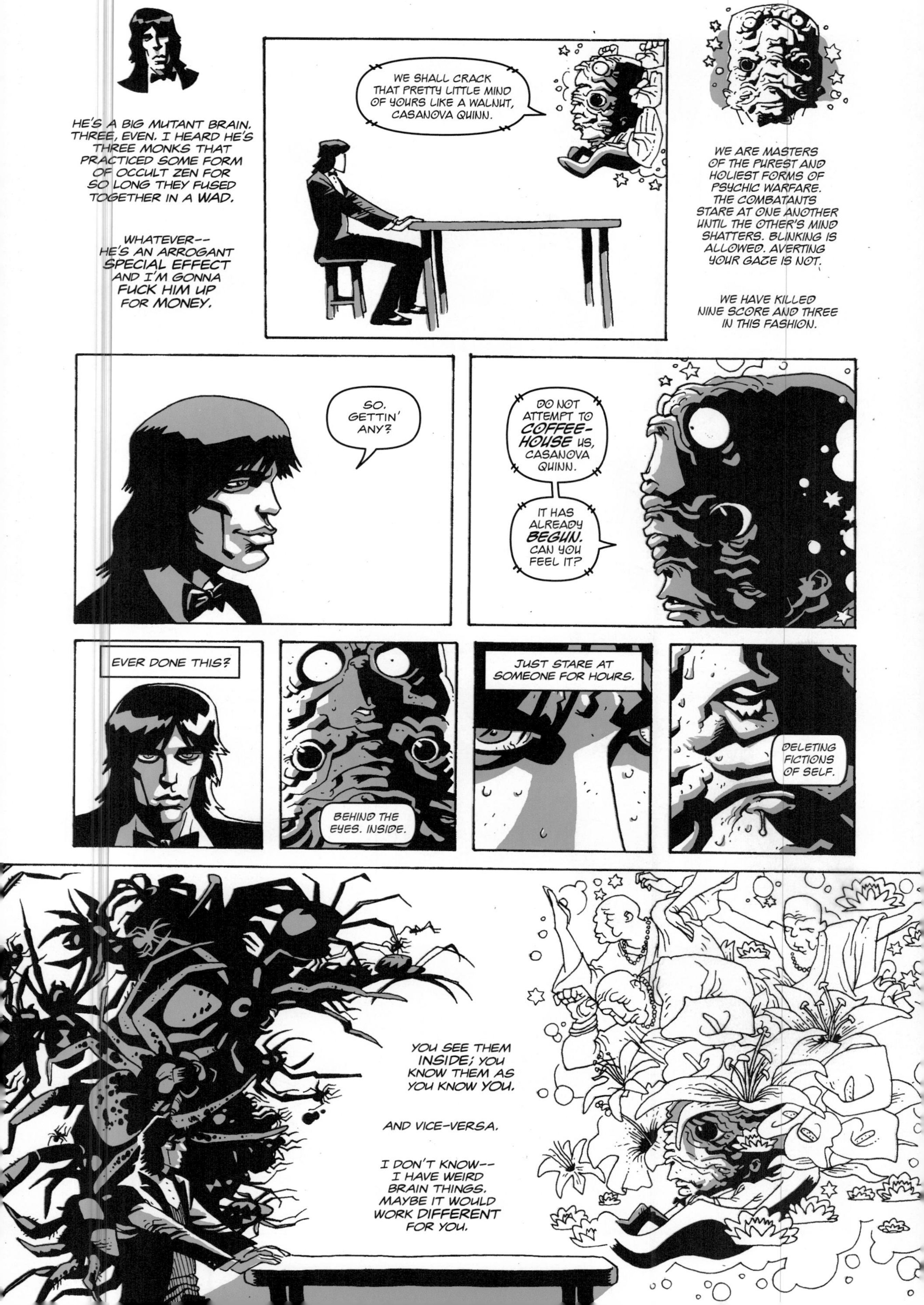
HE'S A BIG MUTANT BRAIN. THREE, EVEN. I HEARD HE'S THREE MONKS THAT PRACTICED SOME FORM OF OCCULT ZEN FOR SO LONG THEY FUSED TOGETHER IN A WAD.
WHATEVER-- HE'S AN ARROGANT SPECIAL EFFECT AND I'M GONNA FUCK HIM UP FOR MONEY.
WE SHALL CRACK THAT PRETTY LITTLE MIND OF YOURS LIKE A WALNUT, CASANOVA QUINN.
WE ARE MASTERS OF THE PUREST AND HOLIEST FORMS OF PSYCHIC WARFARE. THE COMBATANTS STARE AT ONE ANOTHER UNTIL THE OTHER'S MIND SHATTERS. BLINKING IS ALLOWED. AVERTING YOUR GAZE IS NOT.
WE HAVE KILLED NINE SCORE AND THREE IN THIS FASHION.
SO. GETTIN' ANY?
DO NOT ATTEMPT TO COFFEE-HOUSE US, CASANOVA QUINN.
IT HAS ALREADY BEGUN. CAN YOU FEEL IT?
EVER DONE THIS?
BEHIND THE EYES. INSIDE.
JUST STARE AT SOMEONE FOR HOURS.
DELETING FICTIONS OF SELF.
YOU SEE THEM INSIDE; YOU KNOW THEM AS YOU KNOW YOU.
AND VICE-VERSA.
I DON'T KNOW-- I HAVE WEIRD BRAIN THINGS. MAYBE IT WOULD WORK DIFFERENT FOR YOU.

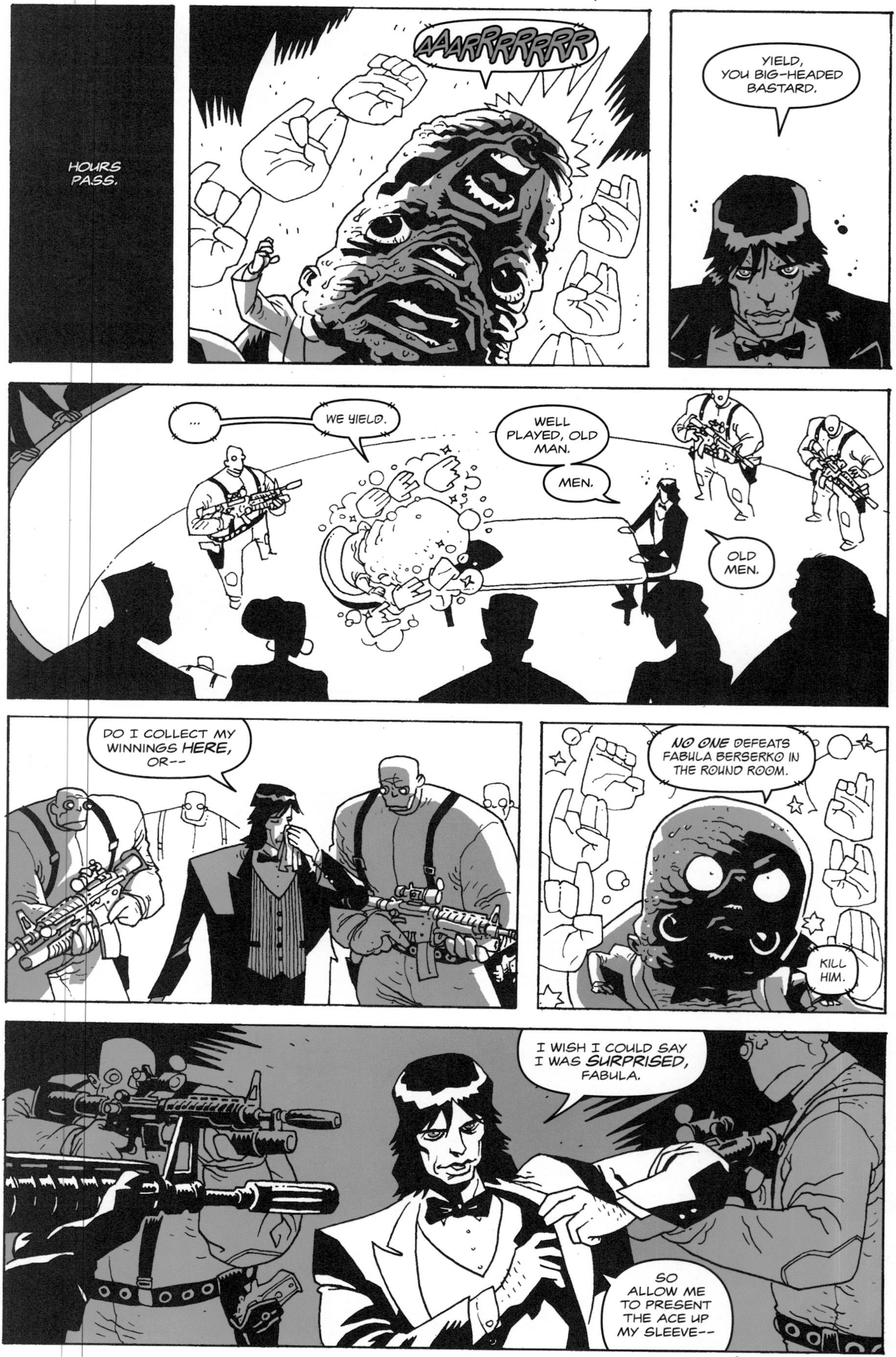
HOURS PASS.
AAARRRRRRR
YIELD, YOU BIG-HEADED BASTARD.
...
WE YIELD.
WELL PLAYED, OLD MAN.
MEN.
OLD MEN.
DO I COLLECT MY WINNINGS HERE, OR--
NO ONE DEFEATS FABULA BERSERKO IN THE ROUND ROOM.
KILL HIM.
I WISH I COULD SAY I WAS SURPRISED, FABULA.
SO ALLOW ME TO PRESENT THE ACE UP MY SLEEVE--

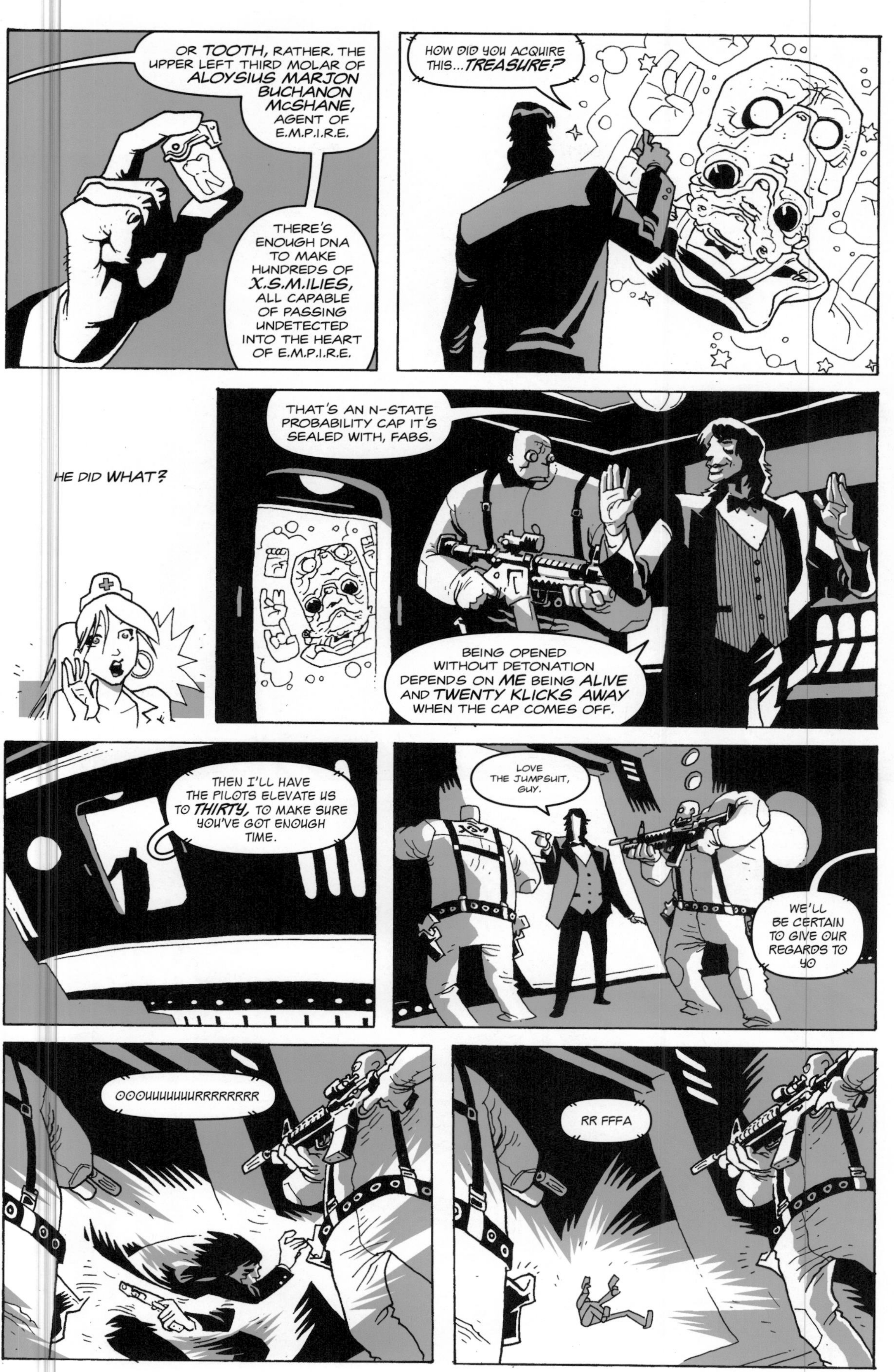
OR TOOTH, RATHER. THE UPPER LEFT THIRD MOLAR OF ALOYSIUS MARJON BUCHANON McSHANE, AGENT OF E.M.P.I.R.E.
THERE'S ENOUGH DNA TO MAKE HUNDREDS OF X.S.M.ILIES, ALL CAPABLE OF PASSING UNDETECTED INTO THE HEART OF E.M.P.I.R.E.
HOW DID YOU ACQUIRE THIS...TREASURE?
HE DID WHAT?
THAT'S AN N-STATE PROBABILITY CAP IT'S SEALED WITH, FABS.
BEING OPENED WITHOUT DETONATION DEPENDS ON ME BEING ALIVE AND TWENTY KLICKS AWAY WHEN THE CAP COMES OFF.
THEN I'LL HAVE THE PILOTS ELEVATE US TO THIRTY, TO MAKE SURE YOU'VE GOT ENOUGH TIME.
LOVE THE JUMPSUIT, GUY.
WE'LL BE CERTAIN TO GIVE OUR REGARDS TO YO
OOOUUUUUUURRRRRRRR
RR FFFA

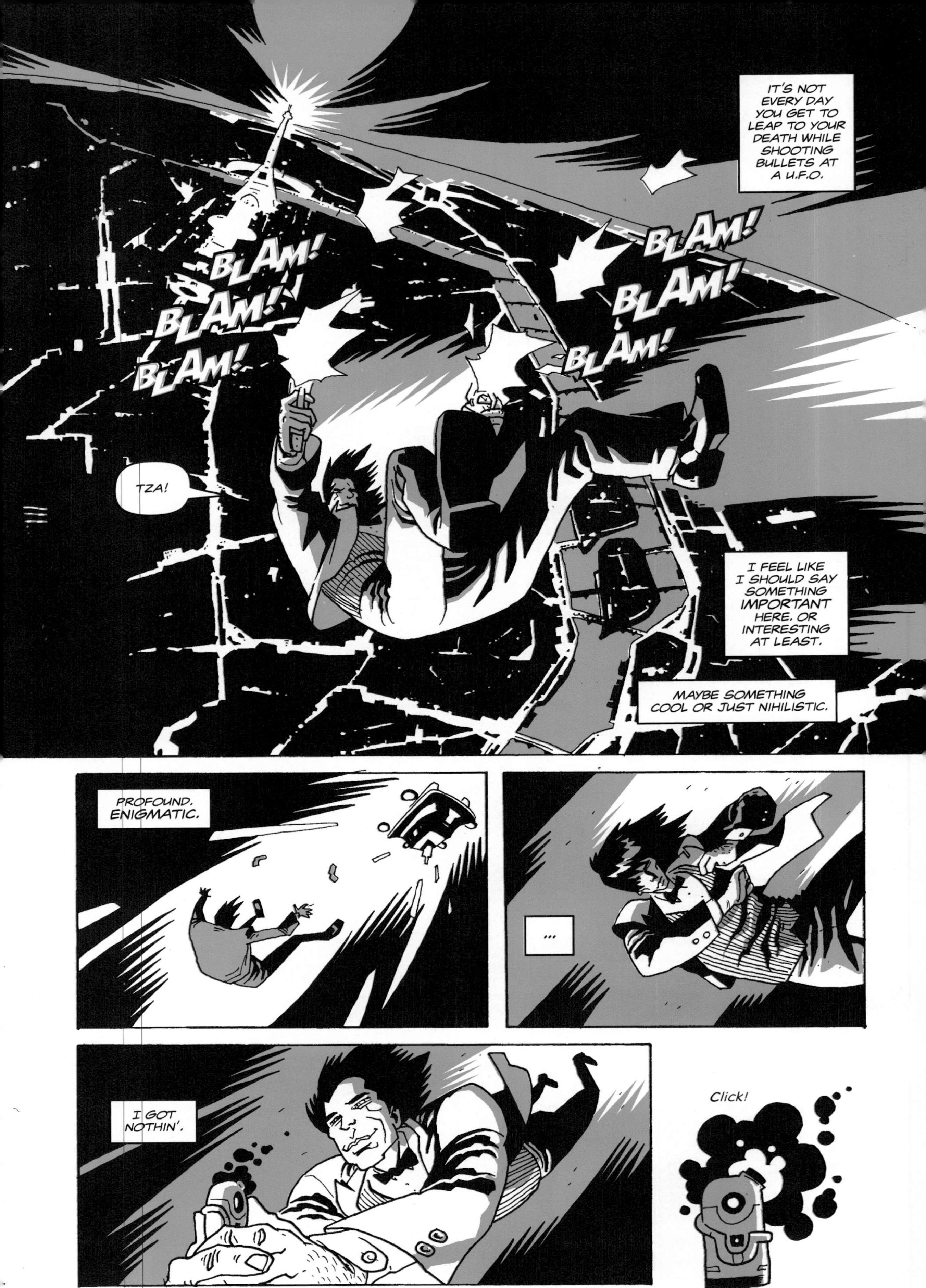
IT'S NOT EVERY DAY YOU GET TO LEAP TO YOUR DEATH WHILE SHOOTING BULLETS AT A U.F.O.
BLAM! BLAM! BLAM!
BLAM! BLAM! BLAM!
TZA!
I FEEL LIKE I SHOULD SAY SOMETHING IMPORTANT HERE. OR INTERESTING AT LEAST.
MAYBE SOMETHING COOL OR JUST NIHILISTIC.
PROFOUND. ENIGMATIC.
...
I GOT NOTHIN'.
Click!

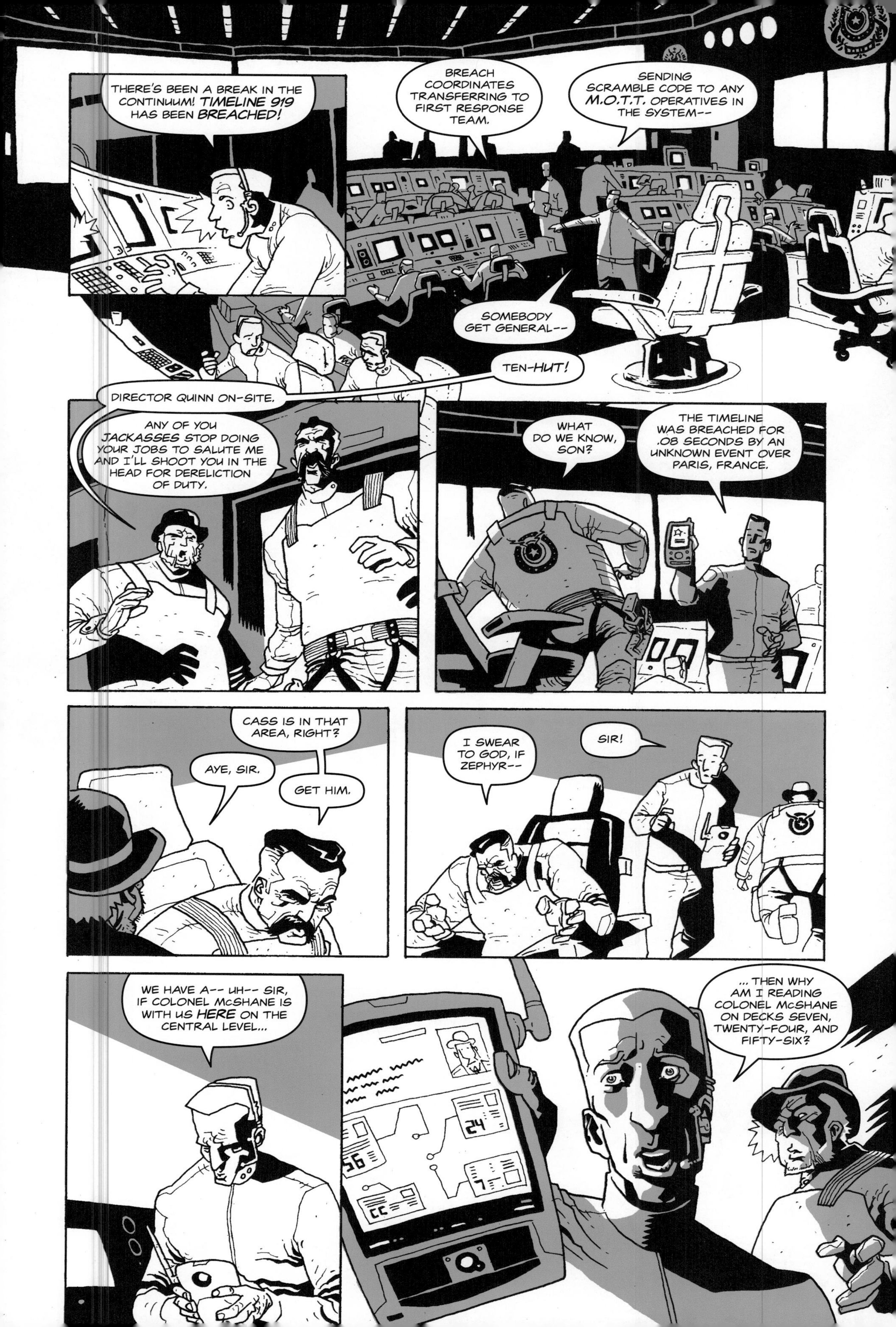
THERE'S BEEN A BREAK IN THE CONTINUUM! TIMELINE 919 HAS BEEN BREACHED!
BREACH COORDINATES TRANSFERRING TO FIRST RESPONSE TEAM.
SENDING SCRAMBLE CODE TO ANY M.O.T.T. OPERATIVES IN THE SYSTEM--
SOMEBODY GET GENERAL--
TEN-HUT!
DIRECTOR QUINN ON-SITE.
ANY OF YOU JACKASSES STOP DOING YOUR JOBS TO SALUTE ME AND I'LL SHOOT YOU IN THE HEAD FOR DERELICTION OF DUTY.
WHAT DO WE KNOW, SON?
THE TIMELINE WAS BREACHED FOR .08 SECONDS BY AN UNKNOWN EVENT OVER PARIS, FRANCE.
CASS IS IN THAT AREA, RIGHT?
AYE, SIR.
GET HIM.
I SWEAR TO GOD, IF ZEPHYR--
SIR!
WE HAVE A-- UH-- SIR, IF COLONEL McSHANE IS WITH US HERE ON THE CENTRAL LEVEL...
... THEN WHY AM I READING COLONEL McSHANE ON DECKS SEVEN, TWENTY-FOUR, AND FIFTY-SIX?
56
24
7
CC

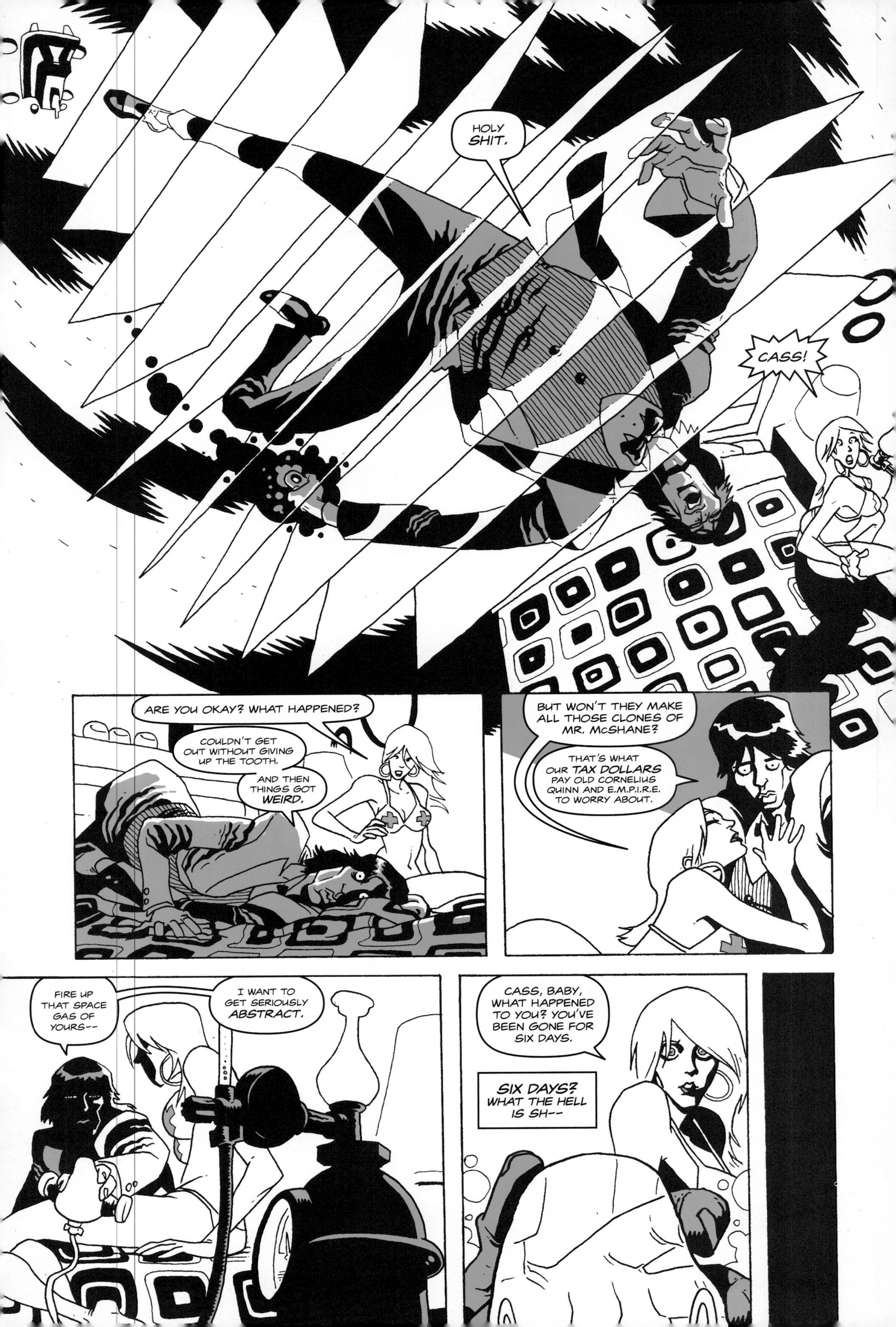
HOLY SHIT.
CASS!
ARE YOU OKAY? WHAT HAPPENED?
COULDN'T GET OUT WITHOUT GIVING UP THE TOOTH.
AND THEN THINGS GOT WEIRD.
BUT WON'T THEY MAKE ALL THOSE CLONES OF MR. McSHANE?
THAT'S WHAT OUR TAX DOLLARS PAY OLD CORNELIUS QUINN AND E.M.P.I.R.E. TO WORRY ABOUT.
FIRE UP THAT SPACE GAS OF YOURS--
I WANT TO GET SERIOUSLY ABSTRACT.
CASS, BABY, WHAT HAPPENED TO YOU? YOU'VE BEEN GONE FOR SIX DAYS.
SIX DAYS? WHAT THE HELL IS SH--

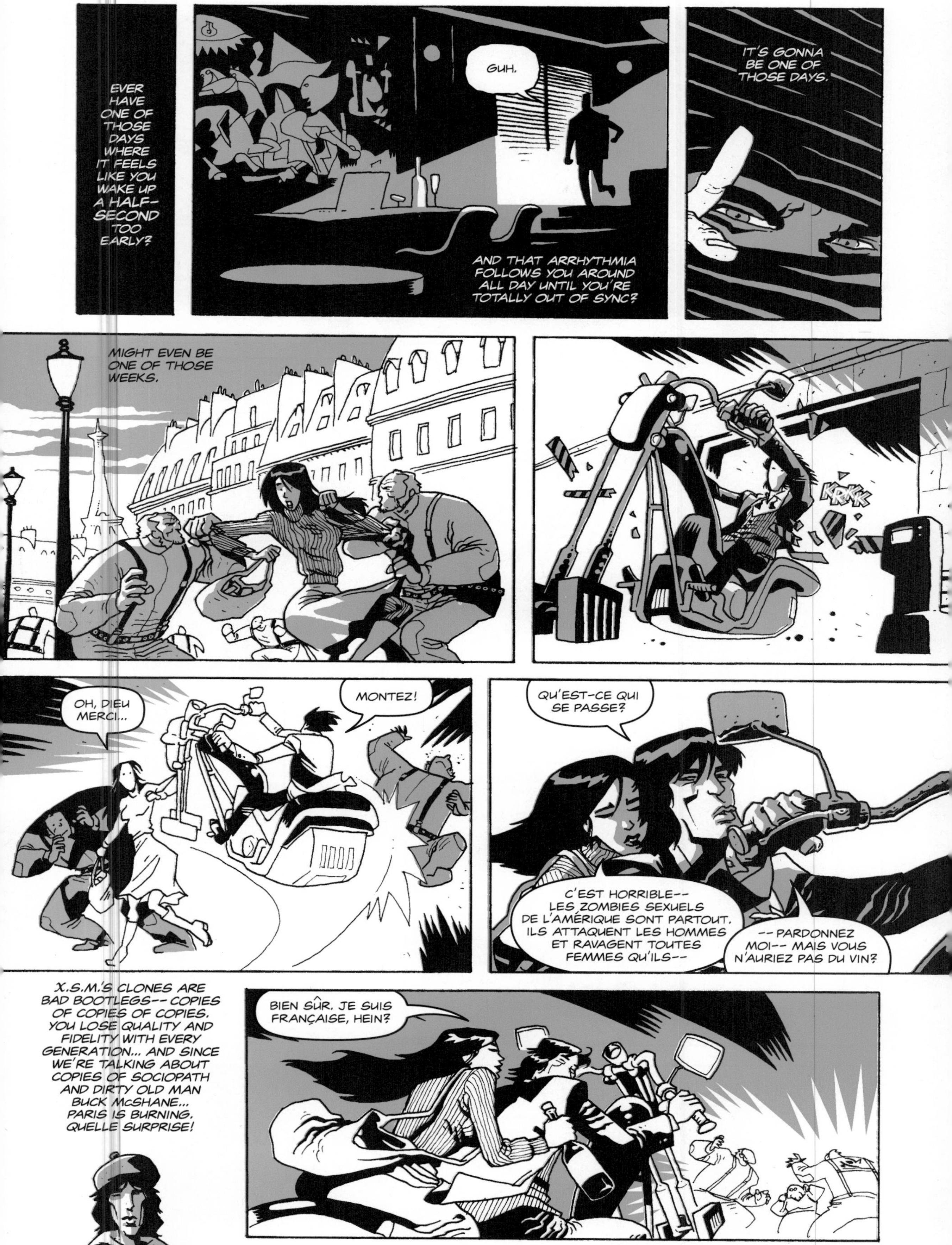
EVER HAVE ONE OF THOSE DAYS WHERE IT FEELS LIKE YOU WAKE UP A HALF-SECOND TOO EARLY?
GUH.
AND THAT ARRHYTHMIA FOLLOWS YOU AROUND ALL DAY UNTIL YOU'RE TOTALLY OUT OF SYNC?
IT'S GONNA BE ONE OF THOSE DAYS.
MIGHT EVEN BE ONE OF THOSE WEEKS.
KRKK
OH, DIEU MERCI...
MONTEZ!
QU'EST-CE QUI SE PASSE?
C'EST HORRIBLE-- LES ZOMBIES SEXUELS DE L'AMÉRIQUE SONT PARTOUT. ILS ATTAQUENT LES HOMMES ET RAVAGENT TOUTES FEMMES QU'ILS--
--PARDONNEZ MOI-- MAIS VOUS N'AURIEZ PAS DU VIN?
X.S.M.'S CLONES ARE BAD BOOTLEGS-- COPIES OF COPIES OF COPIES. YOU LOSE QUALITY AND FIDELITY WITH EVERY GENERATION... AND SINCE WE'RE TALKING ABOUT COPIES OF SOCIOPATH AND DIRTY OLD MAN BUCK McSHANE... PARIS IS BURNING. QUELLE SURPRISE!
BIEN SÛR. JE SUIS FRANÇAISE, HEIN?

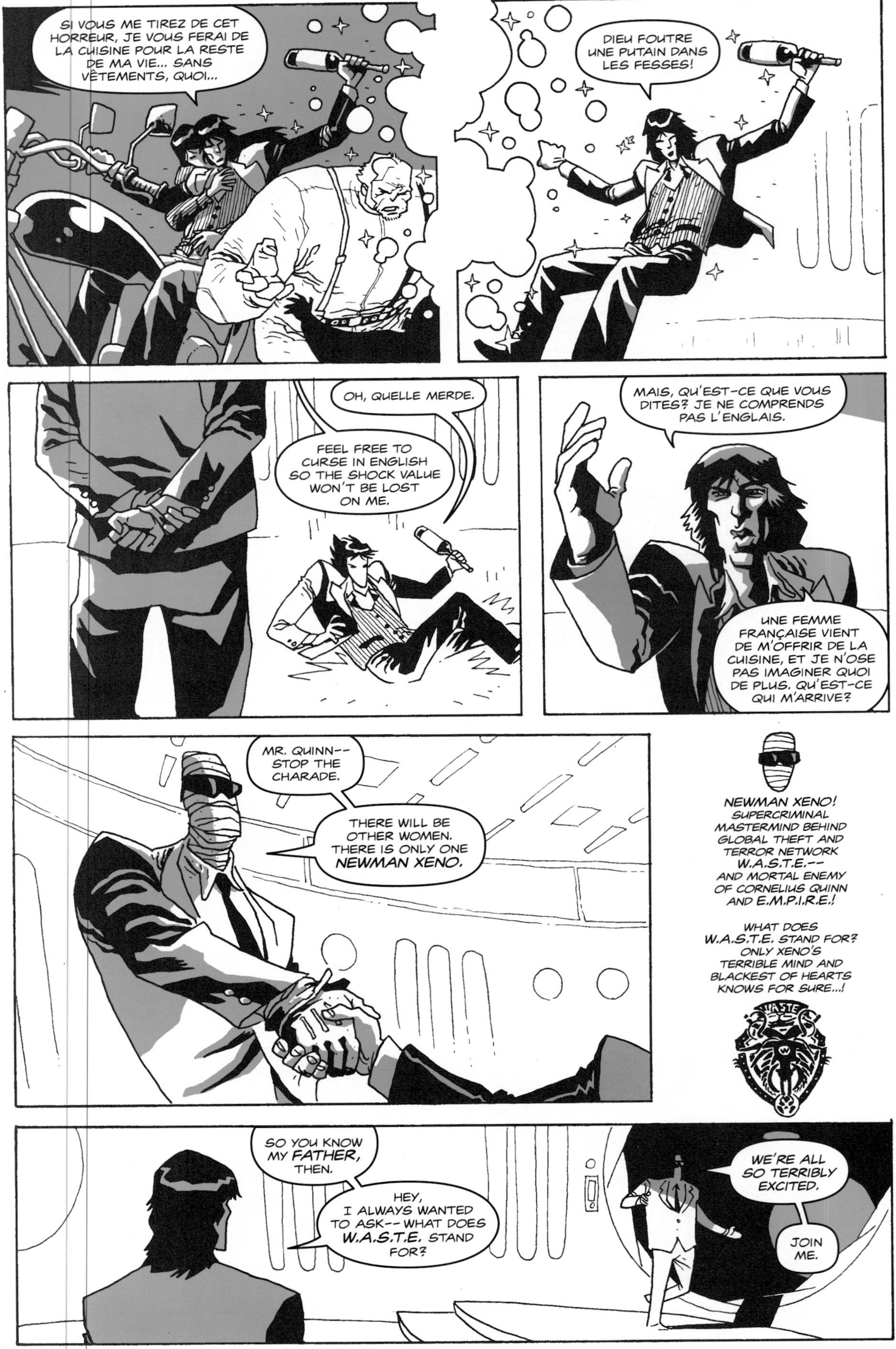
SI VOUS ME TIREZ DE CET HORREUR, JE VOUS FERAI DE LA CUISINE POUR LA RESTE DE MA VIE... SANS VÊTEMENTS, QUOI...
DIEU FOUTRE UNE PUTAIN DANS LES FESSES!
OH, QUELLE MERDE.
FEEL FREE TO CURSE IN ENGLISH SO THE SHOCK VALUE WON'T BE LOST ON ME.
MAIS, QU'EST-CE QUE VOUS DITES? JE NE COMPRENDS PAS L'ENGLAIS.
UNE FEMME FRANÇAISE VIENT DE M'OFFRIR DE LA CUISINE, ET JE N'OSE PAS IMAGINER QUOI DE PLUS. QU'EST-CE QUI M'ARRIVE?
MR. QUINN-- STOP THE CHARADE.
THERE WILL BE OTHER WOMEN. THERE IS ONLY ONE NEWMAN XENO.
NEWMAN XENO! SUPERCRIMINAL MASTERMIND BEHIND GLOBAL THEFT AND TERROR NETWORK W.A.S.T.E.-- AND MORTAL ENEMY OF CORNELIUS QUINN AND E.M.P.I.R.E.!
WHAT DOES W.A.S.T.E. STAND FOR? ONLY XENO'S TERRIBLE MIND AND BLACKEST OF HEARTS KNOWS FOR SURE...!
SO YOU KNOW MY FATHER, THEN.
HEY, I ALWAYS WANTED TO ASK-- WHAT DOES W.A.S.T.E. STAND FOR?
WE'RE ALL SO TERRIBLY EXCITED.
JOIN ME.

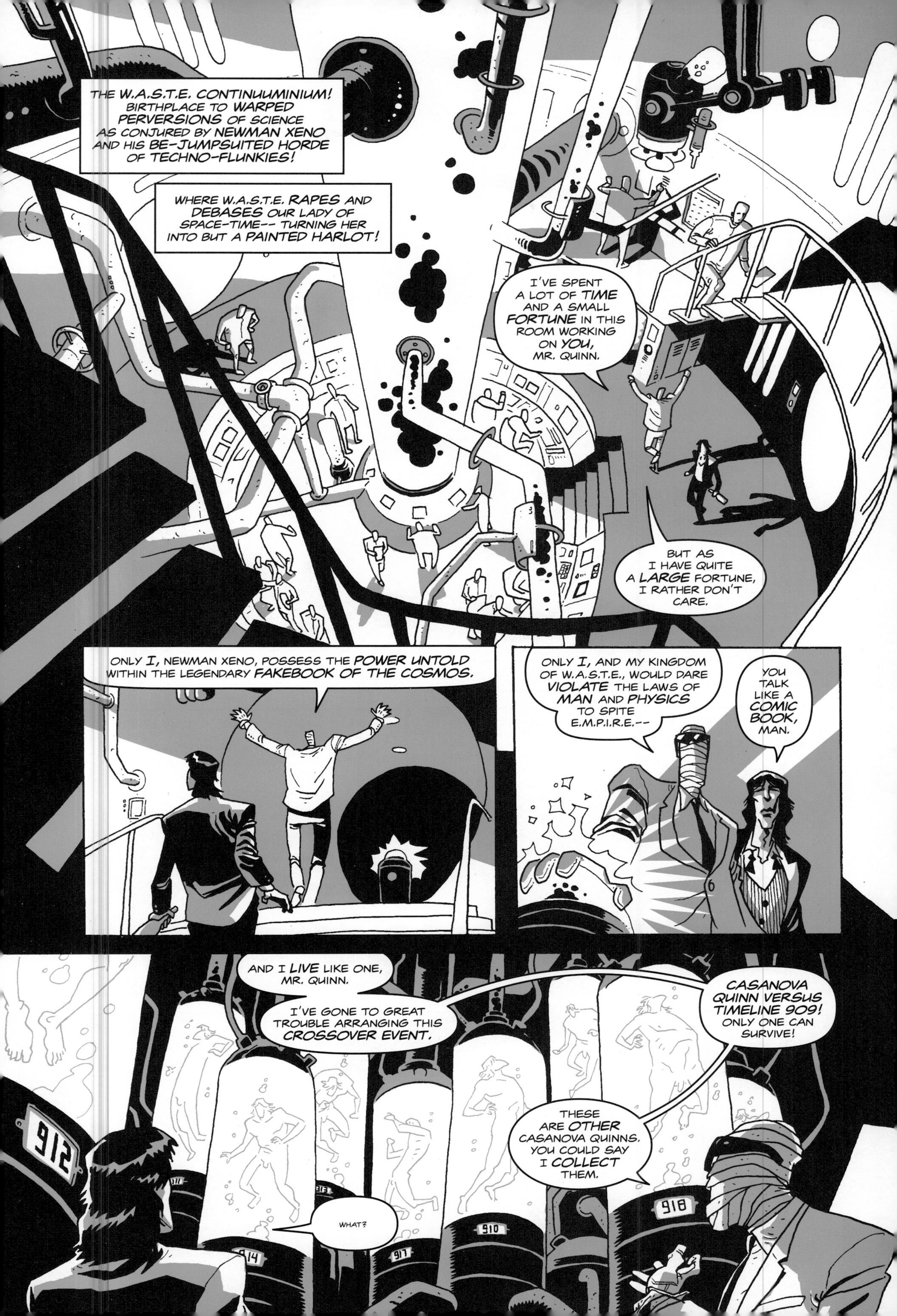
THE W.A.S.T.E. CONTINUUMINIUM! BIRTHPLACE TO WARPED PERVERSIONS OF SCIENCE AS CONJURED BY NEWMAN XENO AND HIS BE-JUMPSUITED HORDE OF TECHNO-FLUNKIES!
WHERE W.A.S.T.E. RAPES AND DEBASES OUR LADY OF SPACE-TIME-- TURNING HER INTO BUT A PAINTED HARLOT!
I'VE SPENT A LOT OF TIME AND A SMALL FORTUNE IN THIS ROOM WORKING ON YOU, MR. QUINN.
BUT AS I HAVE QUITE A LARGE FORTUNE, I RATHER DON'T CARE.
ONLY I, NEWMAN XENO, POSSESS THE POWER UNTOLD WITHIN THE LEGENDARY FAKEBOOK OF THE COSMOS.
ONLY I, AND MY KINGDOM OF W.A.S.T.E., WOULD DARE VIOLATE THE LAWS OF MAN AND PHYSICS TO SPITE E.M.P.I.R.E.--
YOU TALK LIKE A COMIC BOOK, MAN.
AND I LIVE LIKE ONE, MR. QUINN.
I'VE GONE TO GREAT TROUBLE ARRANGING THIS CROSSOVER EVENT.
CASANOVA QUINN VERSUS TIMELINE 909! ONLY ONE CAN SURVIVE!
THESE ARE OTHER CASANOVA QUINNS. YOU COULD SAY I COLLECT THEM.
WHAT?
912
918
910
917
914

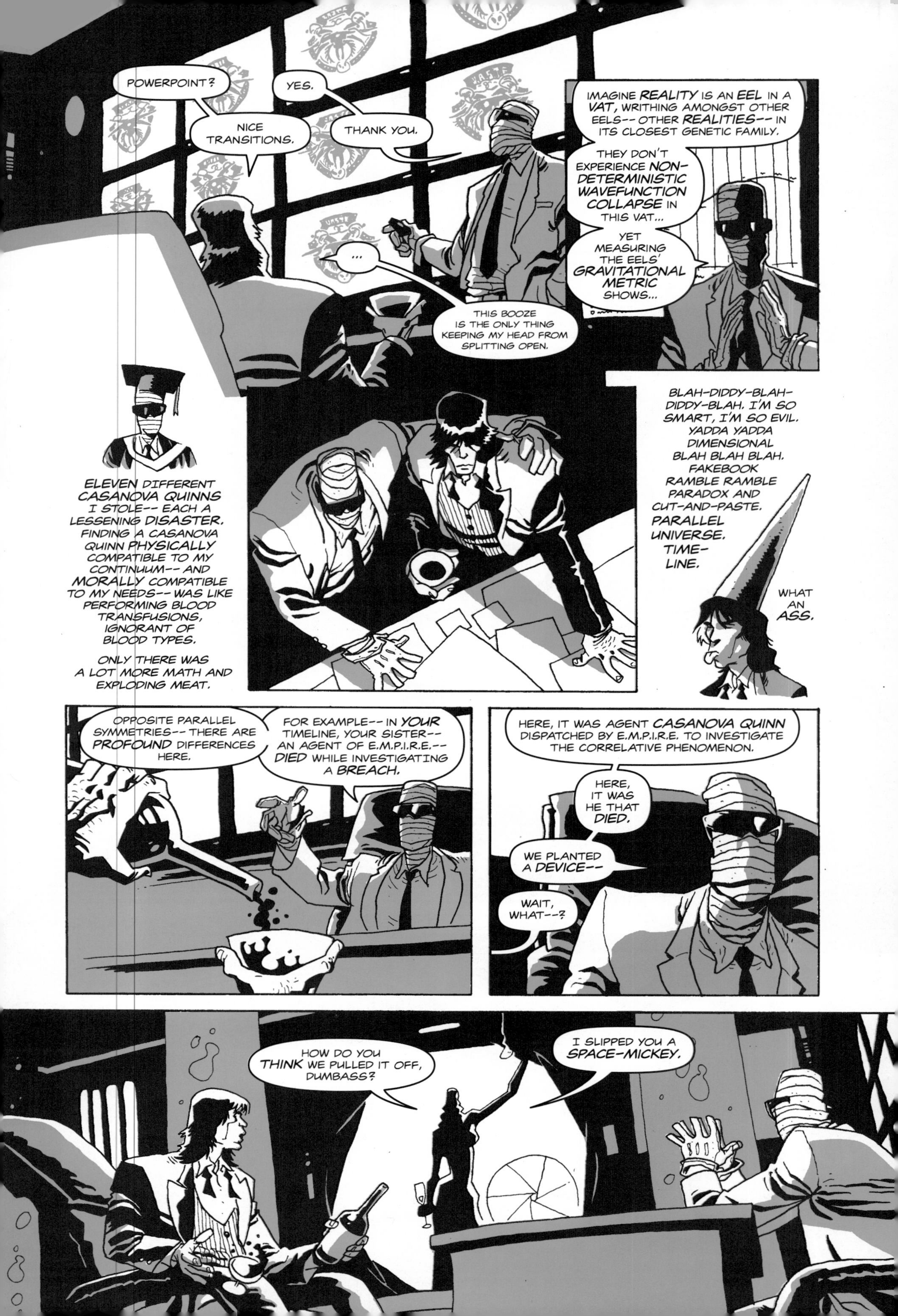
POWERPOINT?
YES.
NICE TRANSITIONS.
THANK YOU.
...
THIS BOOZE IS THE ONLY THING KEEPING MY HEAD FROM SPLITTING OPEN.
IMAGINE REALITY IS AN EEL IN A VAT, WRITHING AMONGST OTHER EELS-- OTHER REALITIES-- IN ITS CLOSEST GENETIC FAMILY.
THEY DON'T EXPERIENCE NON-DETERMINISTIC WAVEFUNCTION COLLAPSE IN THIS VAT...
YET MEASURING THE EELS' GRAVITATIONAL METRIC SHOWS...
ELEVEN DIFFERENT CASANOVA QUINNS I STOLE-- EACH A LESSENING DISASTER. FINDING A CASANOVA QUINN PHYSICALLY COMPATIBLE TO MY CONTINUUM-- AND MORALLY COMPATIBLE TO MY NEEDS-- WAS LIKE PERFORMING BLOOD TRANSFUSIONS, IGNORANT OF BLOOD TYPES.
ONLY THERE WAS A LOT MORE MATH AND EXPLODING MEAT.
BLAH-DIDDY-BLAH-DIDDY-BLAH. I'M SO SMART, I'M SO EVIL. YADDA YADDA DIMENSIONAL BLAH BLAH BLAH. FAKEBOOK RAMBLE RAMBLE PARADOX AND CUT-AND-PASTE. PARALLEL UNIVERSE. TIME-LINE.
WHAT AN ASS.
OPPOSITE PARALLEL SYMMETRIES-- THERE ARE PROFOUND DIFFERENCES HERE.
FOR EXAMPLE-- IN YOUR TIMELINE, YOUR SISTER-- AN AGENT OF E.M.P.I.R.E.-- DIED WHILE INVESTIGATING A BREACH.
HERE, IT WAS AGENT CASANOVA QUINN DISPATCHED BY E.M.P.I.R.E. TO INVESTIGATE THE CORRELATIVE PHENOMENON.
HERE, IT WAS HE THAT DIED.
WE PLANTED A DEVICE--
WAIT, WHAT--?
HOW DO YOU THINK WE PULLED IT OFF, DUMBASS?
I SLIPPED YOU A SPACE-MICKEY.

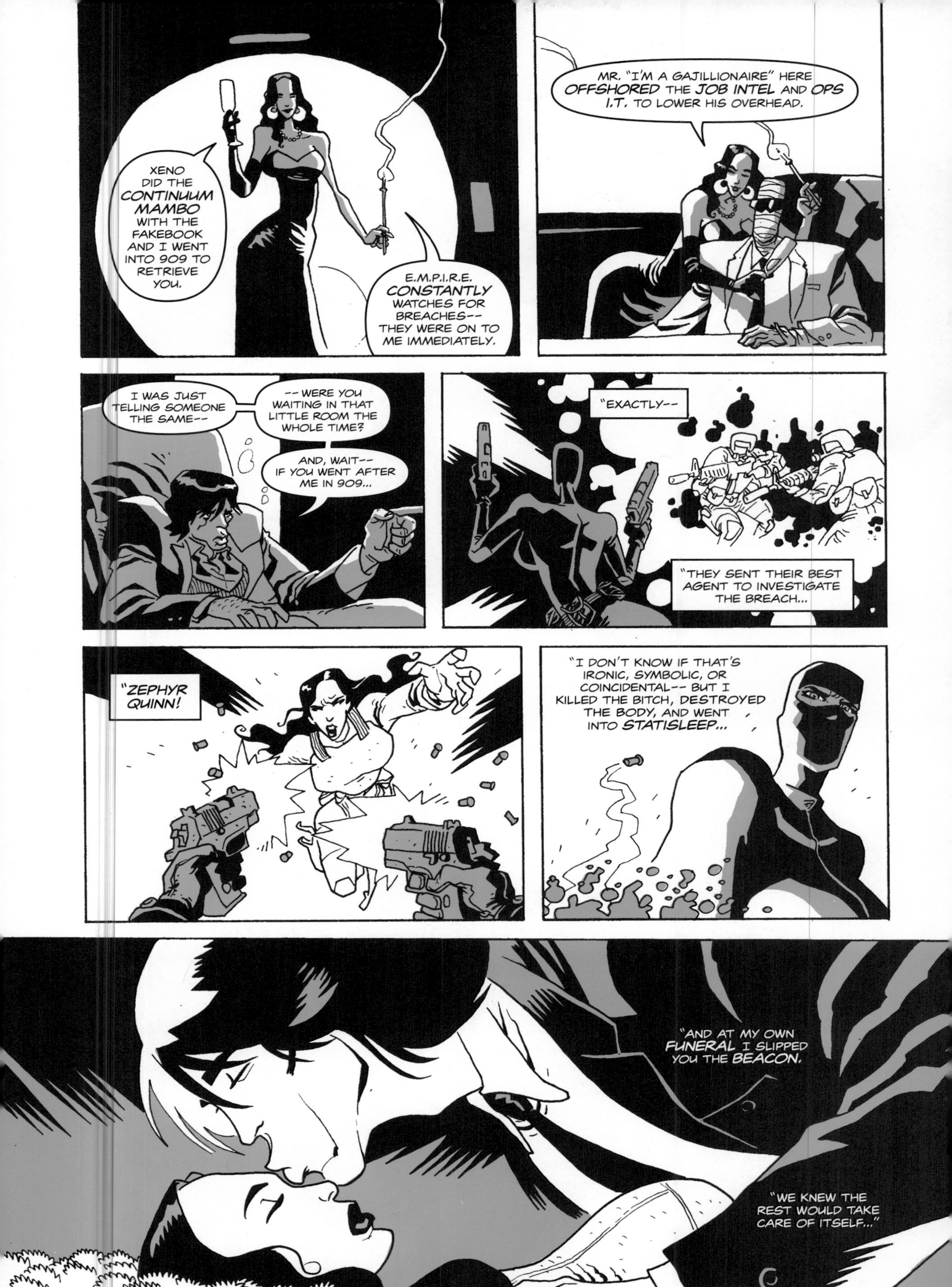
XENO DID THE CONTINUUM MAMBO WITH THE FAKEBOOK AND I WENT INTO 909 TO RETRIEVE YOU.
E.M.P.I.R.E. CONSTANTLY WATCHES FOR BREACHES-- THEY WERE ON TO ME IMMEDIATELY.
MR. "I'M A GAJILLIONAIRE" HERE OFFSHORED THE JOB INTEL AND OPS I.T. TO LOWER HIS OVERHEAD.
I WAS JUST TELLING SOMEONE THE SAME--
--WERE YOU WAITING IN THAT LITTLE ROOM THE WHOLE TIME?
AND, WAIT-- IF YOU WENT AFTER ME IN 909...
"EXACTLY--
"THEY SENT THEIR BEST AGENT TO INVESTIGATE THE BREACH...
"ZEPHYR QUINN!
"I DON'T KNOW IF THAT'S IRONIC, SYMBOLIC, OR COINCIDENTAL-- BUT I KILLED THE BITCH, DESTROYED THE BODY, AND WENT INTO STATISLEEP...
"AND AT MY OWN FUNERAL I SLIPPED YOU THE BEACON.
"WE KNEW THE REST WOULD TAKE CARE OF ITSELF..."

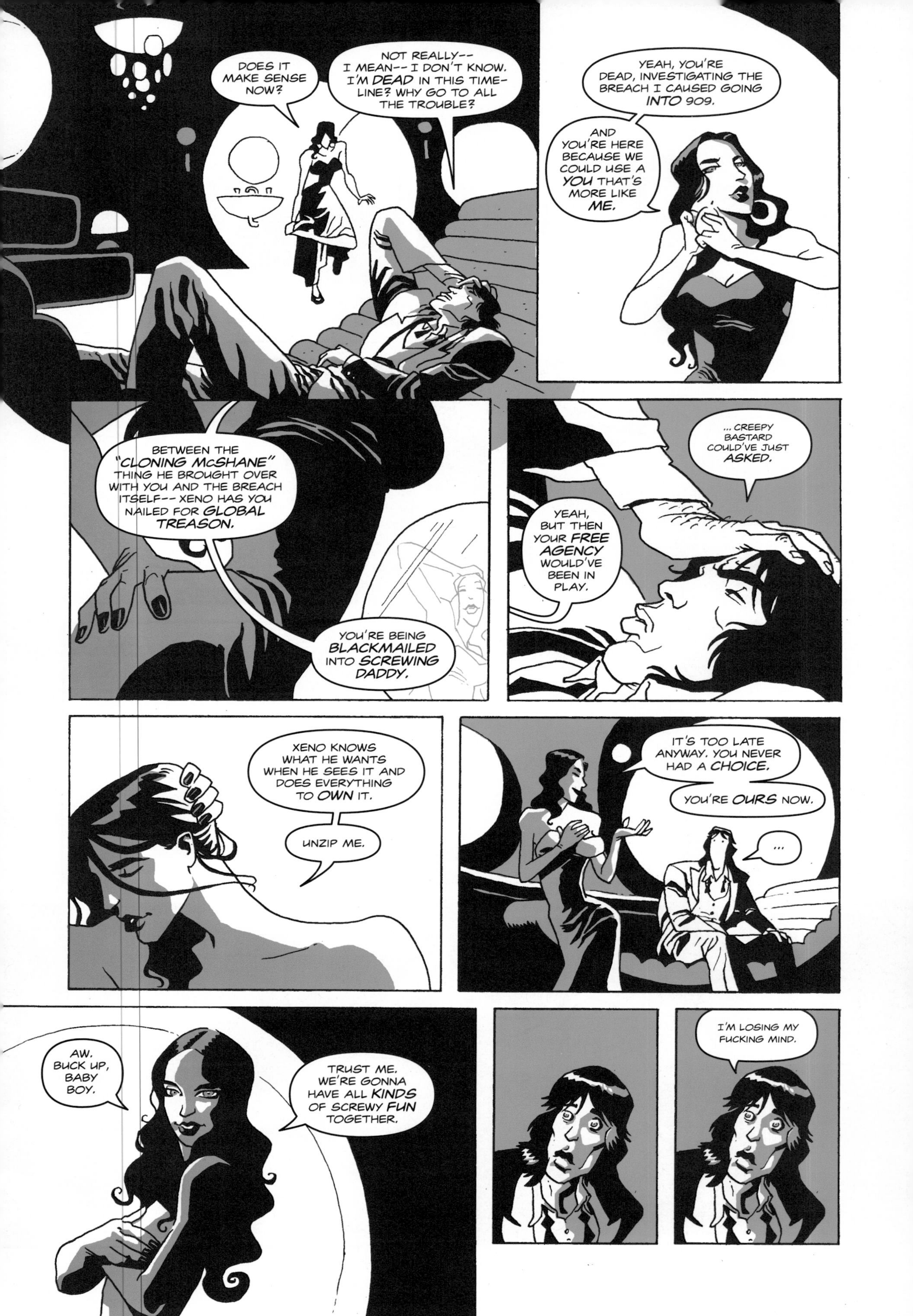
DOES IT MAKE SENSE NOW?
NOT REALLY-- I MEAN-- I DON'T KNOW. I'M DEAD IN THIS TIME-LINE? WHY GO TO ALL THE TROUBLE?
YEAH, YOU'RE DEAD, INVESTIGATING THE BREACH I CAUSED GOING INTO 909.
AND YOU'RE HERE BECAUSE WE COULD USE A YOU THAT'S MORE LIKE ME.
BETWEEN THE "CLONING McSHANE" THING HE BROUGHT OVER WITH YOU AND THE BREACH ITSELF-- XENO HAS YOU NAILED FOR GLOBAL TREASON.
YOU'RE BEING BLACKMAILED INTO SCREWING DADDY.
... CREEPY BASTARD COULD'VE JUST ASKED.
YEAH, BUT THEN YOUR FREE AGENCY WOULD'VE BEEN IN PLAY.
XENO KNOWS WHAT HE WANTS WHEN HE SEES IT AND DOES EVERYTHING TO OWN IT.
UNZIP ME.
IT'S TOO LATE ANYWAY. YOU NEVER HAD A CHOICE.
YOU'RE OURS NOW.
...
AW. BUCK UP, BABY BOY.
TRUST ME. WE'RE GONNA HAVE ALL KINDS OF SCREWY FUN TOGETHER.
I'M LOSING MY FUCKING MIND.

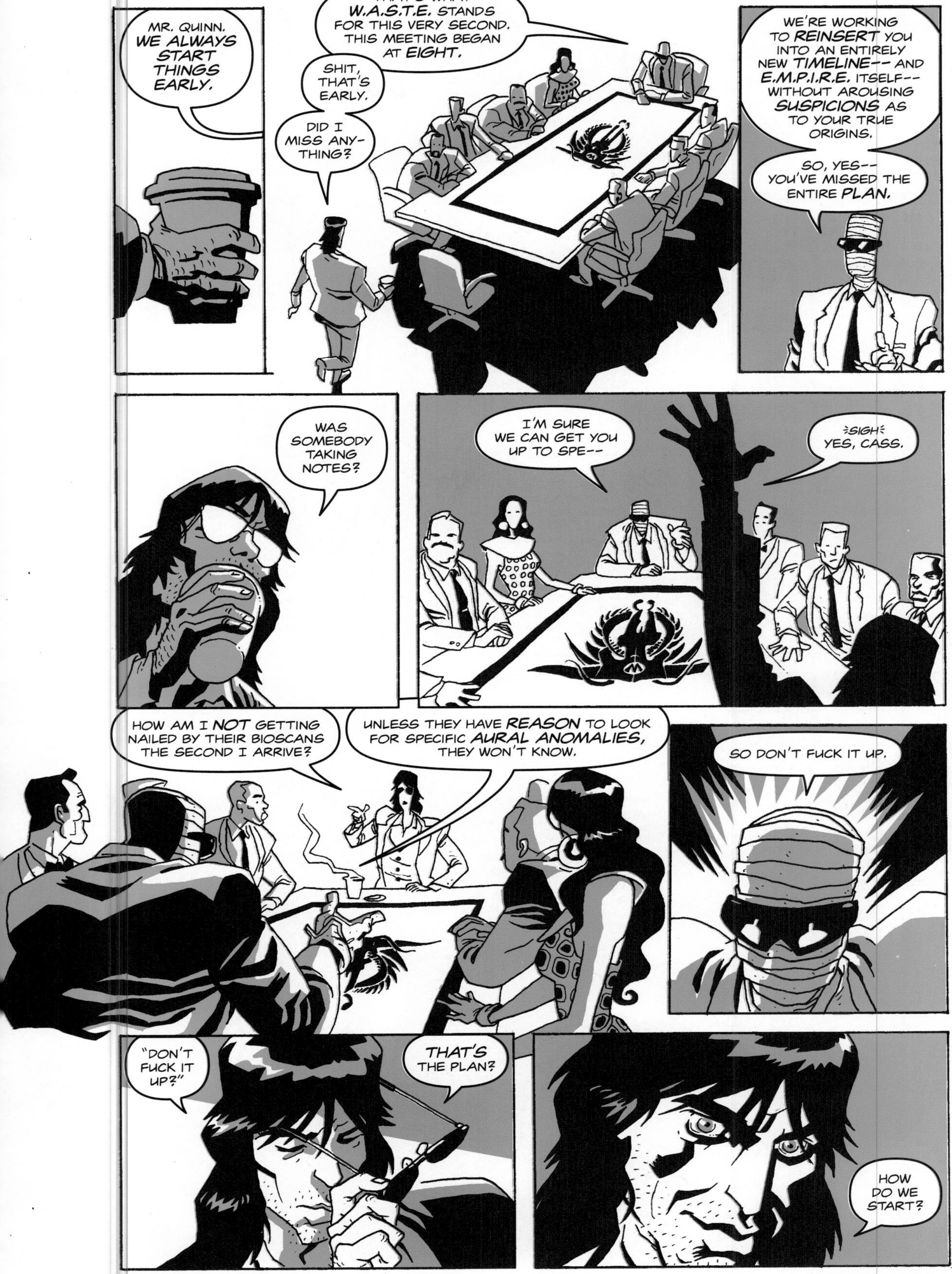

MR. QUINN. WE ALWAYS START THINGS EARLY.
THAT'S WHAT W.A.S.T.E. STANDS FOR THIS VERY SECOND. THIS MEETING BEGAN AT EIGHT.
SHIT, THAT'S EARLY.
DID I MISS ANY-THING?
WE'RE WORKING TO REINSERT YOU INTO AN ENTIRELY NEW TIMELINE-- AND E.M.P.I.R.E. ITSELF-- WITHOUT AROUSING SUSPICIONS AS TO YOUR TRUE ORIGINS.
SO, YES-- YOU'VE MISSED THE ENTIRE PLAN.
WAS SOMEBODY TAKING NOTES?
I'M SURE WE CAN GET YOU UP TO SPE--
SIGH
YES, CASS.
HOW AM I NOT GETTING NAILED BY THEIR BIOSCANS THE SECOND I ARRIVE?
UNLESS THEY HAVE REASON TO LOOK FOR SPECIFIC AURAL ANOMALIES, THEY WON'T KNOW.
SO DON'T FUCK IT UP.
"DON'T FUCK IT UP?"
THAT'S THE PLAN?
HOW DO WE START?

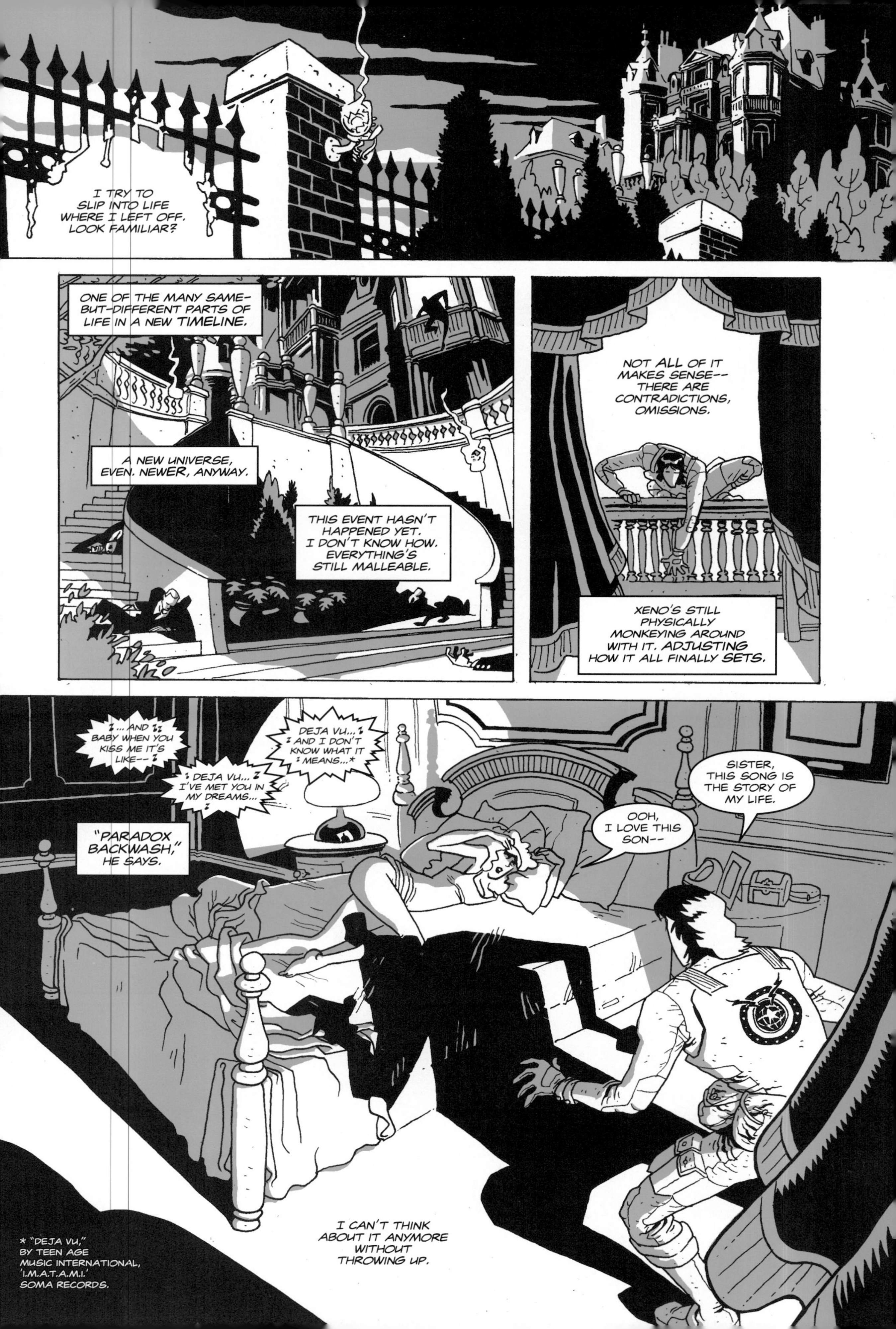
I TRY TO SLIP INTO LIFE WHERE I LEFT OFF. LOOK FAMILIAR?
ONE OF THE MANY SAME-BUT-DIFFERENT PARTS OF LIFE IN A NEW TIMELINE.
A NEW UNIVERSE, EVEN. NEWER, ANYWAY.
THIS EVENT HASN'T HAPPENED YET. I DON'T KNOW HOW. EVERYTHING'S STILL MALLEABLE.
NOT ALL OF IT MAKES SENSE-- THERE ARE CONTRADICTIONS, OMISSIONS.
XENO'S STILL PHYSICALLY MONKEYING AROUND WITH IT. ADJUSTING HOW IT ALL FINALLY SETS.
♪ ...AND ♫ BABY WHEN YOU KISS ME IT'S LIKE-- ♪
♪ DEJA VU... ♪ I'VE MET YOU IN MY DREAMS... ♪
DEJA VU... ♪ AND I DON'T KNOW WHAT IT ♪ MEANS...*
"PARADOX BACKWASH," HE SAYS.
OOH, I LOVE THIS SON--
SISTER, THIS SONG IS THE STORY OF MY LIFE.
I CAN'T THINK ABOUT IT ANYMORE WITHOUT THROWING UP.
* "DEJA VU," BY TEEN AGE MUSIC INTERNATIONAL, 'I.M.A.T.A.M.I.' SOMA RECORDS.

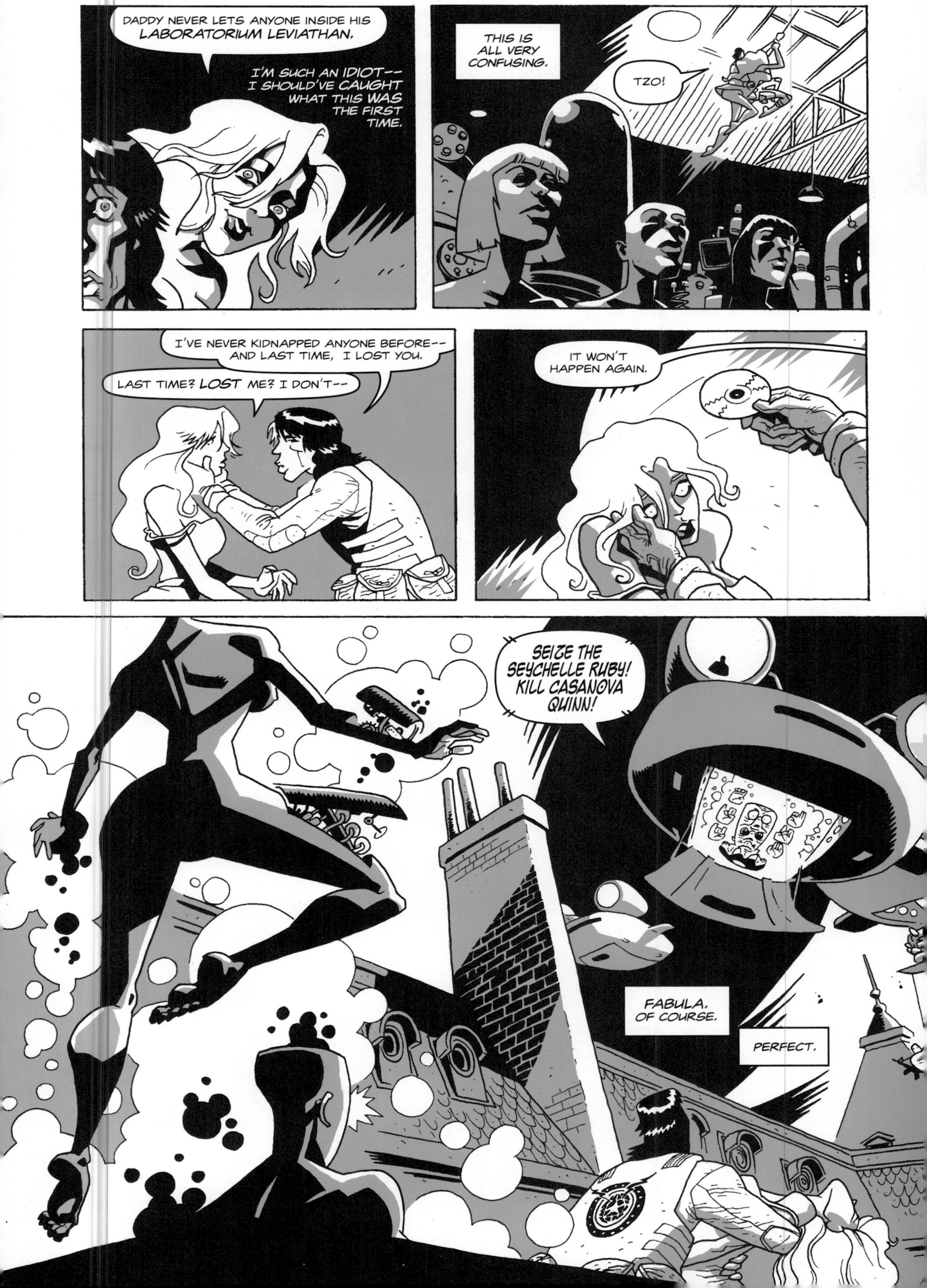
DADDY NEVER LETS ANYONE INSIDE HIS LABORATORIUM LEVIATHAN.
I'M SUCH AN IDIOT-- I SHOULD'VE CAUGHT WHAT THIS WAS THE FIRST TIME.
THIS IS ALL VERY CONFUSING.
TZO!
I'VE NEVER KIDNAPPED ANYONE BEFORE-- AND LAST TIME, I LOST YOU.
LAST TIME? LOST ME? I DON'T--
IT WON'T HAPPEN AGAIN.
SEIZE THE SEYCHELLE RUBY! KILL CASANOVA QUINN!
FABULA, OF COURSE.
PERFECT.

SONG'S RIGHT-- IT *IS* LIKE DEJA VU. EVERYTHING THEY DO, I'M READY FOR.

ALL THEIR OFFENSE, ALL THEIR DEFENSE-- I'VE LIVED THROUGH IT ONCE.

I KNOW WHAT THEY'RE DOING BEFORE THEY DO.

AND I EXPLOIT IT.

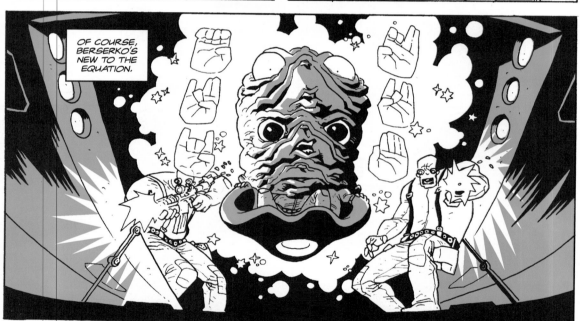

OF COURSE, BERSERKO'S NEW TO THE EQUATION.

BUT WHATEVER, I WENT INTO THE *ROUND ROOM* WITH HIM AND SURVIVED.

I KNOW HIM LIKE I KNOW MYSELF.

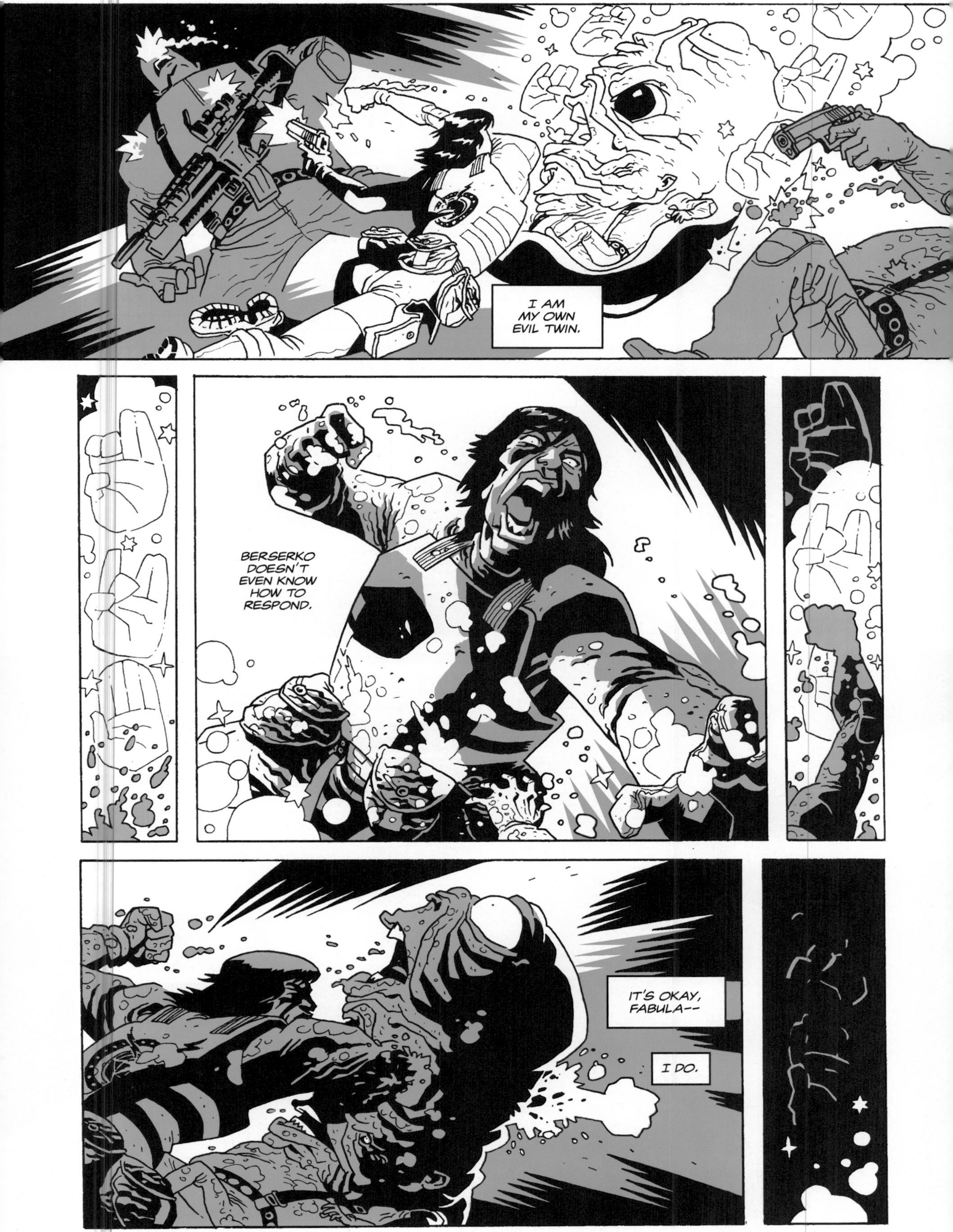
I AM MY OWN EVIL TWIN.
BERSERKO DOESN'T EVEN KNOW HOW TO RESPOND.
IT'S OKAY, FABULA--
I DO.

EVER MEET ANYONE THAT WENT TO THOSE
TECHNICAL SCHOOLS THAT ADVERTISE
ON LATE-NIGHT T.V.?

YOU KNOW--
THE "COLLEGES"
THAT EXIST IN
MINI-MALLS?

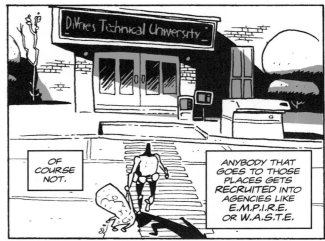

DeVries Technical University

OF
COURSE
NOT.

ANYBODY THAT
GOES TO THOSE
PLACES GETS
RECRUITED INTO
AGENCIES LIKE
E.M.P.I.R.E.
OR W.A.S.T.E.

I MEAN-- EVER WONDER WHERE THOSE JUMPSUIT GUYS
COME FROM? THE KILLER ROBOT FUELERS, THE GIANT
DRILL RUNNERS, THE SPOOKY LASER OPERATORS?

COLLEGES FROM THE T.V.

UH...

SO-- EVER WONDER WHERE THE PLUTONIUM CORES,
THE PLASMA-TEMPERED DRILL-BITS, OR THE DIAMONDS
THAT MAKE THOSE SPOOKY LASERS RUN COME FROM?

ME. THEY COME FROM ME.
THIS IS THE WORLD I LIVE IN.

LIEUTENANT CASANOVA
QUINN REQUESTING IMMEDIATE
EXFILTRATION.

AND TELL DAD
I GOT THE SEYCHELLE RUBY
WITH ME.

I STEAL STUFF.
IN THE END, I DON'T
CARE FOR WHOM.

I LOVE
MY JOB.

GABRIEL
BÁ
2006

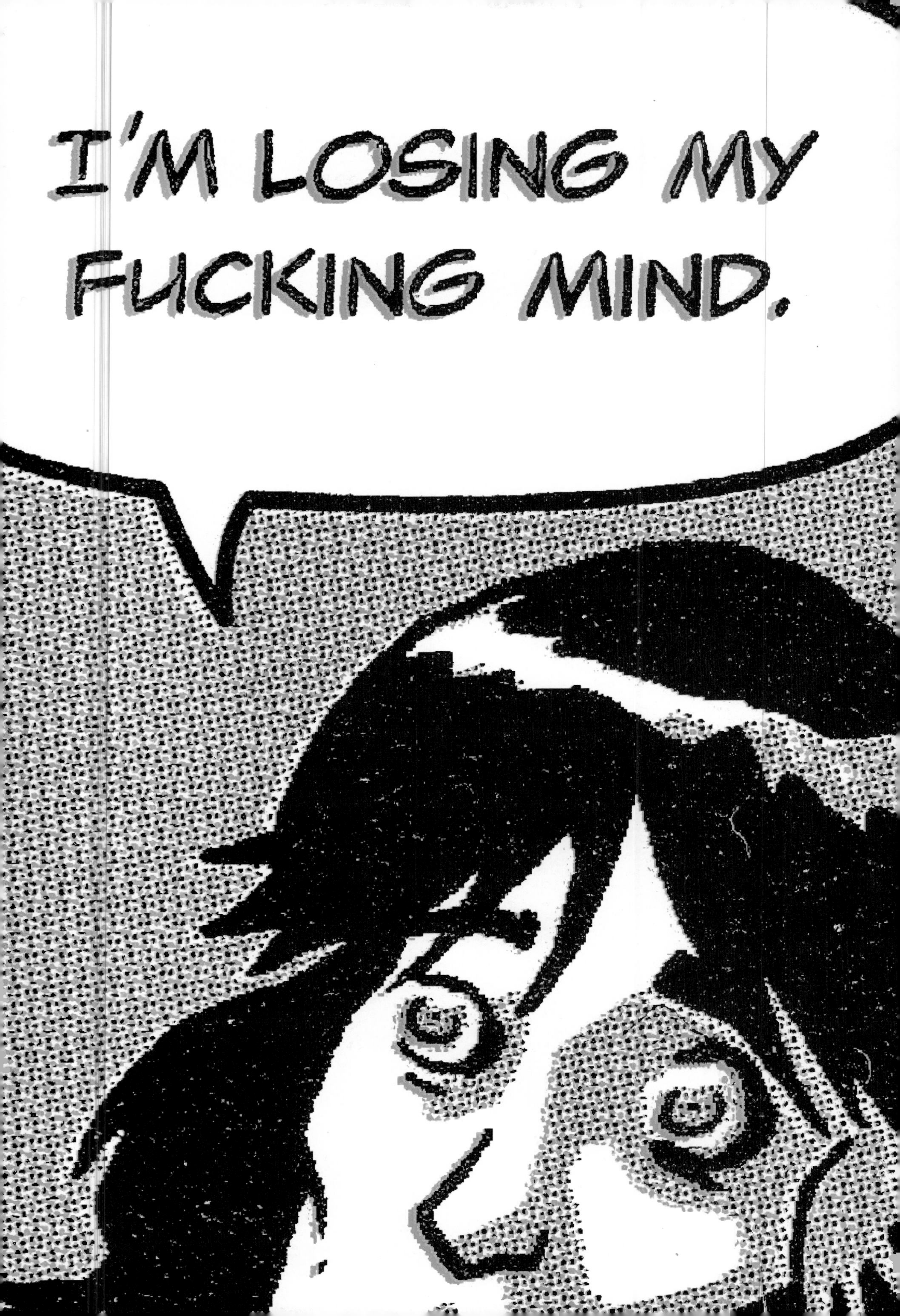
I'M LOSING MY FUCKING MIND.

Chapter Two
Pretty Little Policeman

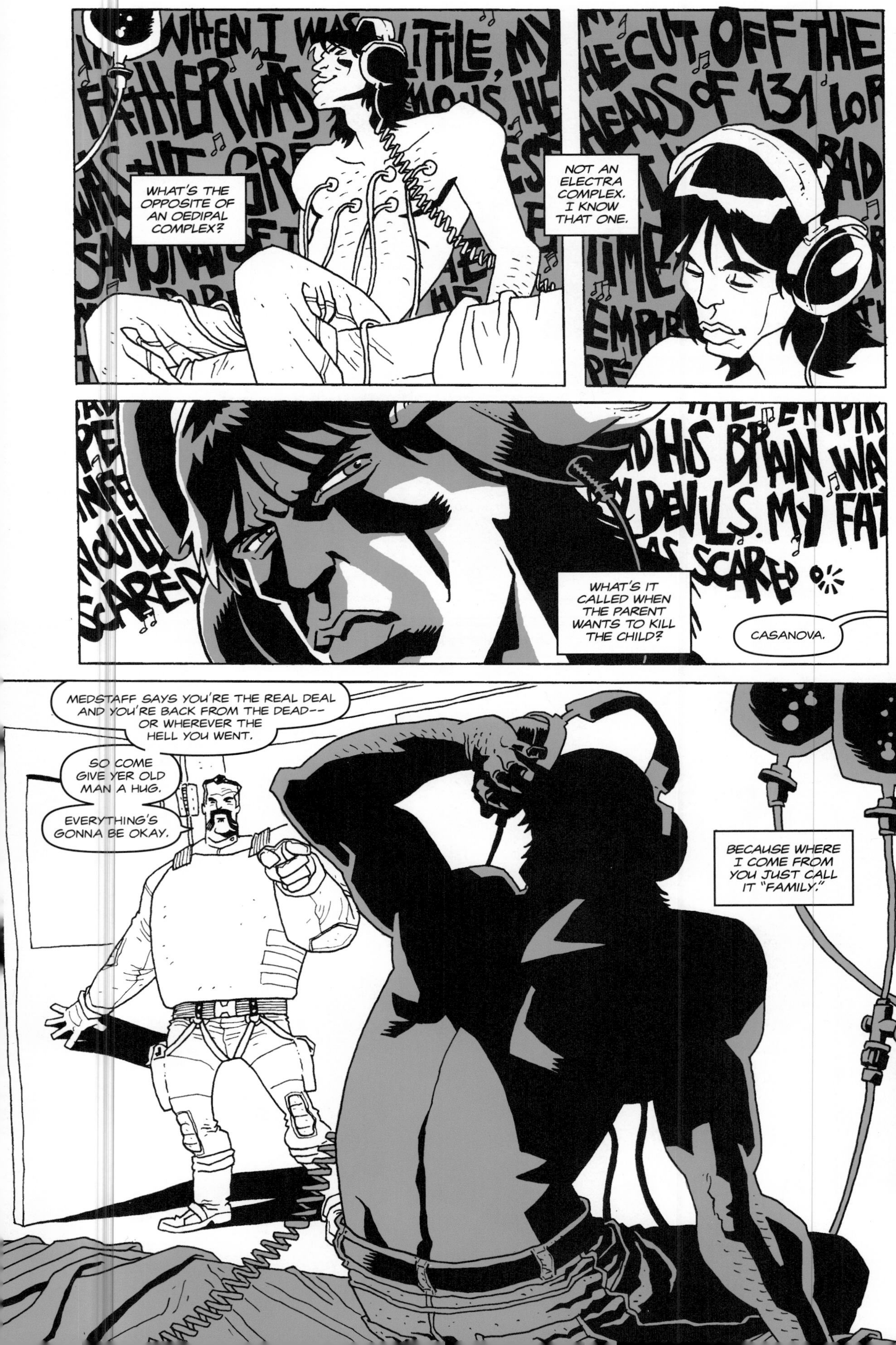

WHAT'S THE OPPOSITE OF AN OEDIPAL COMPLEX?
NOT AN ELECTRA COMPLEX. I KNOW THAT ONE.
WHAT'S IT CALLED WHEN THE PARENT WANTS TO KILL THE CHILD?
CASANOVA.
MEDSTAFF SAYS YOU'RE THE REAL DEAL AND YOU'RE BACK FROM THE DEAD-- OR WHEREVER THE HELL YOU WENT.
SO COME GIVE YER OLD MAN A HUG.
EVERYTHING'S GONNA BE OKAY.
BECAUSE WHERE I COME FROM YOU JUST CALL IT "FAMILY."

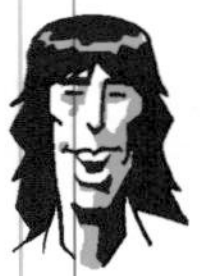

NOBODY COULD EXPLAIN WHAT HAPPENED TO ME-- I WAS *OFF* THE GRID AND THEN BACK ON THE GRID BUT SOMEHOW IT WAS ALL OKAY.

EVERYONE WAS TOLD I HAD A *SPOTTY MEMORY*. GETS ME THROUGH THE SITUATIONS I CAN'T *COVER*.

THEY WERE CONVINCED I WASN'T AN *IMPOSTOR ASSASSIN* FROM ANOTHER DIMENSION, SENT HERE BY *W.A.S.T.E.* TO DESTROY THEM FROM WITHIN-- SO I WAS WELCOMED HOME.

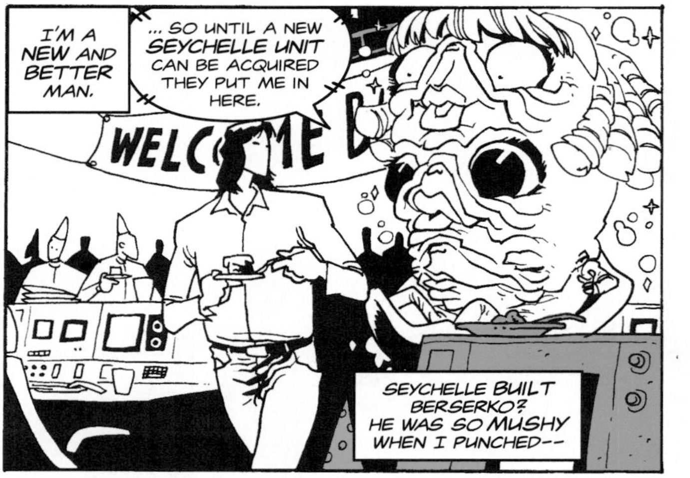

I'M A NEW AND BETTER MAN.
... SO UNTIL A NEW SEYCHELLE UNIT CAN BE ACQUIRED THEY PUT ME IN HERE.
SEYCHELLE BUILT BERSERKO? HE WAS SO MUSHY WHEN I PUNCHED--

DON'T FORGET! THE CASANOVA QUINN YOU SEE HERE IS AN IMPOSTOR ASSASSIN KIDNAPPED FROM ANOTHER DIMENSION AT THE BEHEST OF NEWMAN XENO AND W.A.S.T.E.-- THE SWORN ENEMY OF CORNELIUS QUINN-- TO DESTROY E.M.P.I.R.E. FROM WITHIN!

- ERIC STEPHENSON
EXECUTIVE DIRECTOR,
IMAGE COMICS

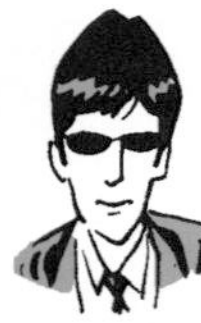

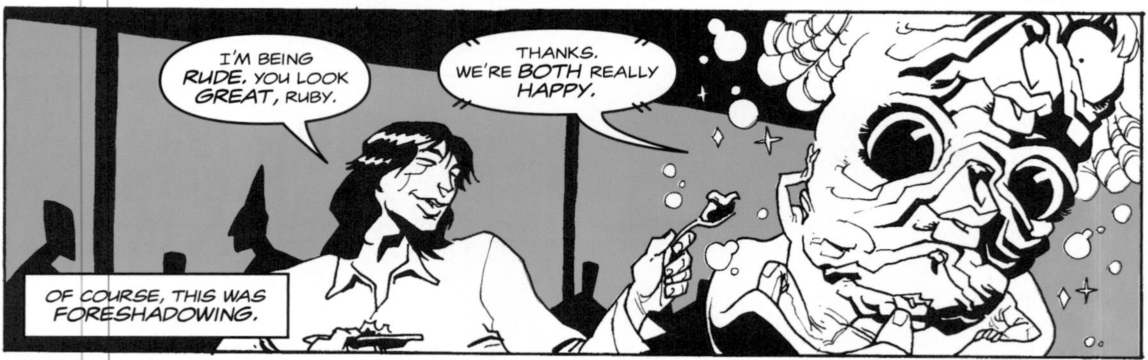

I'M BEING RUDE. YOU LOOK GREAT, RUBY.
THANKS. WE'RE BOTH REALLY HAPPY.
OF COURSE, THIS WAS FORESHADOWING.

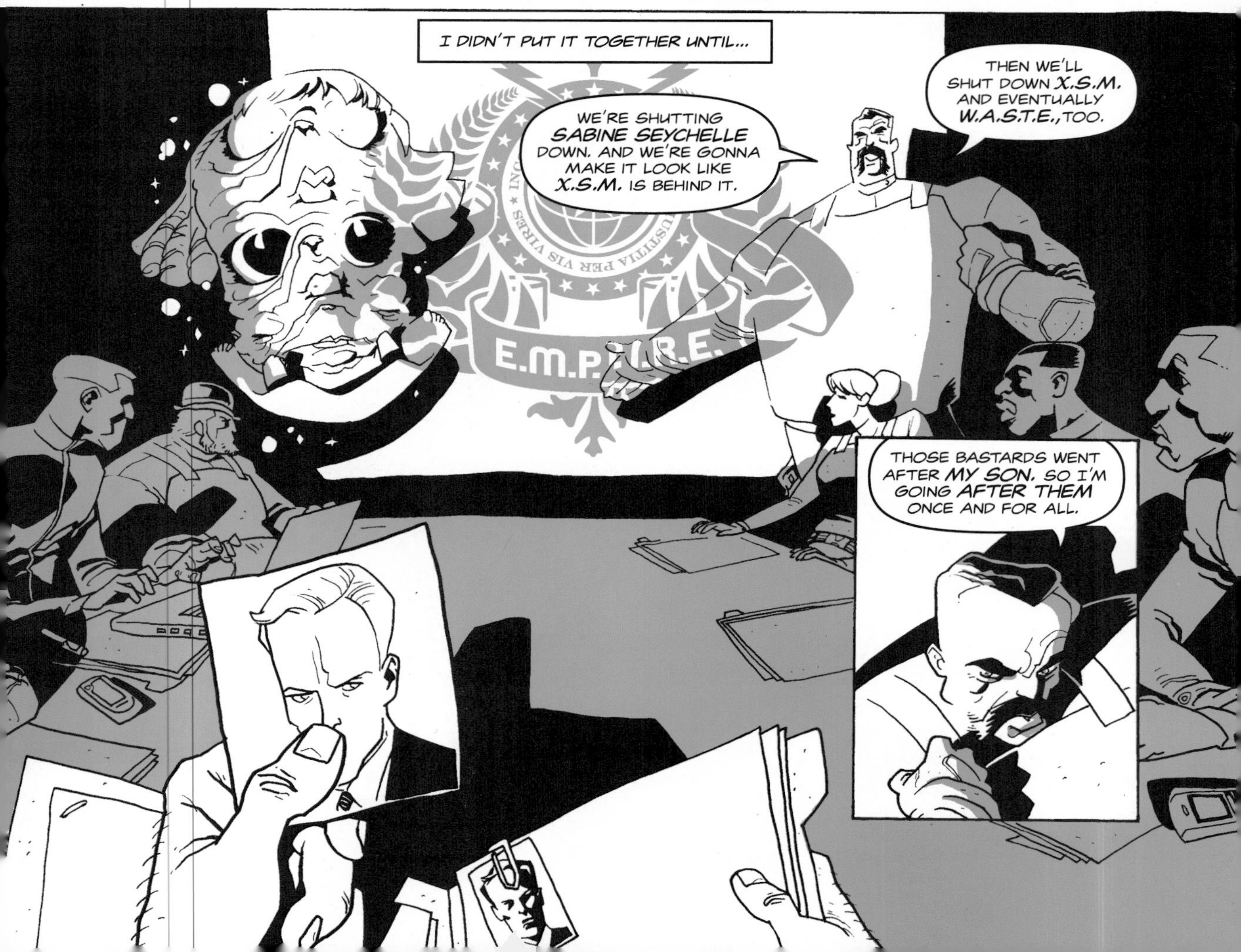

I DIDN'T PUT IT TOGETHER UNTIL...
WE'RE SHUTTING SABINE SEYCHELLE DOWN. AND WE'RE GONNA MAKE IT LOOK LIKE X.S.M. IS BEHIND IT.
THEN WE'LL SHUT DOWN X.S.M. AND EVENTUALLY W.A.S.T.E., TOO.
THOSE BASTARDS WENT AFTER MY SON. SO I'M GOING AFTER THEM ONCE AND FOR ALL.

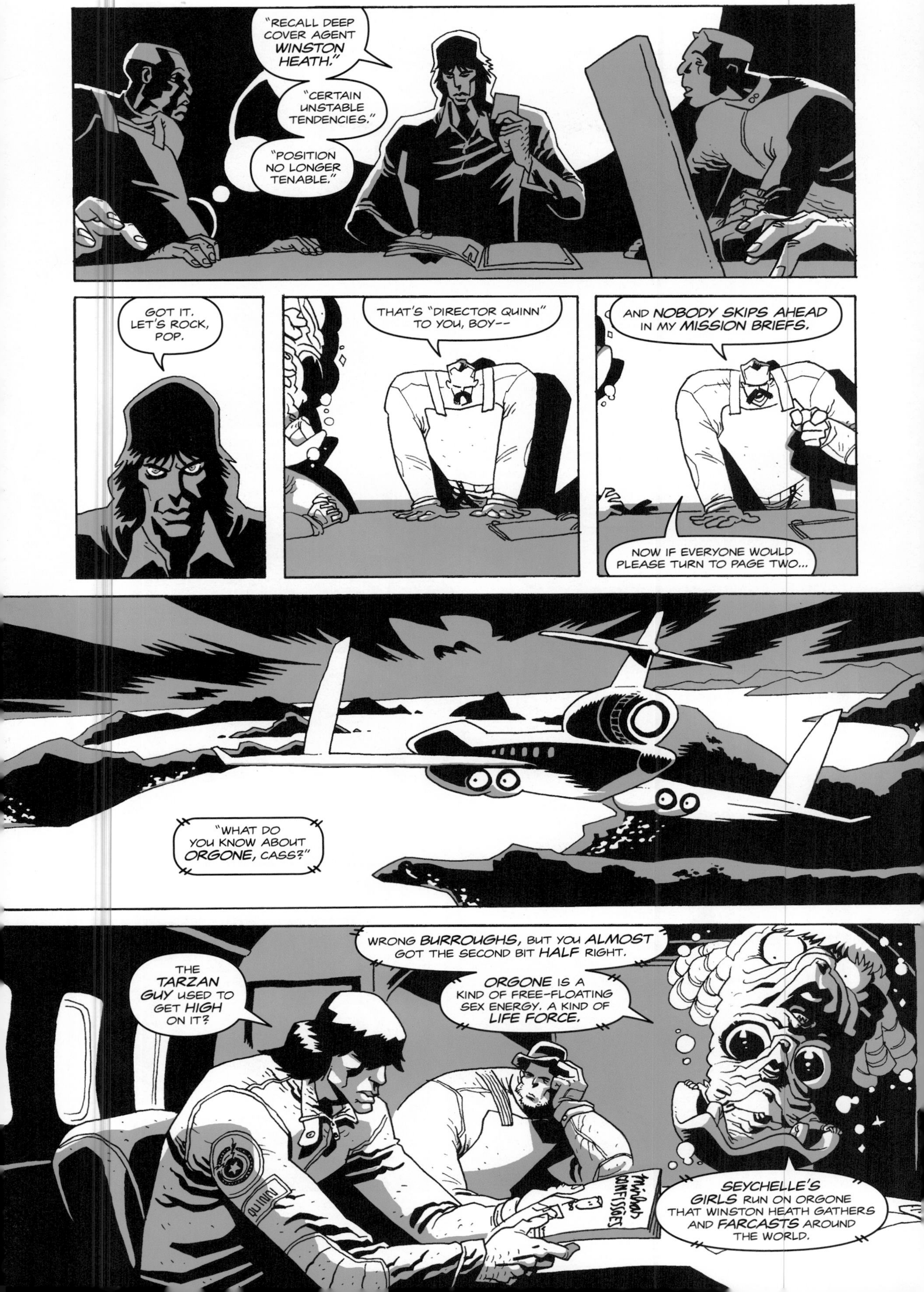

"RECALL DEEP COVER AGENT WINSTON HEATH."
"CERTAIN UNSTABLE TENDENCIES."
"POSITION NO LONGER TENABLE."
GOT IT. LET'S ROCK, POP.
THAT'S "DIRECTOR QUINN" TO YOU, BOY--
AND NOBODY SKIPS AHEAD IN MY MISSION BRIEFS.
NOW IF EVERYONE WOULD PLEASE TURN TO PAGE TWO...
"WHAT DO YOU KNOW ABOUT ORGONE, CASS?"
THE TARZAN GUY USED TO GET HIGH ON IT?
WRONG BURROUGHS, BUT YOU ALMOST GOT THE SECOND BIT HALF RIGHT.
ORGONE IS A KIND OF FREE-FLOATING SEX ENERGY. A KIND OF LIFE FORCE.
SEYCHELLE'S GIRLS RUN ON ORGONE THAT WINSTON HEATH GATHERS AND FARCASTS AROUND THE WORLD.

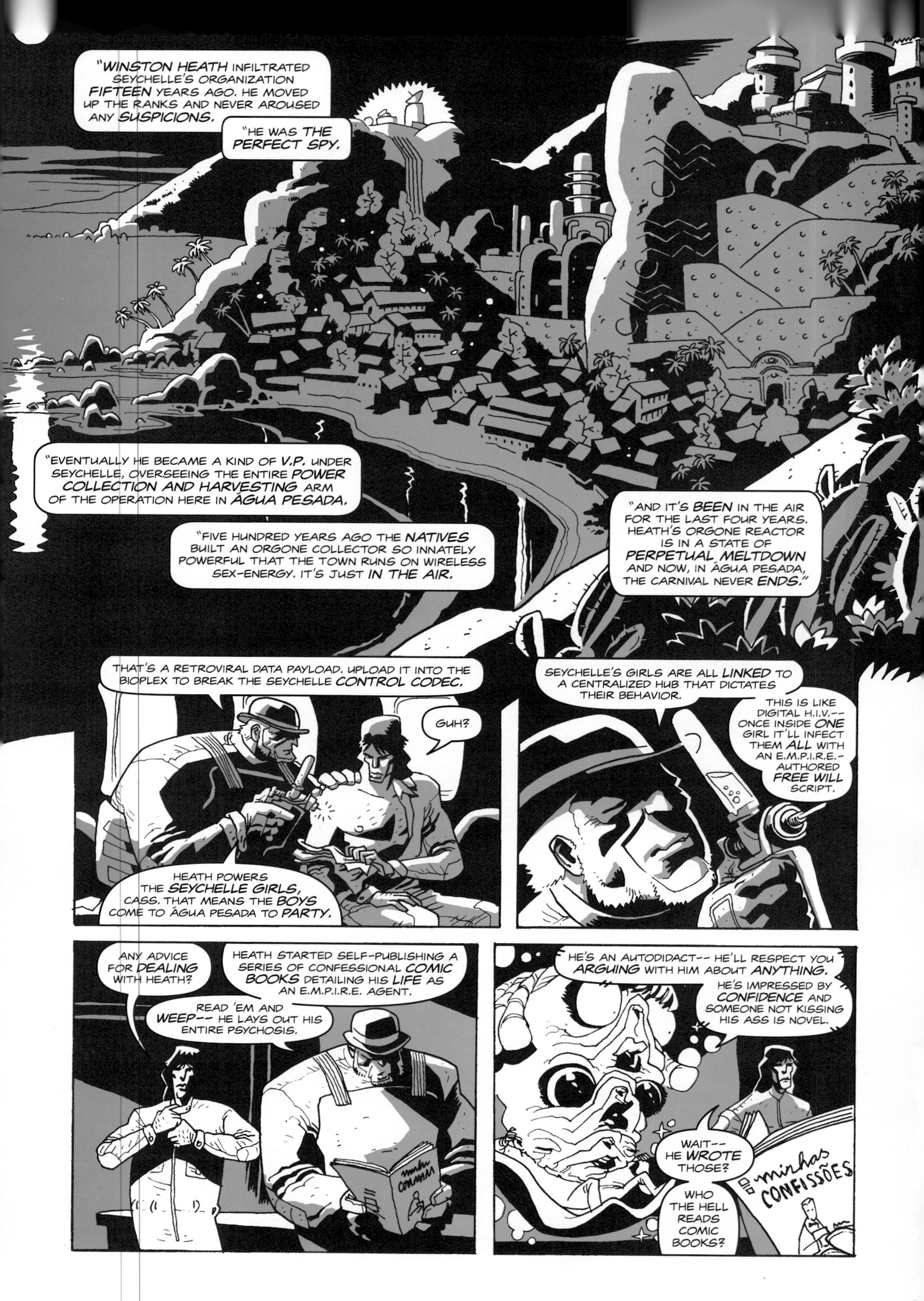
"WINSTON HEATH INFILTRATED SEYCHELLE'S ORGANIZATION FIFTEEN YEARS AGO. HE MOVED UP THE RANKS AND NEVER AROUSED ANY SUSPICIONS.
"HE WAS THE PERFECT SPY.
"EVENTUALLY HE BECAME A KIND OF V.P. UNDER SEYCHELLE, OVERSEEING THE ENTIRE POWER COLLECTION AND HARVESTING ARM OF THE OPERATION HERE IN ÁGUA PESADA.
"FIVE HUNDRED YEARS AGO THE NATIVES BUILT AN ORGONE COLLECTOR SO INNATELY POWERFUL THAT THE TOWN RUNS ON WIRELESS SEX-ENERGY. IT'S JUST IN THE AIR.
"AND IT'S BEEN IN THE AIR FOR THE LAST FOUR YEARS. HEATH'S ORGONE REACTOR IS IN A STATE OF PERPETUAL MELTDOWN AND NOW, IN ÁGUA PESADA, THE CARNIVAL NEVER ENDS."
THAT'S A RETROVIRAL DATA PAYLOAD. UPLOAD IT INTO THE BIOPLEX TO BREAK THE SEYCHELLE CONTROL CODEC.
GUH?
HEATH POWERS THE SEYCHELLE GIRLS, CASS. THAT MEANS THE BOYS COME TO ÁGUA PESADA TO PARTY.
SEYCHELLE'S GIRLS ARE ALL LINKED TO A CENTRALIZED HUB THAT DICTATES THEIR BEHAVIOR.
THIS IS LIKE DIGITAL H.I.V.-- ONCE INSIDE ONE GIRL IT'LL INFECT THEM ALL WITH AN E.M.P.I.R.E.-AUTHORED FREE WILL SCRIPT.
ANY ADVICE FOR DEALING WITH HEATH?
HEATH STARTED SELF-PUBLISHING A SERIES OF CONFESSIONAL COMIC BOOKS DETAILING HIS LIFE AS AN E.M.P.I.R.E. AGENT.
READ 'EM AND WEEP-- HE LAYS OUT HIS ENTIRE PSYCHOSIS.
HE'S AN AUTODIDACT-- HE'LL RESPECT YOU ARGUING WITH HIM ABOUT ANYTHING.
HE'S IMPRESSED BY CONFIDENCE AND SOMEONE NOT KISSING HIS ASS IS NOVEL.
WAIT-- HE WROTE THOSE?
WHO THE HELL READS COMIC BOOKS?
minhas CONFISSÕES

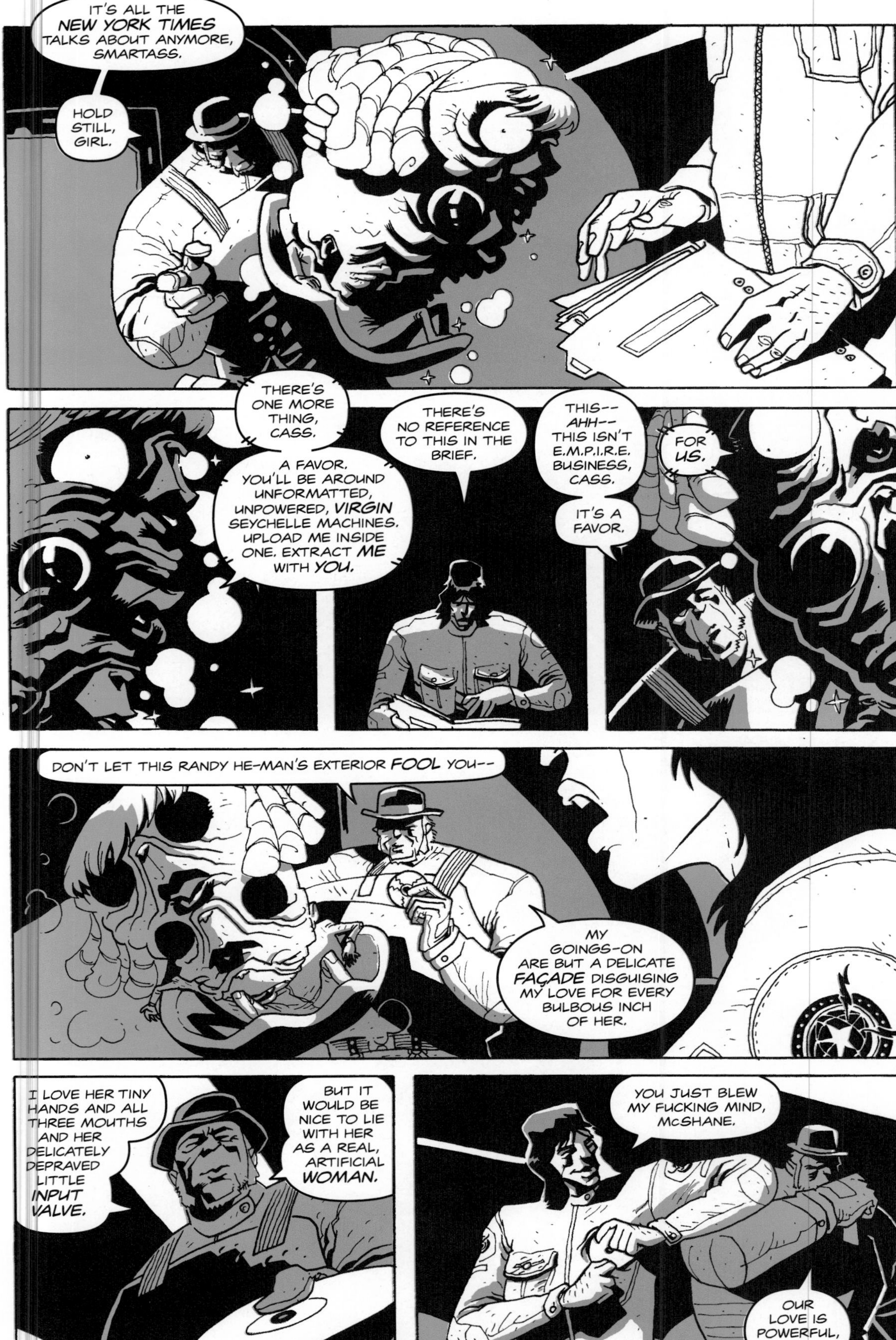
IT'S ALL THE NEW YORK TIMES TALKS ABOUT ANYMORE, SMARTASS.
HOLD STILL, GIRL.
THERE'S ONE MORE THING, CASS.
A FAVOR. YOU'LL BE AROUND UNFORMATTED, UNPOWERED, VIRGIN SEYCHELLE MACHINES. UPLOAD ME INSIDE ONE. EXTRACT ME WITH YOU.
THERE'S NO REFERENCE TO THIS IN THE BRIEF.
THIS-- AHH-- THIS ISN'T E.M.P.I.R.E. BUSINESS, CASS.
IT'S A FAVOR.
FOR US.
DON'T LET THIS RANDY HE-MAN'S EXTERIOR FOOL YOU--
MY GOINGS-ON ARE BUT A DELICATE FAÇADE DISGUISING MY LOVE FOR EVERY BULBOUS INCH OF HER.
I LOVE HER TINY HANDS AND ALL THREE MOUTHS AND HER DELICATELY DEPRAVED LITTLE INPUT VALVE.
BUT IT WOULD BE NICE TO LIE WITH HER AS A REAL, ARTIFICIAL WOMAN.
YOU JUST BLEW MY FUCKING MIND, McSHANE.
OUR LOVE IS POWERFUL, YES.

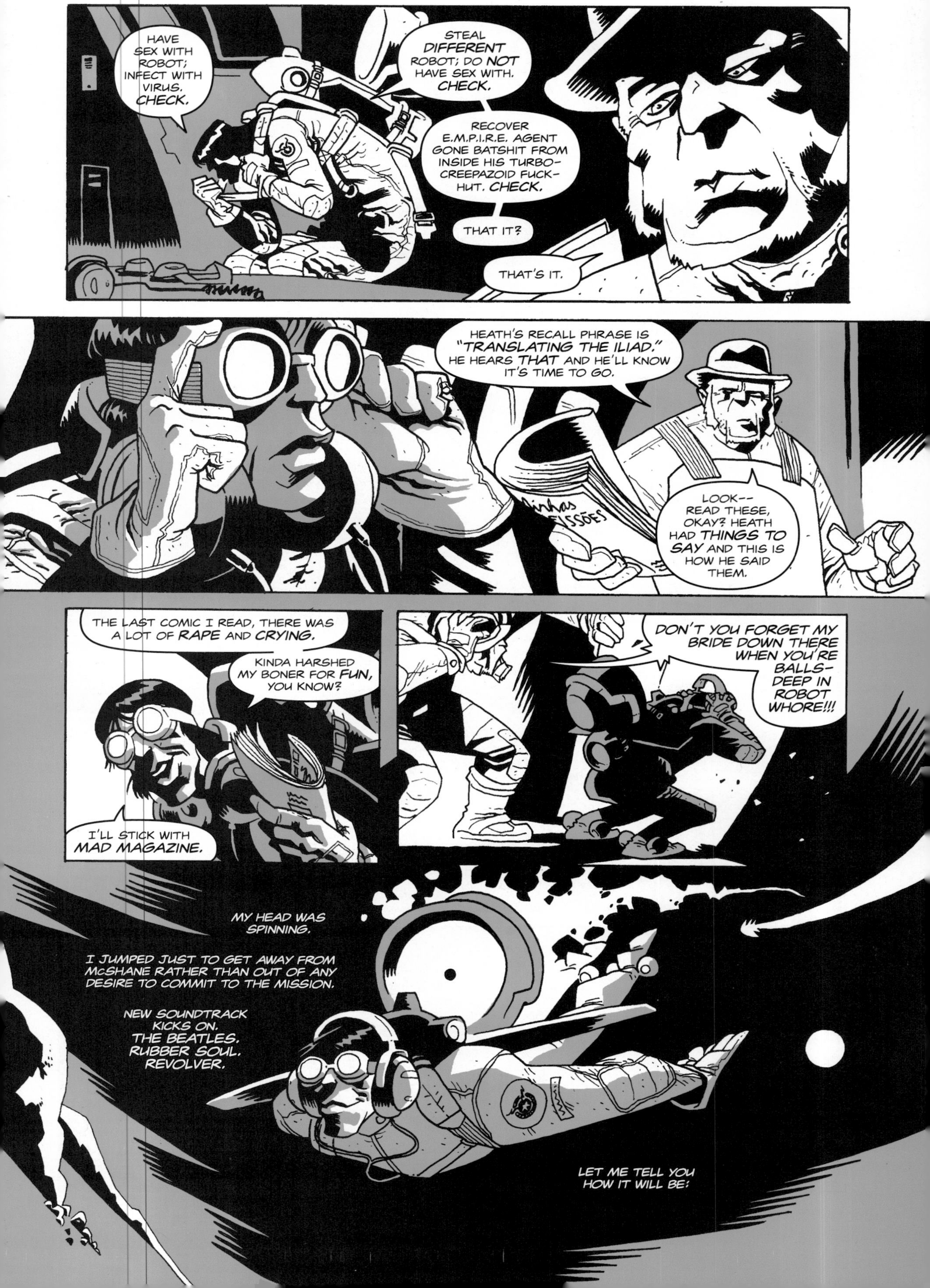
HAVE SEX WITH ROBOT; INFECT WITH VIRUS. CHECK.
STEAL DIFFERENT ROBOT; DO NOT HAVE SEX WITH. CHECK.
RECOVER E.M.P.I.R.E. AGENT GONE BATSHIT FROM INSIDE HIS TURBO-CREEPAZOID FUCK-HUT. CHECK.
THAT IT?
THAT'S IT.
HEATH'S RECALL PHRASE IS "TRANSLATING THE ILIAD." HE HEARS THAT AND HE'LL KNOW IT'S TIME TO GO.
LOOK-- READ THESE, OKAY? HEATH HAD THINGS TO SAY AND THIS IS HOW HE SAID THEM.
THE LAST COMIC I READ, THERE WAS A LOT OF RAPE AND CRYING.
KINDA HARSHED MY BONER FOR FUN, YOU KNOW?
I'LL STICK WITH MAD MAGAZINE.
DON'T YOU FORGET MY BRIDE DOWN THERE WHEN YOU'RE BALLS-DEEP IN ROBOT WHORE!!!
MY HEAD WAS SPINNING.
I JUMPED JUST TO GET AWAY FROM McSHANE RATHER THAN OUT OF ANY DESIRE TO COMMIT TO THE MISSION.
NEW SOUNDTRACK KICKS ON. THE BEATLES. RUBBER SOUL. REVOLVER.
LET ME TELL YOU HOW IT WILL BE:

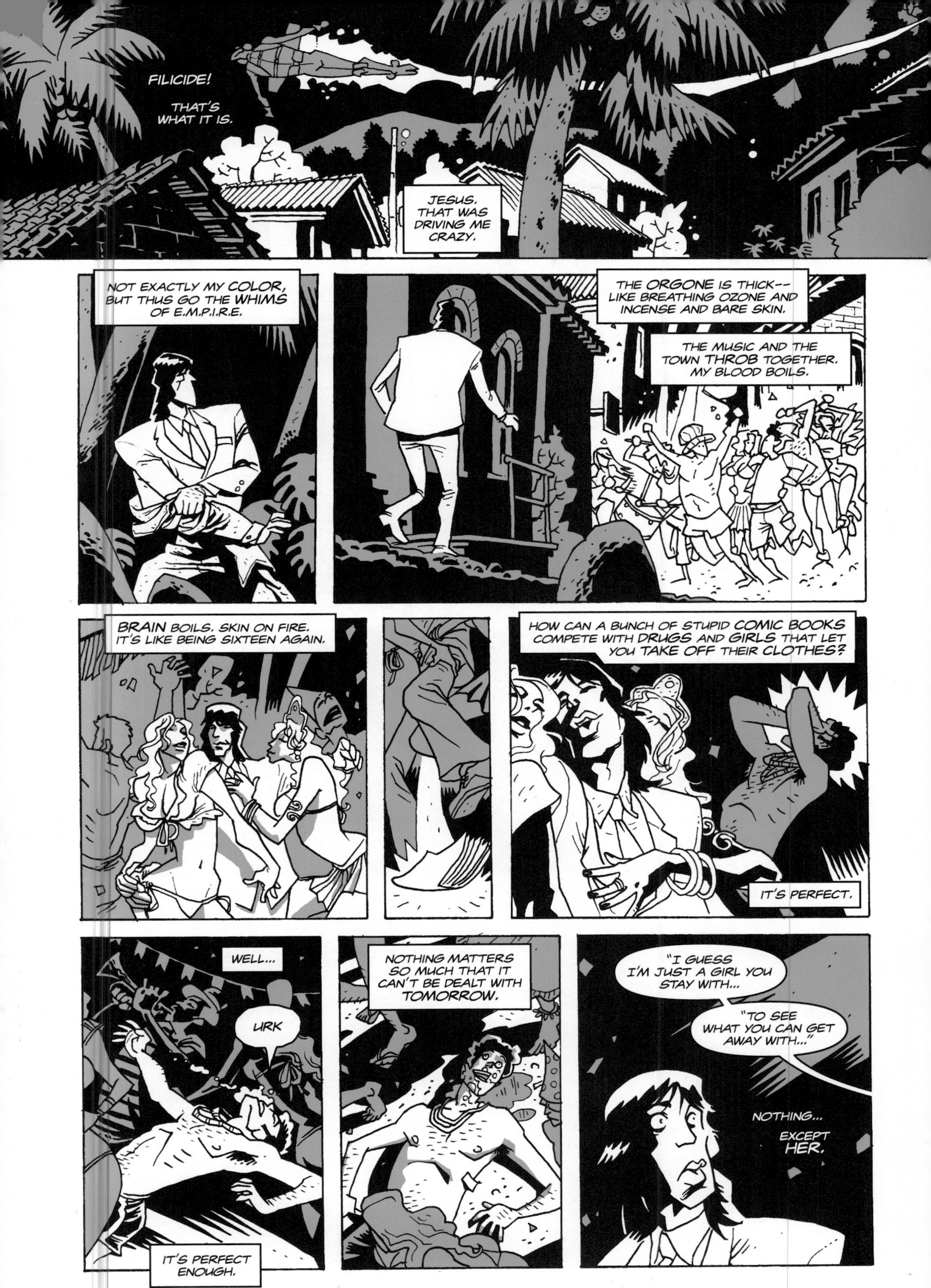
FILICIDE!
THAT'S WHAT IT IS.
JESUS. THAT WAS DRIVING ME CRAZY.
NOT EXACTLY MY COLOR, BUT THUS GO THE WHIMS OF E.M.P.I.R.E.
THE ORGONE IS THICK-- LIKE BREATHING OZONE AND INCENSE AND BARE SKIN.
THE MUSIC AND THE TOWN THROB TOGETHER. MY BLOOD BOILS.
BRAIN BOILS. SKIN ON FIRE. IT'S LIKE BEING SIXTEEN AGAIN.
HOW CAN A BUNCH OF STUPID COMIC BOOKS COMPETE WITH DRUGS AND GIRLS THAT LET YOU TAKE OFF THEIR CLOTHES?
IT'S PERFECT.
WELL...
URK
IT'S PERFECT ENOUGH.
NOTHING MATTERS SO MUCH THAT IT CAN'T BE DEALT WITH TOMORROW.
"I GUESS I'M JUST A GIRL YOU STAY WITH...
"TO SEE WHAT YOU CAN GET AWAY WITH..."
NOTHING... EXCEPT HER.

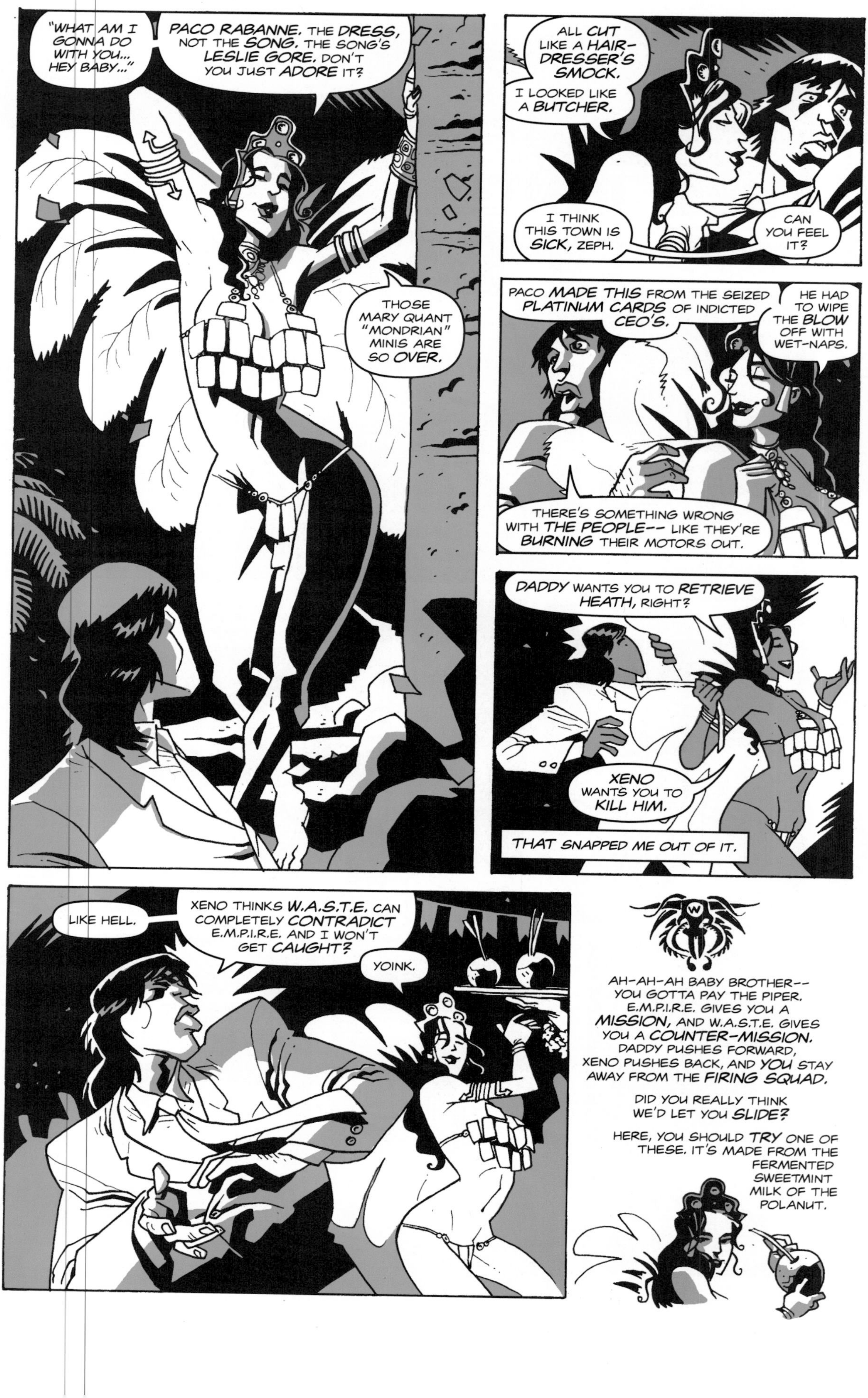
"WHAT AM I GONNA DO WITH YOU... HEY BABY..."
PACO RABANNE. THE DRESS, NOT THE SONG. THE SONG'S LESLIE GORE. DON'T YOU JUST ADORE IT?
THOSE MARY QUANT "MONDRIAN" MINIS ARE SO OVER.
ALL CUT LIKE A HAIR-DRESSER'S SMOCK.
I LOOKED LIKE A BUTCHER.
I THINK THIS TOWN IS SICK, ZEPH.
CAN YOU FEEL IT?
PACO MADE THIS FROM THE SEIZED PLATINUM CARDS OF INDICTED CEO'S.
HE HAD TO WIPE THE BLOW OFF WITH WET-NAPS.
THERE'S SOMETHING WRONG WITH THE PEOPLE-- LIKE THEY'RE BURNING THEIR MOTORS OUT.
DADDY WANTS YOU TO RETRIEVE HEATH, RIGHT?
XENO WANTS YOU TO KILL HIM.
THAT SNAPPED ME OUT OF IT.
LIKE HELL.
XENO THINKS W.A.S.T.E. CAN COMPLETELY CONTRADICT E.M.P.I.R.E. AND I WON'T GET CAUGHT?
YOINK.
AH-AH-AH BABY BROTHER-- YOU GOTTA PAY THE PIPER. E.M.P.I.R.E. GIVES YOU A MISSION, AND W.A.S.T.E. GIVES YOU A COUNTER-MISSION. DADDY PUSHES FORWARD, XENO PUSHES BACK, AND YOU STAY AWAY FROM THE FIRING SQUAD.
DID YOU REALLY THINK WE'D LET YOU SLIDE?
HERE, YOU SHOULD TRY ONE OF THESE. IT'S MADE FROM THE FERMENTED SWEETMINT MILK OF THE POLANUT.

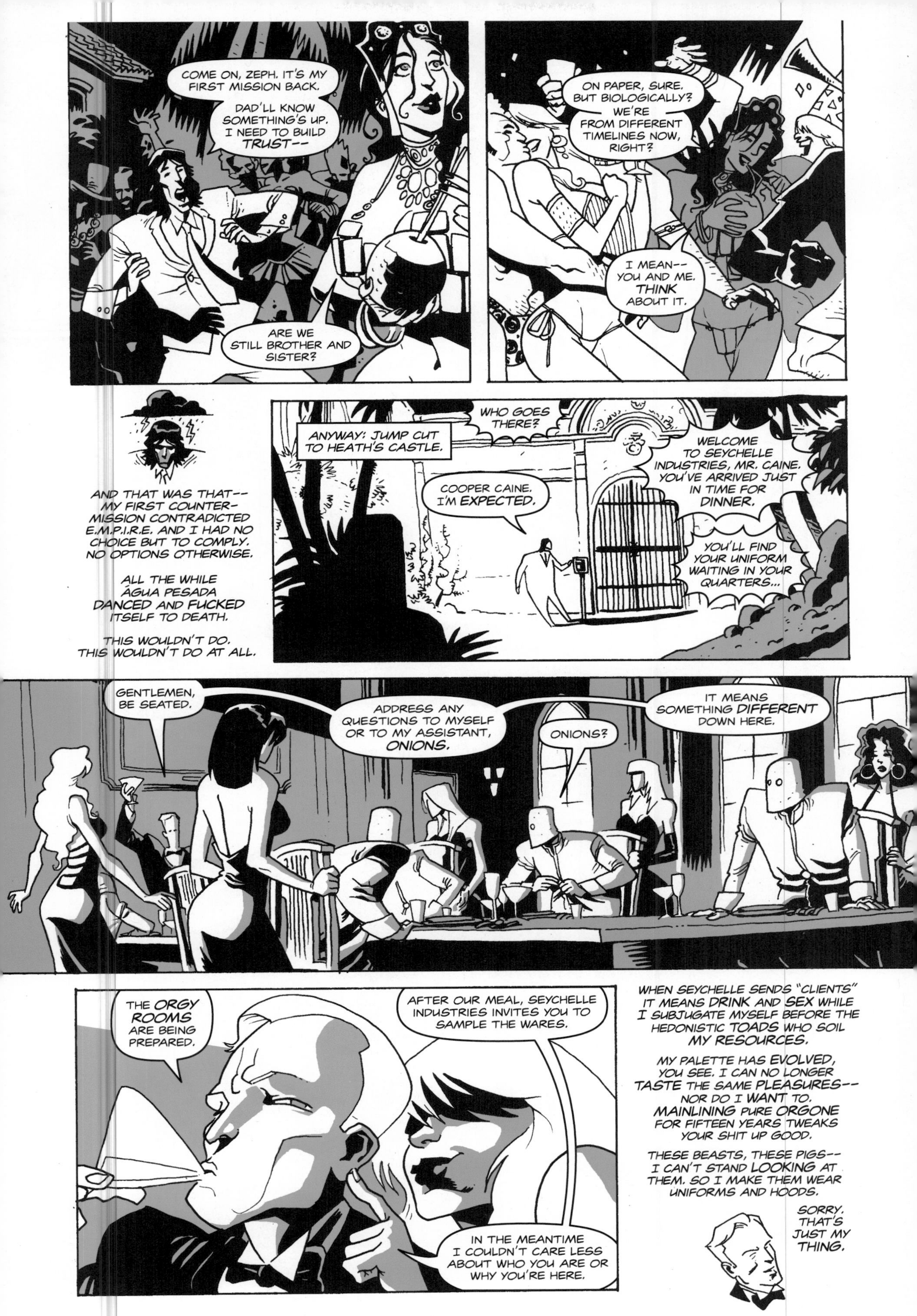
COME ON, ZEPH. IT'S MY FIRST MISSION BACK.
DAD'LL KNOW SOMETHING'S UP. I NEED TO BUILD TRUST--
ARE WE STILL BROTHER AND SISTER?
ON PAPER, SURE. BUT BIOLOGICALLY? WE'RE FROM DIFFERENT TIMELINES NOW, RIGHT?
I MEAN-- YOU AND ME. THINK ABOUT IT.

AND THAT WAS THAT-- MY FIRST COUNTER-MISSION CONTRADICTED E.M.P.I.R.E. AND I HAD NO CHOICE BUT TO COMPLY. NO OPTIONS OTHERWISE.

ALL THE WHILE ÁGUA PESADA DANCED AND FUCKED ITSELF TO DEATH.

THIS WOULDN'T DO. THIS WOULDN'T DO AT ALL.

ANYWAY: JUMP CUT TO HEATH'S CASTLE.
WHO GOES THERE?
COOPER CAINE. I'M EXPECTED.
WELCOME TO SEYCHELLE INDUSTRIES, MR. CAINE. YOU'VE ARRIVED JUST IN TIME FOR DINNER.
YOU'LL FIND YOUR UNIFORM WAITING IN YOUR QUARTERS...
GENTLEMEN, BE SEATED.
ADDRESS ANY QUESTIONS TO MYSELF OR TO MY ASSISTANT, ONIONS.
ONIONS?
IT MEANS SOMETHING DIFFERENT DOWN HERE.
THE ORGY ROOMS ARE BEING PREPARED.
AFTER OUR MEAL, SEYCHELLE INDUSTRIES INVITES YOU TO SAMPLE THE WARES.
IN THE MEANTIME I COULDN'T CARE LESS ABOUT WHO YOU ARE OR WHY YOU'RE HERE.

WHEN SEYCHELLE SENDS "CLIENTS" IT MEANS DRINK AND SEX WHILE I SUBJUGATE MYSELF BEFORE THE HEDONISTIC TOADS WHO SOIL MY RESOURCES.

MY PALETTE HAS EVOLVED, YOU SEE. I CAN NO LONGER TASTE THE SAME PLEASURES-- NOR DO I WANT TO. MAINLINING PURE ORGONE FOR FIFTEEN YEARS TWEAKS YOUR SHIT UP GOOD.

THESE BEASTS, THESE PIGS-- I CAN'T STAND LOOKING AT THEM. SO I MAKE THEM WEAR UNIFORMS AND HOODS.

SORRY. THAT'S JUST MY THING.

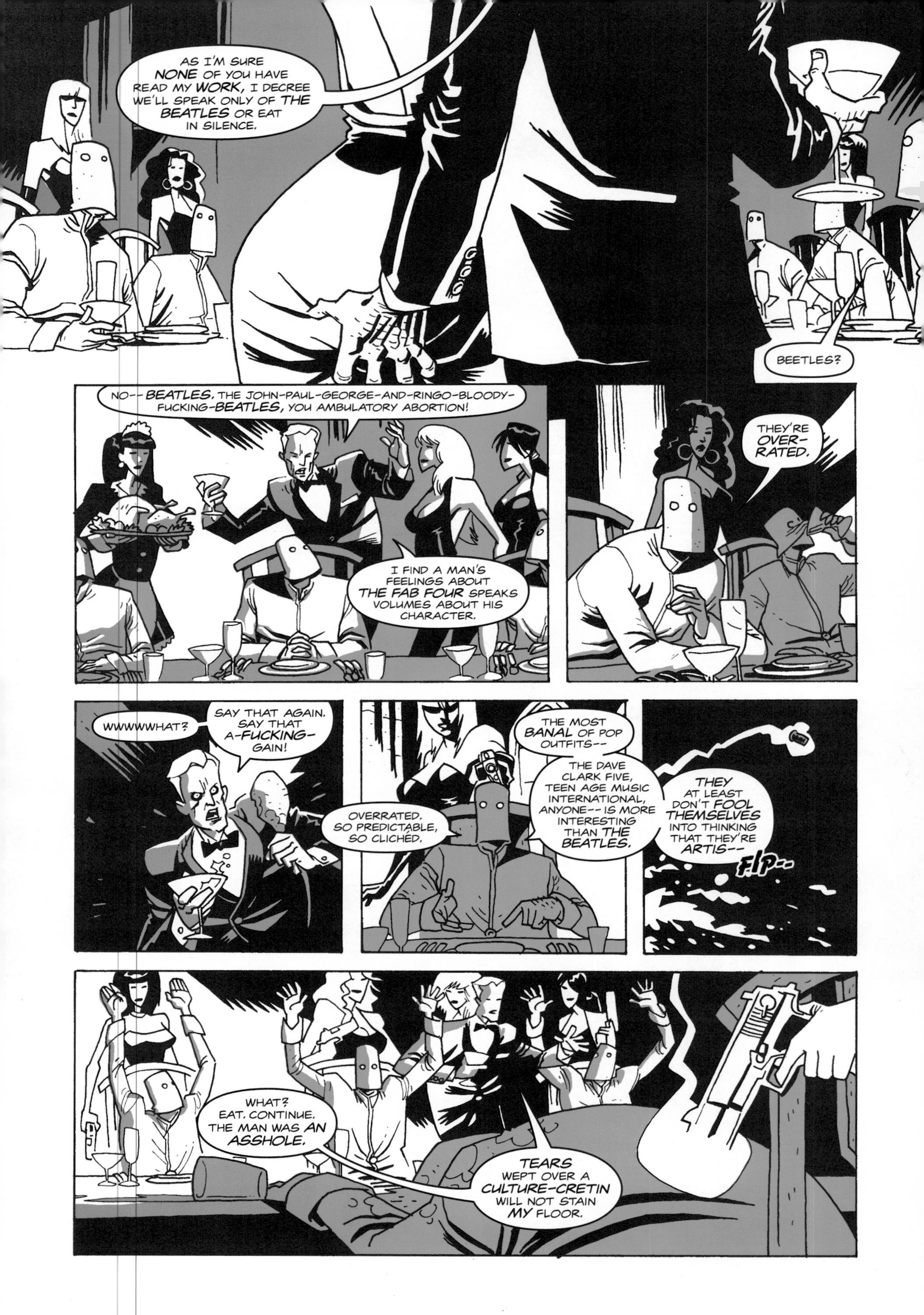
AS I'M SURE NONE OF YOU HAVE READ MY WORK, I DECREE WE'LL SPEAK ONLY OF THE BEATLES OR EAT IN SILENCE.
BEETLES?
NO-- BEATLES. THE JOHN-PAUL-GEORGE-AND-RINGO-BLOODY-FUCKING-BEATLES, YOU AMBULATORY ABORTION!
I FIND A MAN'S FEELINGS ABOUT THE FAB FOUR SPEAKS VOLUMES ABOUT HIS CHARACTER.
THEY'RE OVER-RATED.
WWWWWHAT?
SAY THAT AGAIN. SAY THAT A-FUCKING-GAIN!
OVERRATED. SO PREDICTABLE, SO CLICHÉD.
THE MOST BANAL OF POP OUTFITS--
THE DAVE CLARK FIVE, TEEN AGE MUSIC INTERNATIONAL, ANYONE-- IS MORE INTERESTING THAN THE BEATLES.
THEY AT LEAST DON'T FOOL THEMSELVES INTO THINKING THAT THEY'RE ARTIS--
FIP--
WHAT? EAT. CONTINUE. THE MAN WAS AN ASSHOLE.
TEARS WEPT OVER A CULTURE-CRETIN WILL NOT STAIN MY FLOOR.

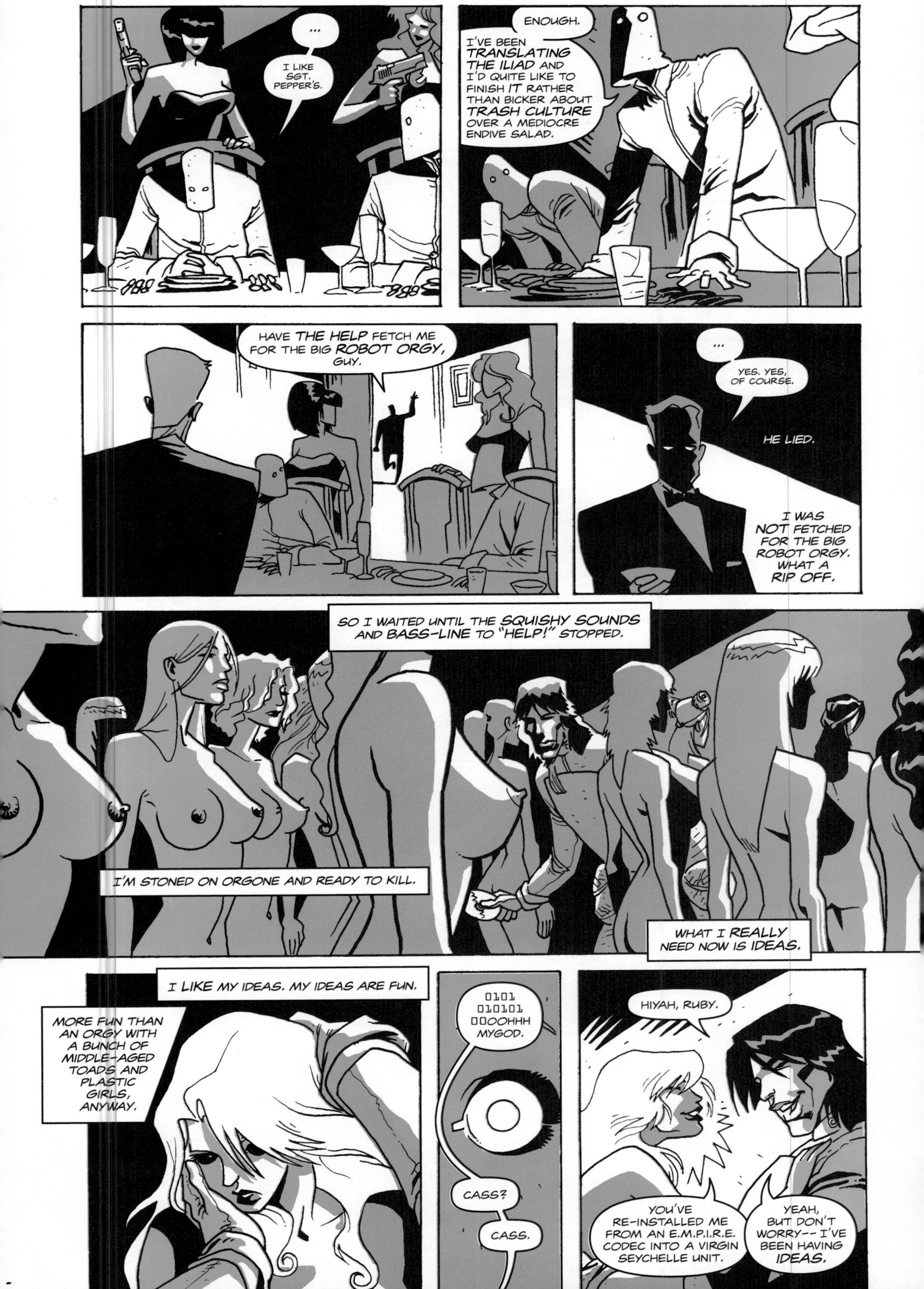
...
I LIKE SGT. PEPPER'S.
ENOUGH.
I'VE BEEN TRANSLATING THE ILIAD AND I'D QUITE LIKE TO FINISH IT RATHER THAN BICKER ABOUT TRASH CULTURE OVER A MEDIOCRE ENDIVE SALAD.
HAVE THE HELP FETCH ME FOR THE BIG ROBOT ORGY, GUY.
...
YES. YES, OF COURSE.
HE LIED.
I WAS NOT FETCHED FOR THE BIG ROBOT ORGY. WHAT A RIP OFF.
SO I WAITED UNTIL THE SQUISHY SOUNDS AND BASS-LINE TO "HELP!" STOPPED.
I'M STONED ON ORGONE AND READY TO KILL.
WHAT I REALLY NEED NOW IS IDEAS.
I LIKE MY IDEAS. MY IDEAS ARE FUN.
MORE FUN THAN AN ORGY WITH A BUNCH OF MIDDLE-AGED TOADS AND PLASTIC GIRLS, ANYWAY.
0101 010101 OOOOHHH MYGOD.
CASS?
CASS.
HIYAH, RUBY.
YOU'VE RE-INSTALLED ME FROM AN E.M.P.I.R.E. CODEC INTO A VIRGIN SEYCHELLE UNIT.
YEAH, BUT DON'T WORRY-- I'VE BEEN HAVING IDEAS.

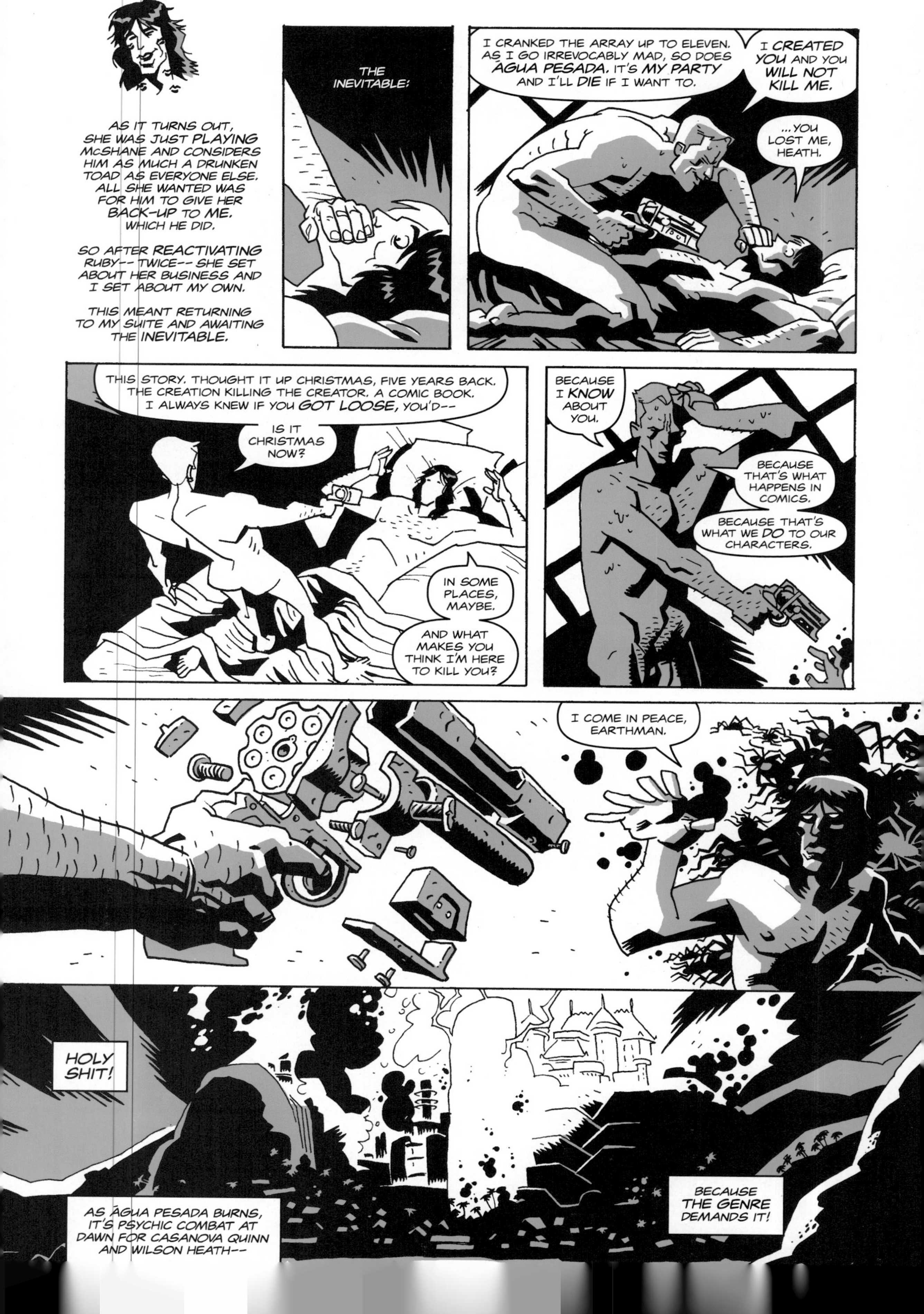
AS IT TURNS OUT, SHE WAS JUST PLAYING McSHANE AND CONSIDERS HIM AS MUCH A DRUNKEN TOAD AS EVERYONE ELSE. ALL SHE WANTED WAS FOR HIM TO GIVE HER BACK-UP TO ME. WHICH HE DID.
SO AFTER REACTIVATING RUBY-- TWICE-- SHE SET ABOUT HER BUSINESS AND I SET ABOUT MY OWN.
THIS MEANT RETURNING TO MY SUITE AND AWAITING THE INEVITABLE.
THE INEVITABLE:
I CRANKED THE ARRAY UP TO ELEVEN. AS I GO IRREVOCABLY MAD, SO DOES ÁGUA PESADA. IT'S MY PARTY AND I'LL DIE IF I WANT TO.
I CREATED YOU AND YOU WILL NOT KILL ME.
...YOU LOST ME, HEATH.
THIS STORY. THOUGHT IT UP CHRISTMAS, FIVE YEARS BACK. THE CREATION KILLING THE CREATOR. A COMIC BOOK. I ALWAYS KNEW IF YOU GOT LOOSE, YOU'D--
IS IT CHRISTMAS NOW?
IN SOME PLACES, MAYBE.
AND WHAT MAKES YOU THINK I'M HERE TO KILL YOU?
BECAUSE I KNOW ABOUT YOU.
BECAUSE THAT'S WHAT HAPPENS IN COMICS.
BECAUSE THAT'S WHAT WE DO TO OUR CHARACTERS.
I COME IN PEACE, EARTHMAN.
HOLY SHIT!
AS ÁGUA PESADA BURNS, IT'S PSYCHIC COMBAT AT DAWN FOR CASANOVA QUINN AND WILSON HEATH--
BECAUSE THE GENRE DEMANDS IT!

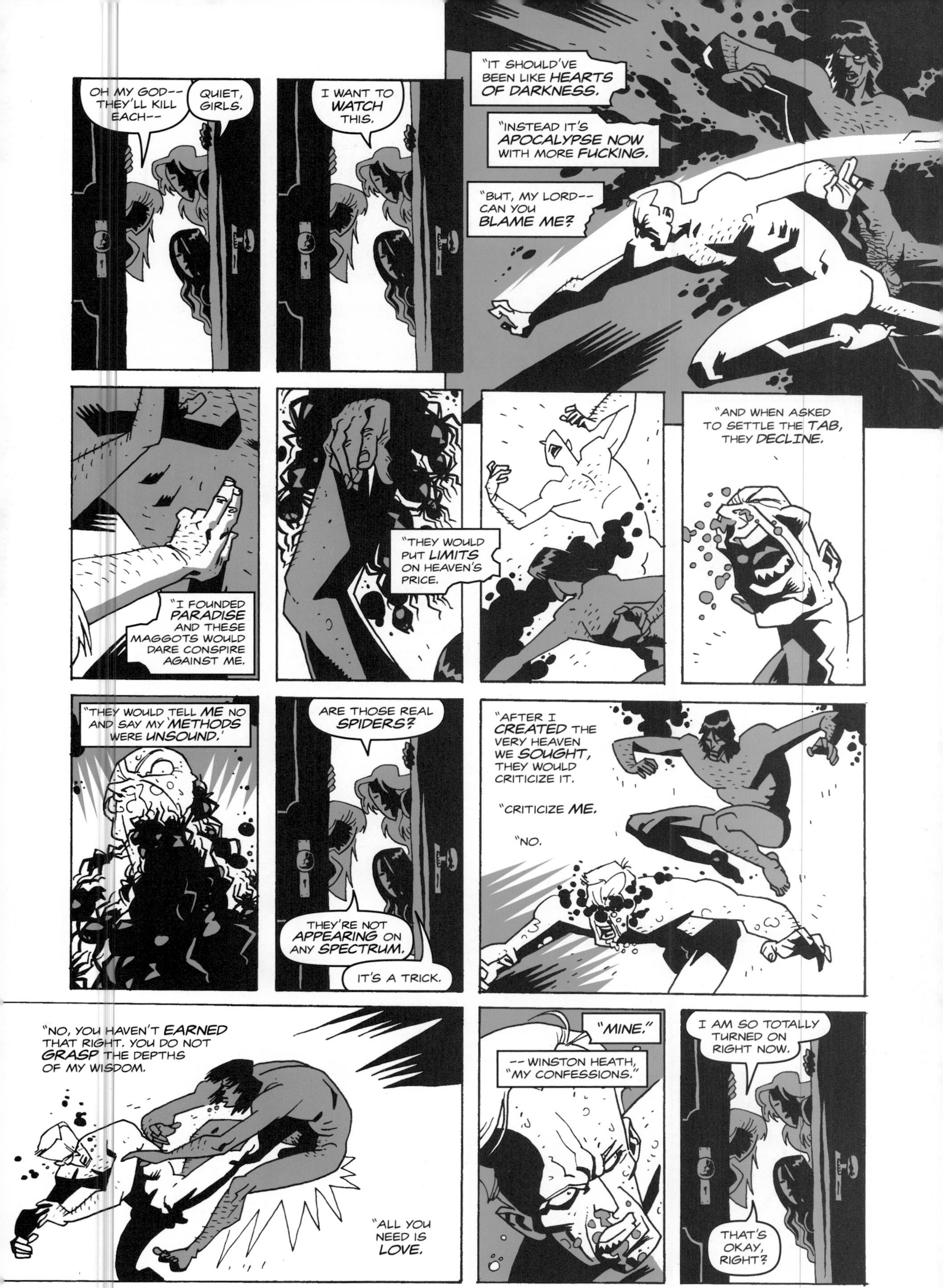
"IT SHOULD'VE BEEN LIKE HEARTS OF DARKNESS.
"INSTEAD IT'S APOCALYPSE NOW WITH MORE FUCKING.
"BUT, MY LORD-- CAN YOU BLAME ME?
OH MY GOD-- THEY'LL KILL EACH--
QUIET, GIRLS.
I WANT TO WATCH THIS.
"I FOUNDED PARADISE AND THESE MAGGOTS WOULD DARE CONSPIRE AGAINST ME.
"THEY WOULD PUT LIMITS ON HEAVEN'S PRICE.
"AND WHEN ASKED TO SETTLE THE TAB, THEY DECLINE.
"THEY WOULD TELL ME NO AND SAY MY 'METHODS WERE UNSOUND.'
ARE THOSE REAL SPIDERS?
THEY'RE NOT APPEARING ON ANY SPECTRUM.
IT'S A TRICK.
"AFTER I CREATED THE VERY HEAVEN WE SOUGHT, THEY WOULD CRITICIZE IT.
"CRITICIZE ME.
"NO.
"NO, YOU HAVEN'T EARNED THAT RIGHT. YOU DO NOT GRASP THE DEPTHS OF MY WISDOM.
"ALL YOU NEED IS LOVE.
"MINE."
--WINSTON HEATH, "MY CONFESSIONS."
I AM SO TOTALLY TURNED ON RIGHT NOW.
THAT'S OKAY, RIGHT?

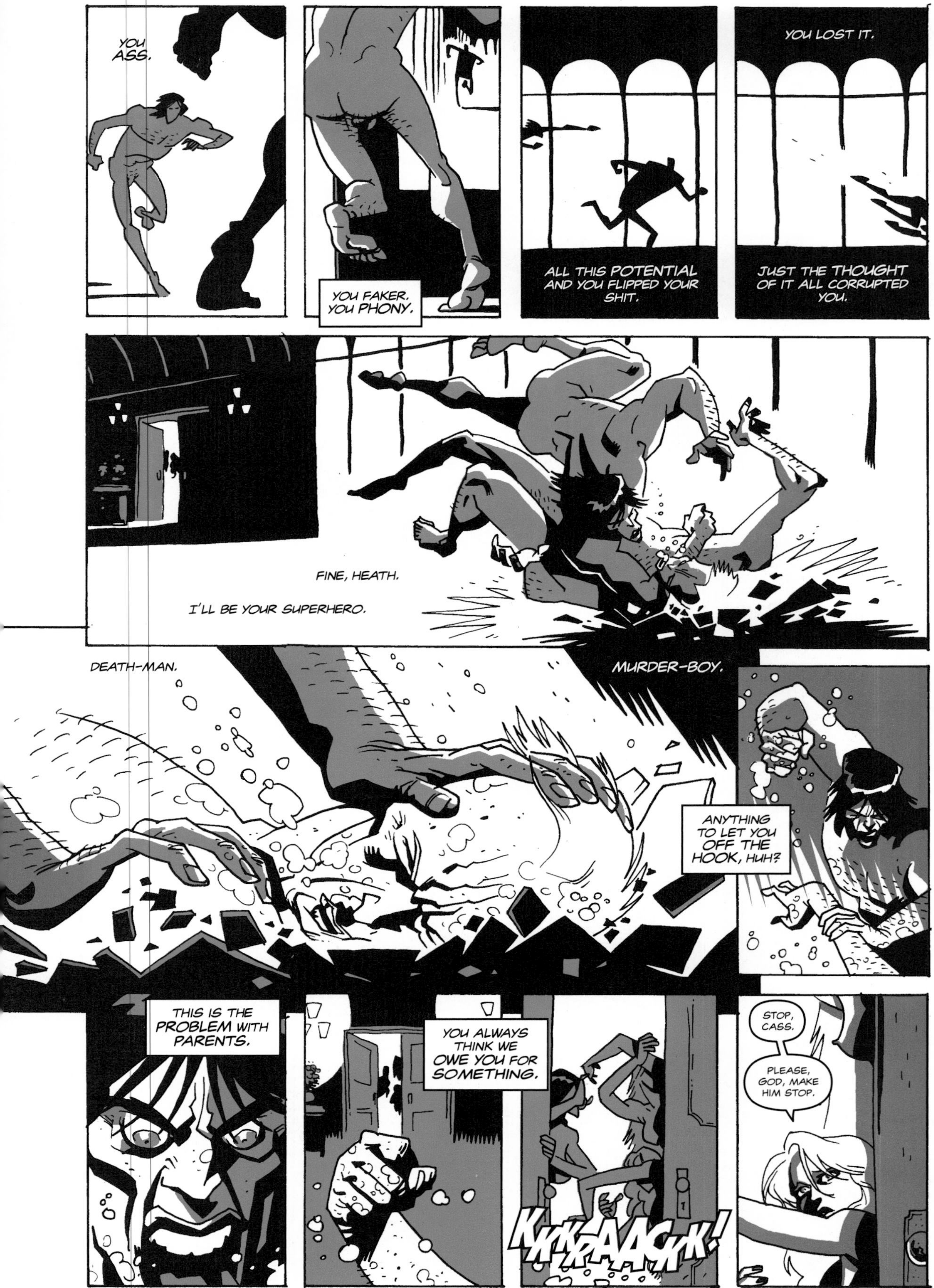

YOU ASS.
YOU FAKER. YOU PHONY.
ALL THIS POTENTIAL AND YOU FLIPPED YOUR SHIT.
YOU LOST IT.
JUST THE THOUGHT OF IT ALL CORRUPTED YOU.
FINE, HEATH.
I'LL BE YOUR SUPERHERO.
DEATH-MAN.
MURDER-BOY.
ANYTHING TO LET YOU OFF THE HOOK, HUH?
THIS IS THE PROBLEM WITH PARENTS.
YOU ALWAYS THINK WE OWE YOU FOR SOMETHING.
KKKRAAACKK!
STOP, CASS.
PLEASE, GOD, MAKE HIM STOP.

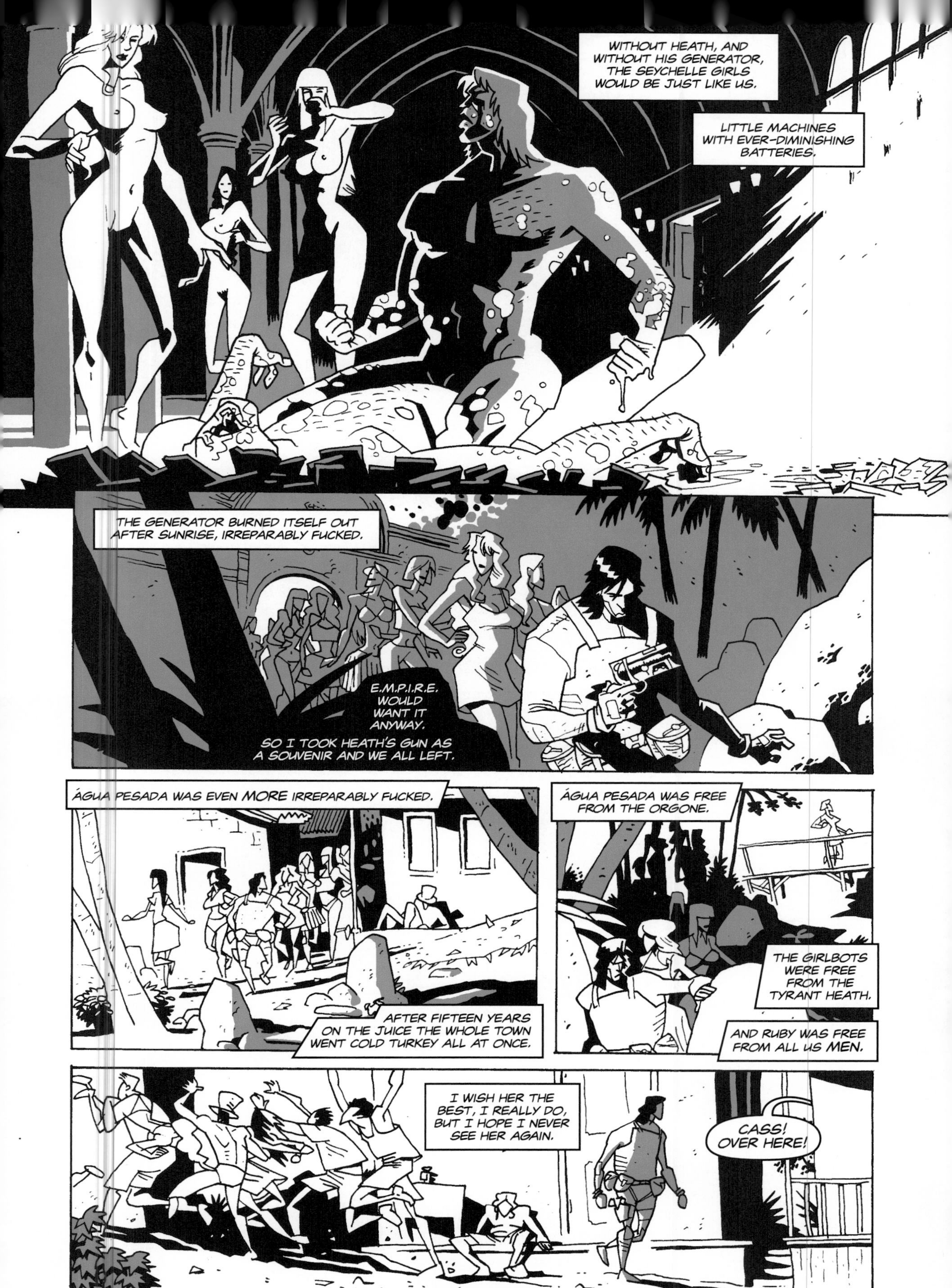
WITHOUT HEATH, AND WITHOUT HIS GENERATOR, THE SEYCHELLE GIRLS WOULD BE JUST LIKE US.
LITTLE MACHINES WITH EVER-DIMINISHING BATTERIES.
THE GENERATOR BURNED ITSELF OUT AFTER SUNRISE, IRREPARABLY FUCKED.
E.M.P.I.R.E. WOULD WANT IT ANYWAY.
SO I TOOK HEATH'S GUN AS A SOUVENIR AND WE ALL LEFT.
ÁGUA PESADA WAS EVEN MORE IRREPARABLY FUCKED.
AFTER FIFTEEN YEARS ON THE JUICE THE WHOLE TOWN WENT COLD TURKEY ALL AT ONCE.
ÁGUA PESADA WAS FREE FROM THE ORGONE.
THE GIRLBOTS WERE FREE FROM THE TYRANT HEATH.
AND RUBY WAS FREE FROM ALL US MEN.
I WISH HER THE BEST, I REALLY DO, BUT I HOPE I NEVER SEE HER AGAIN.
CASS! OVER HERE!

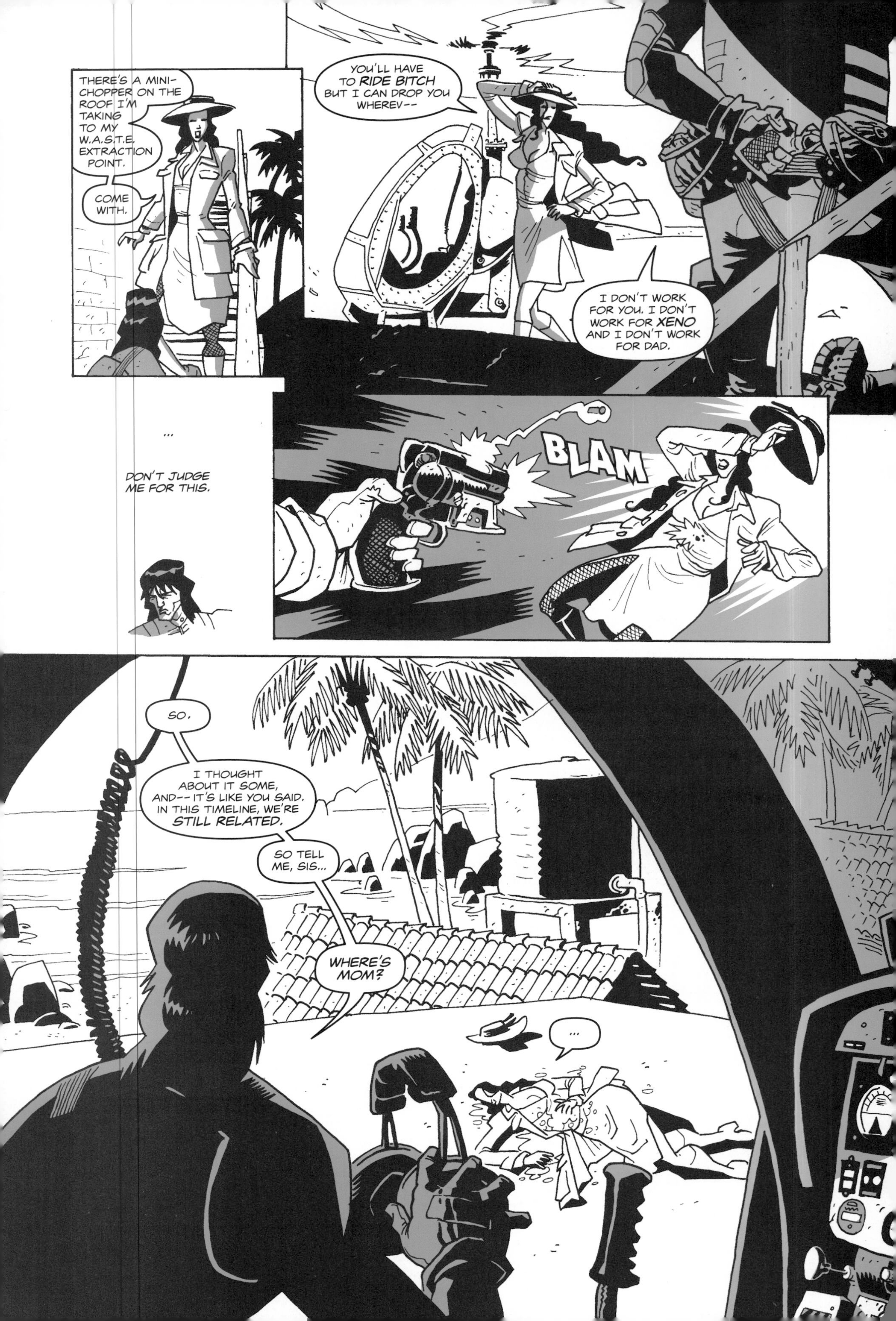

THERE'S A MINI-CHOPPER ON THE ROOF I'M TAKING TO MY W.A.S.T.E. EXTRACTION POINT.
COME WITH.
YOU'LL HAVE TO RIDE BITCH BUT I CAN DROP YOU WHEREV--
I DON'T WORK FOR YOU. I DON'T WORK FOR XENO AND I DON'T WORK FOR DAD.
...
DON'T JUDGE ME FOR THIS.
BLAM
SO.
I THOUGHT ABOUT IT SOME, AND-- IT'S LIKE YOU SAID. IN THIS TIMELINE, WE'RE STILL RELATED.
SO TELL ME, SIS...
WHERE'S MOM?
...

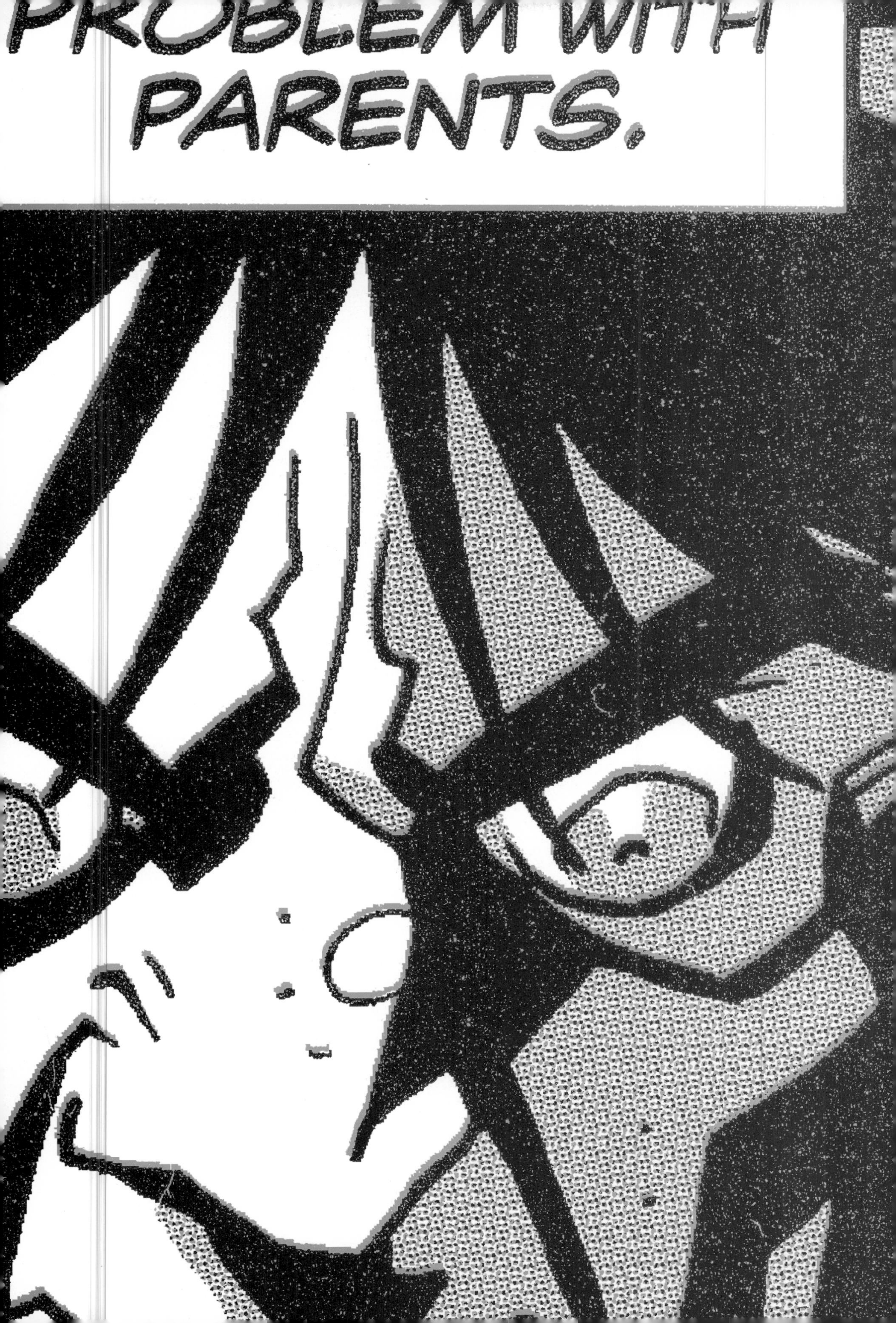
PROBLEM WITH PARENTS.

Chapter Three
Mission To Yerba Muerta

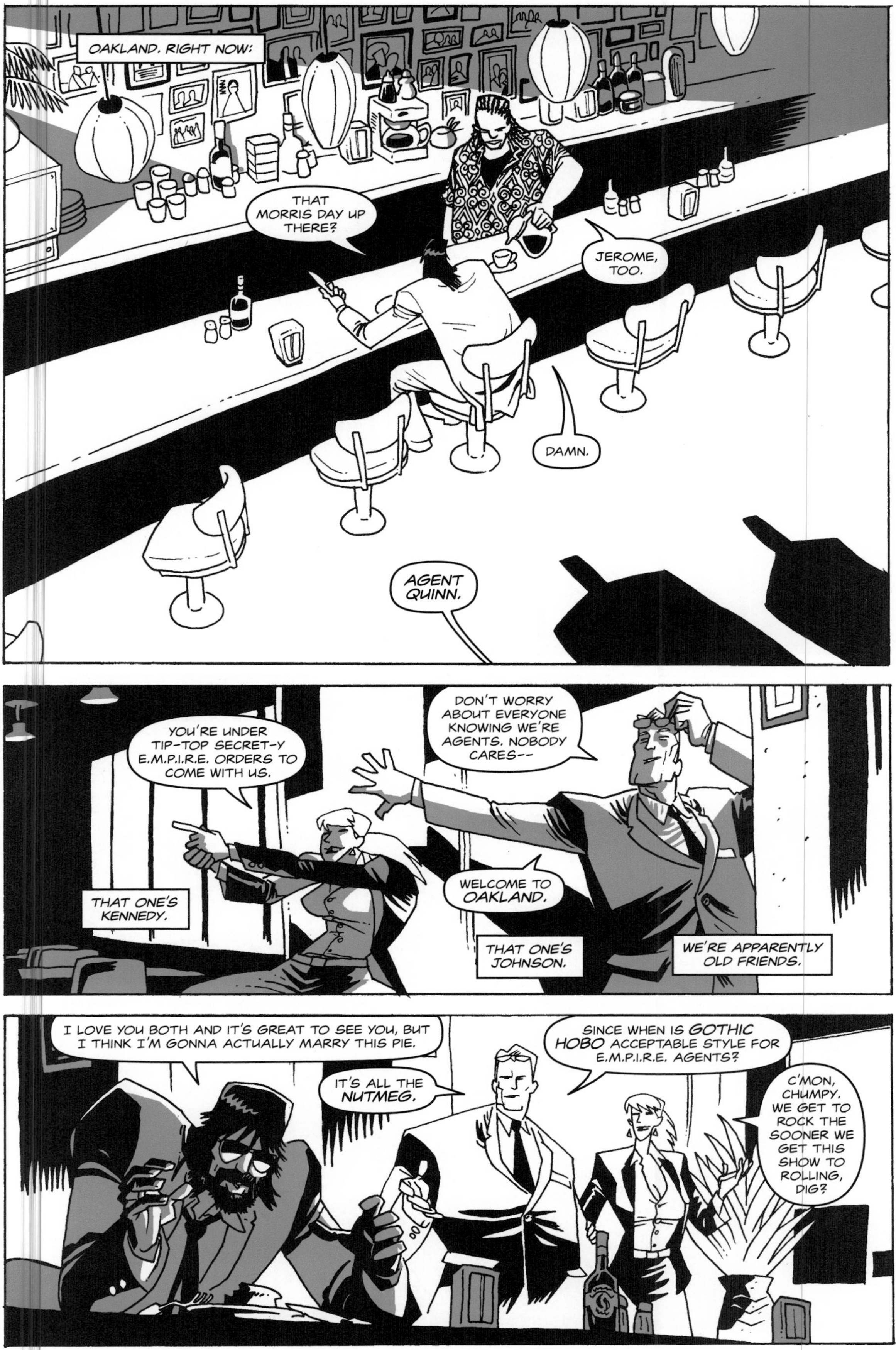
OAKLAND. RIGHT NOW:
THAT MORRIS DAY UP THERE?
JEROME, TOO.
DAMN.
AGENT QUINN.
YOU'RE UNDER TIP-TOP SECRET-Y E.M.P.I.R.E. ORDERS TO COME WITH US.
DON'T WORRY ABOUT EVERYONE KNOWING WE'RE AGENTS. NOBODY CARES--
WELCOME TO OAKLAND.
THAT ONE'S KENNEDY.
THAT ONE'S JOHNSON.
WE'RE APPARENTLY OLD FRIENDS.
I LOVE YOU BOTH AND IT'S GREAT TO SEE YOU, BUT I THINK I'M GONNA ACTUALLY MARRY THIS PIE.
IT'S ALL THE NUTMEG.
SINCE WHEN IS GOTHIC HOBO ACCEPTABLE STYLE FOR E.M.P.I.R.E. AGENTS?
C'MON, CHUMPY. WE GET TO ROCK THE SOONER WE GET THIS SHOW TO ROLLING, DIG?

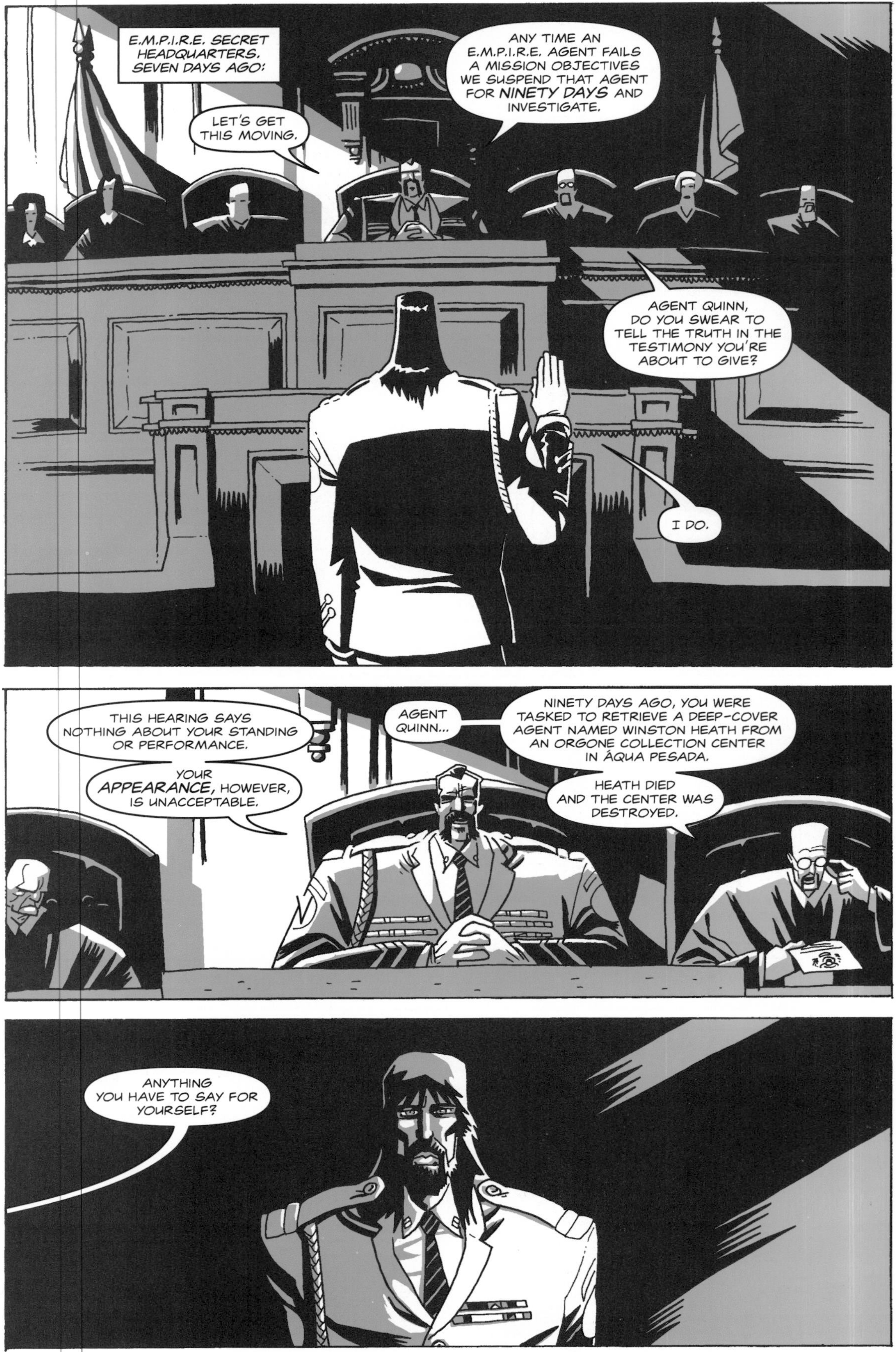
E.M.P.I.R.E. SECRET HEADQUARTERS, SEVEN DAYS AGO:
LET'S GET THIS MOVING.
ANY TIME AN E.M.P.I.R.E. AGENT FAILS A MISSION OBJECTIVES WE SUSPEND THAT AGENT FOR NINETY DAYS AND INVESTIGATE.
AGENT QUINN, DO YOU SWEAR TO TELL THE TRUTH IN THE TESTIMONY YOU'RE ABOUT TO GIVE?
I DO.
THIS HEARING SAYS NOTHING ABOUT YOUR STANDING OR PERFORMANCE.
YOUR APPEARANCE, HOWEVER, IS UNACCEPTABLE.
AGENT QUINN...
NINETY DAYS AGO, YOU WERE TASKED TO RETRIEVE A DEEP-COVER AGENT NAMED WINSTON HEATH FROM AN ORGONE COLLECTION CENTER IN ÁQUA PESADA.
HEATH DIED AND THE CENTER WAS DESTROYED.
ANYTHING YOU HAVE TO SAY FOR YOURSELF?

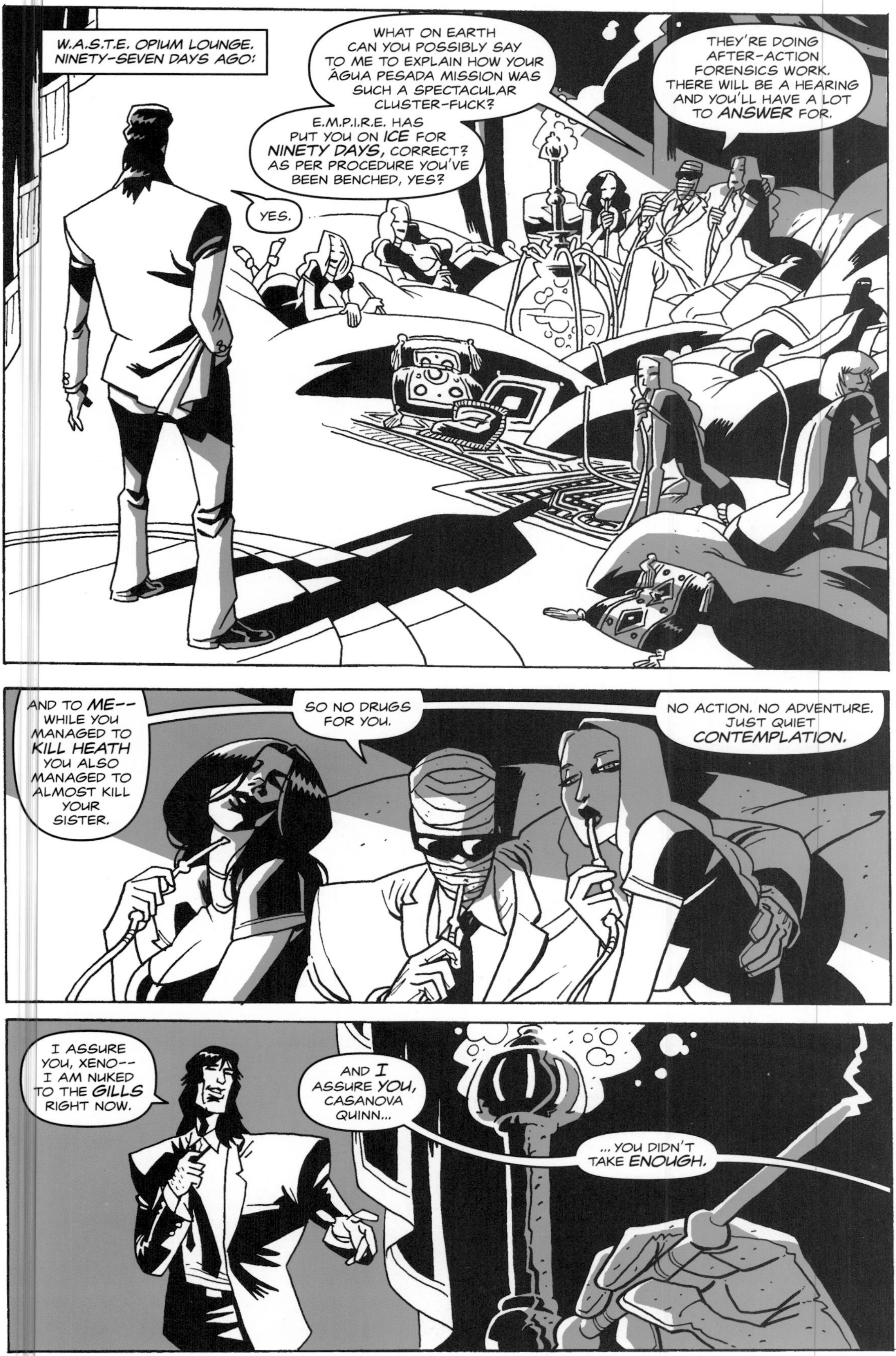
W.A.S.T.E. OPIUM LOUNGE. NINETY-SEVEN DAYS AGO:
WHAT ON EARTH CAN YOU POSSIBLY SAY TO ME TO EXPLAIN HOW YOUR ÁGUA PESADA MISSION WAS SUCH A SPECTACULAR CLUSTER-FUCK?
E.M.P.I.R.E. HAS PUT YOU ON ICE FOR NINETY DAYS, CORRECT? AS PER PROCEDURE YOU'VE BEEN BENCHED, YES?
YES.
THEY'RE DOING AFTER-ACTION FORENSICS WORK. THERE WILL BE A HEARING AND YOU'LL HAVE A LOT TO ANSWER FOR.
AND TO ME-- WHILE YOU MANAGED TO KILL HEATH YOU ALSO MANAGED TO ALMOST KILL YOUR SISTER.
SO NO DRUGS FOR YOU.
NO ACTION. NO ADVENTURE. JUST QUIET CONTEMPLATION.
I ASSURE YOU, XENO-- I AM NUKED TO THE GILLS RIGHT NOW.
AND I ASSURE YOU, CASANOVA QUINN...
...YOU DIDN'T TAKE ENOUGH.

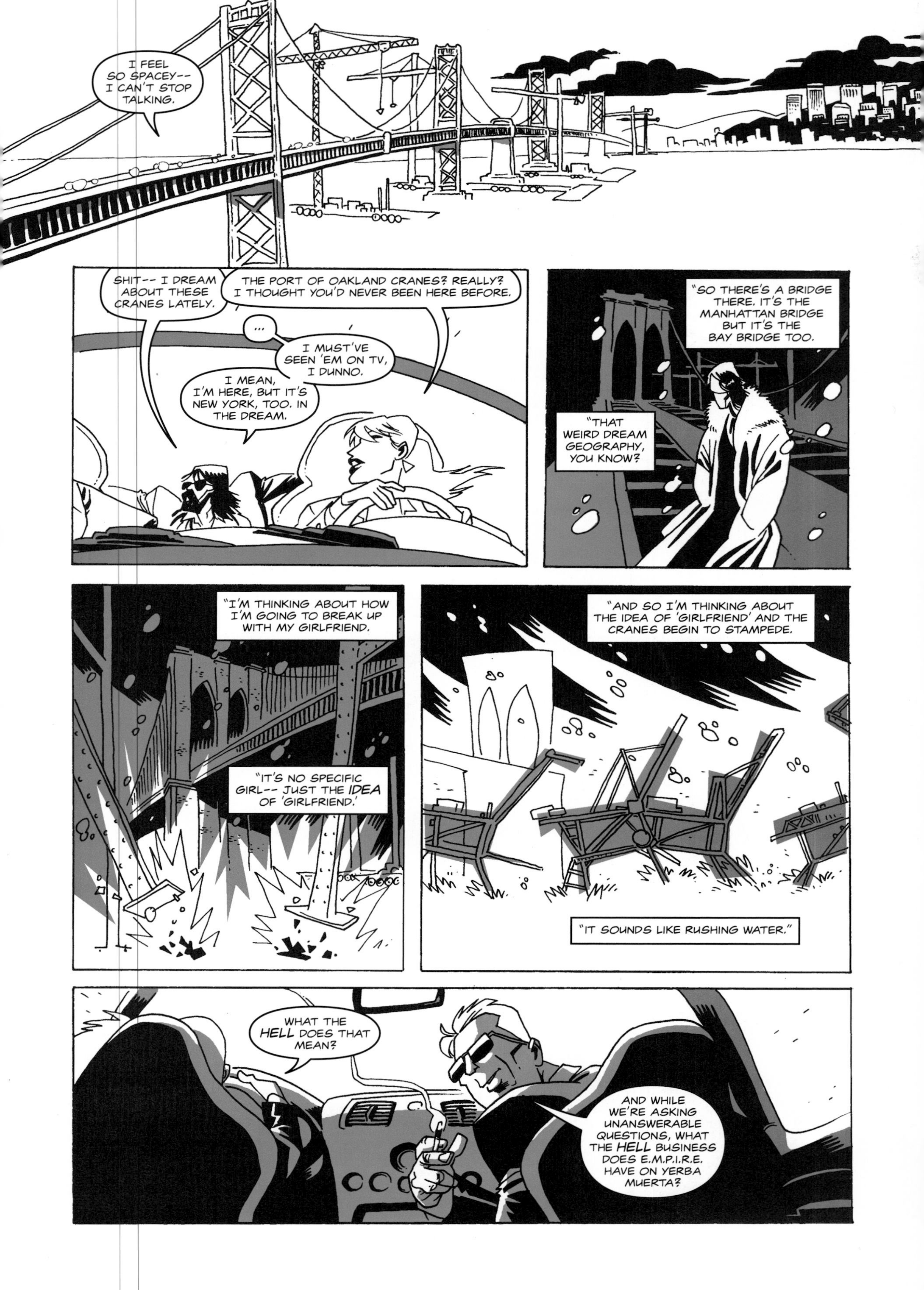
I FEEL SO SPACEY-- I CAN'T STOP TALKING.
SHIT-- I DREAM ABOUT THESE CRANES LATELY.
THE PORT OF OAKLAND CRANES? REALLY? I THOUGHT YOU'D NEVER BEEN HERE BEFORE.
...
I MUST'VE SEEN 'EM ON TV, I DUNNO.
I MEAN, I'M HERE, BUT IT'S NEW YORK, TOO. IN THE DREAM.
"SO THERE'S A BRIDGE THERE. IT'S THE MANHATTAN BRIDGE BUT IT'S THE BAY BRIDGE TOO.
"THAT WEIRD DREAM GEOGRAPHY, YOU KNOW?
"I'M THINKING ABOUT HOW I'M GOING TO BREAK UP WITH MY GIRLFRIEND.
"IT'S NO SPECIFIC GIRL-- JUST THE IDEA OF 'GIRLFRIEND.'
"AND SO I'M THINKING ABOUT THE IDEA OF 'GIRLFRIEND' AND THE CRANES BEGIN TO STAMPEDE.
"IT SOUNDS LIKE RUSHING WATER."
WHAT THE HELL DOES THAT MEAN?
AND WHILE WE'RE ASKING UNANSWERABLE QUESTIONS, WHAT THE HELL BUSINESS DOES E.M.P.I.R.E. HAVE ON YERBA MUERTA?

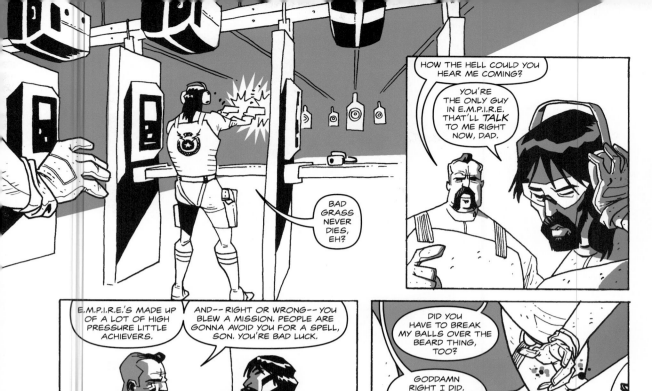

HOW THE HELL COULD YOU HEAR ME COMING?

YOU'RE THE ONLY GUY IN E.M.P.I.R.E. THAT'LL *TALK* TO ME RIGHT NOW, DAD.

BAD GRASS NEVER DIES, EH?

E.M.P.I.R.E.'S MADE UP OF A LOT OF HIGH PRESSURE LITTLE ACHIEVERS.

AND-- RIGHT OR WRONG-- YOU BLEW A MISSION. PEOPLE ARE GONNA AVOID YOU FOR A SPELL, SON. YOU'RE BAD LUCK.

DID YOU HAVE TO BREAK MY BALLS OVER THE BEARD THING, TOO?

GODDAMN RIGHT I DID. THIS IS A MILITARY ORGANIZATION.

MY BOY DOESN'T GET IT ANY EASIER THAN ANYONE ELSE.

LOOK, SON-- WHY DON'T YOU COME TO THE HOUSE FOR A NIGHT BEFORE WE SEND YOU BACK OUT INTO THE WORLD?

BACK--?

WE'VE AGREED ON A SLOW, TACTICAL ENTRY.

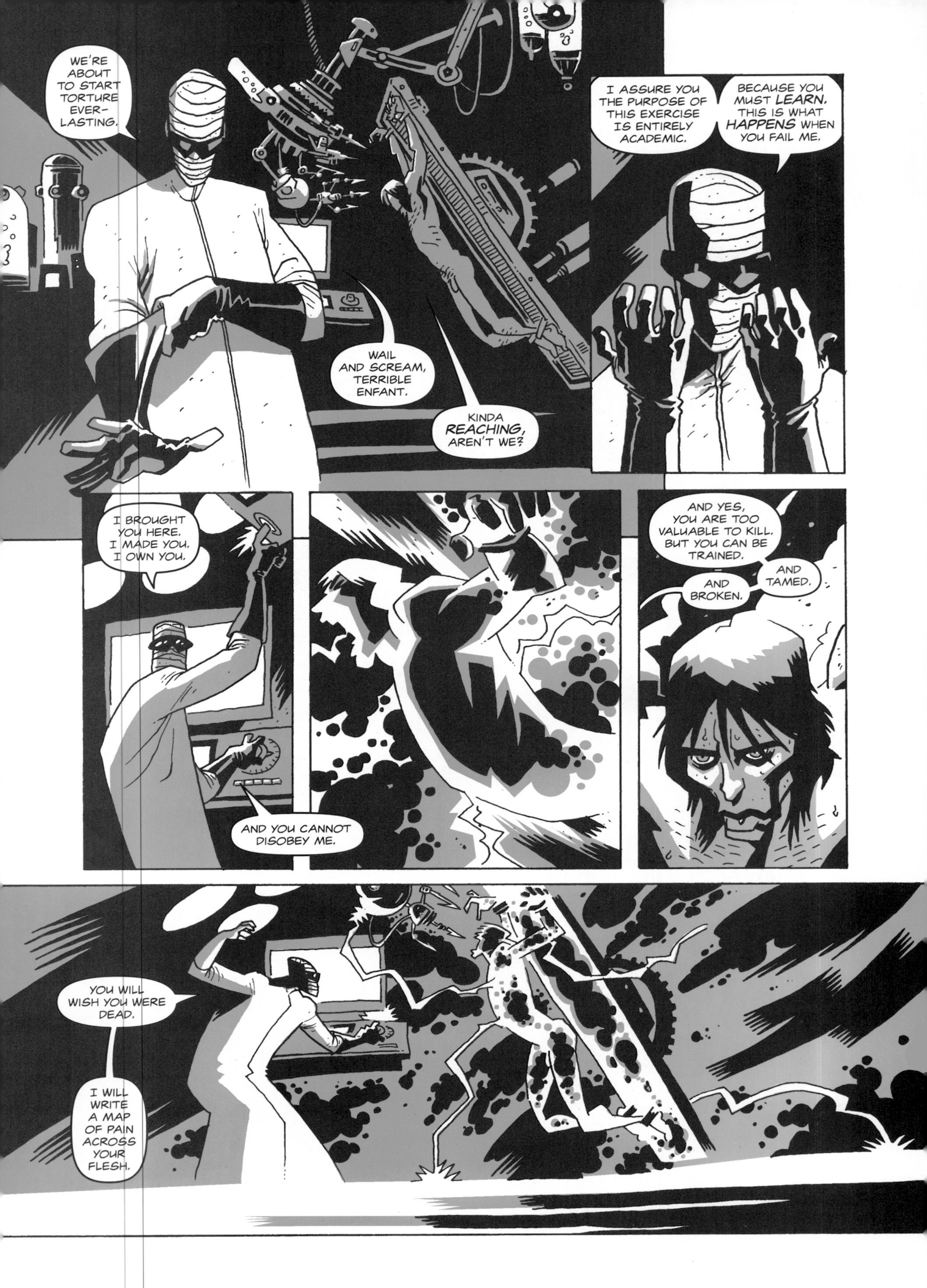
WE'RE ABOUT TO START TORTURE EVER-LASTING.
WAIL AND SCREAM, TERRIBLE ENFANT.
KINDA REACHING, AREN'T WE?
I ASSURE YOU THE PURPOSE OF THIS EXERCISE IS ENTIRELY ACADEMIC.
BECAUSE YOU MUST LEARN. THIS IS WHAT HAPPENS WHEN YOU FAIL ME.
I BROUGHT YOU HERE. I MADE YOU. I OWN YOU.
AND YOU CANNOT DISOBEY ME.
AND YES, YOU ARE TOO VALUABLE TO KILL. BUT YOU CAN BE TRAINED.
AND BROKEN.
AND TAMED.
YOU WILL WISH YOU WERE DEAD.
I WILL WRITE A MAP OF PAIN ACROSS YOUR FLESH.

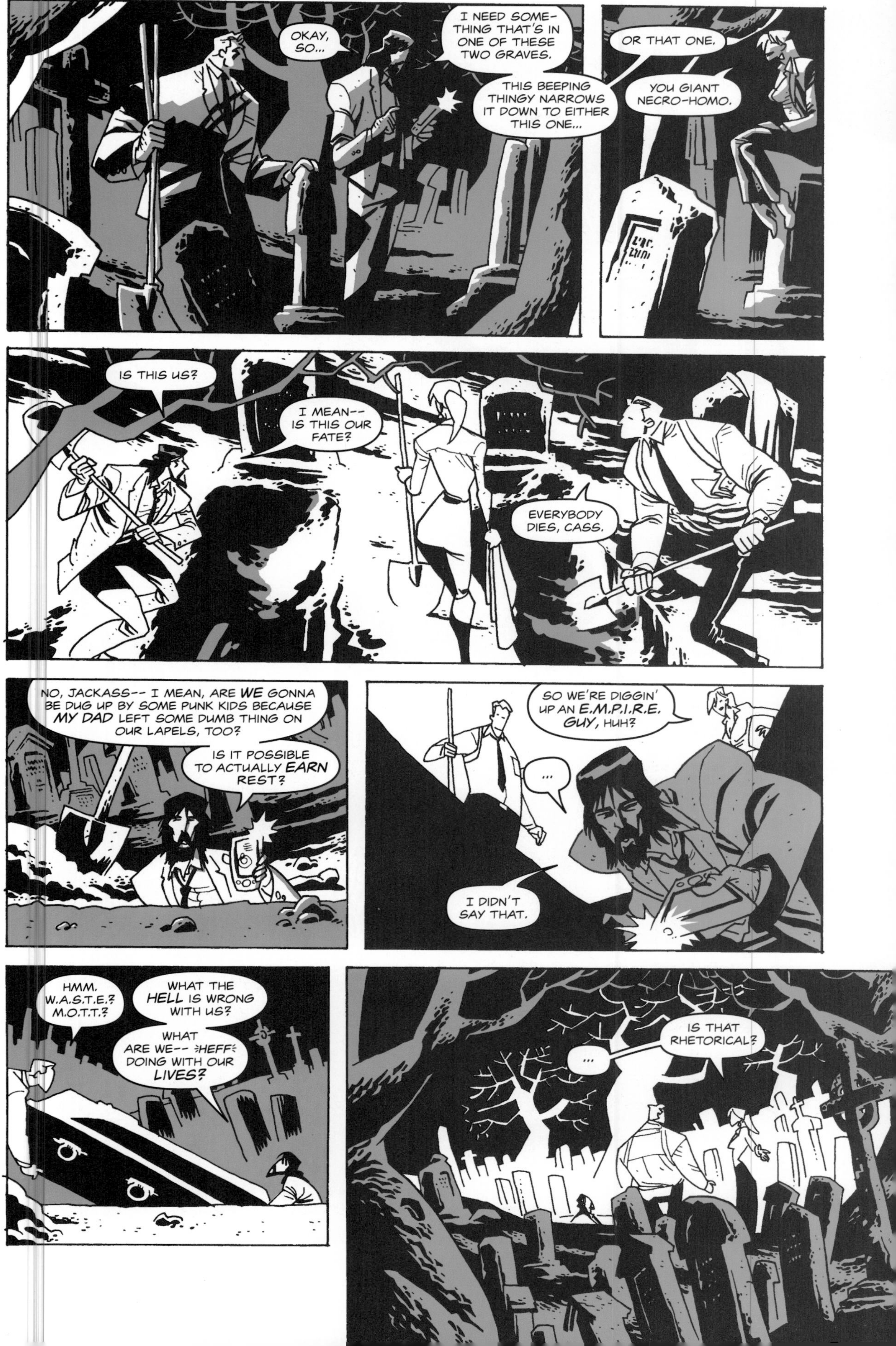
OKAY, SO...
I NEED SOMETHING THAT'S IN ONE OF THESE TWO GRAVES.
THIS BEEPING THINGY NARROWS IT DOWN TO EITHER THIS ONE...
OR THAT ONE.
YOU GIANT NECRO-HOMO.
IS THIS US?
I MEAN-- IS THIS OUR FATE?
EVERYBODY DIES, CASS.
NO, JACKASS-- I MEAN, ARE WE GONNA BE DUG UP BY SOME PUNK KIDS BECAUSE MY DAD LEFT SOME DUMB THING ON OUR LAPELS, TOO?
IS IT POSSIBLE TO ACTUALLY EARN REST?
SO WE'RE DIGGIN' UP AN E.M.P.I.R.E. GUY, HUH?
...
I DIDN'T SAY THAT.
HMM. W.A.S.T.E.? M.O.T.T.?
WHAT THE HELL IS WRONG WITH US?
WHAT ARE WE-- HEFF DOING WITH OUR LIVES?
...
IS THAT RHETORICAL?

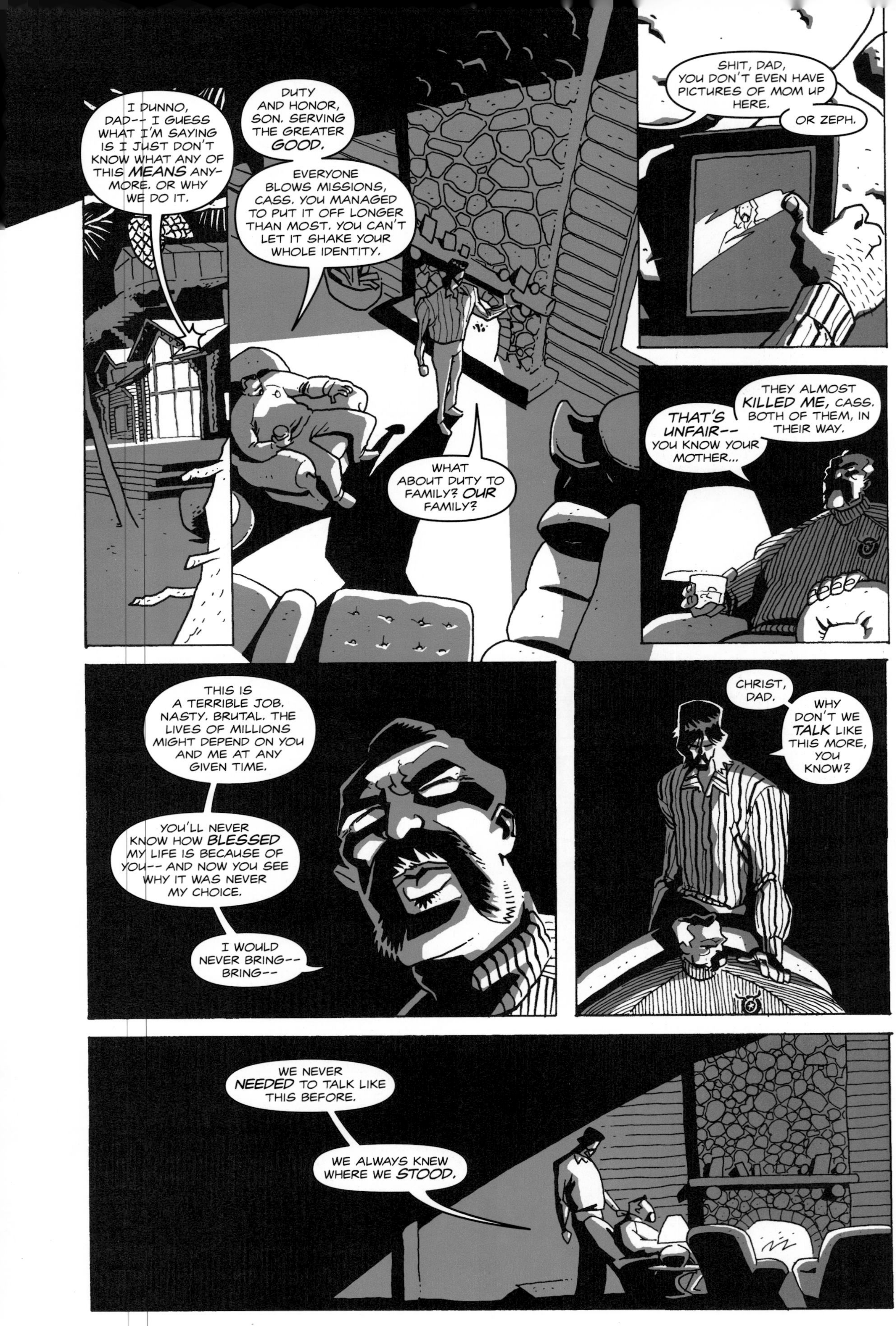
I DUNNO, DAD-- I GUESS WHAT I'M SAYING IS I JUST DON'T KNOW WHAT ANY OF THIS MEANS ANY-MORE. OR WHY WE DO IT.
DUTY AND HONOR, SON. SERVING THE GREATER GOOD.
EVERYONE BLOWS MISSIONS, CASS. YOU MANAGED TO PUT IT OFF LONGER THAN MOST. YOU CAN'T LET IT SHAKE YOUR WHOLE IDENTITY.
WHAT ABOUT DUTY TO FAMILY? OUR FAMILY?
SHIT, DAD, YOU DON'T EVEN HAVE PICTURES OF MOM UP HERE.
OR ZEPH.
THAT'S UNFAIR-- YOU KNOW YOUR MOTHER...
THEY ALMOST KILLED ME, CASS. BOTH OF THEM, IN THEIR WAY.
THIS IS A TERRIBLE JOB. NASTY. BRUTAL. THE LIVES OF MILLIONS MIGHT DEPEND ON YOU AND ME AT ANY GIVEN TIME.
YOU'LL NEVER KNOW HOW BLESSED MY LIFE IS BECAUSE OF YOU-- AND NOW YOU SEE WHY IT WAS NEVER MY CHOICE.
I WOULD NEVER BRING-- BRING--
CHRIST, DAD.
WHY DON'T WE TALK LIKE THIS MORE, YOU KNOW?
WE NEVER NEEDED TO TALK LIKE THIS BEFORE.
WE ALWAYS KNEW WHERE WE STOOD.

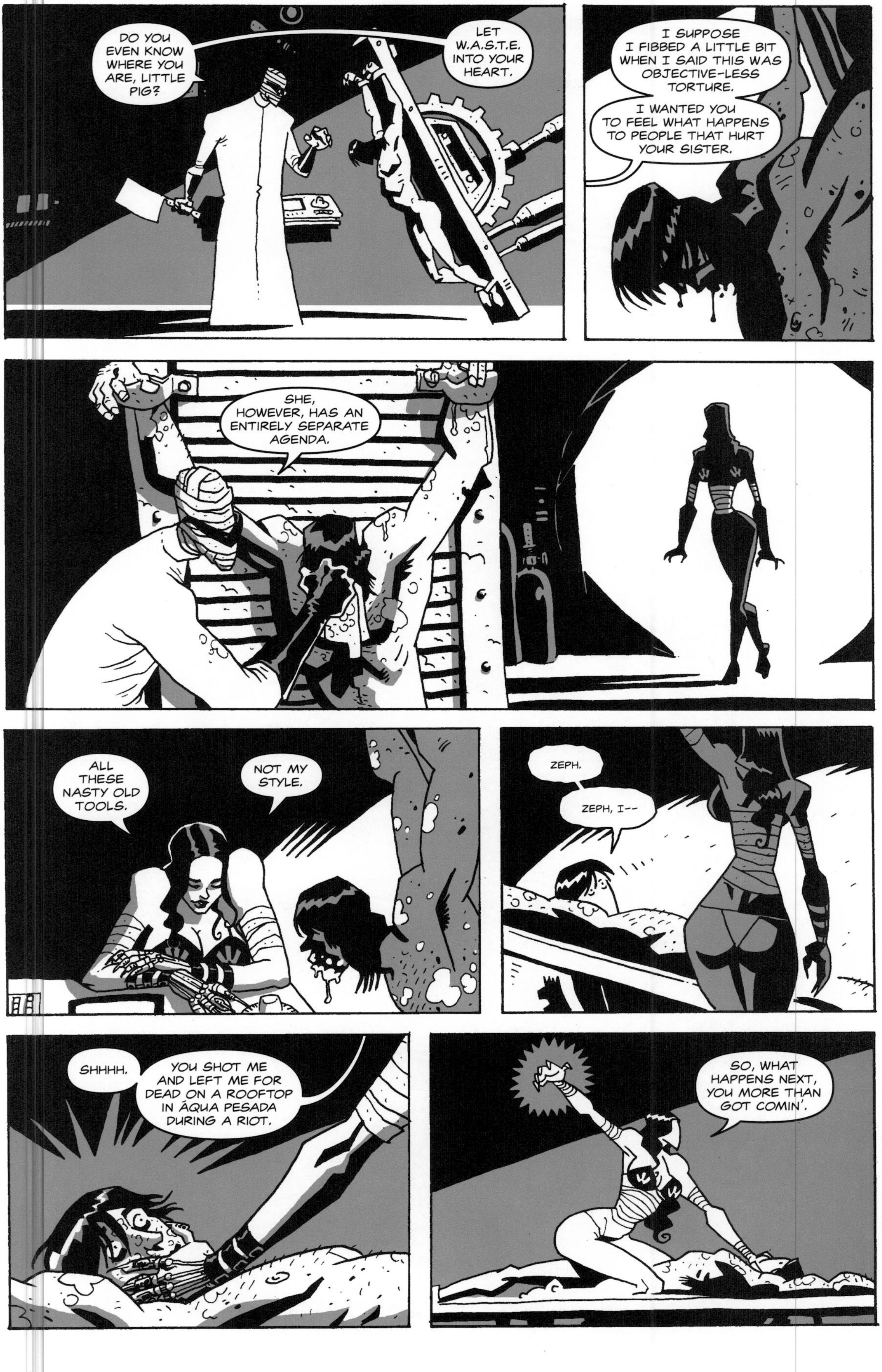
DO YOU EVEN KNOW WHERE YOU ARE, LITTLE PIG?
LET W.A.S.T.E. INTO YOUR HEART.
I SUPPOSE I FIBBED A LITTLE BIT WHEN I SAID THIS WAS OBJECTIVE-LESS TORTURE.
I WANTED YOU TO FEEL WHAT HAPPENS TO PEOPLE THAT HURT YOUR SISTER.
SHE, HOWEVER, HAS AN ENTIRELY SEPARATE AGENDA.
ALL THESE NASTY OLD TOOLS.
NOT MY STYLE.
ZEPH.
ZEPH, I--
SHHHH.
YOU SHOT ME AND LEFT ME FOR DEAD ON A ROOFTOP IN ÁQUA PESADA DURING A RIOT.
SO, WHAT HAPPENS NEXT, YOU MORE THAN GOT COMIN'.

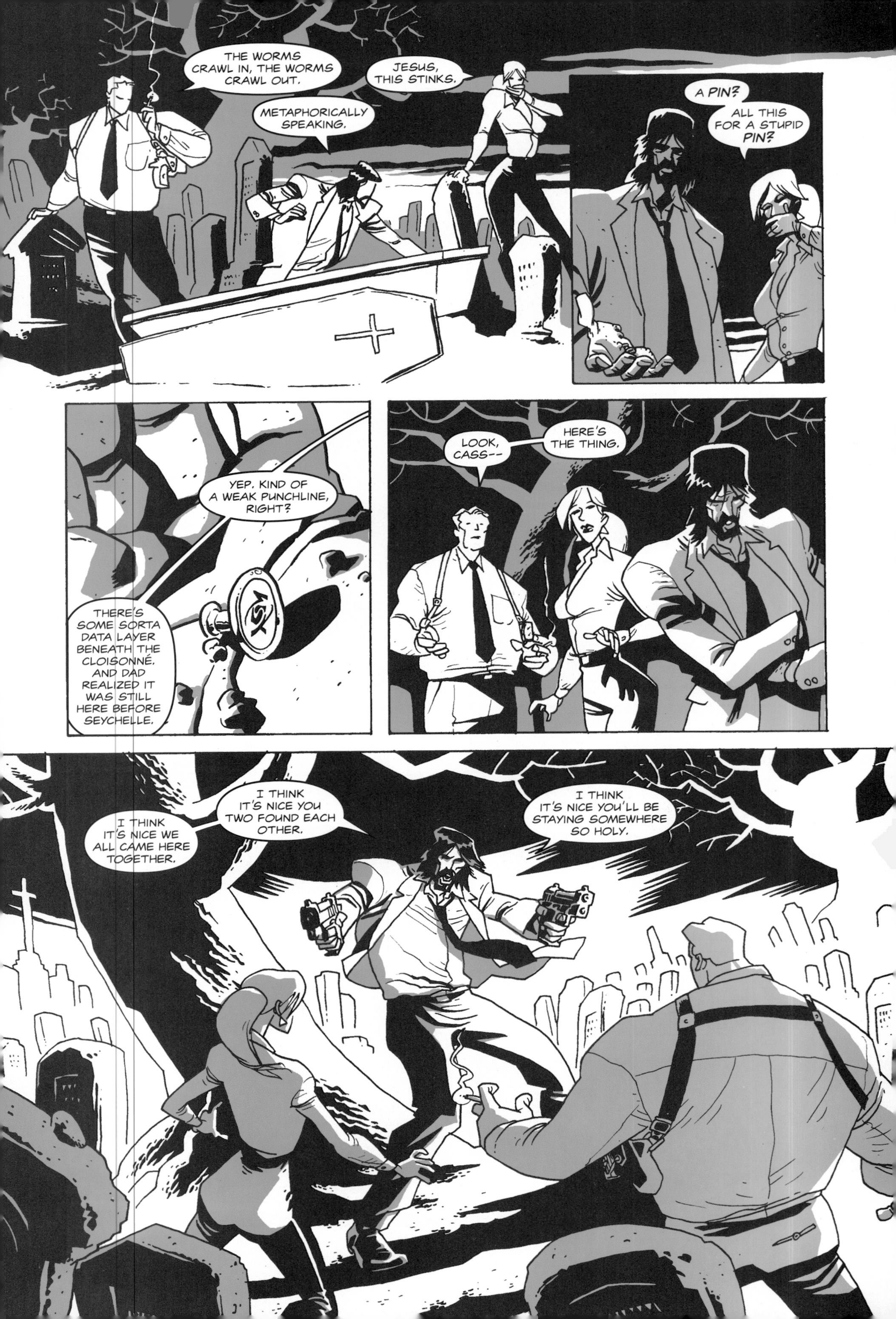
THE WORMS CRAWL IN, THE WORMS CRAWL OUT.
METAPHORICALLY SPEAKING.
JESUS, THIS STINKS.
A PIN?
ALL THIS FOR A STUPID PIN?
YEP. KIND OF A WEAK PUNCHLINE, RIGHT?
THERE'S SOME SORTA DATA LAYER BENEATH THE CLOISONNÉ. AND DAD REALIZED IT WAS STILL HERE BEFORE SEYCHELLE.
LOOK, CASS--
HERE'S THE THING.
I THINK IT'S NICE WE ALL CAME HERE TOGETHER.
I THINK IT'S NICE YOU TWO FOUND EACH OTHER.
I THINK IT'S NICE YOU'LL BE STAYING SOMEWHERE SO HOLY.

YERBA MUERTA IS AN ISLAND IN THE SAN FRANCISCO BAY. IT'S SACRED GROUND TO US.

IT'S NO MAN'S LAND WHERE WE BURY OUR ANONYMOUS DEAD WITH HONOR.

SACRED TO ALL OF US, I MEAN-- E.M.P.I.R.E., W.A.S.T.E., M.O.T.T., X.S.M., EVERYONE.

IT'S A GRAVEYARD FOR SUPER-SPOOKS.

AROUND THE TIME YOU VANISHED, AN R.S.M. HELICASINO WENT DOWN OVER FRANCE.

ON IT WAS A GUY WORKING FOR US.

HE AND YOUR PAL HEATH FED US MOST OF WHAT WE KNOW ABOUT SEYCHELLE'S ORGANIZATION.

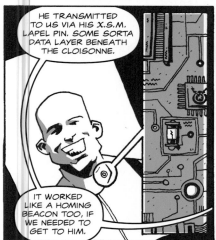

HE TRANSMITTED TO US VIA HIS X.S.M. LAPEL PIN. SOME SORTA DATA LAYER BENEATH THE CLOISONNE.

IT WORKED LIKE A HOMING BEACON TOO, IF WE NEEDED TO GET TO HIM.

HE WAS BURIED WITH THE PIN ON. AND SO NOW WE NEED TO GET TO HIM.

IF SEYCHELLE FIGURES HE WAS OUR MOLE, IT'LL PROVE IT'S US THAT'S TAKING HIM APART AND NOT X.S.M.

SAN FRANCISCO, HUH?

THOUGHT YOU MIGHT LIKE THAT PART-- YOUR ACADEMY PALS KENNEDY AND JOHNSON ARE TASKED TO OAKLAND THESE DAYS. THEY'LL BE YOUR CONTACTS UP THERE.

THAT'S GREAT. I'VE BEEN STAYING UP IN BIG SUR LATELY ANYWAY.

...

WHY ON EARTH HAVE YOU BEEN UP THERE?

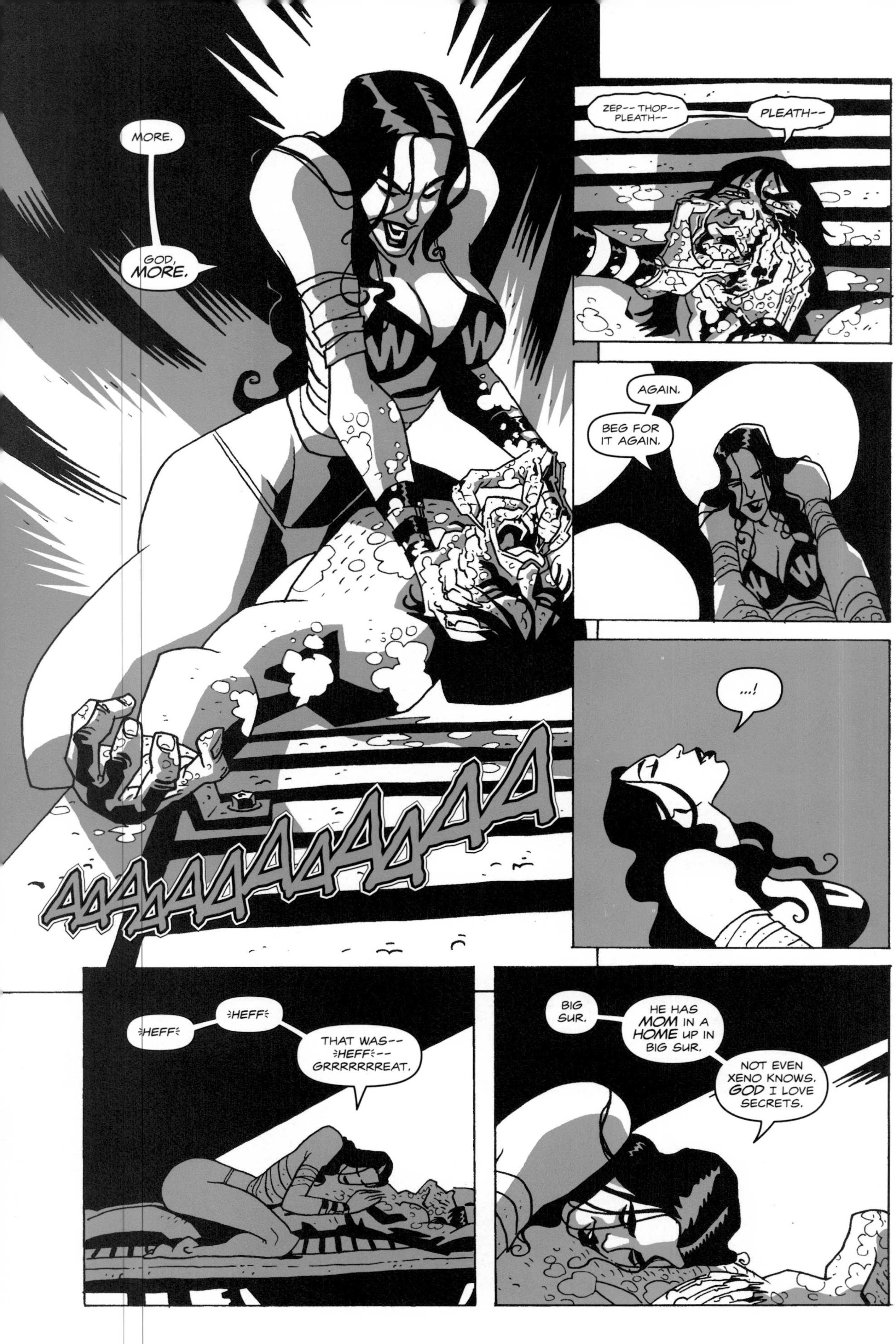
MORE.
GOD, MORE.
AAAAAAAAAAAAA
ZEP-- THOP-- PLEATH--
PLEATH--
AGAIN.
BEG FOR IT AGAIN.
...!
HEFF
HEFF
THAT WAS-- HEFF-- GRRRRRRREAT.
BIG SUR.
HE HAS MOM IN A HOME UP IN BIG SUR.
NOT EVEN XENO KNOWS. GOD I LOVE SECRETS.

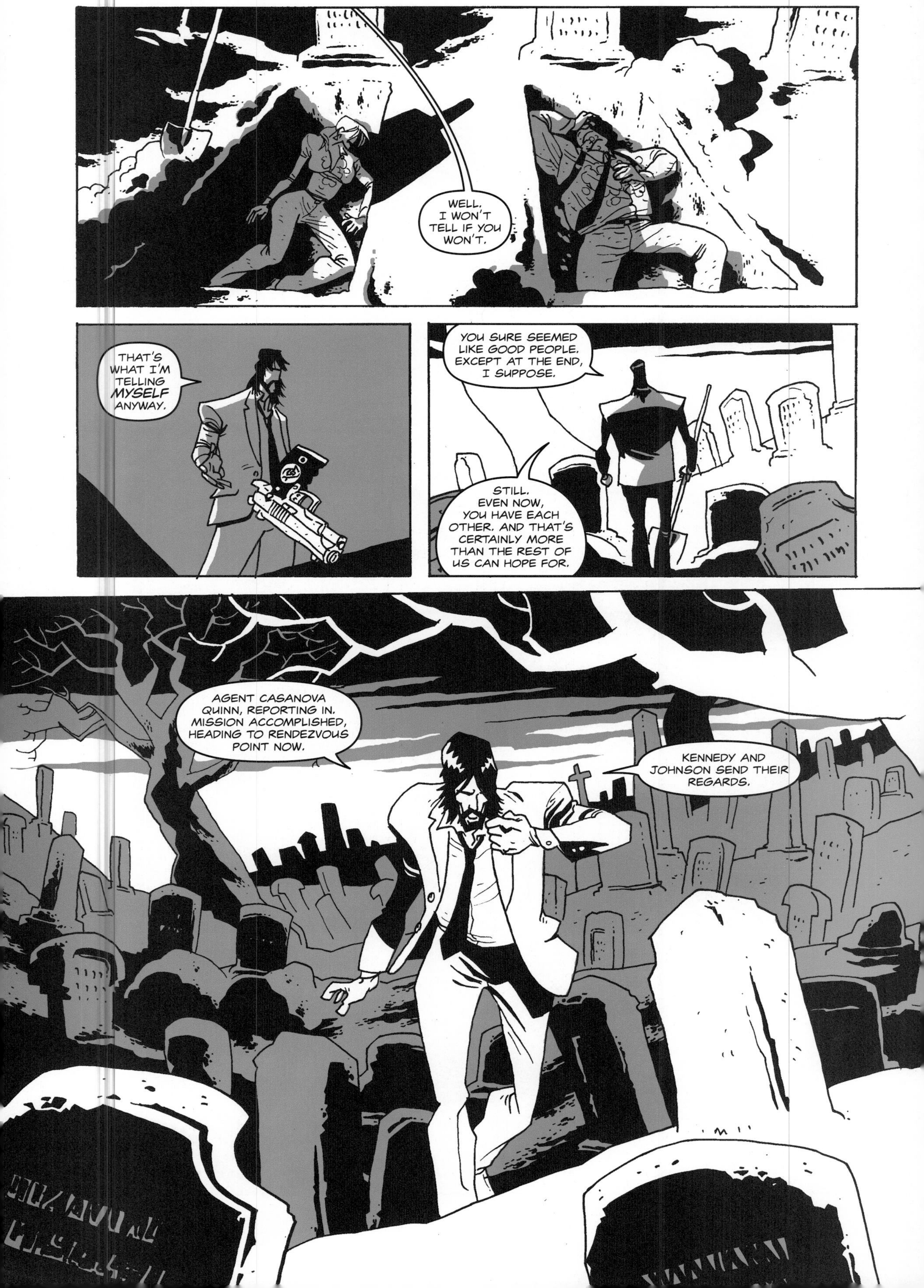
WELL, I WON'T TELL IF YOU WON'T.
THAT'S WHAT I'M TELLING *MYSELF* ANYWAY.
YOU SURE SEEMED LIKE GOOD PEOPLE. EXCEPT AT THE END, I SUPPOSE.
STILL. EVEN NOW, YOU HAVE EACH OTHER. AND THAT'S CERTAINLY MORE THAN THE REST OF US CAN HOPE FOR.
AGENT CASANOVA QUINN, REPORTING IN. MISSION ACCOMPLISHED, HEADING TO RENDEZVOUS POINT NOW.
KENNEDY AND JOHNSON SEND THEIR REGARDS.

WHEN KENNEDY AND JOHNSON TAKE YOU THERE, THIS'LL FIND THE E.M. SIGNATURE, ACCURATE DOWN TO A TWO-GRAVE RADIUS.

OKAY.

LISTEN, RUBY... THINGS IN ÁGUA PESADA WERE NUTS--

NO, IT'S OKAY. THEY JUST RE-INSTALLED ME FROM BACK-UP.

I DIDN'T EVEN NOTICE THE TIME I WAS OUT.

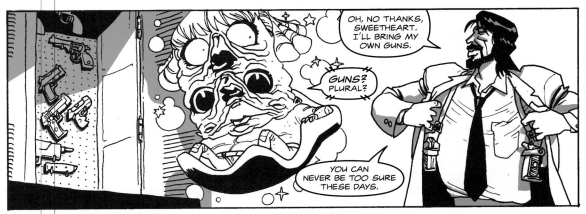

OH, NO THANKS, SWEETHEART. I'LL BRING MY OWN GUNS.

GUNS? PLURAL?

YOU CAN NEVER BE TOO SURE THESE DAYS.

LOTS OF DANGEROUS PEOPLE IN THE WORLD TO WATCH OUT FOR.

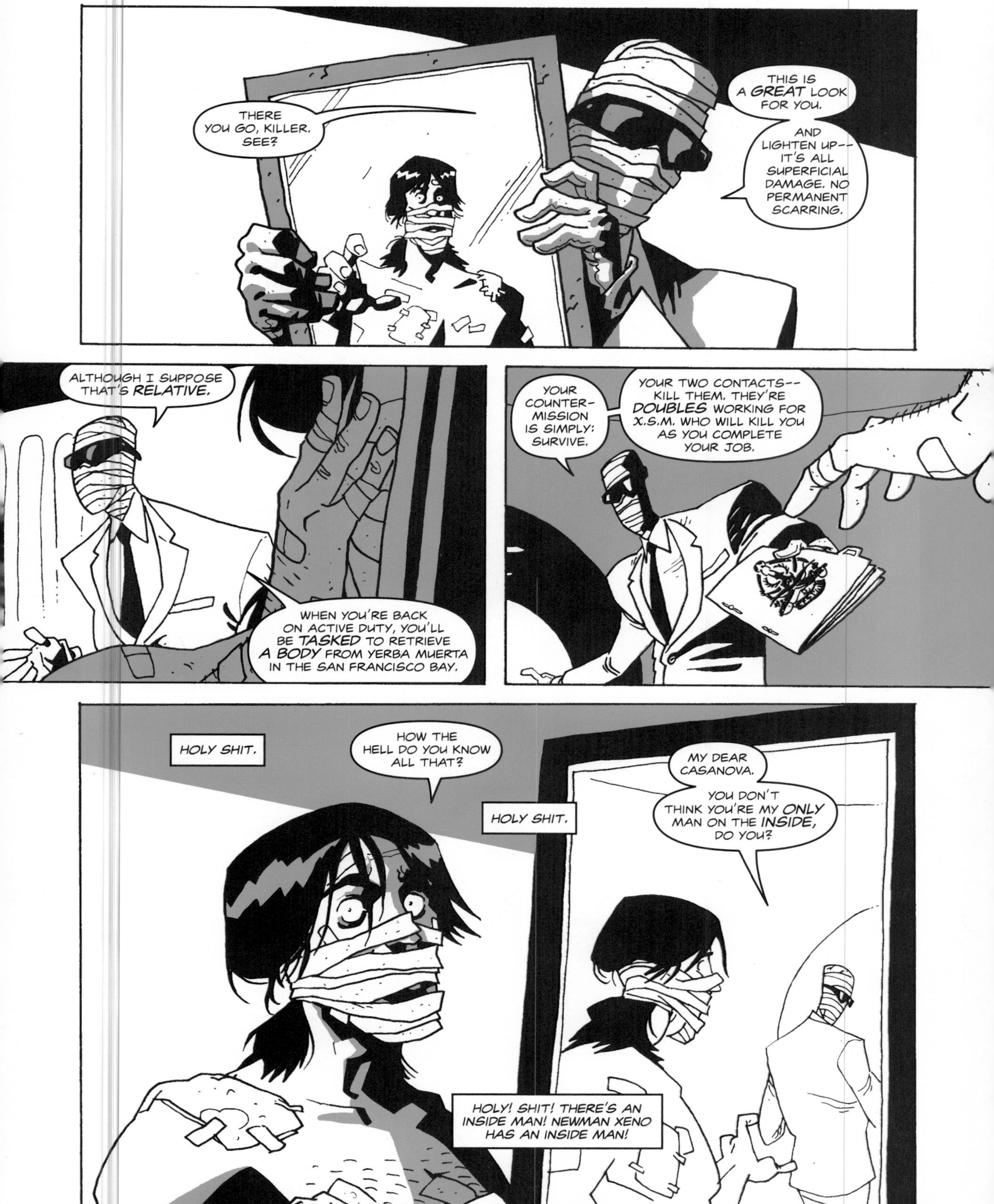
THERE YOU GO, KILLER. SEE?
THIS IS A GREAT LOOK FOR YOU.
AND LIGHTEN UP-- IT'S ALL SUPERFICIAL DAMAGE. NO PERMANENT SCARRING.
ALTHOUGH I SUPPOSE THAT'S RELATIVE.
WHEN YOU'RE BACK ON ACTIVE DUTY, YOU'LL BE TASKED TO RETRIEVE A BODY FROM YERBA MUERTA IN THE SAN FRANCISCO BAY.
YOUR TWO CONTACTS-- KILL THEM. THEY'RE DOUBLES WORKING FOR X.S.M. WHO WILL KILL YOU AS YOU COMPLETE YOUR JOB.
YOUR COUNTER-MISSION IS SIMPLY: SURVIVE.
HOLY SHIT.
HOW THE HELL DO YOU KNOW ALL THAT?
HOLY SHIT.
MY DEAR CASANOVA.
YOU DON'T THINK YOU'RE MY ONLY MAN ON THE INSIDE, DO YOU?
HOLY! SHIT! THERE'S AN INSIDE MAN! NEWMAN XENO HAS AN INSIDE MAN!

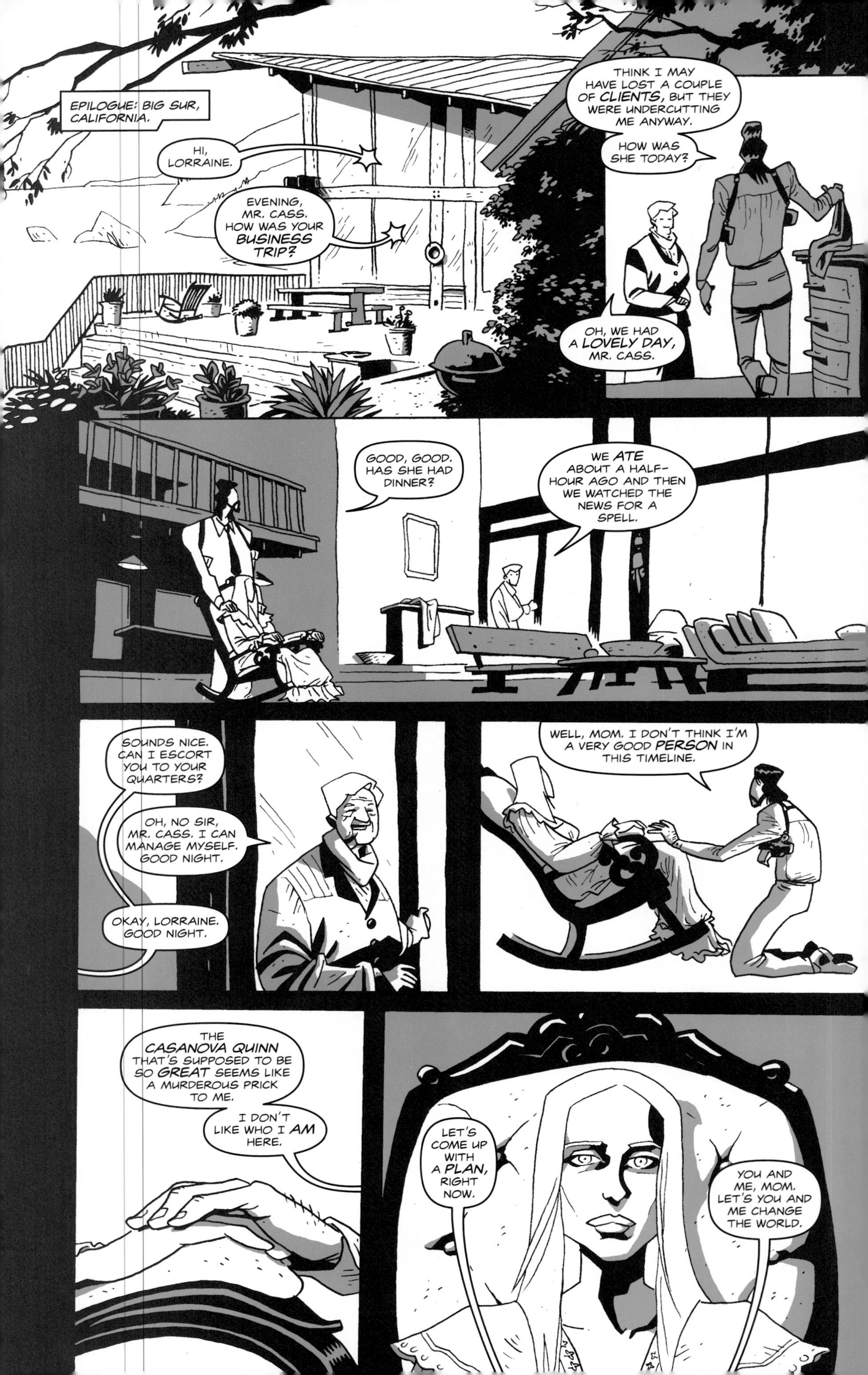

EPILOGUE: BIG SUR, CALIFORNIA.
HI, LORRAINE.
EVENING, MR. CASS. HOW WAS YOUR BUSINESS TRIP?
THINK I MAY HAVE LOST A COUPLE OF CLIENTS, BUT THEY WERE UNDERCUTTING ME ANYWAY.
HOW WAS SHE TODAY?
OH, WE HAD A LOVELY DAY, MR. CASS.
GOOD, GOOD. HAS SHE HAD DINNER?
WE ATE ABOUT A HALF-HOUR AGO AND THEN WE WATCHED THE NEWS FOR A SPELL.
SOUNDS NICE. CAN I ESCORT YOU TO YOUR QUARTERS?
OH, NO SIR, MR. CASS. I CAN MANAGE MYSELF. GOOD NIGHT.
OKAY, LORRAINE. GOOD NIGHT.
WELL, MOM. I DON'T THINK I'M A VERY GOOD PERSON IN THIS TIMELINE.
THE CASANOVA QUINN THAT'S SUPPOSED TO BE SO GREAT SEEMS LIKE A MURDEROUS PRICK TO ME.
I DON'T LIKE WHO I AM HERE.
LET'S COME UP WITH A PLAN, RIGHT NOW.
YOU AND ME, MOM. LET'S YOU AND ME CHANGE THE WORLD.

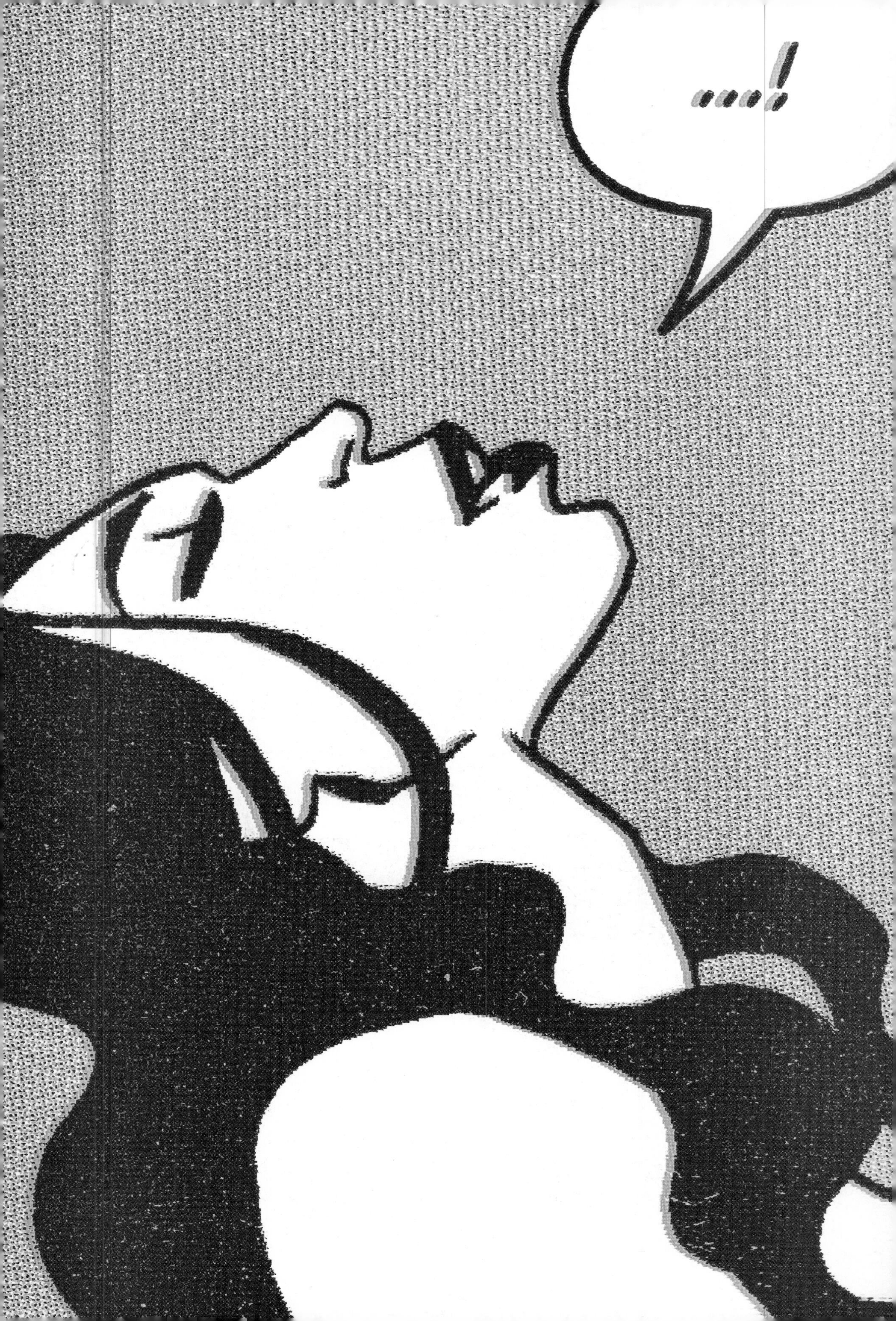
....!

Chapter Four
Dètournement

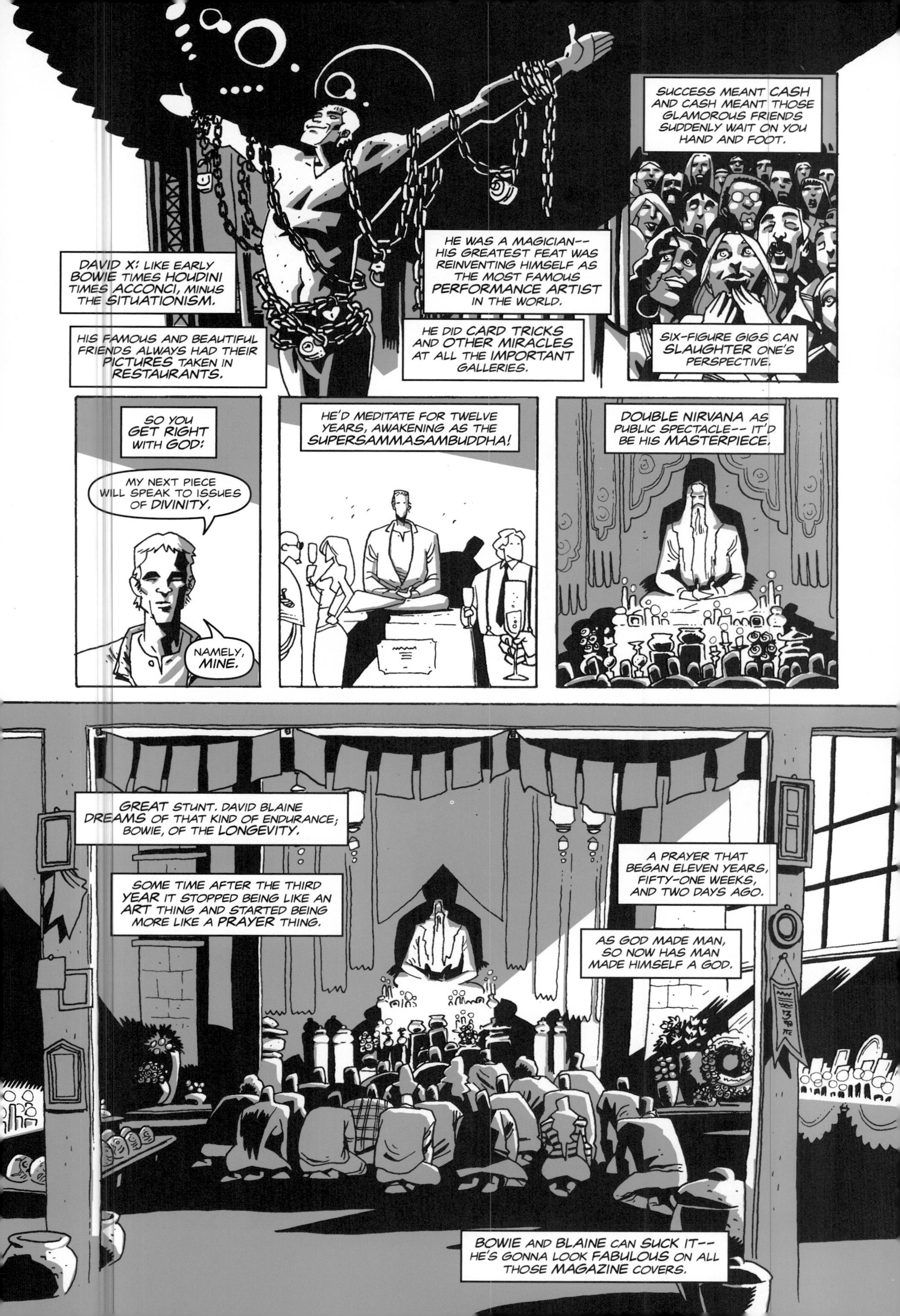
DAVID X: LIKE EARLY BOWIE TIMES HOUDINI TIMES ACCONCI, MINUS THE SITUATIONISM.
HIS FAMOUS AND BEAUTIFUL FRIENDS ALWAYS HAD THEIR PICTURES TAKEN IN RESTAURANTS.
HE WAS A MAGICIAN-- HIS GREATEST FEAT WAS REINVENTING HIMSELF AS THE MOST FAMOUS PERFORMANCE ARTIST IN THE WORLD.
HE DID CARD TRICKS AND OTHER MIRACLES AT ALL THE IMPORTANT GALLERIES.
SUCCESS MEANT CASH AND CASH MEANT THOSE GLAMOROUS FRIENDS SUDDENLY WAIT ON YOU HAND AND FOOT.
SIX-FIGURE GIGS CAN SLAUGHTER ONE'S PERSPECTIVE.
SO YOU GET RIGHT WITH GOD:
MY NEXT PIECE WILL SPEAK TO ISSUES OF DIVINITY.
NAMELY, MINE.
HE'D MEDITATE FOR TWELVE YEARS, AWAKENING AS THE SUPERSAMMASAMBUDDHA!
DOUBLE NIRVANA AS PUBLIC SPECTACLE-- IT'D BE HIS MASTERPIECE.
GREAT STUNT. DAVID BLAINE DREAMS OF THAT KIND OF ENDURANCE; BOWIE, OF THE LONGEVITY.
SOME TIME AFTER THE THIRD YEAR IT STOPPED BEING LIKE AN ART THING AND STARTED BEING MORE LIKE A PRAYER THING.
A PRAYER THAT BEGAN ELEVEN YEARS, FIFTY-ONE WEEKS, AND TWO DAYS AGO.
AS GOD MADE MAN, SO NOW HAS MAN MADE HIMSELF A GOD.
BOWIE AND BLAINE CAN SUCK IT-- HE'S GONNA LOOK FABULOUS ON ALL THOSE MAGAZINE COVERS.

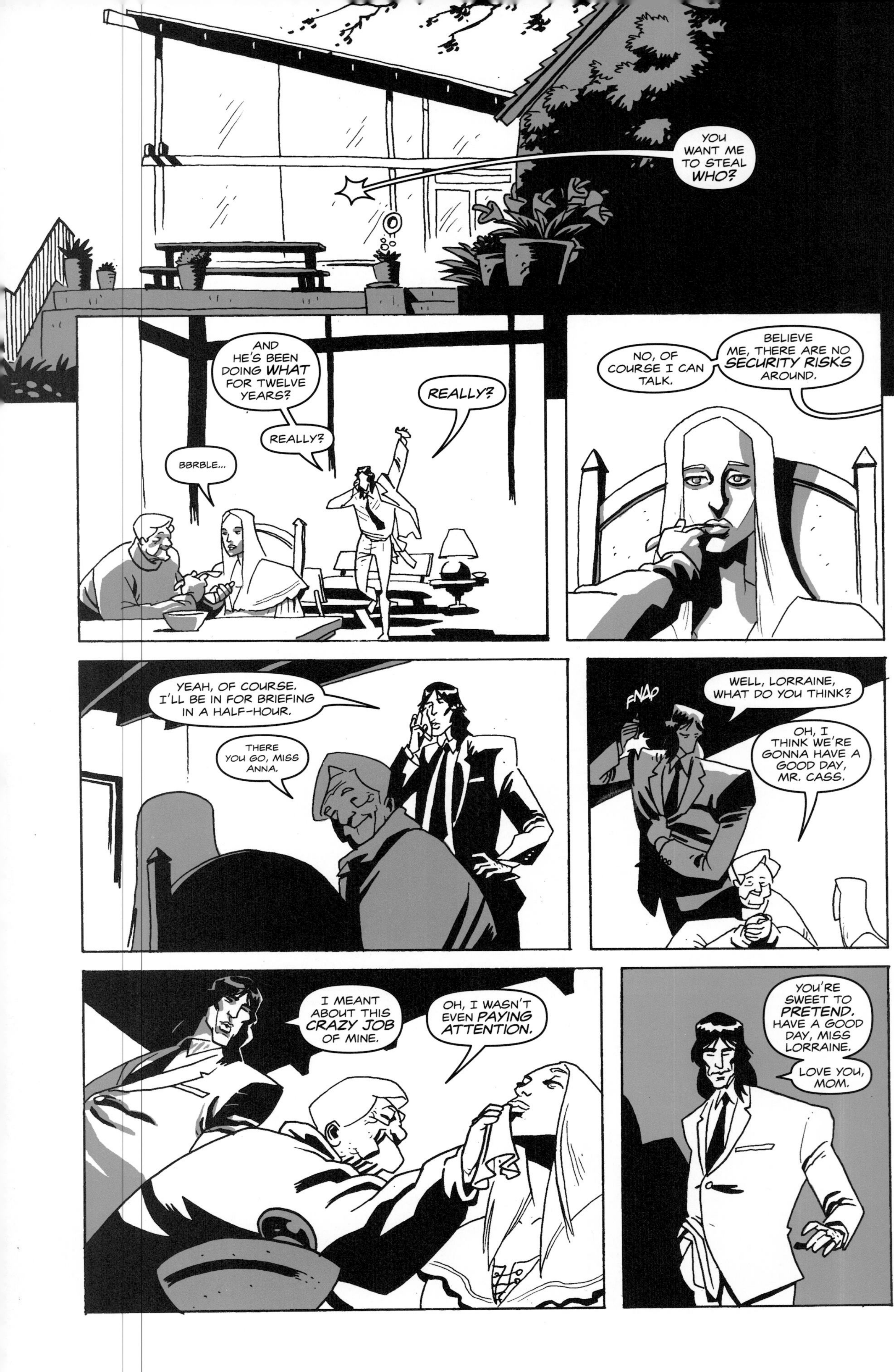
YOU WANT ME TO STEAL WHO?
AND HE'S BEEN DOING WHAT FOR TWELVE YEARS?
REALLY?
REALLY?
BBRBLE...
NO, OF COURSE I CAN TALK.
BELIEVE ME, THERE ARE NO SECURITY RISKS AROUND.
YEAH, OF COURSE. I'LL BE IN FOR BRIEFING IN A HALF-HOUR.
THERE YOU GO, MISS ANNA.
FNAP
WELL, LORRAINE, WHAT DO YOU THINK?
OH, I THINK WE'RE GONNA HAVE A GOOD DAY, MR. CASS.
I MEANT ABOUT THIS CRAZY JOB OF MINE.
OH, I WASN'T EVEN PAYING ATTENTION.
YOU'RE SWEET TO PRETEND. HAVE A GOOD DAY, MISS LORRAINE.
LOVE YOU, MOM.

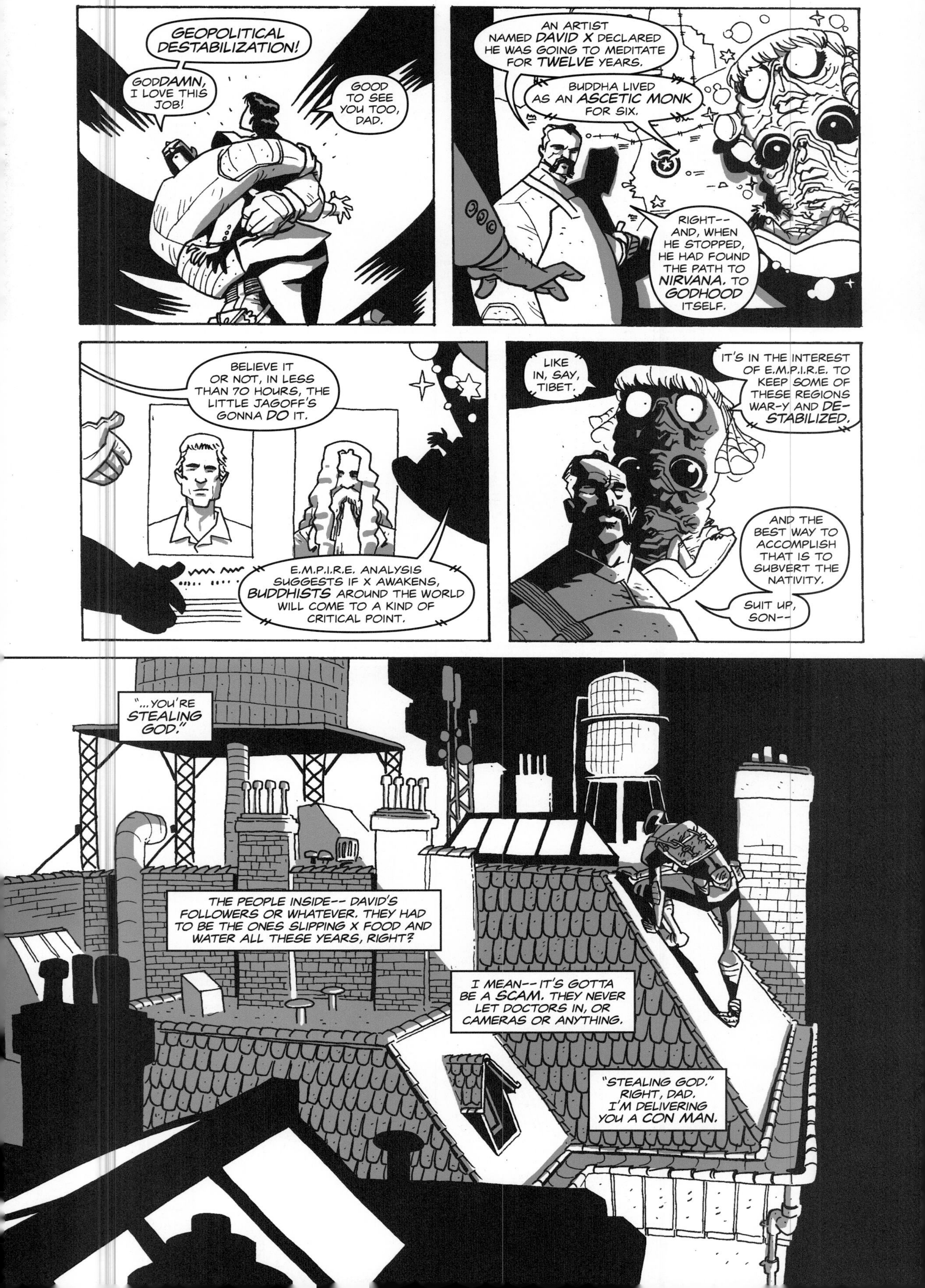
GEOPOLITICAL DESTABILIZATION!
GODDAMN, I LOVE THIS JOB!
GOOD TO SEE YOU TOO, DAD.
AN ARTIST NAMED DAVID X DECLARED HE WAS GOING TO MEDITATE FOR TWELVE YEARS.
BUDDHA LIVED AS AN ASCETIC MONK FOR SIX.
RIGHT-- AND, WHEN HE STOPPED, HE HAD FOUND THE PATH TO NIRVANA. TO GODHOOD ITSELF.
BELIEVE IT OR NOT, IN LESS THAN 70 HOURS, THE LITTLE JAGOFF'S GONNA DO IT.
E.M.P.I.R.E. ANALYSIS SUGGESTS IF X AWAKENS, BUDDHISTS AROUND THE WORLD WILL COME TO A KIND OF CRITICAL POINT.
LIKE IN, SAY, TIBET.
IT'S IN THE INTEREST OF E.M.P.I.R.E. TO KEEP SOME OF THESE REGIONS WAR-Y AND DE-STABILIZED.
AND THE BEST WAY TO ACCOMPLISH THAT IS TO SUBVERT THE NATIVITY.
SUIT UP, SON--
"...YOU'RE STEALING GOD."
THE PEOPLE INSIDE-- DAVID'S FOLLOWERS OR WHATEVER. THEY HAD TO BE THE ONES SLIPPING X FOOD AND WATER ALL THESE YEARS, RIGHT?
I MEAN-- IT'S GOTTA BE A SCAM. THEY NEVER LET DOCTORS IN, OR CAMERAS OR ANYTHING.
"STEALING GOD." RIGHT, DAD. I'M DELIVERING YOU A CON MAN.

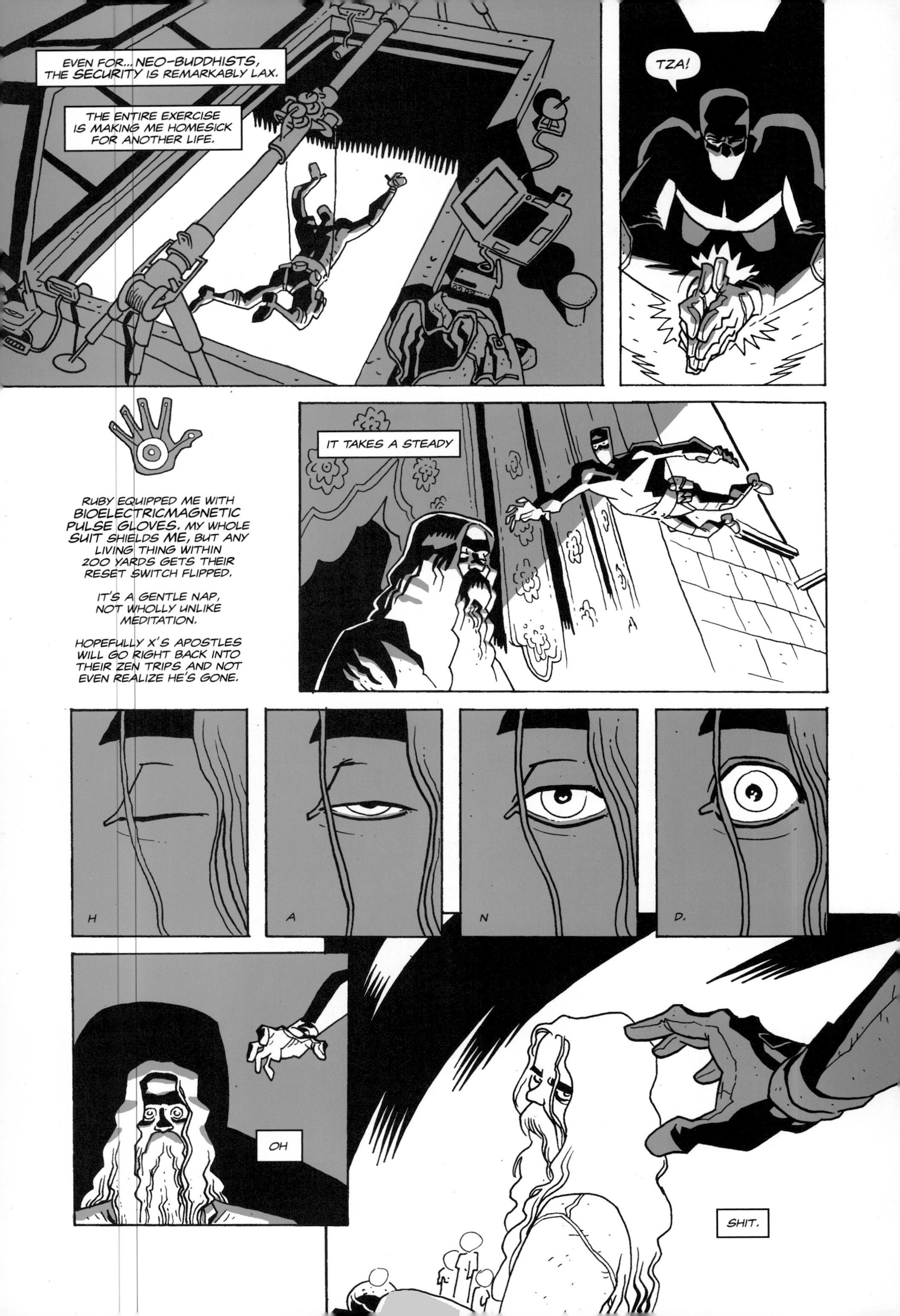
EVEN FOR... NEO-BUDDHISTS, THE SECURITY IS REMARKABLY LAX.
THE ENTIRE EXERCISE IS MAKING ME HOMESICK FOR ANOTHER LIFE.
TZA!
RUBY EQUIPPED ME WITH BIOELECTRICMAGNETIC PULSE GLOVES. MY WHOLE SUIT SHIELDS ME, BUT ANY LIVING THING WITHIN 200 YARDS GETS THEIR RESET SWITCH FLIPPED.
IT'S A GENTLE NAP, NOT WHOLLY UNLIKE MEDITATION.
HOPEFULLY X'S APOSTLES WILL GO RIGHT BACK INTO THEIR ZEN TRIPS AND NOT EVEN REALIZE HE'S GONE.
IT TAKES A STEADY
H
A
N
D.
OH
SHIT.

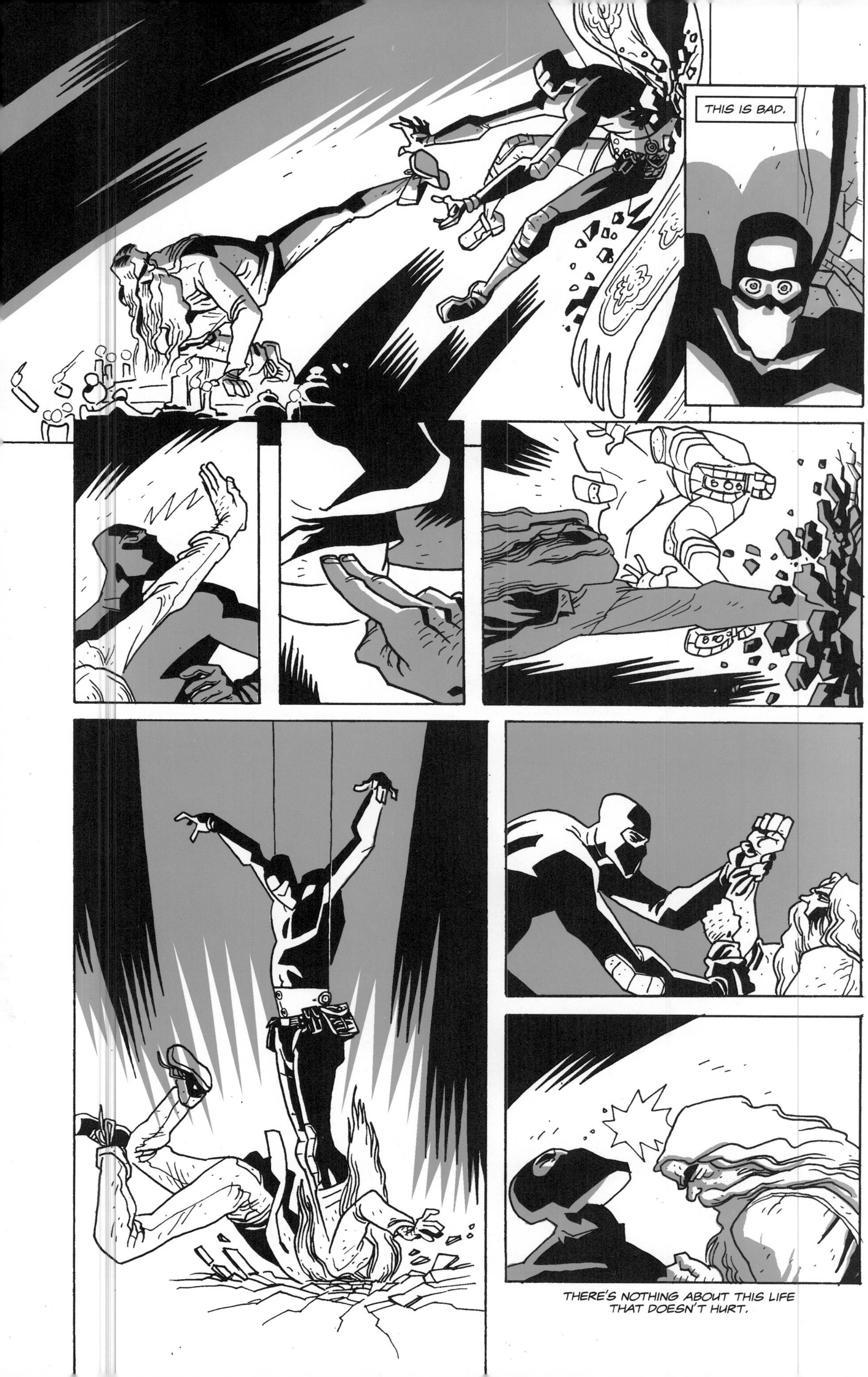
THIS IS BAD.
THERE'S NOTHING ABOUT THIS LIFE
THAT DOESN'T HURT.

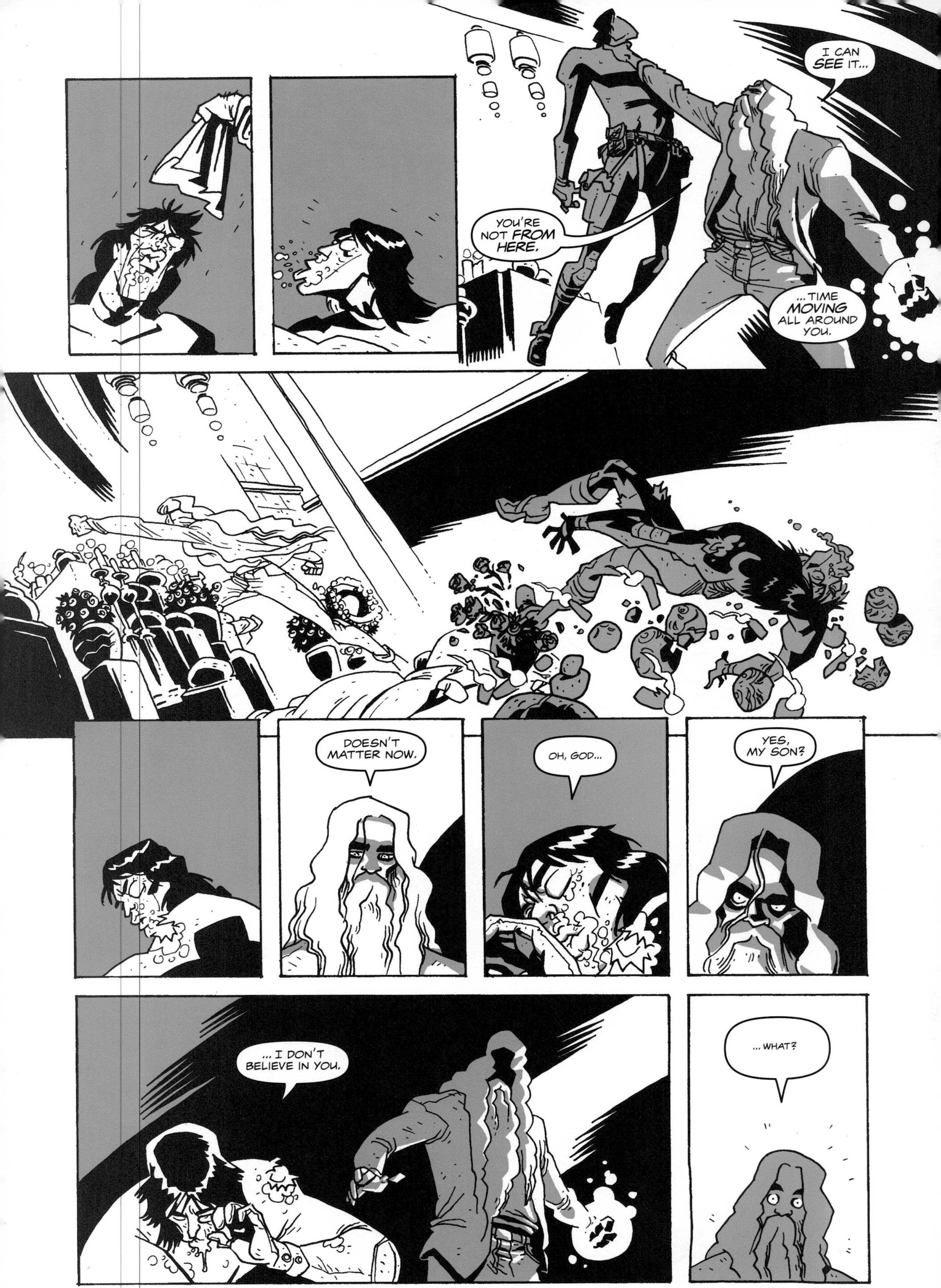
I CAN SEE IT...
YOU'RE NOT FROM HERE.
...TIME MOVING ALL AROUND YOU.
DOESN'T MATTER NOW.
OH, GOD...
YES, MY SON?
...I DON'T BELIEVE IN YOU.
...WHAT?

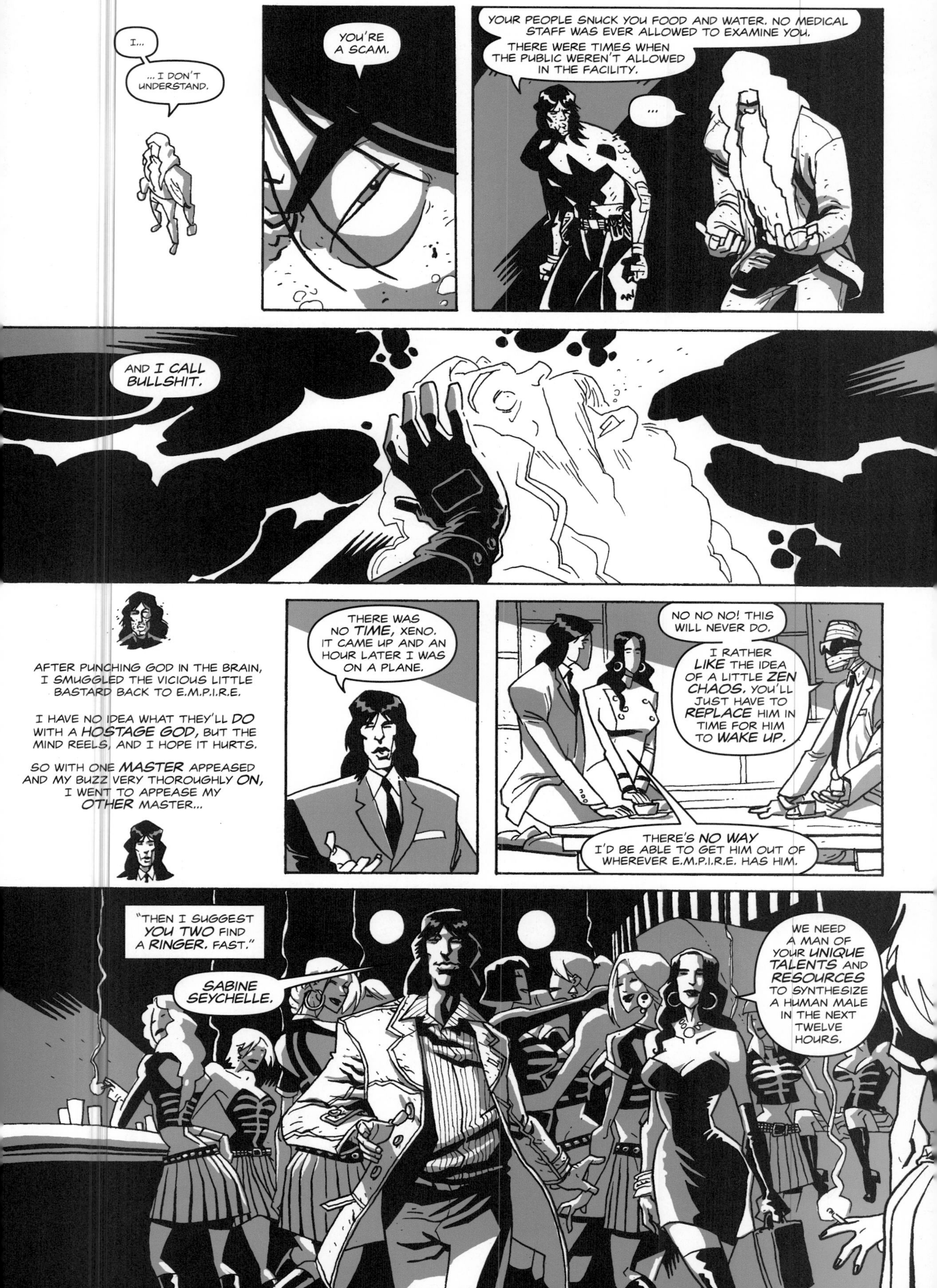
I...
...I DON'T UNDERSTAND.
YOU'RE A SCAM.
YOUR PEOPLE SNUCK YOU FOOD AND WATER. NO MEDICAL STAFF WAS EVER ALLOWED TO EXAMINE YOU.
THERE WERE TIMES WHEN THE PUBLIC WEREN'T ALLOWED IN THE FACILITY.
...
AND I CALL BULLSHIT.
AFTER PUNCHING GOD IN THE BRAIN, I SMUGGLED THE VICIOUS LITTLE BASTARD BACK TO E.M.P.I.R.E.
I HAVE NO IDEA WHAT THEY'LL DO WITH A HOSTAGE GOD, BUT THE MIND REELS, AND I HOPE IT HURTS.
SO WITH ONE MASTER APPEASED AND MY BUZZ VERY THOROUGHLY ON, I WENT TO APPEASE MY OTHER MASTER...
THERE WAS NO TIME, XENO. IT CAME UP AND AN HOUR LATER I WAS ON A PLANE.
NO NO NO! THIS WILL NEVER DO.
I RATHER LIKE THE IDEA OF A LITTLE ZEN CHAOS. YOU'LL JUST HAVE TO REPLACE HIM IN TIME FOR HIM TO WAKE UP.
THERE'S NO WAY I'D BE ABLE TO GET HIM OUT OF WHEREVER E.M.P.I.R.E. HAS HIM.
"THEN I SUGGEST YOU TWO FIND A RINGER. FAST."
SABINE SEYCHELLE.
WE NEED A MAN OF YOUR UNIQUE TALENTS AND RESOURCES TO SYNTHESIZE A HUMAN MALE IN THE NEXT TWELVE HOURS.

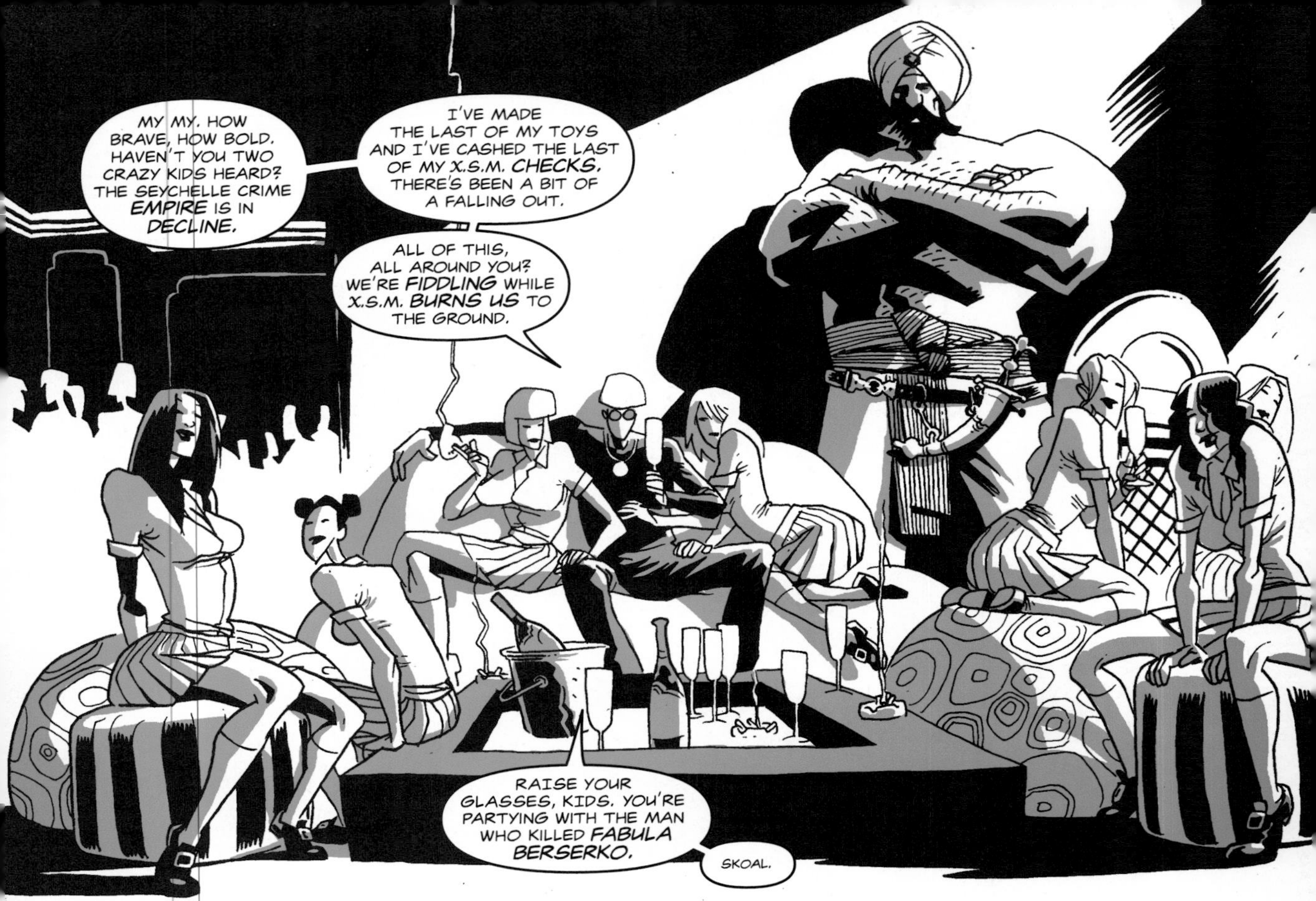
MY MY. HOW BRAVE, HOW BOLD. HAVEN'T YOU TWO CRAZY KIDS HEARD? THE SEYCHELLE CRIME EMPIRE IS IN DECLINE.
I'VE MADE THE LAST OF MY TOYS AND I'VE CASHED THE LAST OF MY X.S.M. CHECKS. THERE'S BEEN A BIT OF A FALLING OUT.
ALL OF THIS, ALL AROUND YOU? WE'RE FIDDLING WHILE X.S.M. BURNS US TO THE GROUND.
RAISE YOUR GLASSES, KIDS. YOU'RE PARTYING WITH THE MAN WHO KILLED FABULA BERSERKO.
SKOAL.

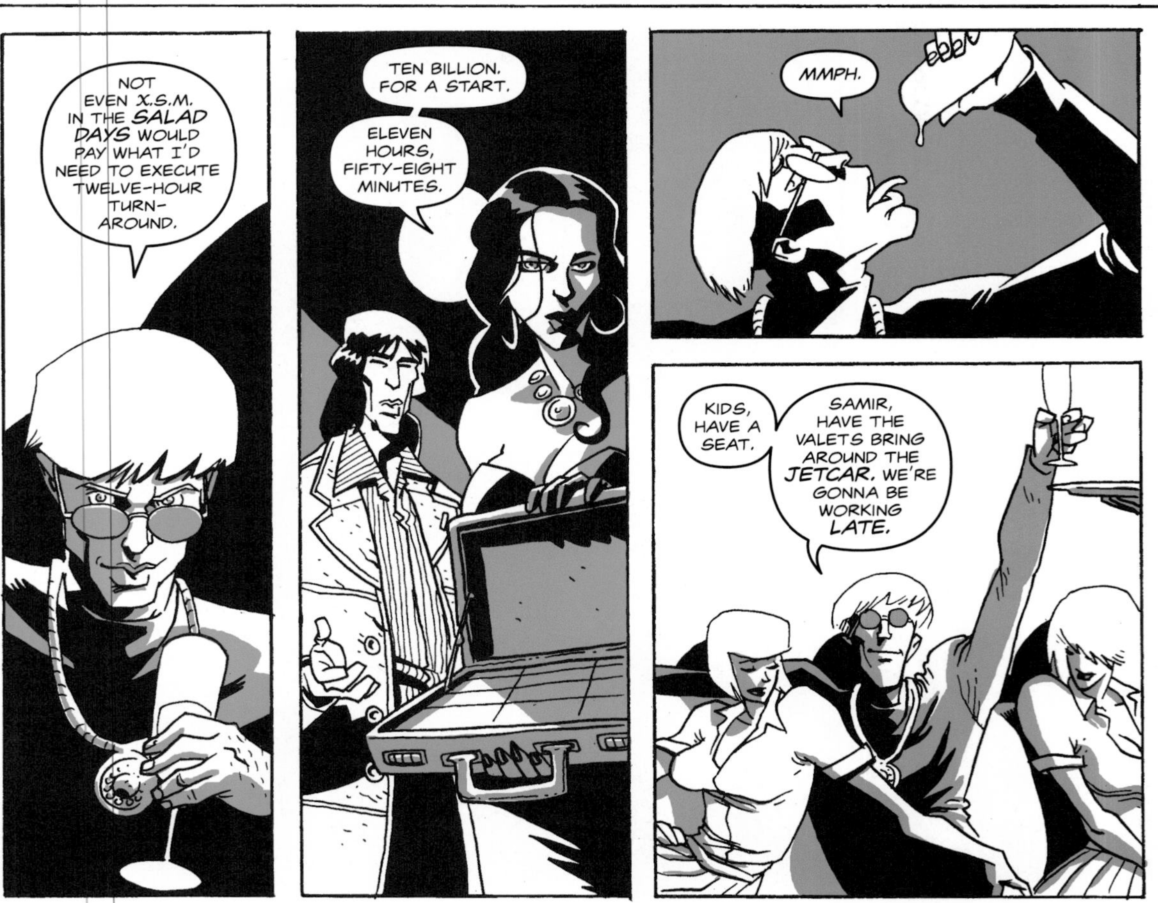
NOT EVEN X.S.M. IN THE SALAD DAYS WOULD PAY WHAT I'D NEED TO EXECUTE TWELVE-HOUR TURN-AROUND.
TEN BILLION. FOR A START.
ELEVEN HOURS, FIFTY-EIGHT MINUTES.
MMPH.
KIDS, HAVE A SEAT.
SAMIR, HAVE THE VALETS BRING AROUND THE JETCAR. WE'RE GONNA BE WORKING LATE.

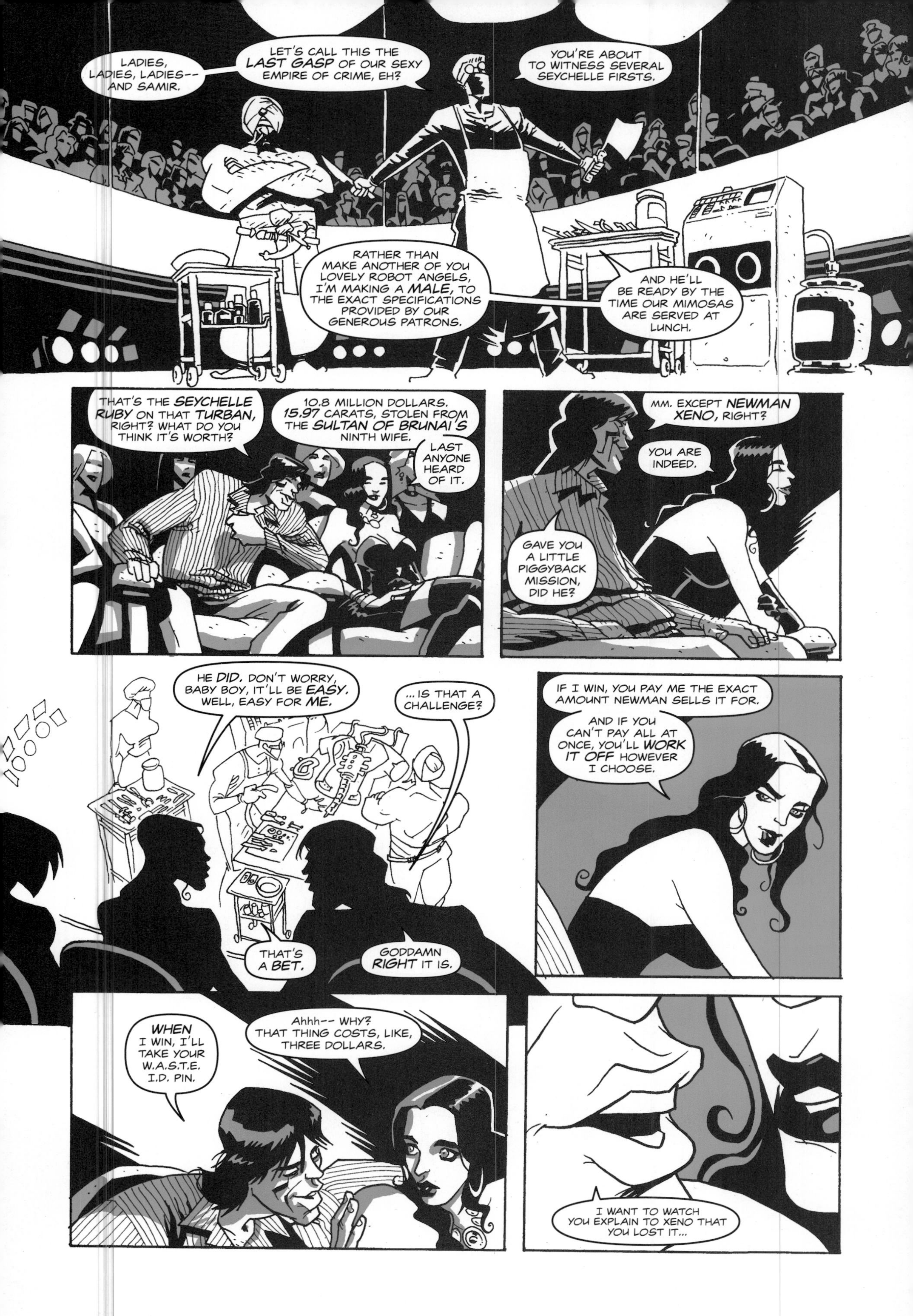
LADIES, LADIES, LADIES-- AND SAMIR.
LET'S CALL THIS THE LAST GASP OF OUR SEXY EMPIRE OF CRIME, EH?
YOU'RE ABOUT TO WITNESS SEVERAL SEYCHELLE FIRSTS.
RATHER THAN MAKE ANOTHER OF YOU LOVELY ROBOT ANGELS, I'M MAKING A MALE, TO THE EXACT SPECIFICATIONS PROVIDED BY OUR GENEROUS PATRONS.
AND HE'LL BE READY BY THE TIME OUR MIMOSAS ARE SERVED AT LUNCH.
THAT'S THE SEYCHELLE RUBY ON THAT TURBAN, RIGHT? WHAT DO YOU THINK IT'S WORTH?
10.8 MILLION DOLLARS. 15.97 CARATS, STOLEN FROM THE SULTAN OF BRUNAI'S NINTH WIFE.
LAST ANYONE HEARD OF IT.
MM. EXCEPT NEWMAN XENO, RIGHT?
YOU ARE INDEED.
GAVE YOU A LITTLE PIGGYBACK MISSION, DID HE?
HE DID. DON'T WORRY, BABY BOY, IT'LL BE EASY. WELL, EASY FOR ME.
...IS THAT A CHALLENGE?
THAT'S A BET.
GODDAMN RIGHT IT IS.
IF I WIN, YOU PAY ME THE EXACT AMOUNT NEWMAN SELLS IT FOR.
AND IF YOU CAN'T PAY ALL AT ONCE, YOU'LL WORK IT OFF HOWEVER I CHOOSE.
WHEN I WIN, I'LL TAKE YOUR W.A.S.T.E. I.D. PIN.
Ahhh-- WHY? THAT THING COSTS, LIKE, THREE DOLLARS.
I WANT TO WATCH YOU EXPLAIN TO XENO THAT YOU LOST IT...

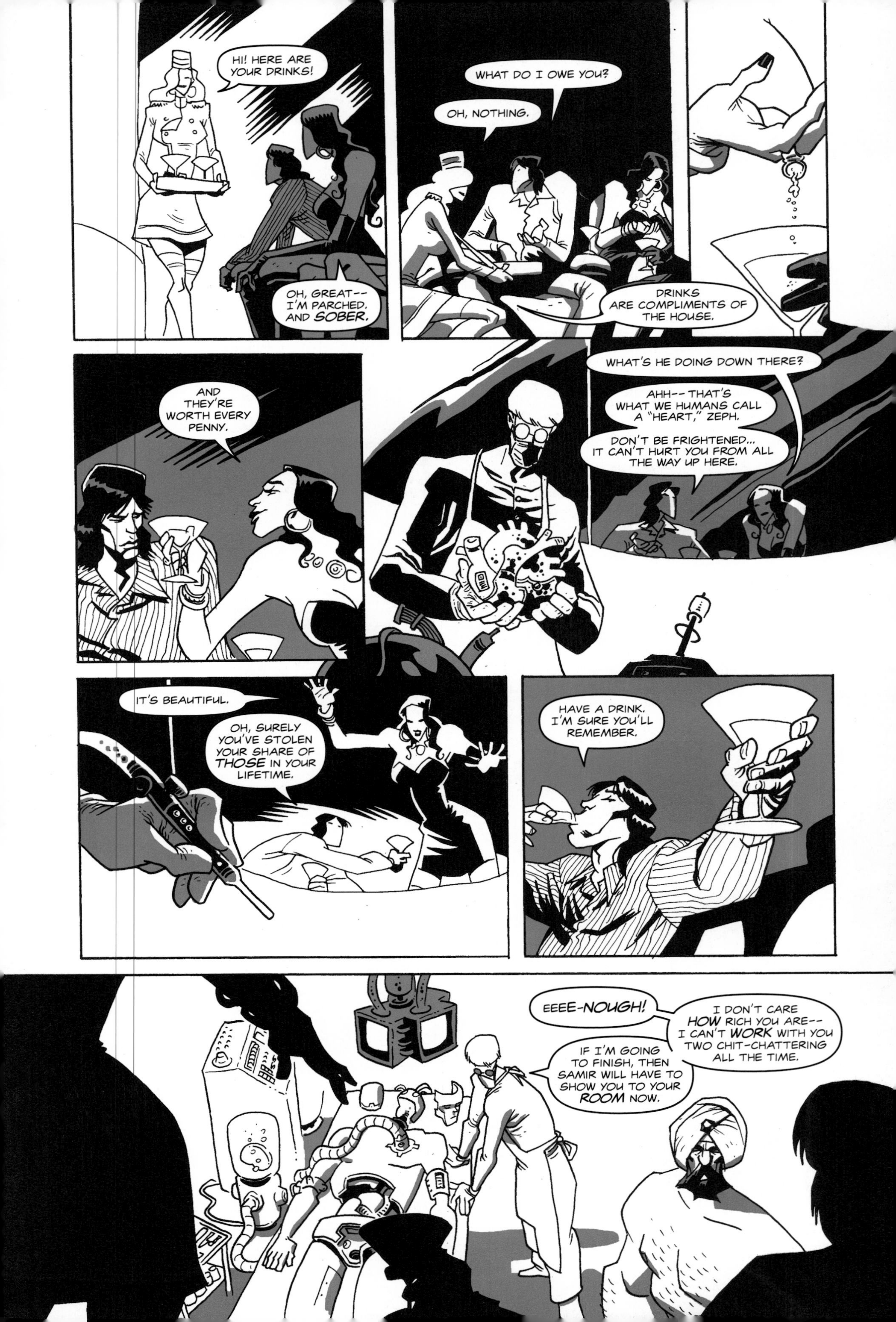
HI! HERE ARE YOUR DRINKS!
OH, GREAT-- I'M PARCHED. AND SOBER.
WHAT DO I OWE YOU?
OH, NOTHING.
DRINKS ARE COMPLIMENTS OF THE HOUSE.
AND THEY'RE WORTH EVERY PENNY.
WHAT'S HE DOING DOWN THERE?
AHH-- THAT'S WHAT WE HUMANS CALL A "HEART," ZEPH.
DON'T BE FRIGHTENED... IT CAN'T HURT YOU FROM ALL THE WAY UP HERE.
IT'S BEAUTIFUL.
OH, SURELY YOU'VE STOLEN YOUR SHARE OF THOSE IN YOUR LIFETIME.
HAVE A DRINK. I'M SURE YOU'LL REMEMBER.
EEEE-NOUGH!
I DON'T CARE HOW RICH YOU ARE-- I CAN'T WORK WITH YOU TWO CHIT-CHATTERING ALL THE TIME.
IF I'M GOING TO FINISH, THEN SAMIR WILL HAVE TO SHOW YOU TO YOUR ROOM NOW.

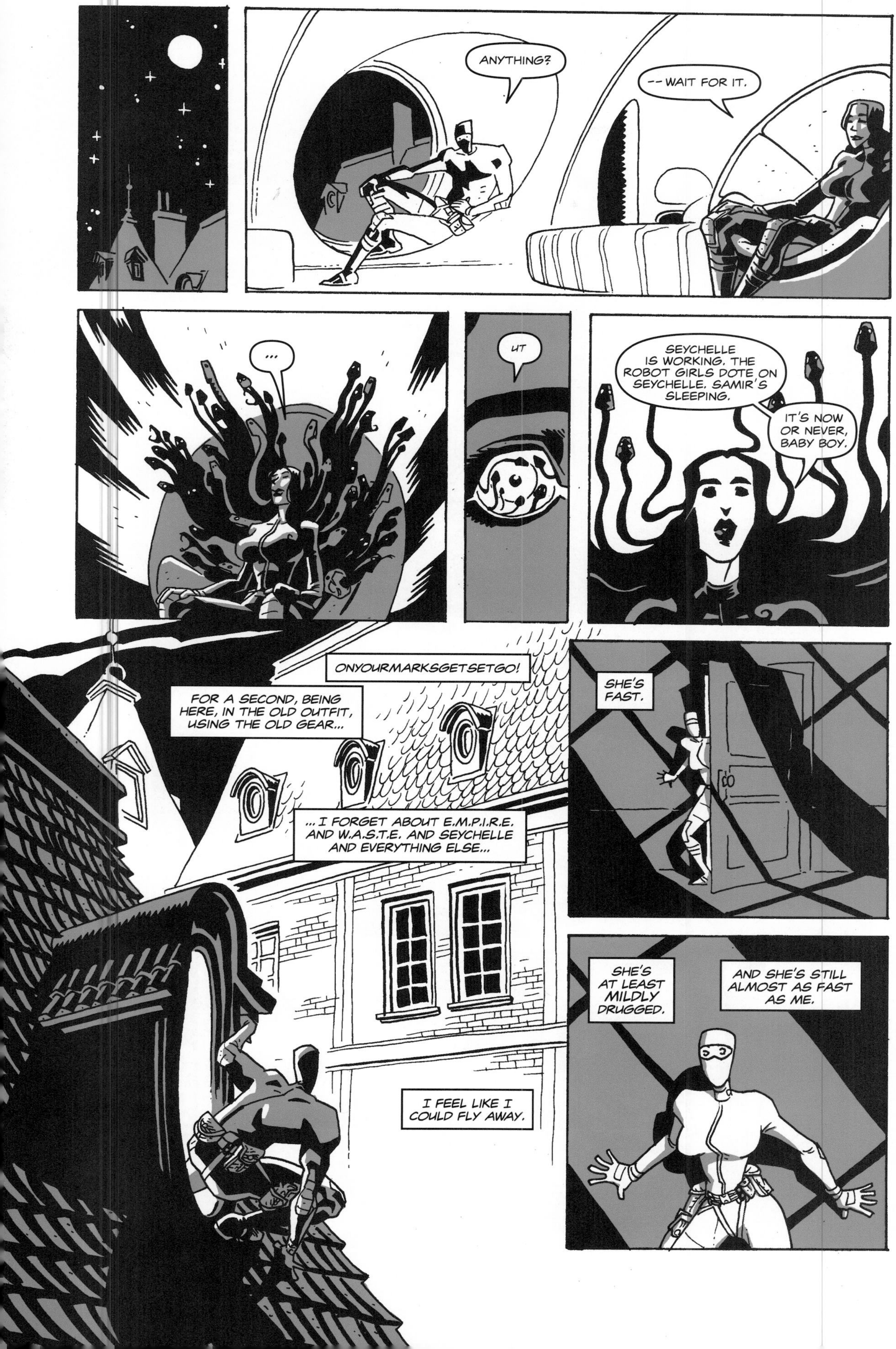
ANYTHING?
-- WAIT FOR IT.
...
UT
SEYCHELLE IS WORKING. THE ROBOT GIRLS DOTE ON SEYCHELLE. SAMIR'S SLEEPING.
IT'S NOW OR NEVER, BABY BOY.
ONYOURMARKSGETSETGO!
FOR A SECOND, BEING HERE, IN THE OLD OUTFIT, USING THE OLD GEAR...
...I FORGET ABOUT E.M.P.I.R.E. AND W.A.S.T.E. AND SEYCHELLE AND EVERYTHING ELSE...
I FEEL LIKE I COULD FLY AWAY.
SHE'S FAST.
SHE'S AT LEAST MILDLY DRUGGED.
AND SHE'S STILL ALMOST AS FAST AS ME.

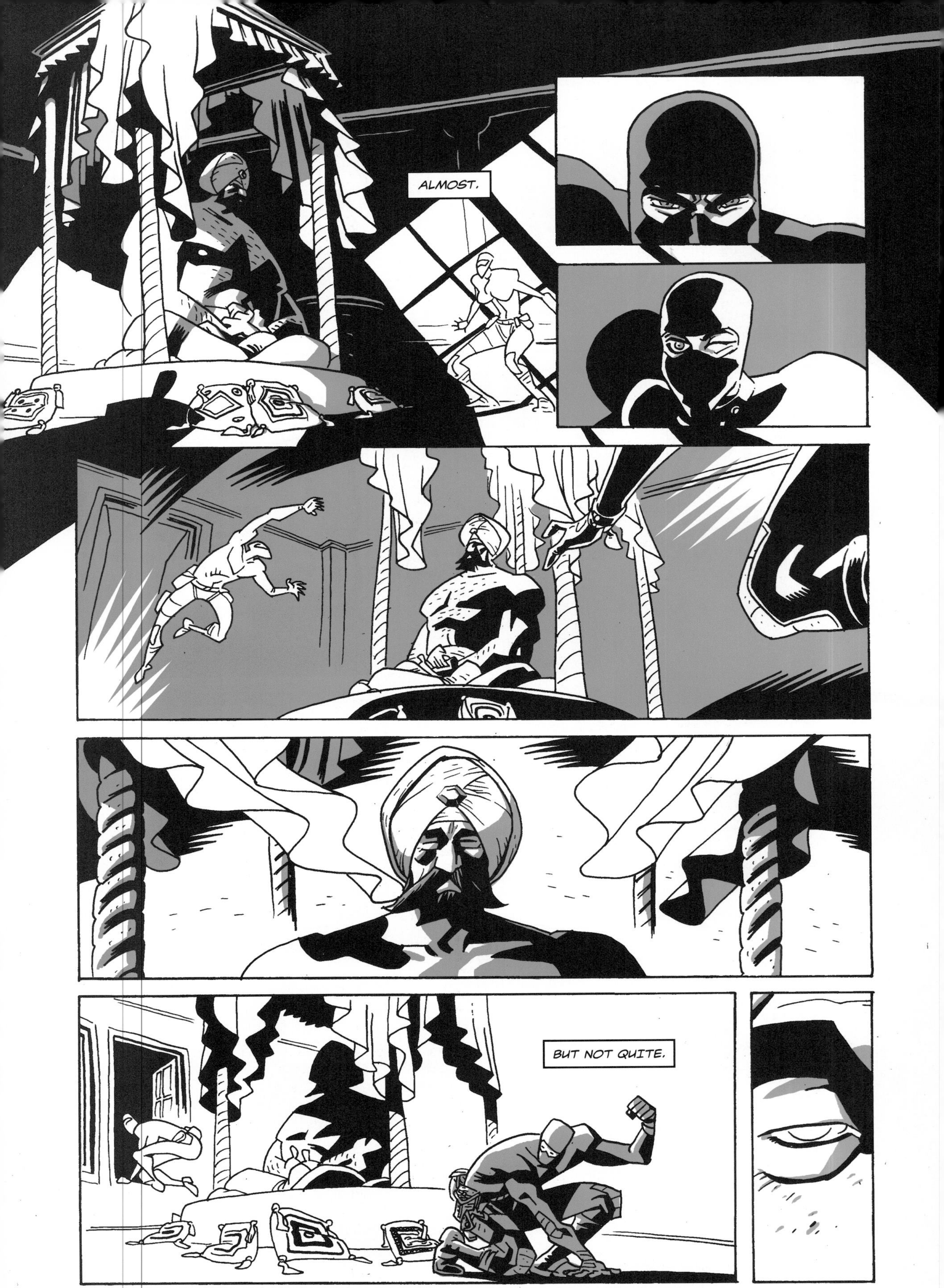
ALMOST.
BUT NOT QUITE.

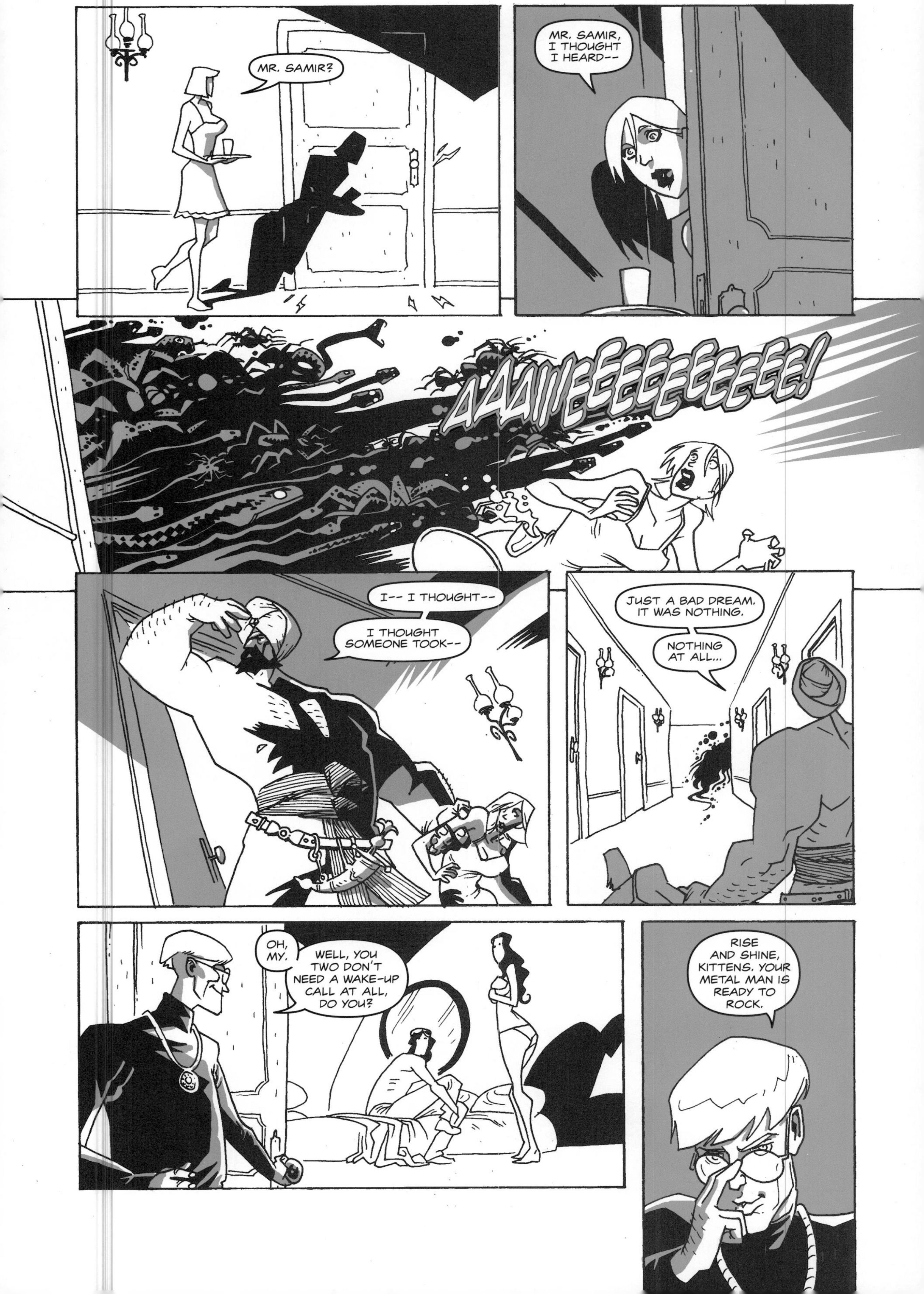

MR. SAMIR?
MR. SAMIR, I THOUGHT I HEARD--
AAAIIEEEEEEEEEEEE!
I-- I THOUGHT--
I THOUGHT SOMEONE TOOK--
JUST A BAD DREAM. IT WAS NOTHING.
NOTHING AT ALL...
OH, MY.
WELL, YOU TWO DON'T NEED A WAKE-UP CALL AT ALL, DO YOU?
RISE AND SHINE, KITTENS. YOUR METAL MAN IS READY TO ROCK.

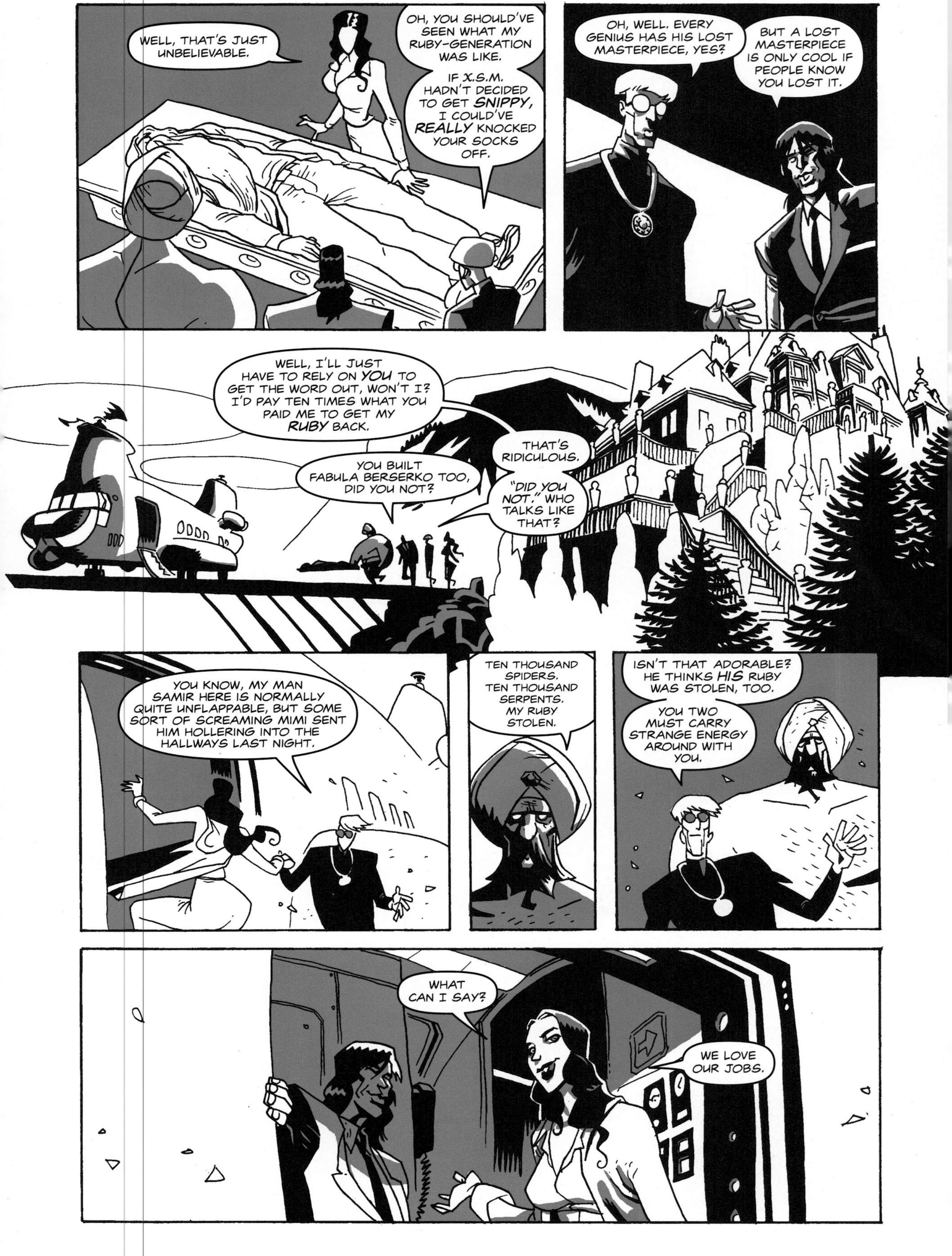
WELL, THAT'S JUST UNBELIEVABLE.
OH, YOU SHOULD'VE SEEN WHAT MY RUBY-GENERATION WAS LIKE.
IF X.S.M. HADN'T DECIDED TO GET SNIPPY, I COULD'VE REALLY KNOCKED YOUR SOCKS OFF.
OH, WELL. EVERY GENIUS HAS HIS LOST MASTERPIECE, YES?
BUT A LOST MASTERPIECE IS ONLY COOL IF PEOPLE KNOW YOU LOST IT.
WELL, I'LL JUST HAVE TO RELY ON YOU TO GET THE WORD OUT, WON'T I? I'D PAY TEN TIMES WHAT YOU PAID ME TO GET MY RUBY BACK.
YOU BUILT FABULA BERSERKO TOO, DID YOU NOT?
THAT'S RIDICULOUS.
"DID YOU NOT." WHO TALKS LIKE THAT?
YOU KNOW, MY MAN SAMIR HERE IS NORMALLY QUITE UNFLAPPABLE, BUT SOME SORT OF SCREAMING MIMI SENT HIM HOLLERING INTO THE HALLWAYS LAST NIGHT.
TEN THOUSAND SPIDERS. TEN THOUSAND SERPENTS. MY RUBY STOLEN.
ISN'T THAT ADORABLE? HE THINKS HIS RUBY WAS STOLEN, TOO.
YOU TWO MUST CARRY STRANGE ENERGY AROUND WITH YOU.
WHAT CAN I SAY?
WE LOVE OUR JOBS.

NICE WORK REPLACING THE RUBY.

ONE OF US HAD TO SAVE OUR ASSES WHILE YOU WERE THINKING OF YOURSELF.

IS THAT REALLY WHAT THIS WAS ABOUT? TAKING THE ACTUAL SEYCHELLE RUBY?

I MEAN, WHAT IS THAT? A PUN? DOES XENO THINK THAT'S FUNNY?

AND DON'T THINK JUST BECAUSE YOU THOUGHT TO LEAVE THE RINGER BEHIND THAT I'M NOT GONNA COLLECT.

YOUR W.A.S.T.E. PIN. PAY UP. NOW.

PLEASURE DOING BUSINESS WITH YOU, SIS.

ARE YOU SURE, McSHANE?

AND YOU'VE-- YOU'VE MADE SURE THAT DAVID X IS STILL IN E.M.P.I.R.E. CUSTODY?

YES, I'M SERIOUS. HE'S A GODDAMN ESCAPE ARTIST, ISN'T HE?

WELL, HOW THE HELL ELSE CAN YOU EXPLAIN THAT HE WAS BACK THIS MORN--

I'LL CALL YOU BACK.

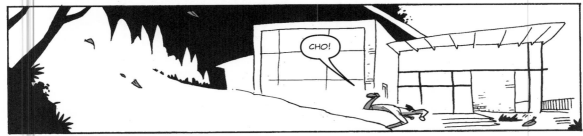

CHO!

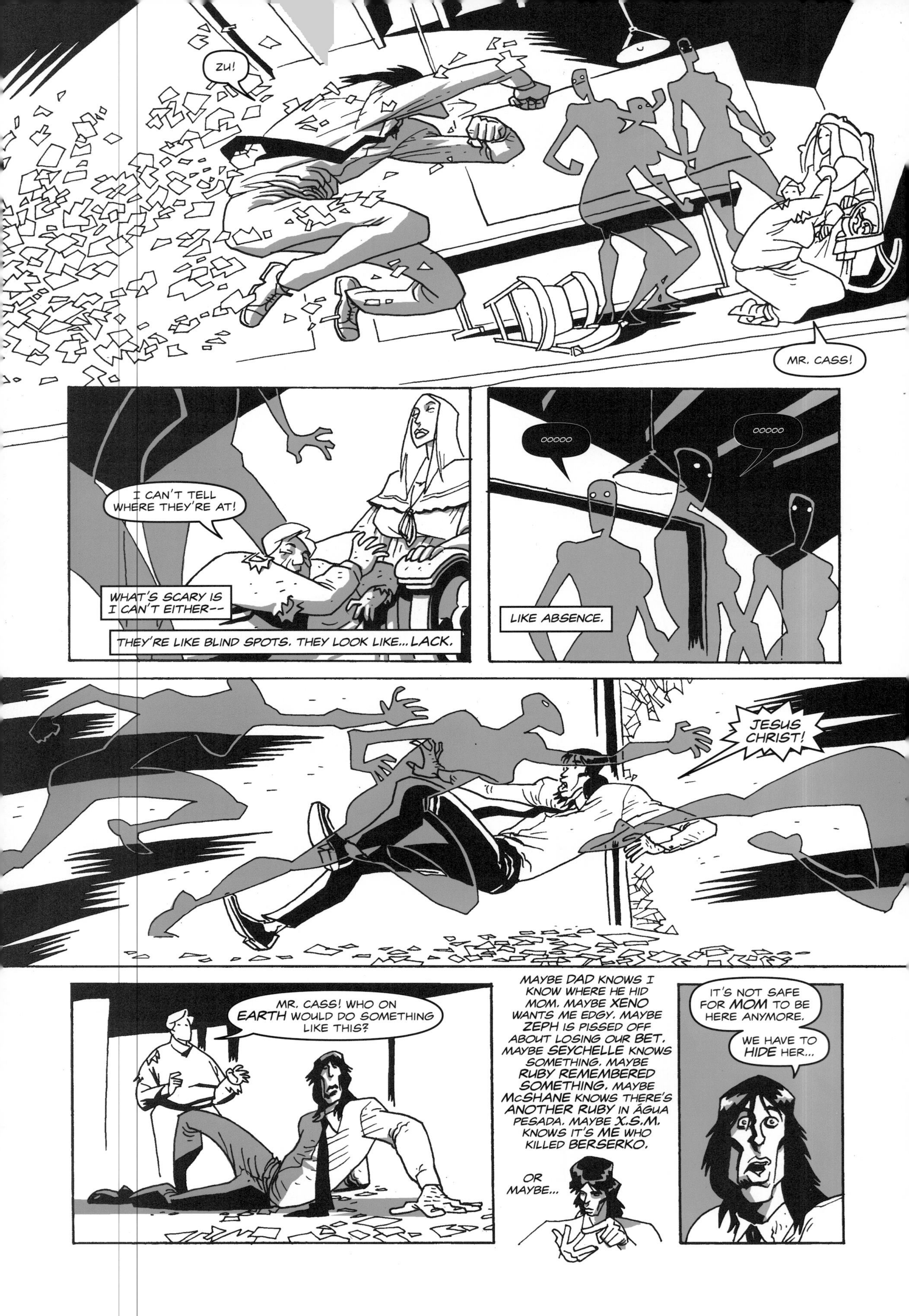

ZU!
MR. CASS!
I CAN'T TELL WHERE THEY'RE AT!
WHAT'S SCARY IS I CAN'T EITHER--
THEY'RE LIKE BLIND SPOTS. THEY LOOK LIKE... LACK.
OOOOO
OOOOO
LIKE ABSENCE.
JESUS CHRIST!
MR. CASS! WHO ON EARTH WOULD DO SOMETHING LIKE THIS?
MAYBE DAD KNOWS I KNOW WHERE HE HID MOM. MAYBE XENO WANTS ME EDGY. MAYBE ZEPH IS PISSED OFF ABOUT LOSING OUR BET. MAYBE SEYCHELLE KNOWS SOMETHING. MAYBE RUBY REMEMBERED SOMETHING. MAYBE McSHANE KNOWS THERE'S ANOTHER RUBY IN ÁGUA PESADA. MAYBE X.S.M. KNOWS IT'S ME WHO KILLED BERSERKO.
OR MAYBE...
IT'S NOT SAFE FOR MOM TO BE HERE ANYMORE.
WE HAVE TO HIDE HER...

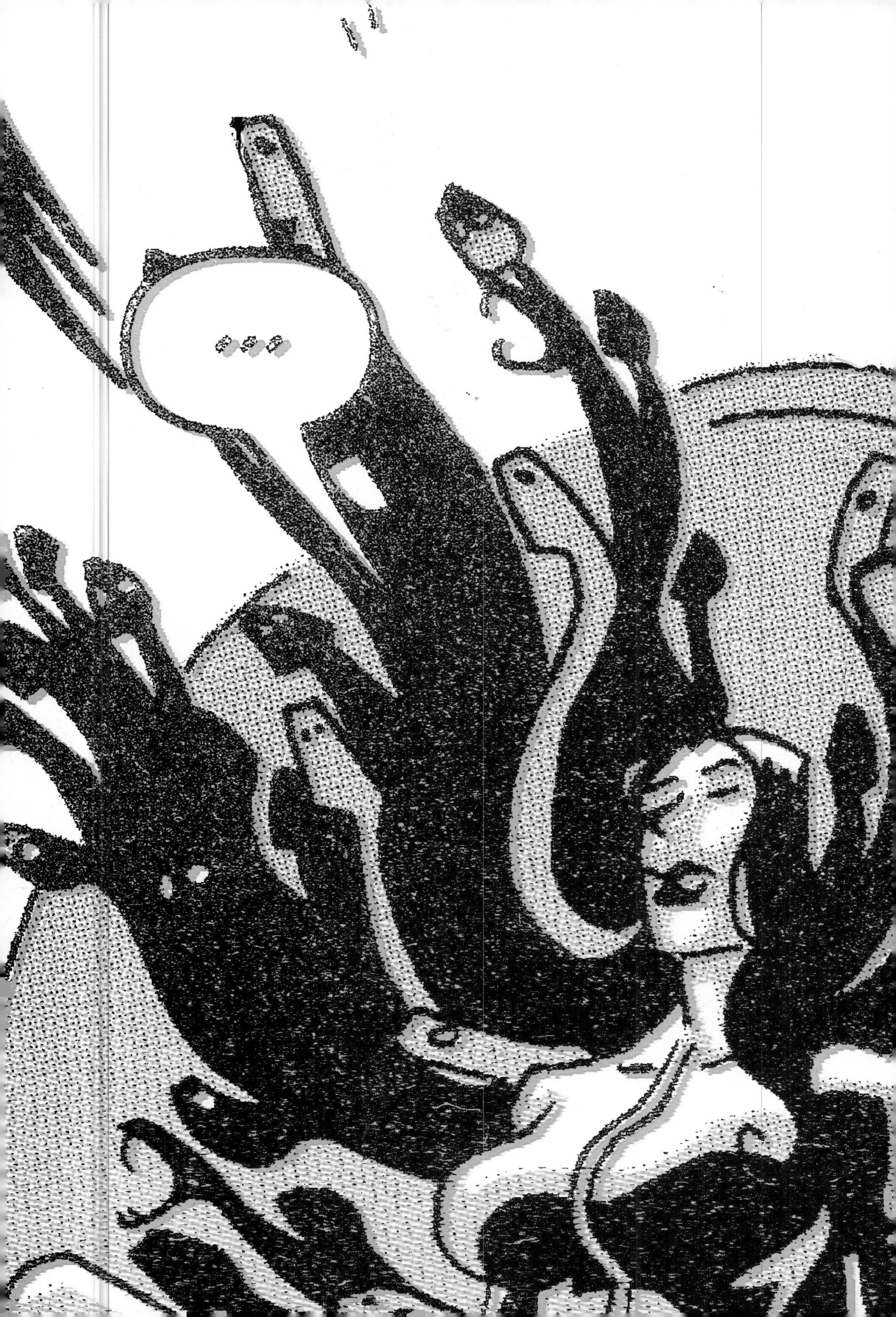
...

Chapter Five
Coldheart

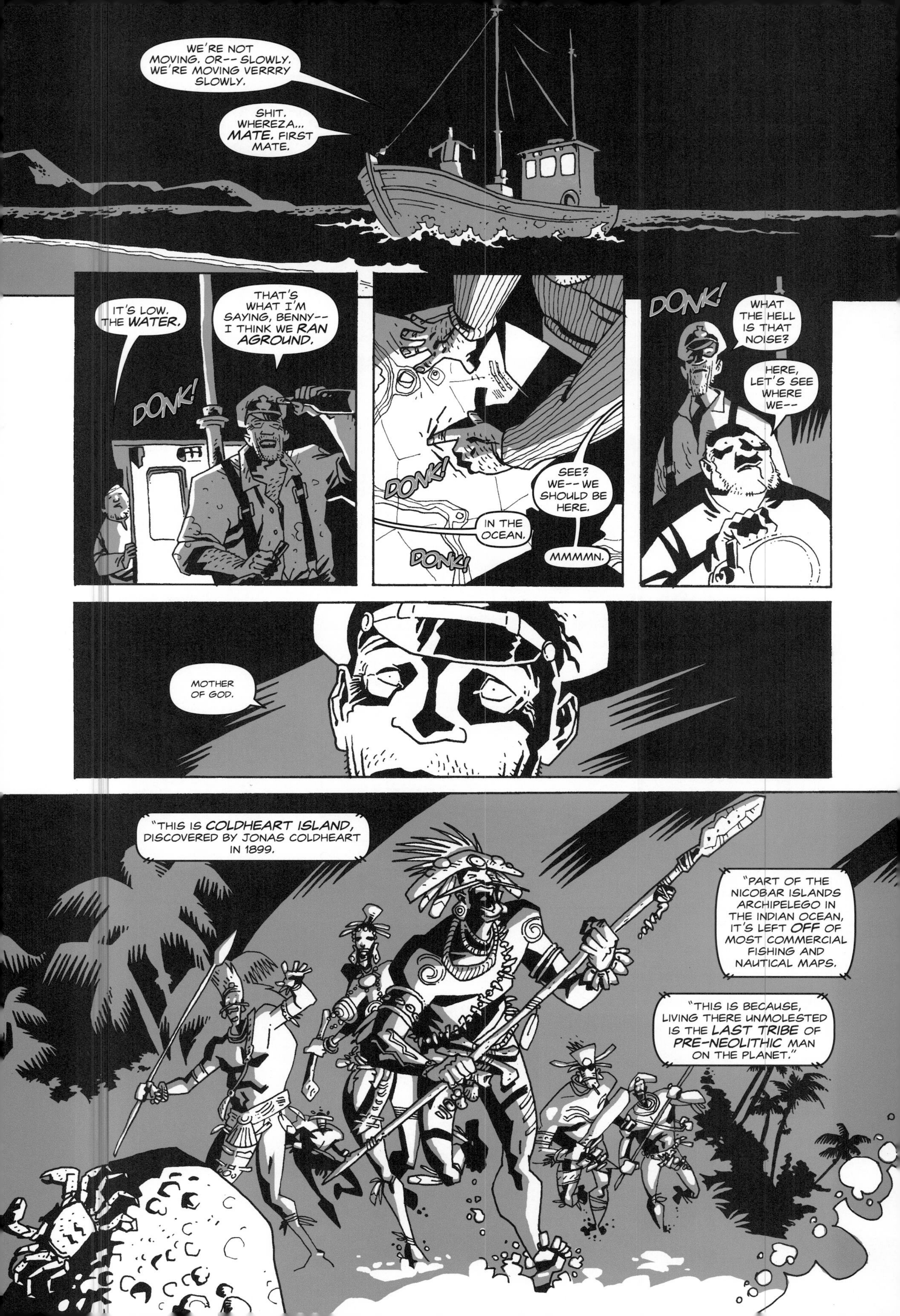
WE'RE NOT MOVING. OR-- SLOWLY. WE'RE MOVING VERRRY SLOWLY.
SHIT. WHEREZA... MATE. FIRST MATE.
IT'S LOW. THE WATER.
THAT'S WHAT I'M SAYING, BENNY-- I THINK WE RAN AGROUND.
DONK!
DONK!
IN THE OCEAN.
SEE? WE-- WE SHOULD BE HERE.
DONK!
MMMMN.
DONK!
WHAT THE HELL IS THAT NOISE?
HERE, LET'S SEE WHERE WE--
MOTHER OF GOD.
"THIS IS COLDHEART ISLAND, DISCOVERED BY JONAS COLDHEART IN 1899.
"PART OF THE NICOBAR ISLANDS ARCHIPELEGO IN THE INDIAN OCEAN, IT'S LEFT OFF OF MOST COMMERCIAL FISHING AND NAUTICAL MAPS.
"THIS IS BECAUSE, LIVING THERE UNMOLESTED IS THE LAST TRIBE OF PRE-NEOLITHIC MAN ON THE PLANET."

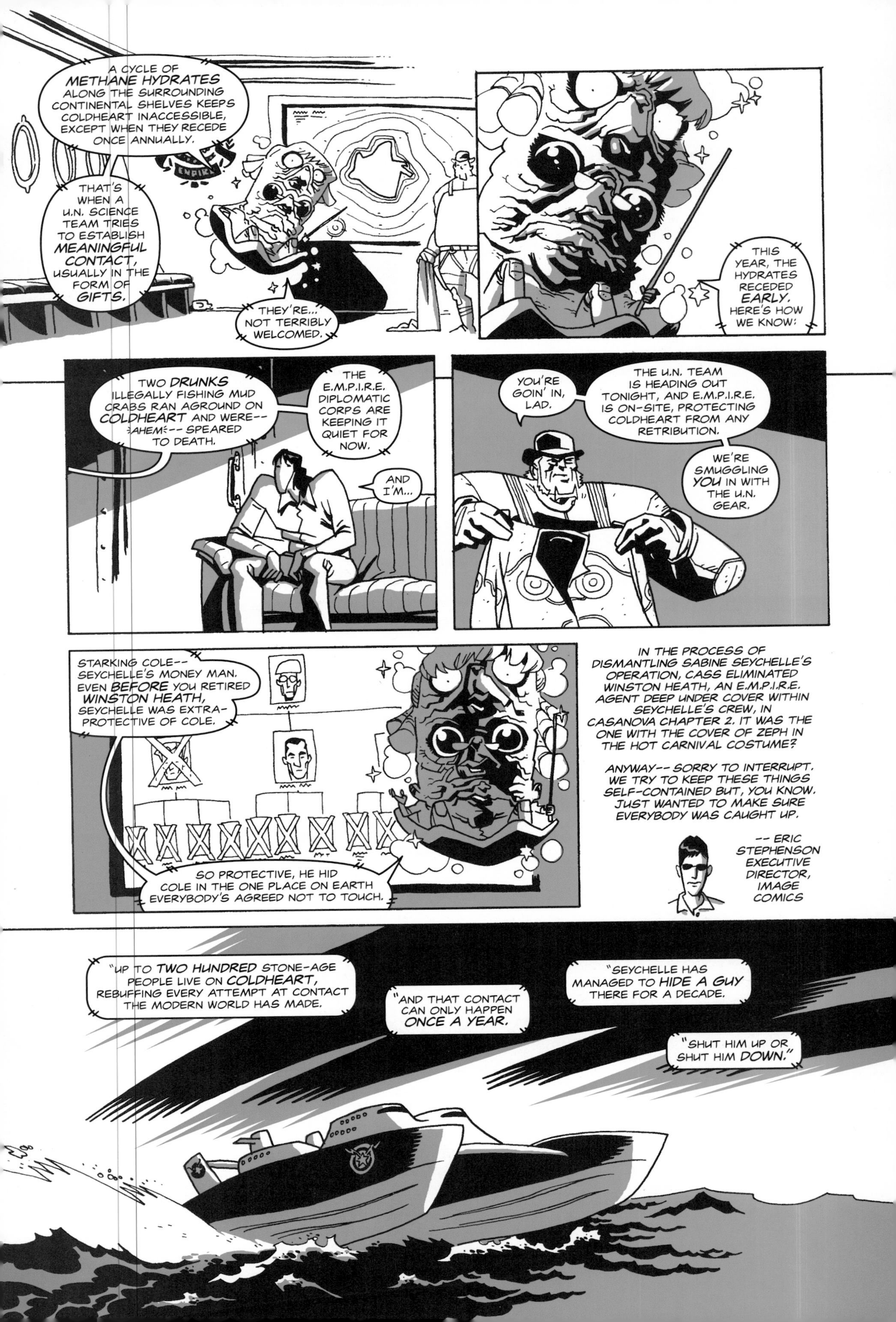

A CYCLE OF METHANE HYDRATES ALONG THE SURROUNDING CONTINENTAL SHELVES KEEPS COLDHEART INACCESSIBLE, EXCEPT WHEN THEY RECEDE ONCE ANNUALLY.
THAT'S WHEN A U.N. SCIENCE TEAM TRIES TO ESTABLISH MEANINGFUL CONTACT, USUALLY IN THE FORM OF GIFTS.
THEY'RE... NOT TERRIBLY WELCOMED.
EMPIRE
THIS YEAR, THE HYDRATES RECEDED EARLY. HERE'S HOW WE KNOW:
TWO DRUNKS ILLEGALLY FISHING MUD CRABS RAN AGROUND ON COLDHEART AND WERE-- AHEM-- SPEARED TO DEATH.
THE E.M.P.I.R.E. DIPLOMATIC CORPS ARE KEEPING IT QUIET FOR NOW.
AND I'M...
YOU'RE GOIN' IN, LAD.
THE U.N. TEAM IS HEADING OUT TONIGHT, AND E.M.P.I.R.E. IS ON-SITE, PROTECTING COLDHEART FROM ANY RETRIBUTION.
WE'RE SMUGGLING YOU IN WITH THE U.N. GEAR.
STARKING COLE-- SEYCHELLE'S MONEY MAN. EVEN BEFORE YOU RETIRED WINSTON HEATH, SEYCHELLE WAS EXTRA-PROTECTIVE OF COLE.
SO PROTECTIVE, HE HID COLE IN THE ONE PLACE ON EARTH EVERYBODY'S AGREED NOT TO TOUCH.
IN THE PROCESS OF DISMANTLING SABINE SEYCHELLE'S OPERATION, CASS ELIMINATED WINSTON HEATH, AN E.M.P.I.R.E. AGENT DEEP UNDER COVER WITHIN SEYCHELLE'S CREW, IN CASANOVA CHAPTER 2. IT WAS THE ONE WITH THE COVER OF ZEPH IN THE HOT CARNIVAL COSTUME?
ANYWAY-- SORRY TO INTERRUPT. WE TRY TO KEEP THESE THINGS SELF-CONTAINED BUT, YOU KNOW. JUST WANTED TO MAKE SURE EVERYBODY WAS CAUGHT UP.
-- ERIC STEPHENSON EXECUTIVE DIRECTOR, IMAGE COMICS
"UP TO TWO HUNDRED STONE-AGE PEOPLE LIVE ON COLDHEART, REBUFFING EVERY ATTEMPT AT CONTACT THE MODERN WORLD HAS MADE.
"AND THAT CONTACT CAN ONLY HAPPEN ONCE A YEAR.
"SEYCHELLE HAS MANAGED TO HIDE A GUY THERE FOR A DECADE.
"SHUT HIM UP OR SHUT HIM DOWN."

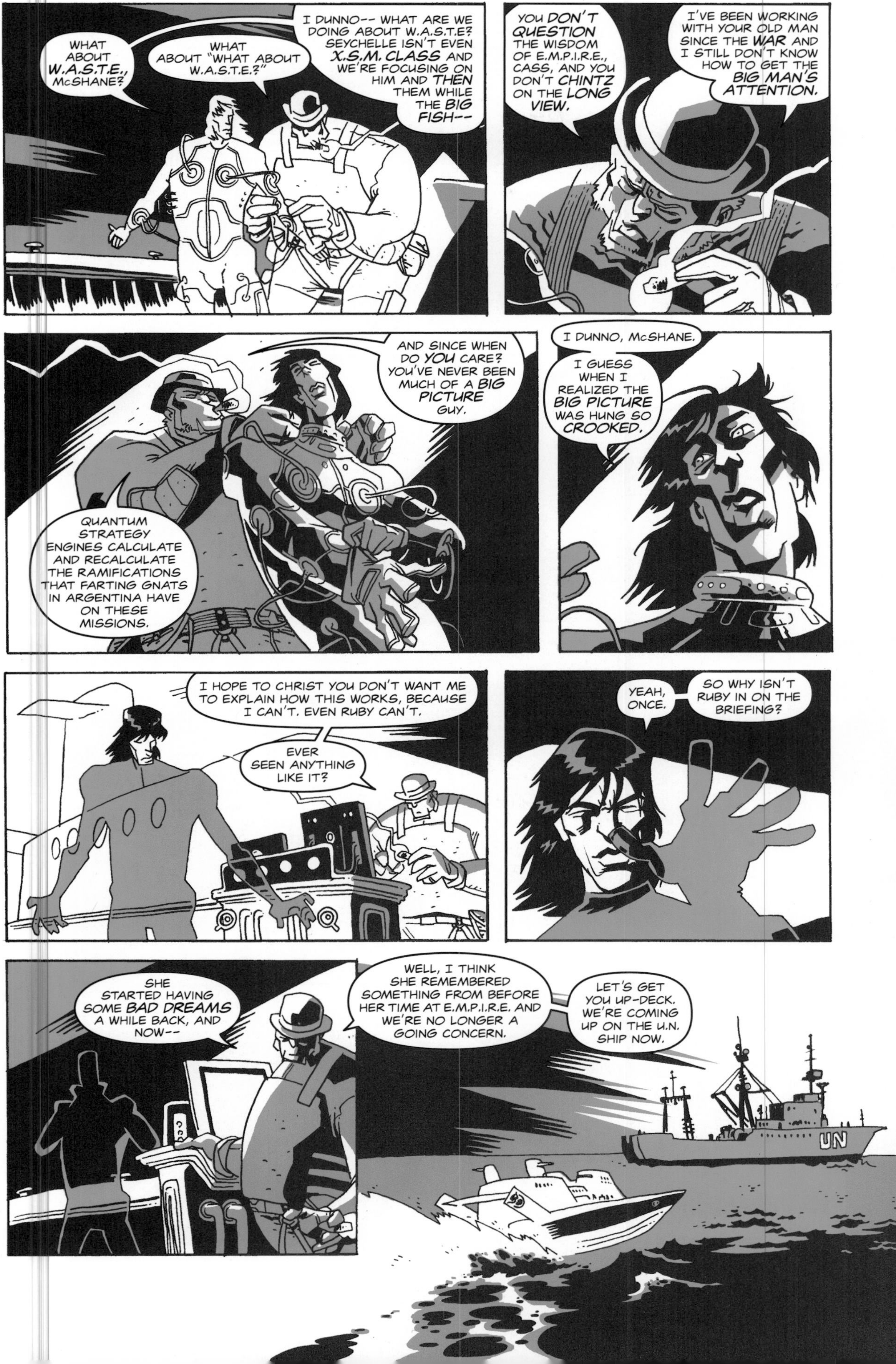
WHAT ABOUT W.A.S.T.E., McSHANE?
WHAT ABOUT "WHAT ABOUT W.A.S.T.E.?"
I DUNNO-- WHAT ARE WE DOING ABOUT W.A.S.T.E.? SEYCHELLE ISN'T EVEN X.S.M. CLASS AND WE'RE FOCUSING ON HIM AND THEN THEM WHILE THE BIG FISH--
YOU DON'T QUESTION THE WISDOM OF E.M.P.I.R.E., CASS, AND YOU DON'T CHINTZ ON THE LONG VIEW.
I'VE BEEN WORKING WITH YOUR OLD MAN SINCE THE WAR AND I STILL DON'T KNOW HOW TO GET THE BIG MAN'S ATTENTION.
AND SINCE WHEN DO YOU CARE? YOU'VE NEVER BEEN MUCH OF A BIG PICTURE GUY.
QUANTUM STRATEGY ENGINES CALCULATE AND RECALCULATE THE RAMIFICATIONS THAT FARTING GNATS IN ARGENTINA HAVE ON THESE MISSIONS.
I DUNNO, McSHANE.
I GUESS WHEN I REALIZED THE BIG PICTURE WAS HUNG SO CROOKED.
I HOPE TO CHRIST YOU DON'T WANT ME TO EXPLAIN HOW THIS WORKS, BECAUSE I CAN'T. EVEN RUBY CAN'T.
EVER SEEN ANYTHING LIKE IT?
YEAH, ONCE.
SO WHY ISN'T RUBY IN ON THE BRIEFING?
SHE STARTED HAVING SOME BAD DREAMS A WHILE BACK, AND NOW--
WELL, I THINK SHE REMEMBERED SOMETHING FROM BEFORE HER TIME AT E.M.P.I.R.E. AND WE'RE NO LONGER A GOING CONCERN.
LET'S GET YOU UP-DECK. WE'RE COMING UP ON THE U.N. SHIP NOW.
UN

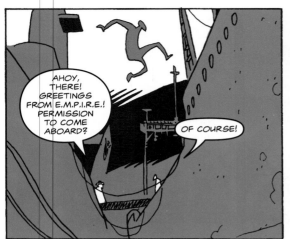

AHOY, THERE! GREETINGS FROM E.M.P.I.R.E.! PERMISSION TO COME ABOARD?

OF COURSE!

AND HERE WE GO AGAIN: A BAD MAN STALKS A WORSE MAN.

A MAN THAT LET HIMSELF GET WARPED AND BLACKENED BY THE PROXIMITY OF POWER AND MONEY.

HIM, NOT ME, YOU ASSHOLES.

SEYCHELLE'S COURIER, AND THE SUBJECT OF MY COUNTER-MISSION.

YOUR COUNTER-MISSION IS TOTALLY FUCKING EASY, BUCKAROO.

WE COOKED SEYCHELLE'S BOOKS FOR HIM. SWITCH 'EM OUT-- WE NEED SEYCHELLE THINKING HE'S BROKE.

LAND HO!

I ALWAYS WANTED TO SAY THAT.

FUHHH.

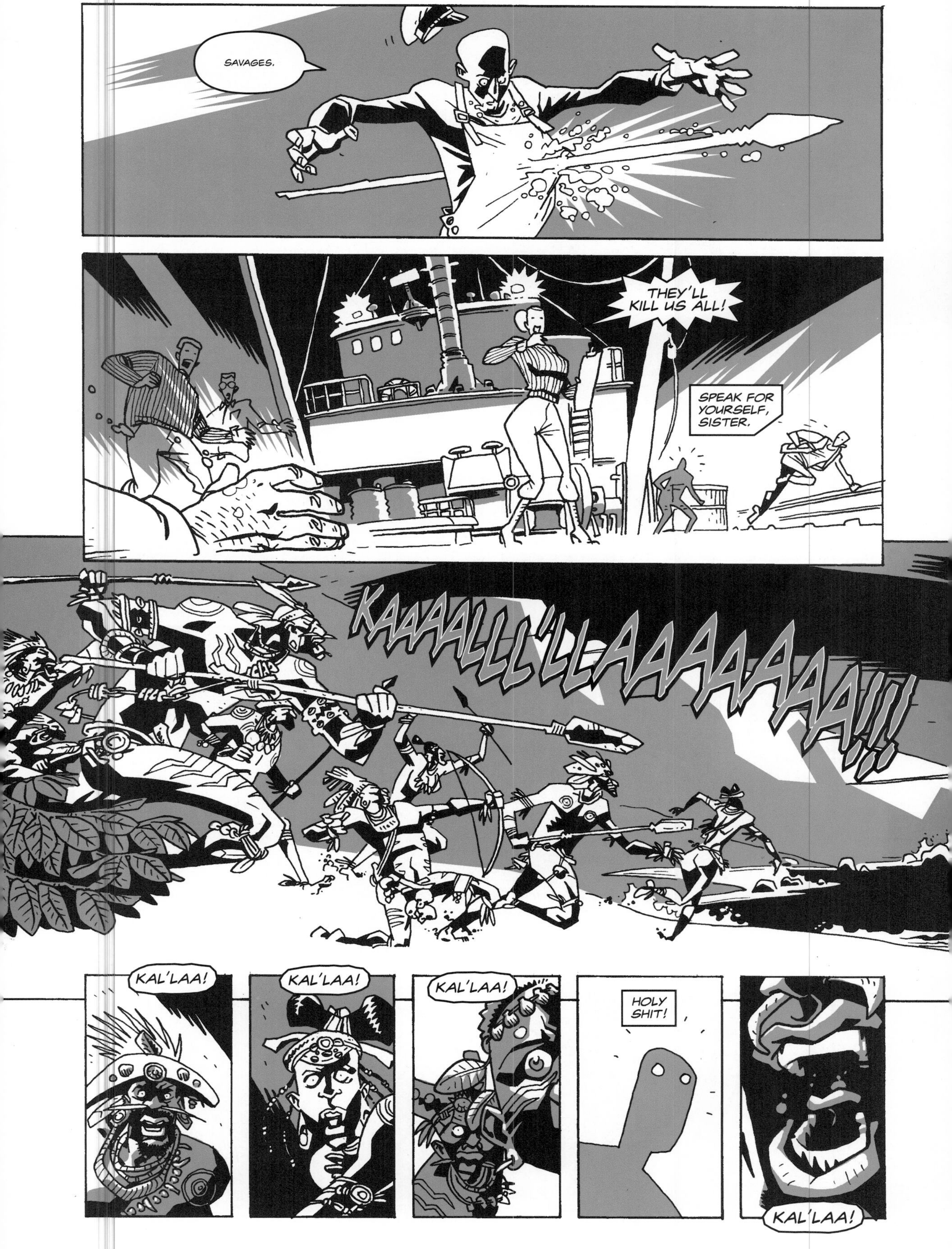
SAVAGES.
THEY'LL KILL US ALL!
SPEAK FOR YOURSELF, SISTER.
KAAAALLL'LLAAAAAAAA!!!
KAL'LAA!
KAL'LAA!
KAL'LAA!
HOLY SHIT!
KAL'LAA!

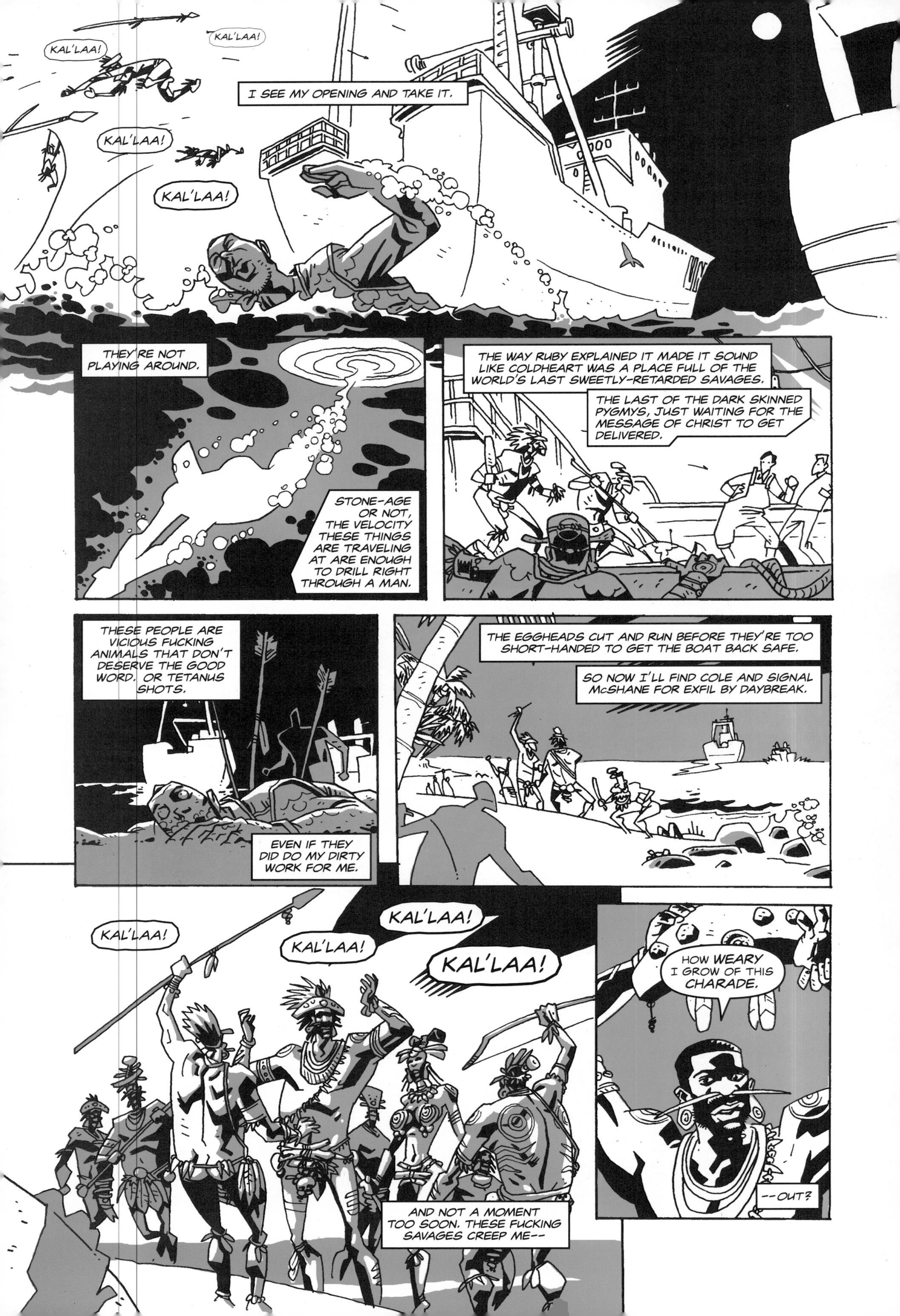
KAL'LAA!
KAL'LAA!
KAL'LAA!
KAL'LAA!
I SEE MY OPENING AND TAKE IT.
THEY'RE NOT PLAYING AROUND.
STONE-AGE OR NOT, THE VELOCITY THESE THINGS ARE TRAVELING AT ARE ENOUGH TO DRILL RIGHT THROUGH A MAN.
THE WAY RUBY EXPLAINED IT MADE IT SOUND LIKE COLDHEART WAS A PLACE FULL OF THE WORLD'S LAST SWEETLY-RETARDED SAVAGES.
THE LAST OF THE DARK SKINNED PYGMYS, JUST WAITING FOR THE MESSAGE OF CHRIST TO GET DELIVERED.
THESE PEOPLE ARE VICIOUS FUCKING ANIMALS THAT DON'T DESERVE THE GOOD WORD. OR TETANUS SHOTS.
EVEN IF THEY DID DO MY DIRTY WORK FOR ME.
THE EGGHEADS CUT AND RUN BEFORE THEY'RE TOO SHORT-HANDED TO GET THE BOAT BACK SAFE.
SO NOW I'LL FIND COLE AND SIGNAL McSHANE FOR EXFIL BY DAYBREAK.
KAL'LAA!
KAL'LAA!
KAL'LAA!
KAL'LAA!
AND NOT A MOMENT TOO SOON. THESE FUCKING SAVAGES CREEP ME--
HOW WEARY I GROW OF THIS CHARADE.
--OUT?

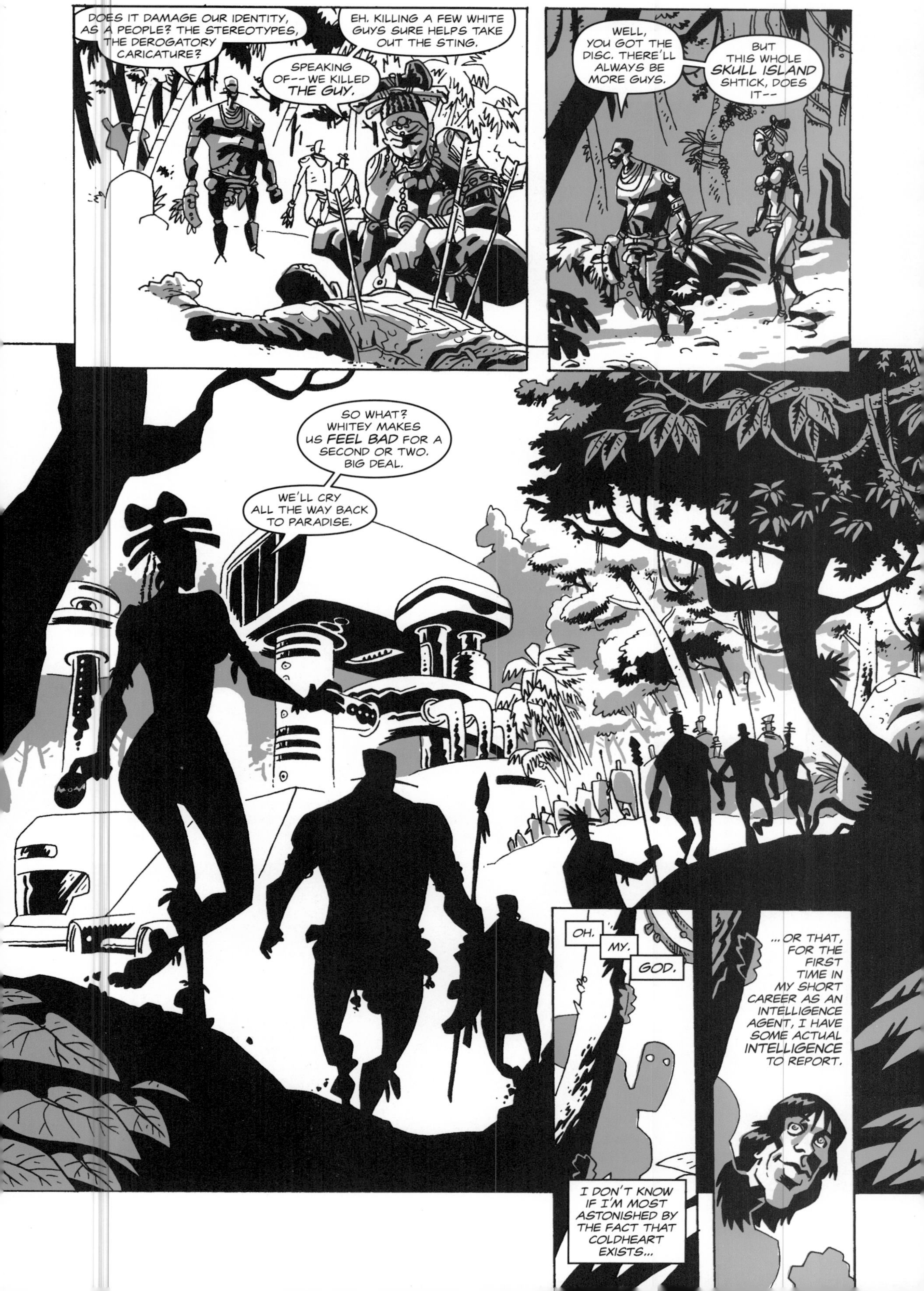
DOES IT DAMAGE OUR IDENTITY, AS A PEOPLE? THE STEREOTYPES, THE DEROGATORY CARICATURE?
EH. KILLING A FEW WHITE GUYS SURE HELPS TAKE OUT THE STING.
SPEAKING OF-- WE KILLED THE GUY.
WELL, YOU GOT THE DISC. THERE'LL ALWAYS BE MORE GUYS.
BUT THIS WHOLE SKULL ISLAND SHTICK, DOES IT--
SO WHAT? WHITEY MAKES US FEEL BAD FOR A SECOND OR TWO. BIG DEAL.
WE'LL CRY ALL THE WAY BACK TO PARADISE.
OH.
MY.
GOD.
I DON'T KNOW IF I'M MOST ASTONISHED BY THE FACT THAT COLDHEART EXISTS...
...OR THAT, FOR THE FIRST TIME IN MY SHORT CAREER AS AN INTELLIGENCE AGENT, I HAVE SOME ACTUAL INTELLIGENCE TO REPORT.

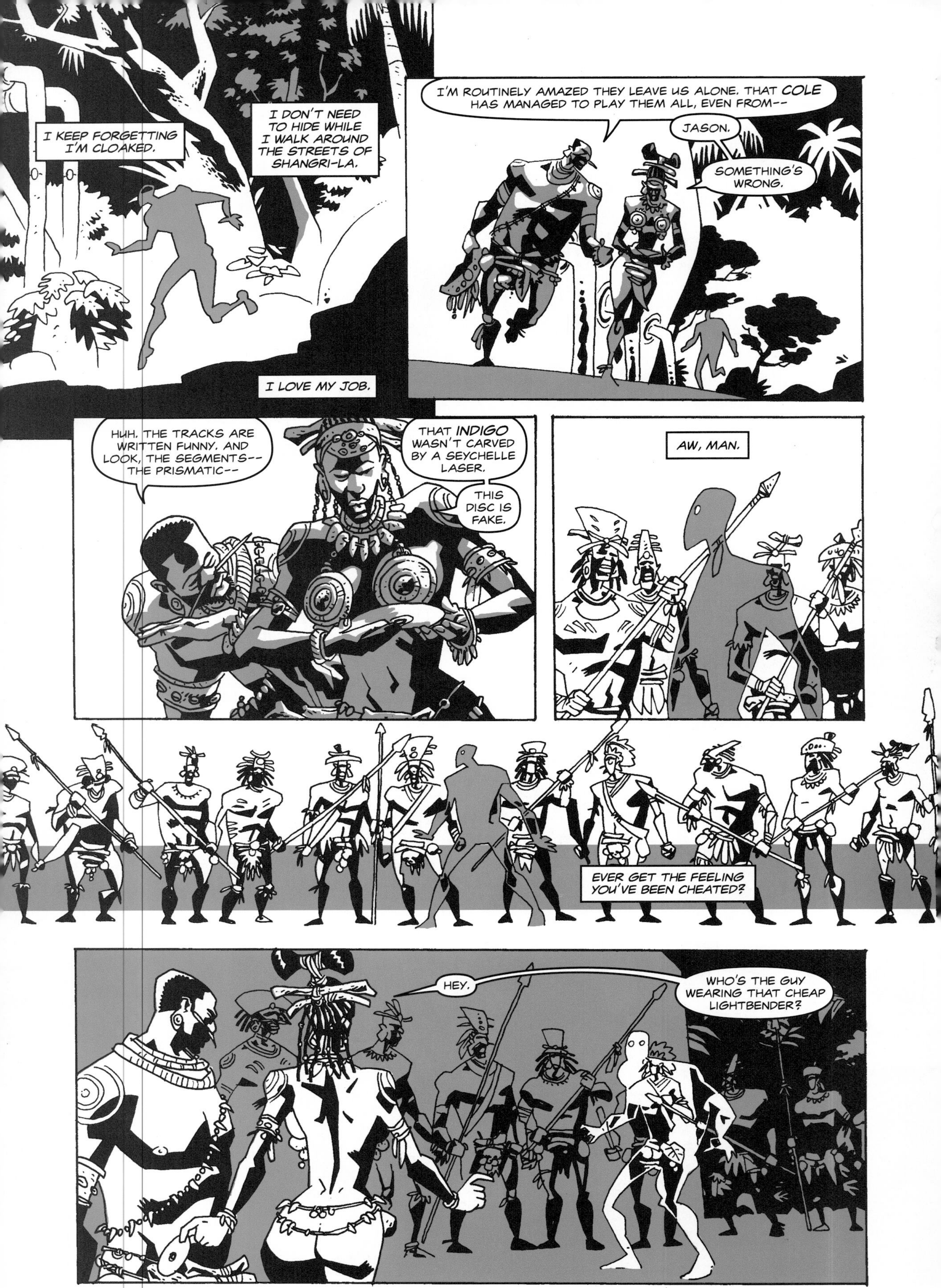
I KEEP FORGETTING I'M CLOAKED.
I DON'T NEED TO HIDE WHILE I WALK AROUND THE STREETS OF SHANGRI-LA.
I LOVE MY JOB.
I'M ROUTINELY AMAZED THEY LEAVE US ALONE. THAT COLE HAS MANAGED TO PLAY THEM ALL, EVEN FROM--
JASON.
SOMETHING'S WRONG.
HUH. THE TRACKS ARE WRITTEN FUNNY. AND LOOK, THE SEGMENTS-- THE PRISMATIC--
THAT INDIGO WASN'T CARVED BY A SEYCHELLE LASER.
THIS DISC IS FAKE.
AW, MAN.
EVER GET THE FEELING YOU'VE BEEN CHEATED?
HEY.
WHO'S THE GUY WEARING THAT CHEAP LIGHTBENDER?

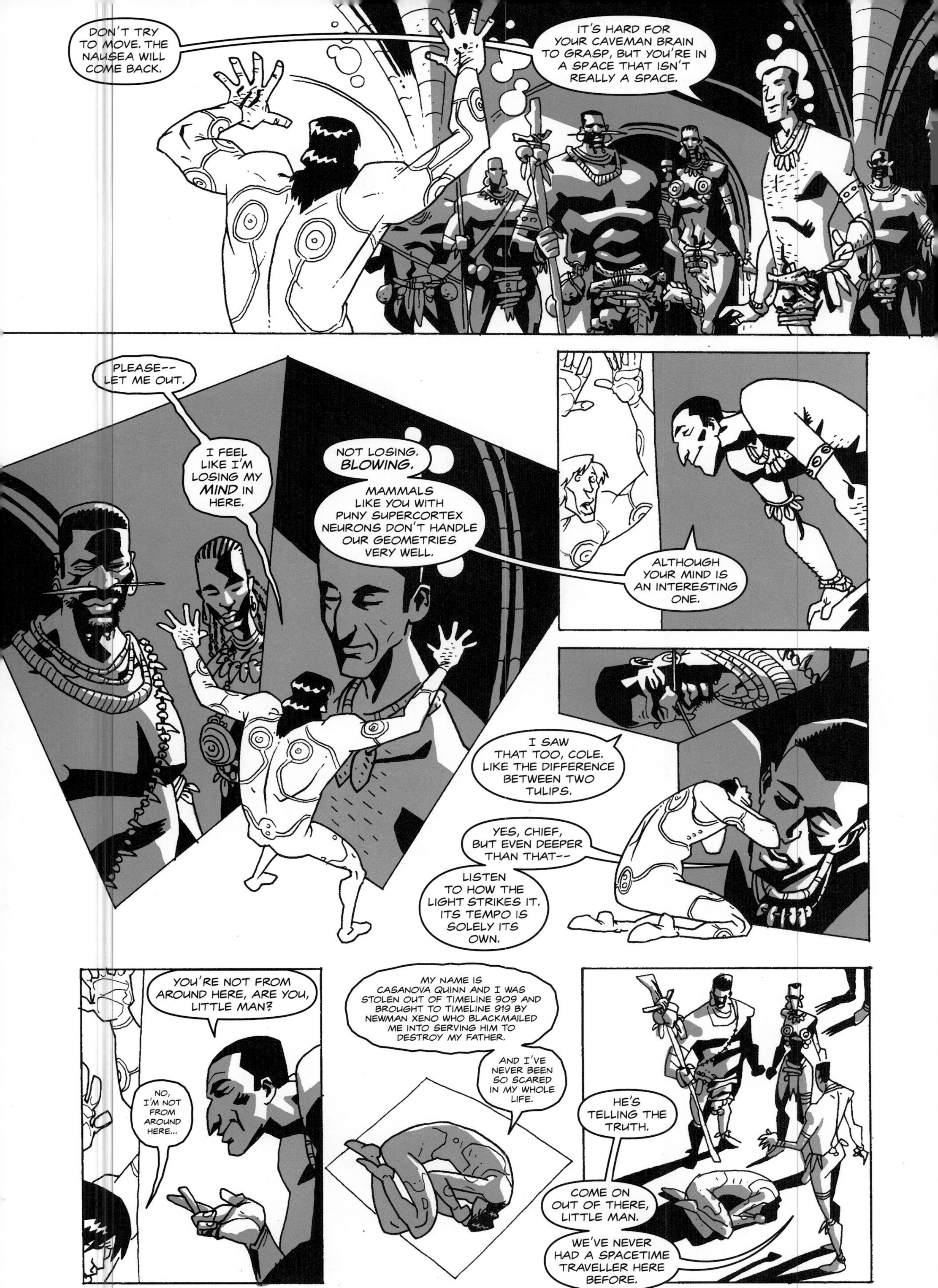
DON'T TRY TO MOVE. THE NAUSEA WILL COME BACK.
IT'S HARD FOR YOUR CAVEMAN BRAIN TO GRASP, BUT YOU'RE IN A SPACE THAT ISN'T REALLY A SPACE.
PLEASE-- LET ME OUT.
I FEEL LIKE I'M LOSING MY MIND IN HERE.
NOT LOSING. BLOWING.
MAMMALS LIKE YOU WITH PUNY SUPERCORTEX NEURONS DON'T HANDLE OUR GEOMETRIES VERY WELL.
ALTHOUGH YOUR MIND IS AN INTERESTING ONE.
I SAW THAT TOO, COLE. LIKE THE DIFFERENCE BETWEEN TWO TULIPS.
YES, CHIEF, BUT EVEN DEEPER THAN THAT--
LISTEN TO HOW THE LIGHT STRIKES IT. ITS TEMPO IS SOLELY ITS OWN.
YOU'RE NOT FROM AROUND HERE, ARE YOU, LITTLE MAN?
NO, I'M NOT FROM AROUND HERE...
MY NAME IS CASANOVA QUINN AND I WAS STOLEN OUT OF TIMELINE 909 AND BROUGHT TO TIMELINE 919 BY NEWMAN XENO WHO BLACKMAILED ME INTO SERVING HIM TO DESTROY MY FATHER.
AND I'VE NEVER BEEN SO SCARED IN MY WHOLE LIFE.
HE'S TELLING THE TRUTH.
COME ON OUT OF THERE, LITTLE MAN.
WE'VE NEVER HAD A SPACETIME TRAVELLER HERE BEFORE.

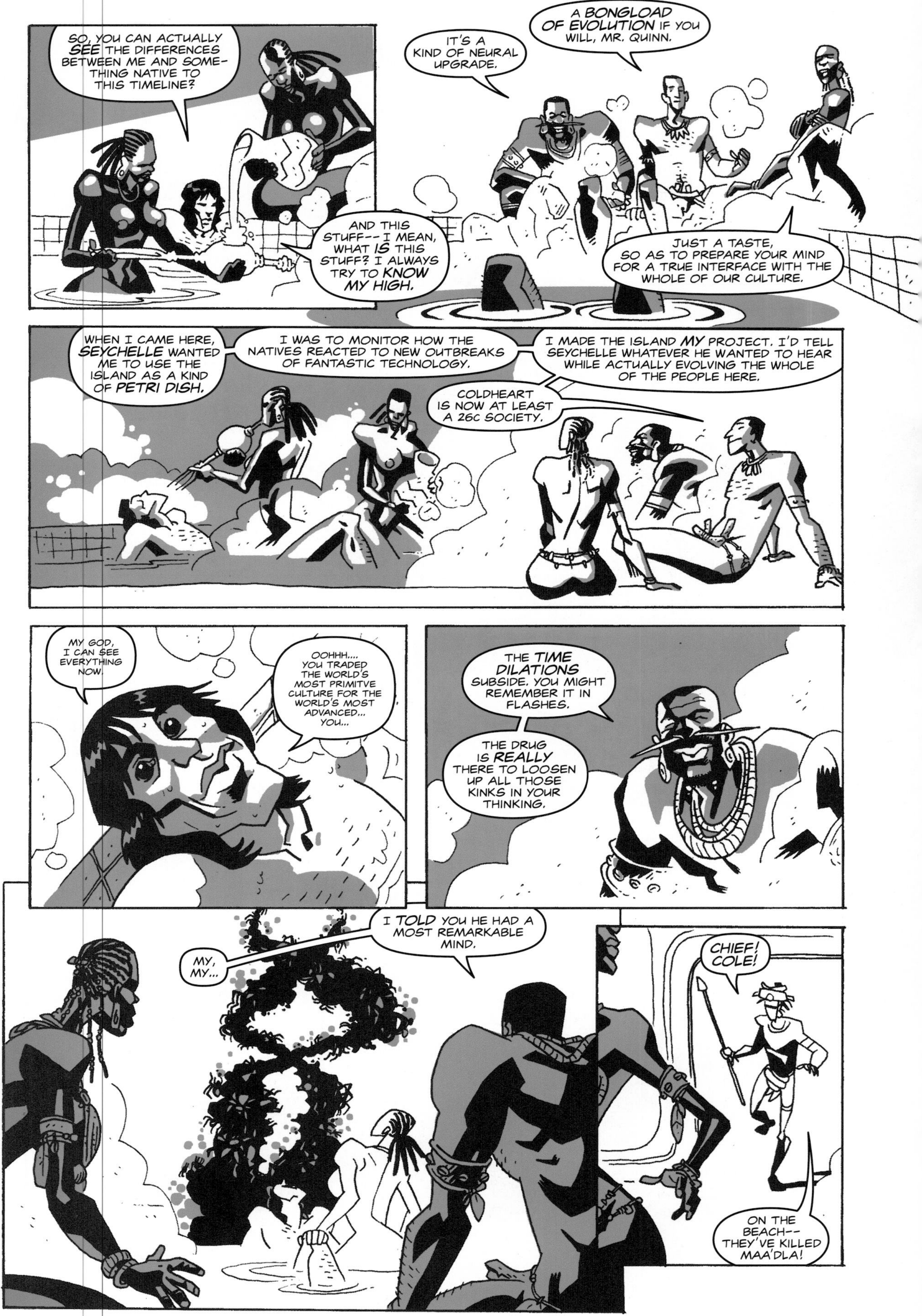
SO, YOU CAN ACTUALLY SEE THE DIFFERENCES BETWEEN ME AND SOMETHING NATIVE TO THIS TIMELINE?
AND THIS STUFF-- I MEAN, WHAT IS THIS STUFF? I ALWAYS TRY TO KNOW MY HIGH.
IT'S A KIND OF NEURAL UPGRADE.
A BONGLOAD OF EVOLUTION IF YOU WILL, MR. QUINN.
JUST A TASTE, SO AS TO PREPARE YOUR MIND FOR A TRUE INTERFACE WITH THE WHOLE OF OUR CULTURE.
WHEN I CAME HERE, SEYCHELLE WANTED ME TO USE THE ISLAND AS A KIND OF PETRI DISH.
I WAS TO MONITOR HOW THE NATIVES REACTED TO NEW OUTBREAKS OF FANTASTIC TECHNOLOGY.
I MADE THE ISLAND MY PROJECT. I'D TELL SEYCHELLE WHATEVER HE WANTED TO HEAR WHILE ACTUALLY EVOLVING THE WHOLE OF THE PEOPLE HERE.
COLDHEART IS NOW AT LEAST A 26C SOCIETY.
MY GOD, I CAN SEE EVERYTHING NOW.
OOHHH.... YOU TRADED THE WORLD'S MOST PRIMITVE CULTURE FOR THE WORLD'S MOST ADVANCED... YOU...
THE TIME DILATIONS SUBSIDE. YOU MIGHT REMEMBER IT IN FLASHES.
THE DRUG IS REALLY THERE TO LOOSEN UP ALL THOSE KINKS IN YOUR THINKING.
MY, MY...
I TOLD YOU HE HAD A MOST REMARKABLE MIND.
CHIEF! COLE!
ON THE BEACH-- THEY'VE KILLED MAA'DLA!

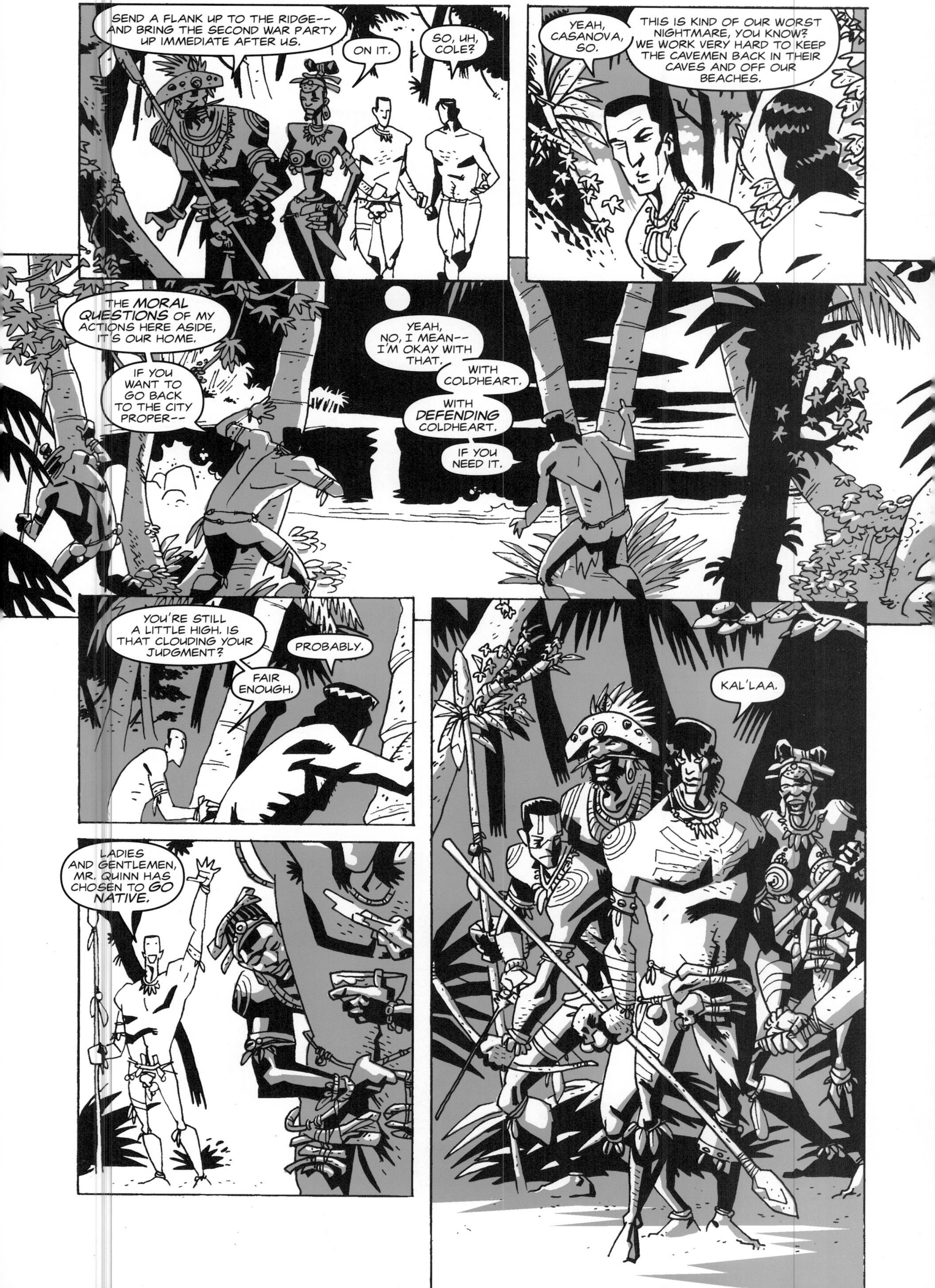
SEND A FLANK UP TO THE RIDGE-- AND BRING THE SECOND WAR PARTY UP IMMEDIATE AFTER US.
ON IT.
SO, UH, COLE?
YEAH, CASANOVA, SO.
THIS IS KIND OF OUR WORST NIGHTMARE, YOU KNOW? WE WORK VERY HARD TO KEEP THE CAVEMEN BACK IN THEIR CAVES AND OFF OUR BEACHES.
THE MORAL QUESTIONS OF MY ACTIONS HERE ASIDE, IT'S OUR HOME.
IF YOU WANT TO GO BACK TO THE CITY PROPER--
YEAH, NO, I MEAN-- I'M OKAY WITH THAT.
WITH COLDHEART.
WITH DEFENDING COLDHEART.
IF YOU NEED IT.
YOU'RE STILL A LITTLE HIGH. IS THAT CLOUDING YOUR JUDGMENT?
PROBABLY.
FAIR ENOUGH.
LADIES AND GENTLEMEN, MR. QUINN HAS CHOSEN TO GO NATIVE.
KAL'LAA.

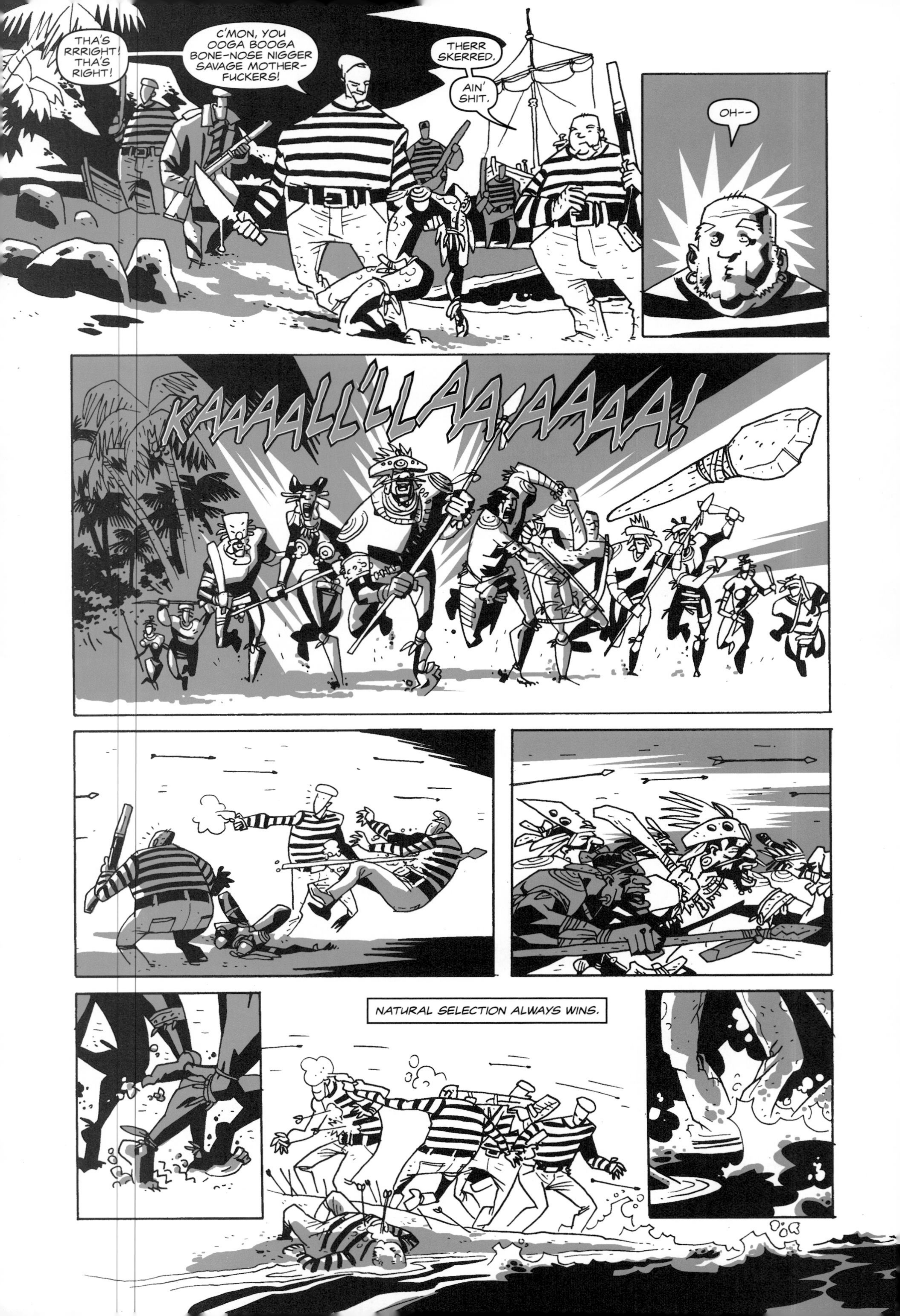
THA'S RRRIGHT! THA'S RIGHT!
C'MON, YOU OOGA BOOGA BONE-NOSE NIGGER SAVAGE MOTHER-FUCKERS!
THERR SKERRED.
AIN' SHIT.
OH--
KAAAALL'LLAAAAAA!
NATURAL SELECTION ALWAYS WINS.

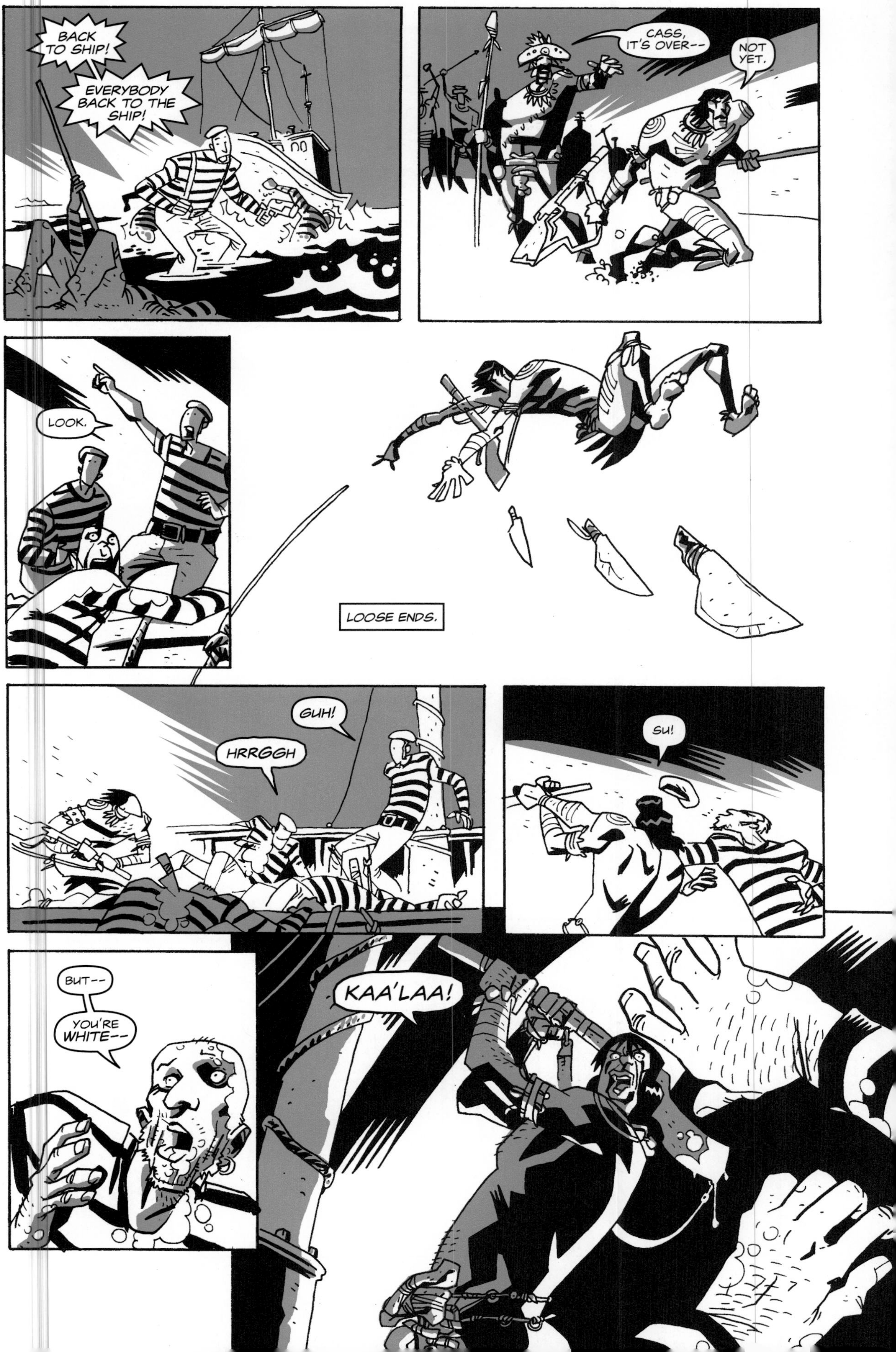
BACK TO SHIP!
EVERYBODY BACK TO THE SHIP!
CASS, IT'S OVER--
NOT YET.
LOOK.
LOOSE ENDS.
GUH!
HRRGGH
SU!
BUT--
YOU'RE WHITE--
KAA'LAA!

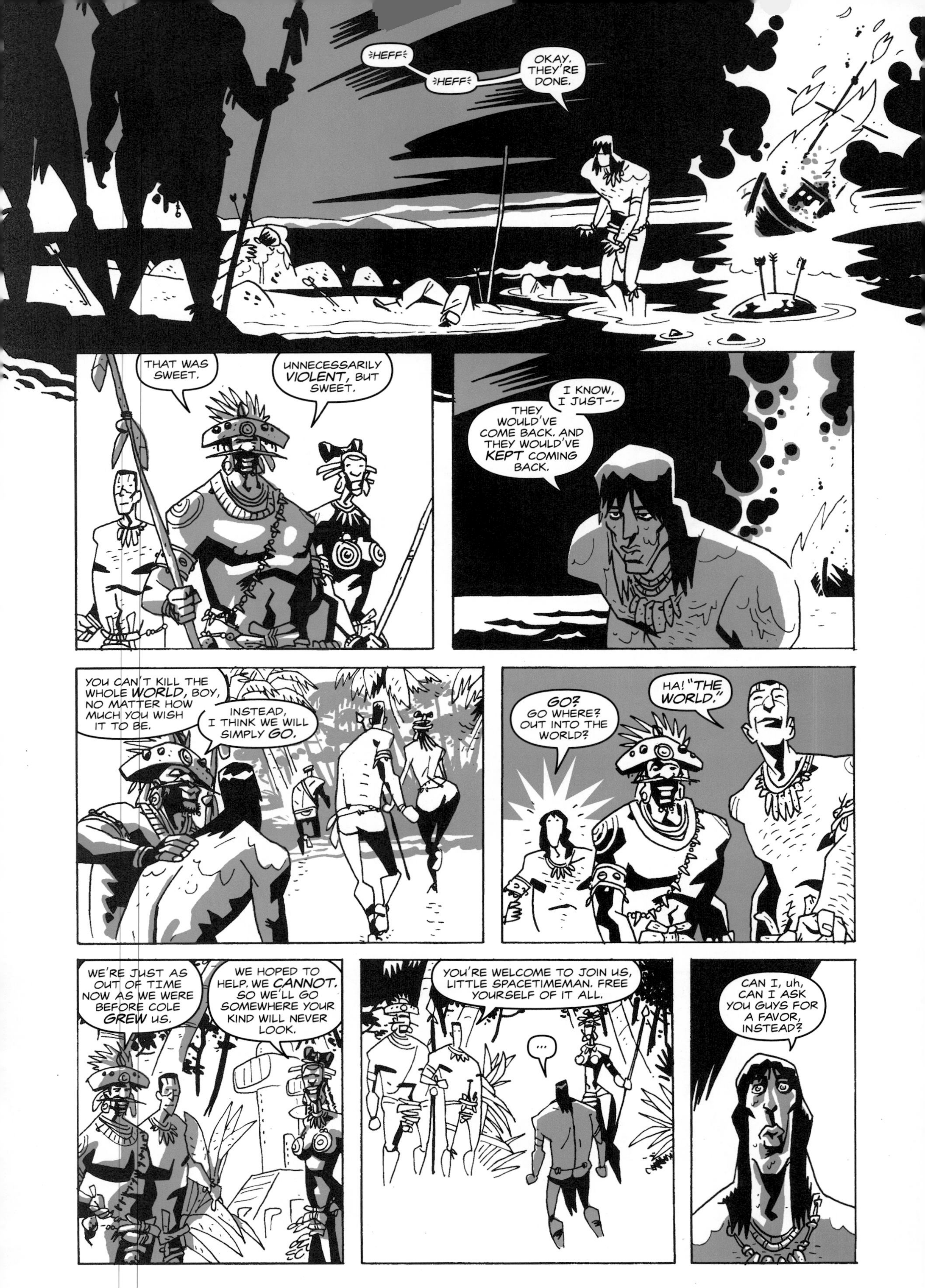
HEFF
HEFF
OKAY. THEY'RE DONE.
THAT WAS SWEET.
UNNECESSARILY VIOLENT, BUT SWEET.
I KNOW, I JUST--
THEY WOULD'VE COME BACK. AND THEY WOULD'VE KEPT COMING BACK.
YOU CAN'T KILL THE WHOLE WORLD, BOY, NO MATTER HOW MUCH YOU WISH IT TO BE.
INSTEAD, I THINK WE WILL SIMPLY GO.
GO? GO WHERE? OUT INTO THE WORLD?
HA! "THE WORLD."
WE'RE JUST AS OUT OF TIME NOW AS WE WERE BEFORE COLE GREW US.
WE HOPED TO HELP. WE CANNOT. SO WE'LL GO SOMEWHERE YOUR KIND WILL NEVER LOOK.
YOU'RE WELCOME TO JOIN US, LITTLE SPACETIMEMAN. FREE YOURSELF OF IT ALL.
...
CAN I, uh, CAN I ASK YOU GUYS FOR A FAVOR, INSTEAD?

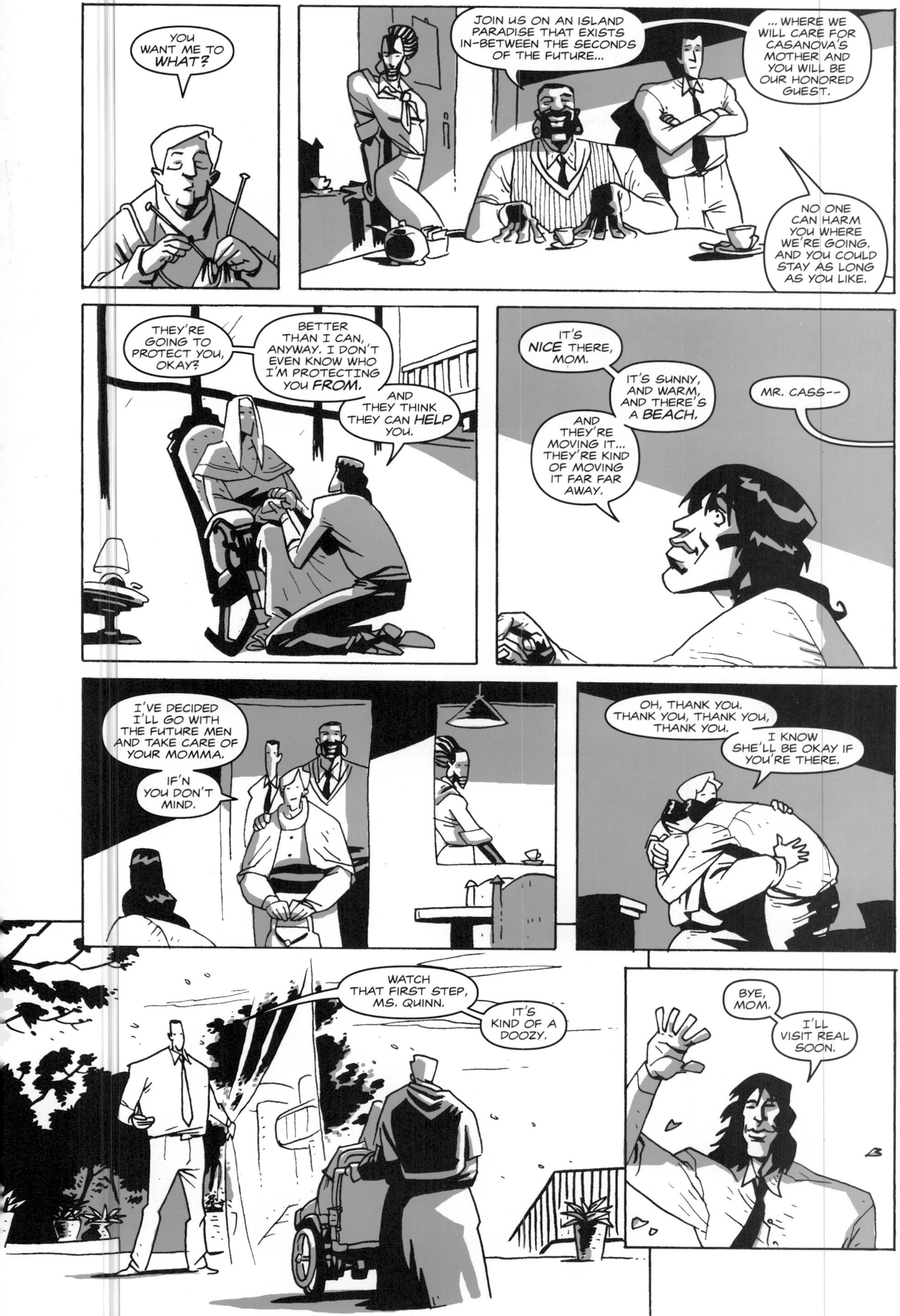
YOU WANT ME TO WHAT?
JOIN US ON AN ISLAND PARADISE THAT EXISTS IN-BETWEEN THE SECONDS OF THE FUTURE...
...WHERE WE WILL CARE FOR CASANOVA'S MOTHER AND YOU WILL BE OUR HONORED GUEST.
NO ONE CAN HARM YOU WHERE WE'RE GOING. AND YOU COULD STAY AS LONG AS YOU LIKE.
THEY'RE GOING TO PROTECT YOU, OKAY?
BETTER THAN I CAN, ANYWAY. I DON'T EVEN KNOW WHO I'M PROTECTING YOU FROM.
AND THEY THINK THEY CAN HELP YOU.
IT'S NICE THERE, MOM.
IT'S SUNNY, AND WARM, AND THERE'S A BEACH.
AND THEY'RE MOVING IT... THEY'RE KIND OF MOVING IT FAR FAR AWAY.
MR. CASS--
I'VE DECIDED I'LL GO WITH THE FUTURE MEN AND TAKE CARE OF YOUR MOMMA.
IF'N YOU DON'T MIND.
OH, THANK YOU. THANK YOU, THANK YOU, THANK YOU.
I KNOW SHE'LL BE OKAY IF YOU'RE THERE.
WATCH THAT FIRST STEP, MS. QUINN.
IT'S KIND OF A DOOZY.
BYE, MOM.
I'LL VISIT REAL SOON.

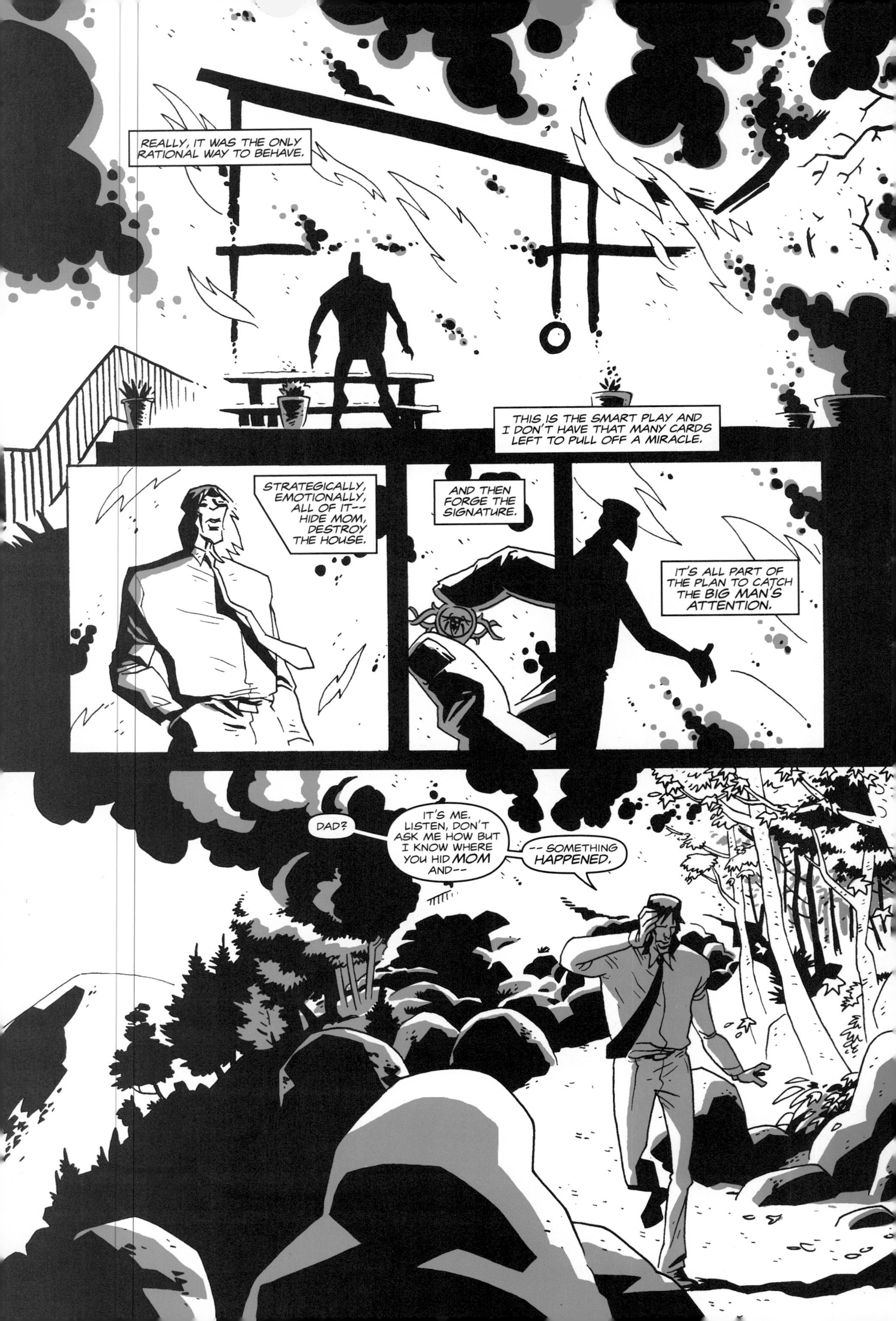
REALLY, IT WAS THE ONLY RATIONAL WAY TO BEHAVE.
THIS IS THE SMART PLAY AND I DON'T HAVE THAT MANY CARDS LEFT TO PULL OFF A MIRACLE.
STRATEGICALLY, EMOTIONALLY, ALL OF IT-- HIDE MOM, DESTROY THE HOUSE.
AND THEN FORGE THE SIGNATURE.
IT'S ALL PART OF THE PLAN TO CATCH THE BIG MAN'S ATTENTION.
DAD?
IT'S ME. LISTEN, DON'T ASK ME HOW BUT I KNOW WHERE YOU HID MOM AND--
-- SOMETHING HAPPENED.

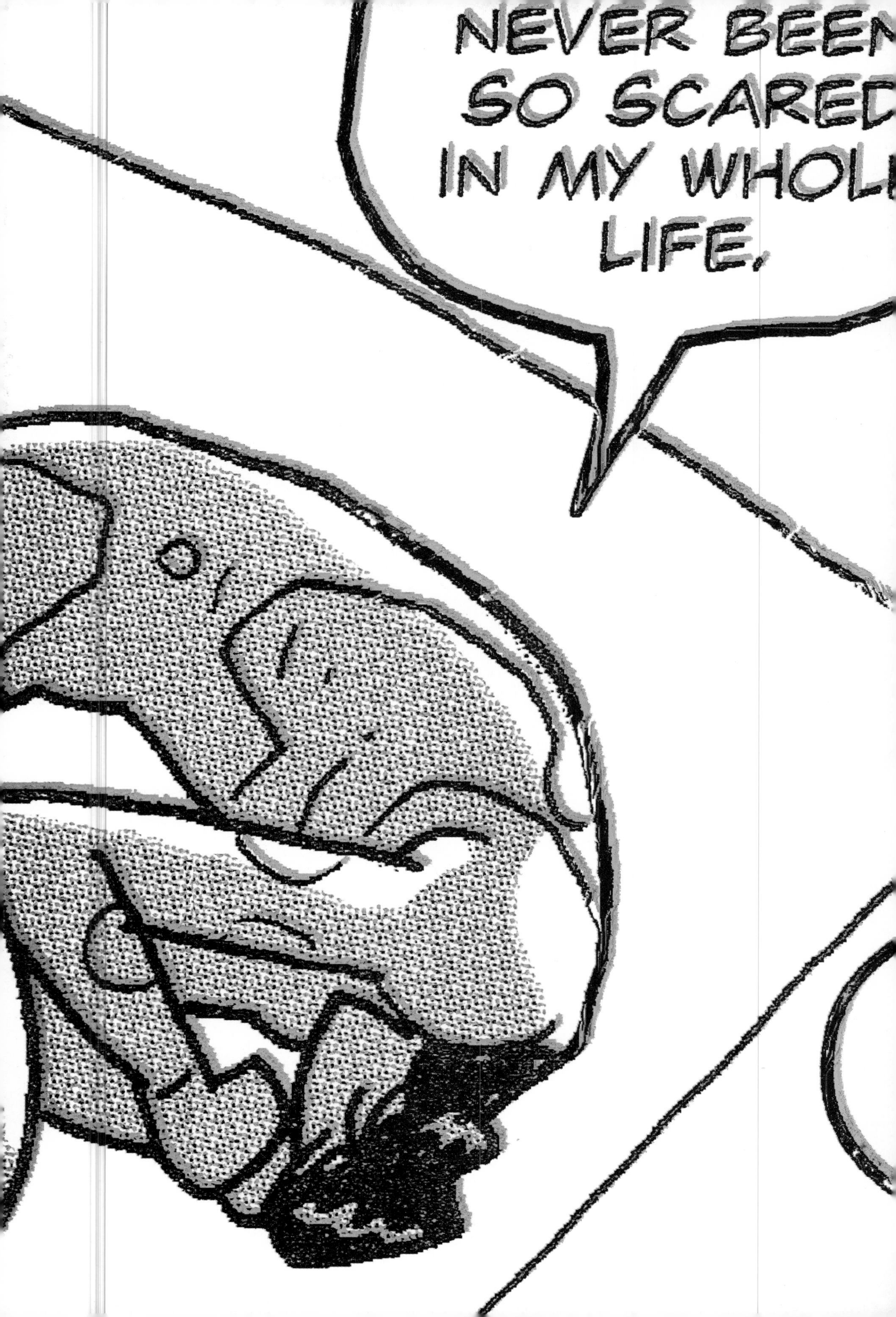
NEVER BEEN SO SCARED IN MY WHOLE LIFE.

Chapter Six
Women and Men (Part One)

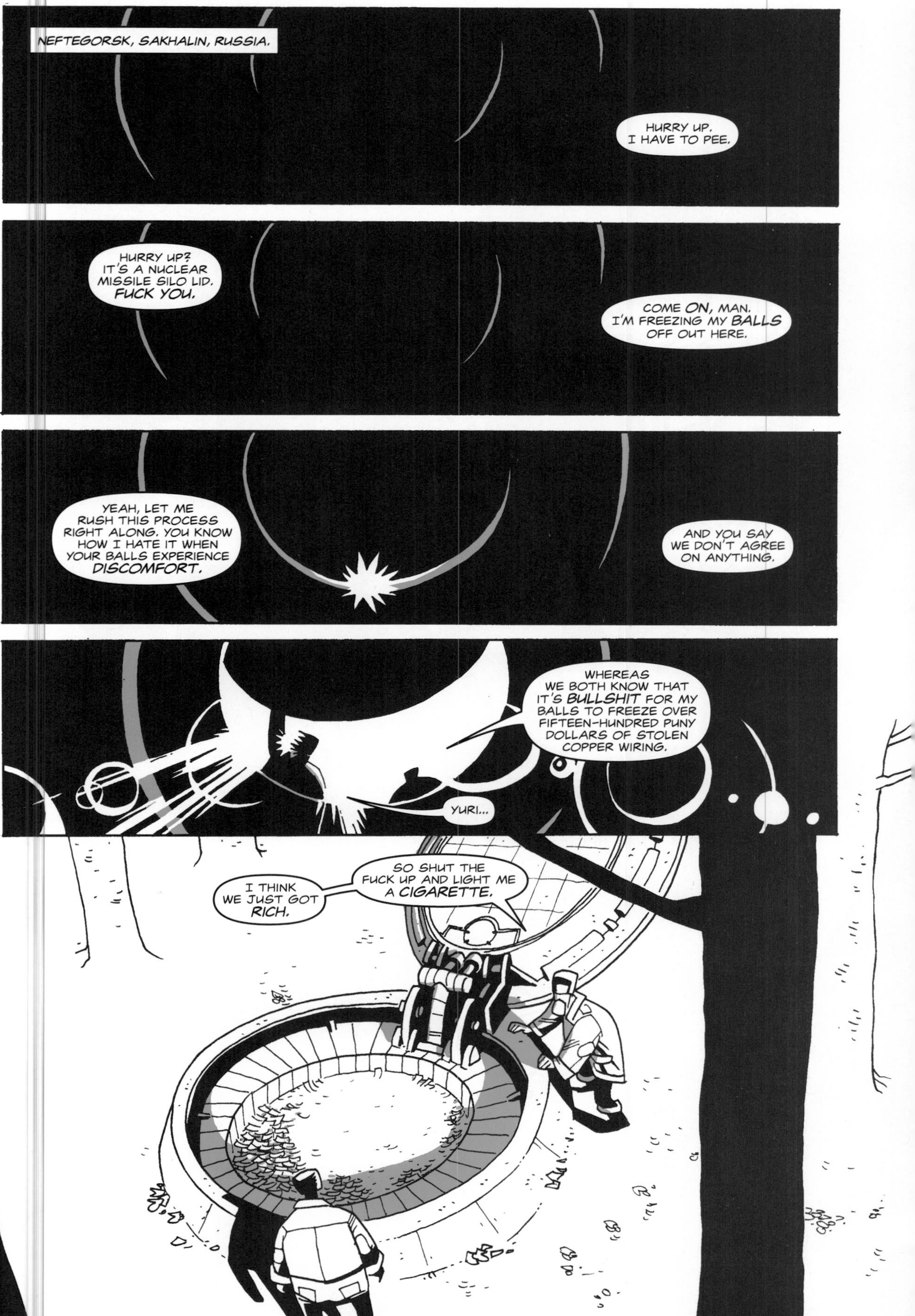
NEFTEGORSK, SAKHALIN, RUSSIA.
HURRY UP. I HAVE TO PEE.
HURRY UP? IT'S A NUCLEAR MISSILE SILO LID. FUCK YOU.
COME ON, MAN. I'M FREEZING MY BALLS OFF OUT HERE.
YEAH, LET ME RUSH THIS PROCESS RIGHT ALONG. YOU KNOW HOW I HATE IT WHEN YOUR BALLS EXPERIENCE DISCOMFORT.
AND YOU SAY WE DON'T AGREE ON ANYTHING.
WHEREAS WE BOTH KNOW THAT IT'S BULLSHIT FOR MY BALLS TO FREEZE OVER FIFTEEN-HUNDRED PUNY DOLLARS OF STOLEN COPPER WIRING.
YURI...
SO SHUT THE FUCK UP AND LIGHT ME A CIGARETTE.
I THINK WE JUST GOT RICH.

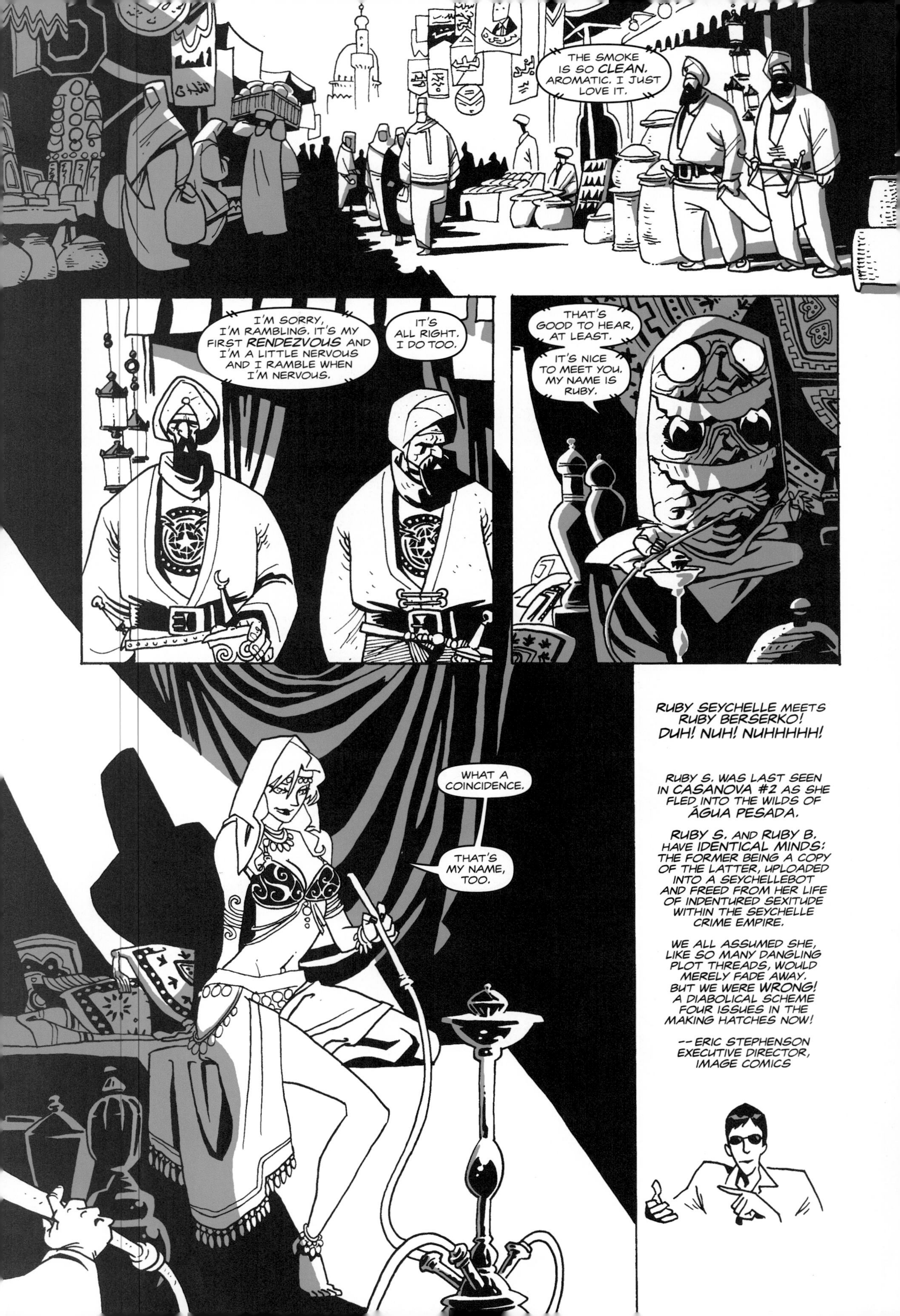
THE SMOKE IS SO CLEAN, AROMATIC. I JUST LOVE IT.
I'M SORRY, I'M RAMBLING. IT'S MY FIRST RENDEZVOUS AND I'M A LITTLE NERVOUS AND I RAMBLE WHEN I'M NERVOUS.
IT'S ALL RIGHT. I DO TOO.
THAT'S GOOD TO HEAR, AT LEAST.
IT'S NICE TO MEET YOU. MY NAME IS RUBY.
WHAT A COINCIDENCE.
THAT'S MY NAME, TOO.
RUBY SEYCHELLE MEETS RUBY BERSERKO! DUH! NUH! NUHHHHH!
RUBY S. WAS LAST SEEN IN CASANOVA #2 AS SHE FLED INTO THE WILDS OF ÁGUA PESADA.
RUBY S. AND RUBY B. HAVE IDENTICAL MINDS: THE FORMER BEING A COPY OF THE LATTER, UPLOADED INTO A SEYCHELLEBOT AND FREED FROM HER LIFE OF INDENTURED SEXITUDE WITHIN THE SEYCHELLE CRIME EMPIRE.
WE ALL ASSUMED SHE, LIKE SO MANY DANGLING PLOT THREADS, WOULD MERELY FADE AWAY. BUT WE WERE WRONG! A DIABOLICAL SCHEME FOUR ISSUES IN THE MAKING HATCHES NOW!
-- ERIC STEPHENSON EXECUTIVE DIRECTOR, IMAGE COMICS

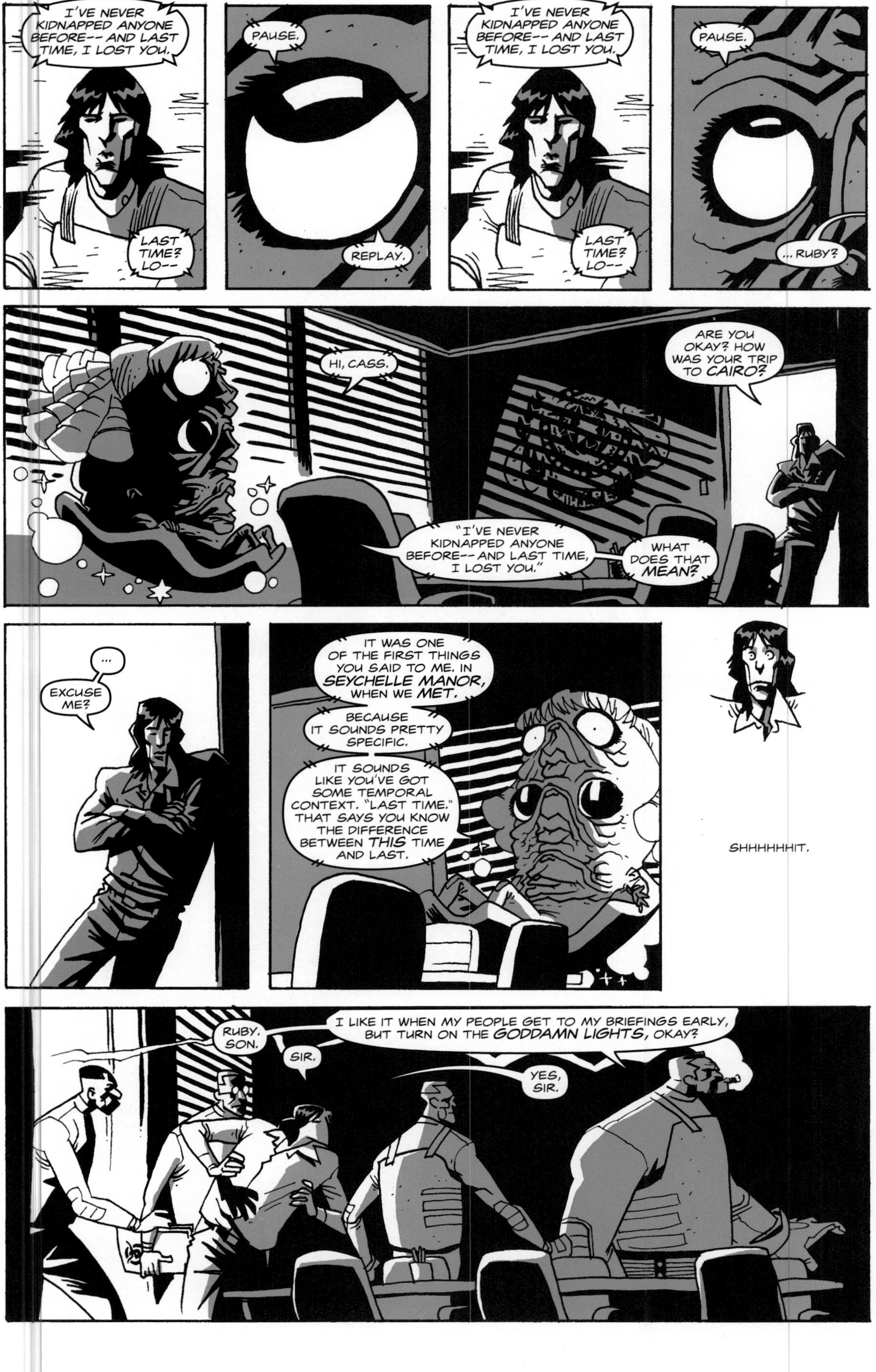
I'VE NEVER KIDNAPPED ANYONE BEFORE-- AND LAST TIME, I LOST YOU.
LAST TIME? LO--
PAUSE.
REPLAY.
I'VE NEVER KIDNAPPED ANYONE BEFORE-- AND LAST TIME, I LOST YOU.
LAST TIME? LO--
PAUSE.
...RUBY?
HI, CASS.
ARE YOU OKAY? HOW WAS YOUR TRIP TO CAIRO?
"I'VE NEVER KIDNAPPED ANYONE BEFORE-- AND LAST TIME, I LOST YOU."
WHAT DOES THAT MEAN?
...
EXCUSE ME?
IT WAS ONE OF THE FIRST THINGS YOU SAID TO ME, IN SEYCHELLE MANOR, WHEN WE MET.
BECAUSE IT SOUNDS PRETTY SPECIFIC.
IT SOUNDS LIKE YOU'VE GOT SOME TEMPORAL CONTEXT. "LAST TIME." THAT SAYS YOU KNOW THE DIFFERENCE BETWEEN THIS TIME AND LAST.
SHHHHHHIT.
RUBY. SON.
SIR.
I LIKE IT WHEN MY PEOPLE GET TO MY BRIEFINGS EARLY, BUT TURN ON THE GODDAMN LIGHTS, OKAY?
YES, SIR.

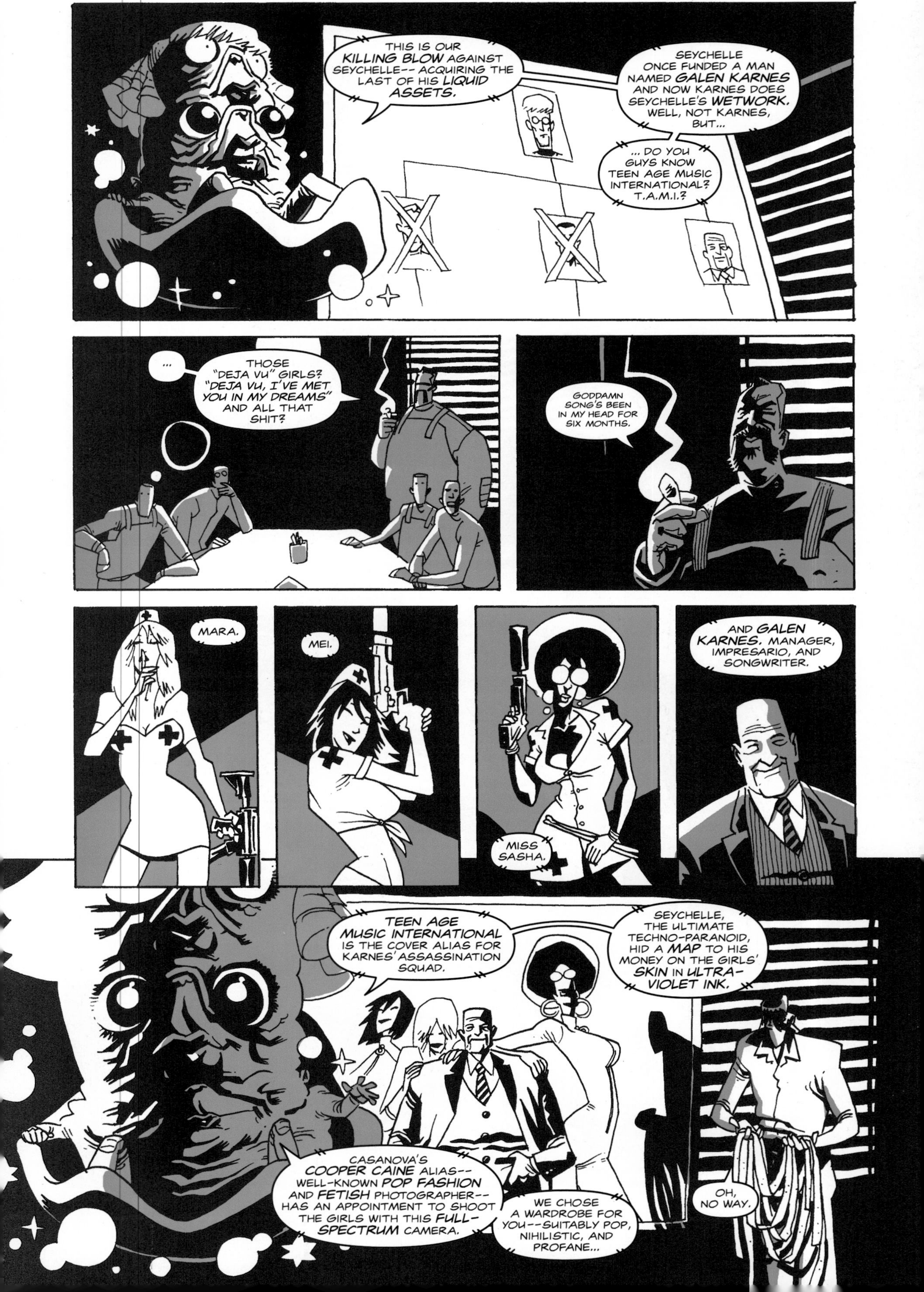
THIS IS OUR KILLING BLOW AGAINST SEYCHELLE-- ACQUIRING THE LAST OF HIS LIQUID ASSETS.
SEYCHELLE ONCE FUNDED A MAN NAMED GALEN KARNES AND NOW KARNES DOES SEYCHELLE'S WETWORK. WELL, NOT KARNES, BUT...
... DO YOU GUYS KNOW TEEN AGE MUSIC INTERNATIONAL? T.A.M.I.?
...
THOSE "DEJA VU" GIRLS? "DEJA VU, I'VE MET YOU IN MY DREAMS" AND ALL THAT SHIT?
GODDAMN SONG'S BEEN IN MY HEAD FOR SIX MONTHS.
MARA.
MEI.
MISS SASHA.
AND GALEN KARNES. MANAGER, IMPRESARIO, AND SONGWRITER.
TEEN AGE MUSIC INTERNATIONAL IS THE COVER ALIAS FOR KARNES' ASSASSINATION SQUAD.
SEYCHELLE, THE ULTIMATE TECHNO-PARANOID, HID A MAP TO HIS MONEY ON THE GIRLS' SKIN IN ULTRA-VIOLET INK.
CASANOVA'S COOPER CAINE ALIAS-- WELL-KNOWN POP FASHION AND FETISH PHOTOGRAPHER-- HAS AN APPOINTMENT TO SHOOT THE GIRLS WITH THIS FULL-SPECTRUM CAMERA.
WE CHOSE A WARDROBE FOR YOU--SUITABLY POP, NIHILISTIC, AND PROFANE...
OH, NO WAY.

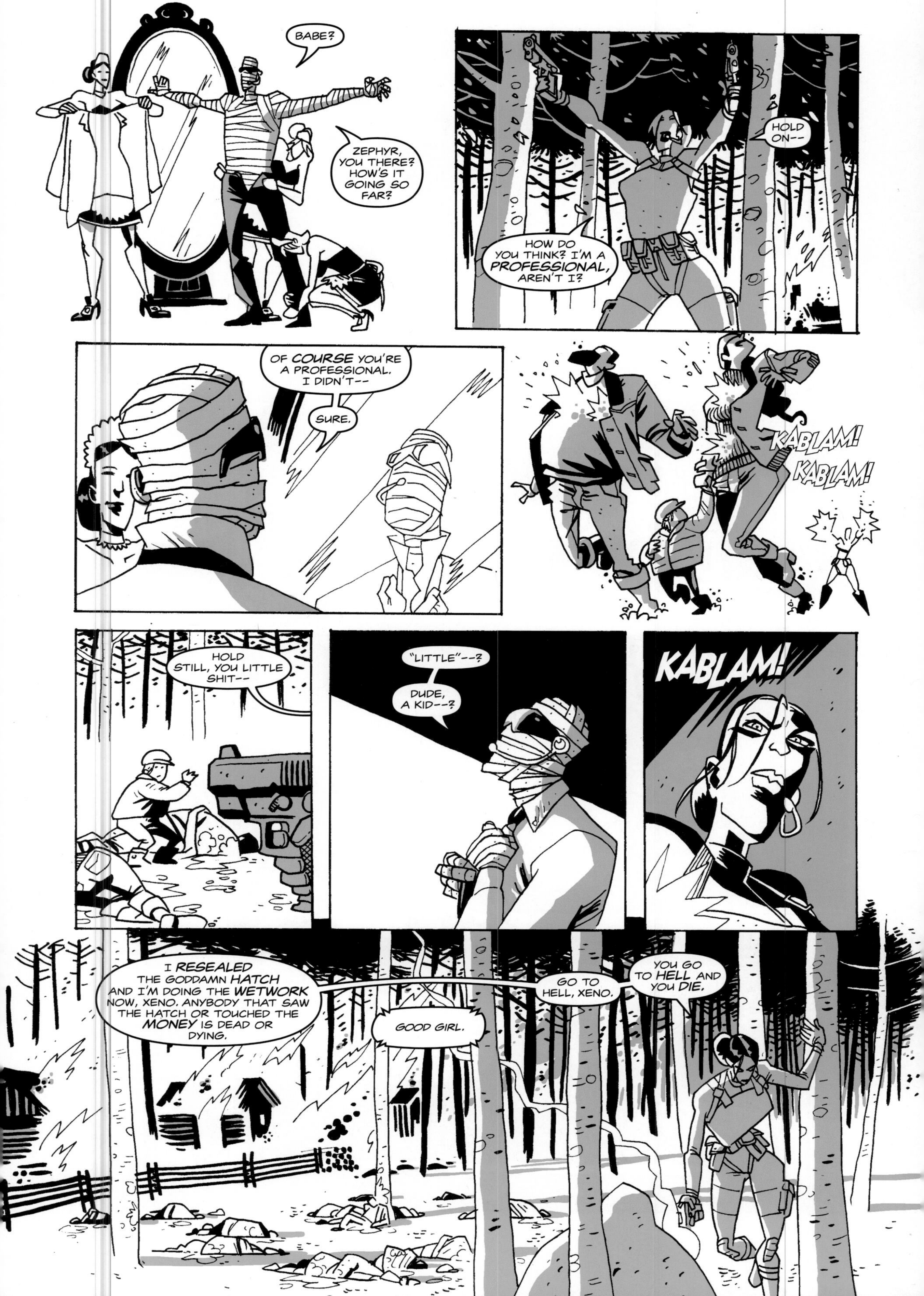
BABE?
ZEPHYR, YOU THERE? HOW'S IT GOING SO FAR?
HOLD ON--
HOW DO YOU THINK? I'M A PROFESSIONAL, AREN'T I?
OF COURSE YOU'RE A PROFESSIONAL. I DIDN'T--
SURE.
KABLAM!
KABLAM!
HOLD STILL, YOU LITTLE SHIT--
"LITTLE"--?
DUDE, A KID--?
KABLAM!
I RESEALED THE GODDAMN HATCH AND I'M DOING THE WETWORK NOW, XENO. ANYBODY THAT SAW THE HATCH OR TOUCHED THE MONEY IS DEAD OR DYING.
GOOD GIRL.
GO TO HELL, XENO.
YOU GO TO HELL AND YOU DIE.

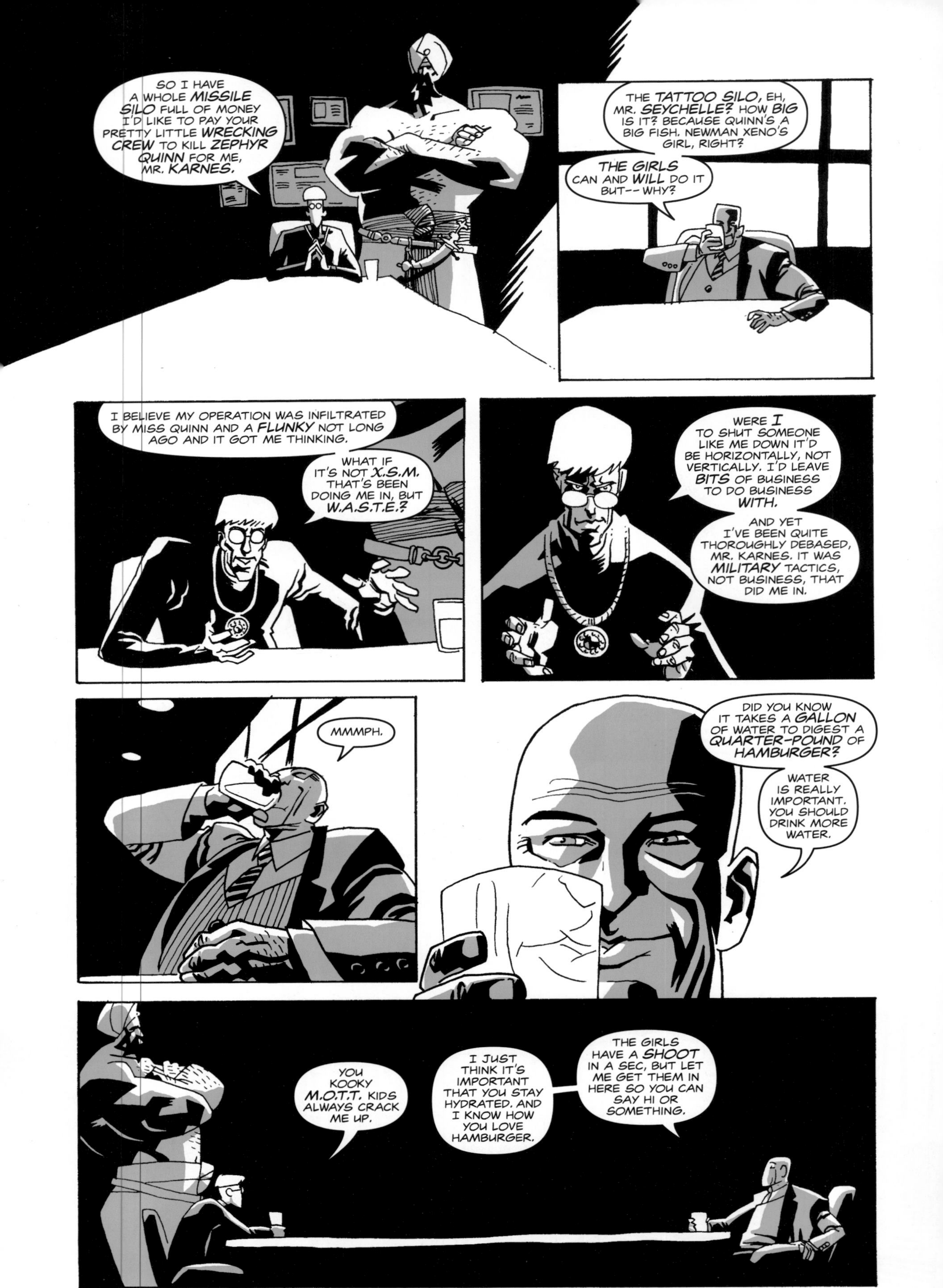

SO I HAVE A WHOLE MISSILE SILO FULL OF MONEY I'D LIKE TO PAY YOUR PRETTY LITTLE WRECKING CREW TO KILL ZEPHYR QUINN FOR ME, MR. KARNES.
THE TATTOO SILO, EH, MR. SEYCHELLE? HOW BIG IS IT? BECAUSE QUINN'S A BIG FISH. NEWMAN XENO'S GIRL, RIGHT?
THE GIRLS CAN AND WILL DO IT BUT-- WHY?
I BELIEVE MY OPERATION WAS INFILTRATED BY MISS QUINN AND A FLUNKY NOT LONG AGO AND IT GOT ME THINKING.
WHAT IF IT'S NOT X.S.M. THAT'S BEEN DOING ME IN, BUT W.A.S.T.E.?
WERE I TO SHUT SOMEONE LIKE ME DOWN IT'D BE HORIZONTALLY, NOT VERTICALLY. I'D LEAVE BITS OF BUSINESS TO DO BUSINESS WITH.
AND YET I'VE BEEN QUITE THOROUGHLY DEBASED, MR. KARNES. IT WAS MILITARY TACTICS, NOT BUSINESS, THAT DID ME IN.
MMMPH.
DID YOU KNOW IT TAKES A GALLON OF WATER TO DIGEST A QUARTER-POUND OF HAMBURGER?
WATER IS REALLY IMPORTANT. YOU SHOULD DRINK MORE WATER.
YOU KOOKY M.O.T.T. KIDS ALWAYS CRACK ME UP.
I JUST THINK IT'S IMPORTANT THAT YOU STAY HYDRATED. AND I KNOW HOW YOU LOVE HAMBURGER.
THE GIRLS HAVE A SHOOT IN A SEC, BUT LET ME GET THEM IN HERE SO YOU CAN SAY HI OR SOMETHING.

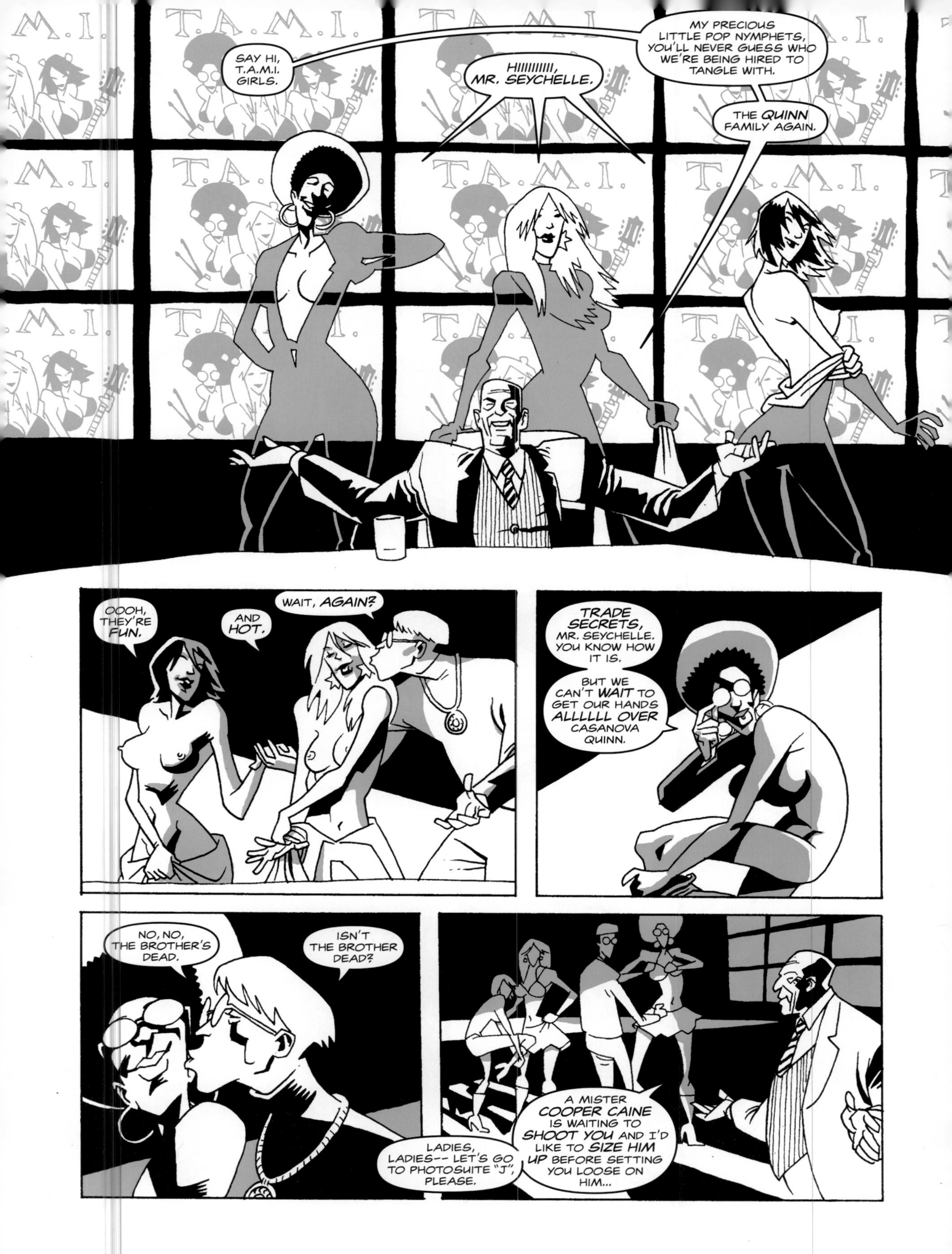
T.A.M.I.
SAY HI, T.A.M.I. GIRLS.
MY PRECIOUS LITTLE POP NYMPHETS, YOU'LL NEVER GUESS WHO WE'RE BEING HIRED TO TANGLE WITH.
HIIIIIIIII, MR. SEYCHELLE.
THE QUINN FAMILY AGAIN.
OOOH, THEY'RE FUN.
AND HOT.
WAIT, AGAIN?
TRADE SECRETS, MR. SEYCHELLE. YOU KNOW HOW IT IS.
BUT WE CAN'T WAIT TO GET OUR HANDS ALLLLLL OVER CASANOVA QUINN.
NO, NO, THE BROTHER'S DEAD.
ISN'T THE BROTHER DEAD?
LADIES, LADIES-- LET'S GO TO PHOTOSUITE "J", PLEASE.
A MISTER COOPER CAINE IS WAITING TO SHOOT YOU AND I'D LIKE TO SIZE HIM UP BEFORE SETTING YOU LOOSE ON HIM...

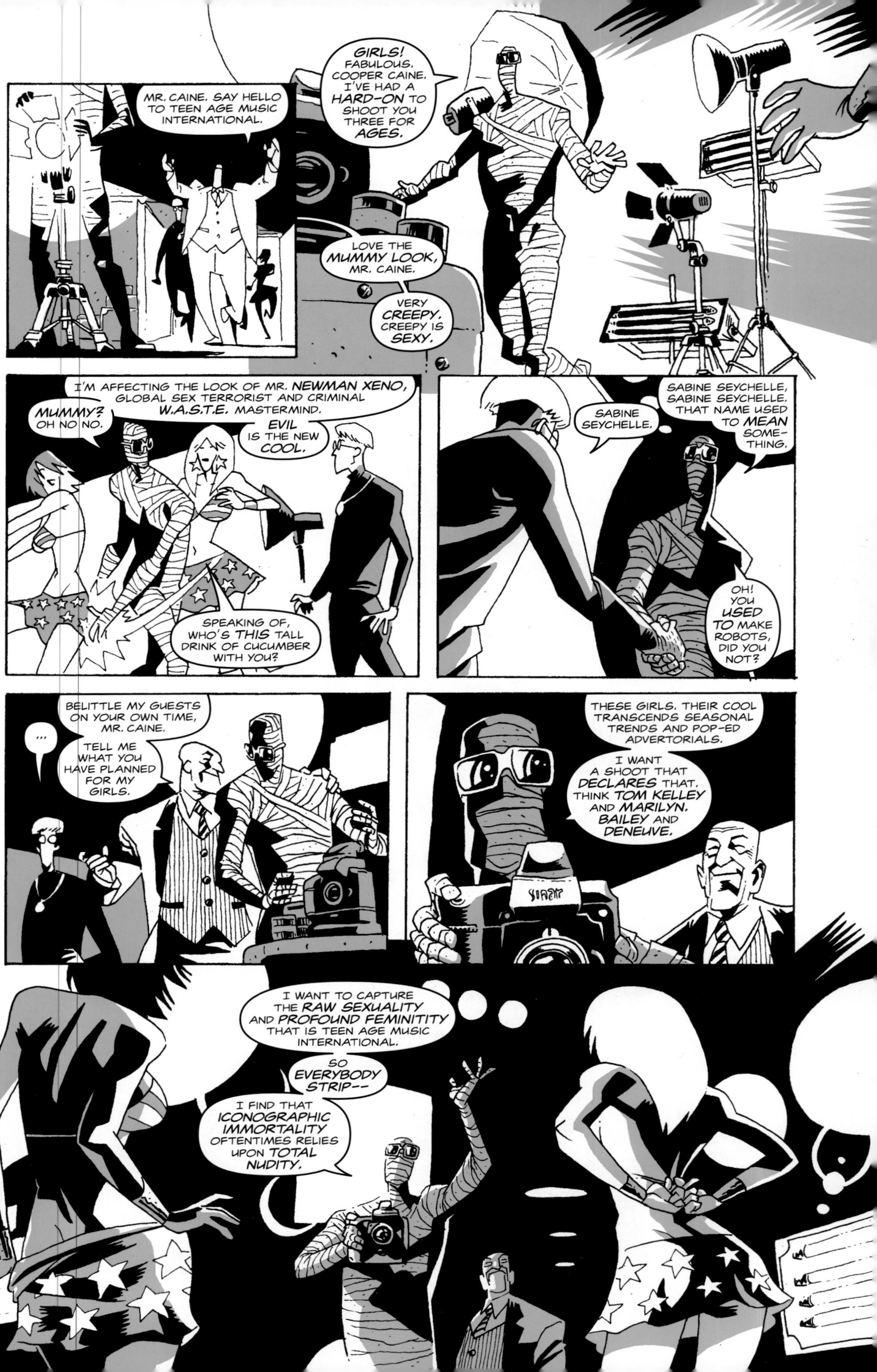

MR. CAINE. SAY HELLO TO TEEN AGE MUSIC INTERNATIONAL.
GIRLS! FABULOUS. COOPER CAINE. I'VE HAD A HARD-ON TO SHOOT YOU THREE FOR AGES.
LOVE THE MUMMY LOOK, MR. CAINE.
VERY CREEPY. CREEPY IS SEXY.
I'M AFFECTING THE LOOK OF MR. NEWMAN XENO, GLOBAL SEX TERRORIST AND CRIMINAL W.A.S.T.E. MASTERMIND.
MUMMY? OH NO NO.
EVIL IS THE NEW COOL.
SPEAKING OF, WHO'S THIS TALL DRINK OF CUCUMBER WITH YOU?
SABINE SEYCHELLE.
SABINE SEYCHELLE, SABINE SEYCHELLE. THAT NAME USED TO MEAN SOMETHING.
OH! YOU USED TO MAKE ROBOTS, DID YOU NOT?
...
BELITTLE MY GUESTS ON YOUR OWN TIME, MR. CAINE.
TELL ME WHAT YOU HAVE PLANNED FOR MY GIRLS.
THESE GIRLS. THEIR COOL TRANSCENDS SEASONAL TRENDS AND POP-ED ADVERTORIALS.
I WANT A SHOOT THAT DECLARES THAT. THINK TOM KELLEY AND MARILYN. BAILEY AND DENEUVE.
I WANT TO CAPTURE THE RAW SEXUALITY AND PROFOUND FEMINITITY THAT IS TEEN AGE MUSIC INTERNATIONAL.
SO EVERYBODY STRIP--
I FIND THAT ICONOGRAPHIC IMMORTALITY OFTENTIMES RELIES UPON TOTAL NUDITY.

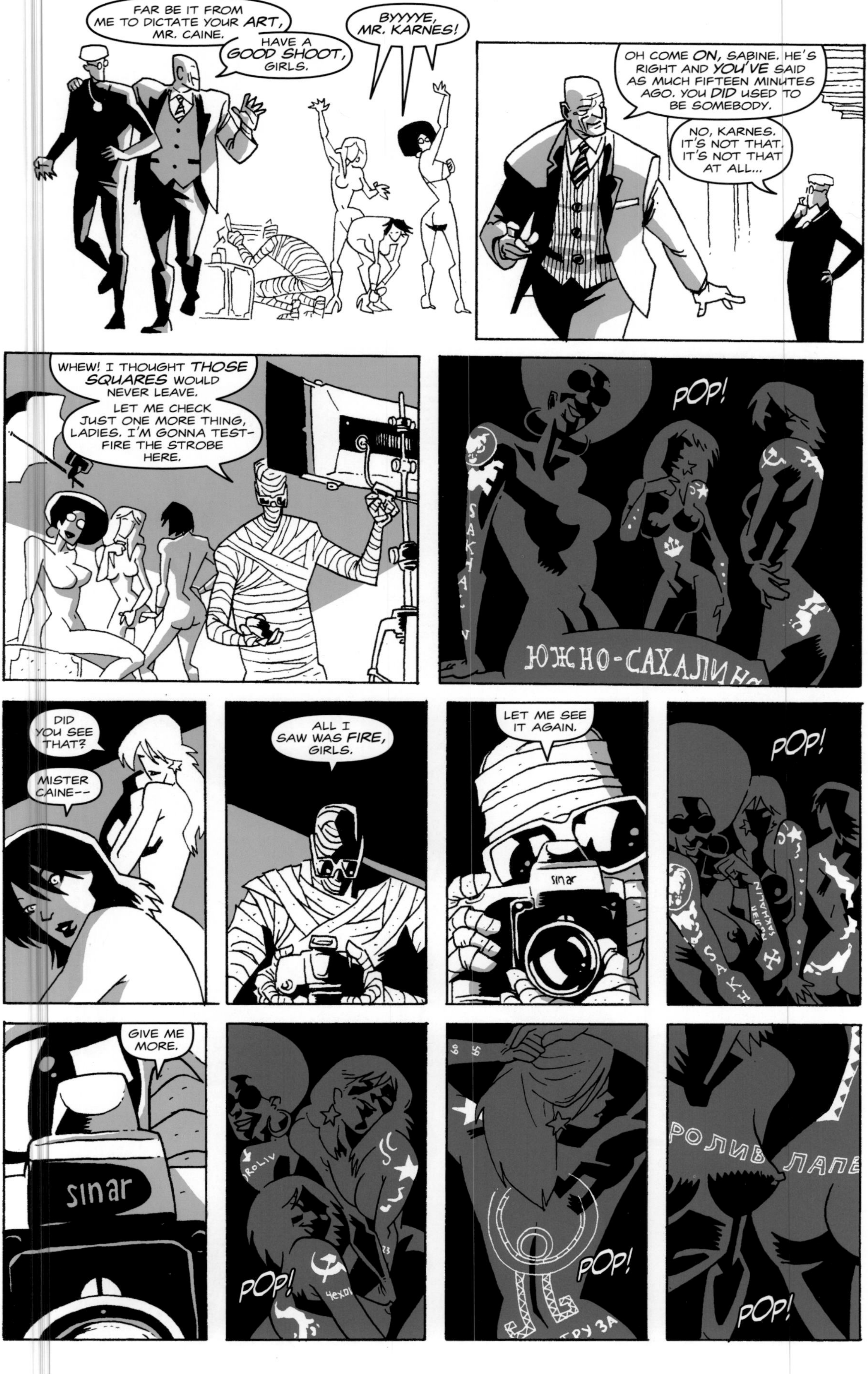
FAR BE IT FROM ME TO DICTATE YOUR ART, MR. CAINE.
HAVE A GOOD SHOOT, GIRLS.
BYYYYE, MR. KARNES!
OH COME ON, SABINE. HE'S RIGHT AND YOU'VE SAID AS MUCH FIFTEEN MINUTES AGO. YOU DID USED TO BE SOMEBODY.
NO, KARNES. IT'S NOT THAT. IT'S NOT THAT AT ALL...
WHEW! I THOUGHT THOSE SQUARES WOULD NEVER LEAVE.
LET ME CHECK JUST ONE MORE THING, LADIES. I'M GONNA TEST-FIRE THE STROBE HERE.
POP!
ЮЖНО-САХАЛИН
DID YOU SEE THAT?
MISTER CAINE--
ALL I SAW WAS FIRE, GIRLS.
LET ME SEE IT AGAIN.
sinar
POP!
GIVE ME MORE.
sinar
POP!
POP!
РОЛИВ
ЛАПЕ
POP!

THAT'S THE ONE, GIRLS.

THE ONE THEY'LL STARE AT FOR HOURS.

SO MUCH WORK. NO FUN.

NO FUN? I LOVE MY JOB.

OH YEAH? IS IT HARD?

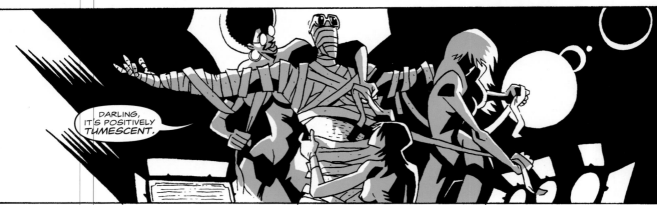

DARLING, IT'S POSITIVELY TUMESCENT.

LOOK, I'M SORRY TO INTERRUPT AND I DON'T MEAN TO OBSESS BUT-- THAT FELLOW GAVE ME THE ODDEST SENSE OF DEJA VU.

APPROPRIATE, PERHAPS, BUT UNSETTLING ALL THE SAME. THE COINCIDENCE OF A GUY LOOKING LIKE NEWMAN XENO AND THE WHOLE THING WITH--

--OH, SON OF A BITCH, IT WAS TWO CHAPTERS BACK:

YOU BUILT FABULA BERSERKO TOO, DID YOU NOT?

"DID YOU NOT." THE BROTHER ISN'T DEAD.

THAT MAN IS CASANOVA QUINN!

OH, MY GOD.

CASANOVA QUINN.

HOW'S YOUR MOM?

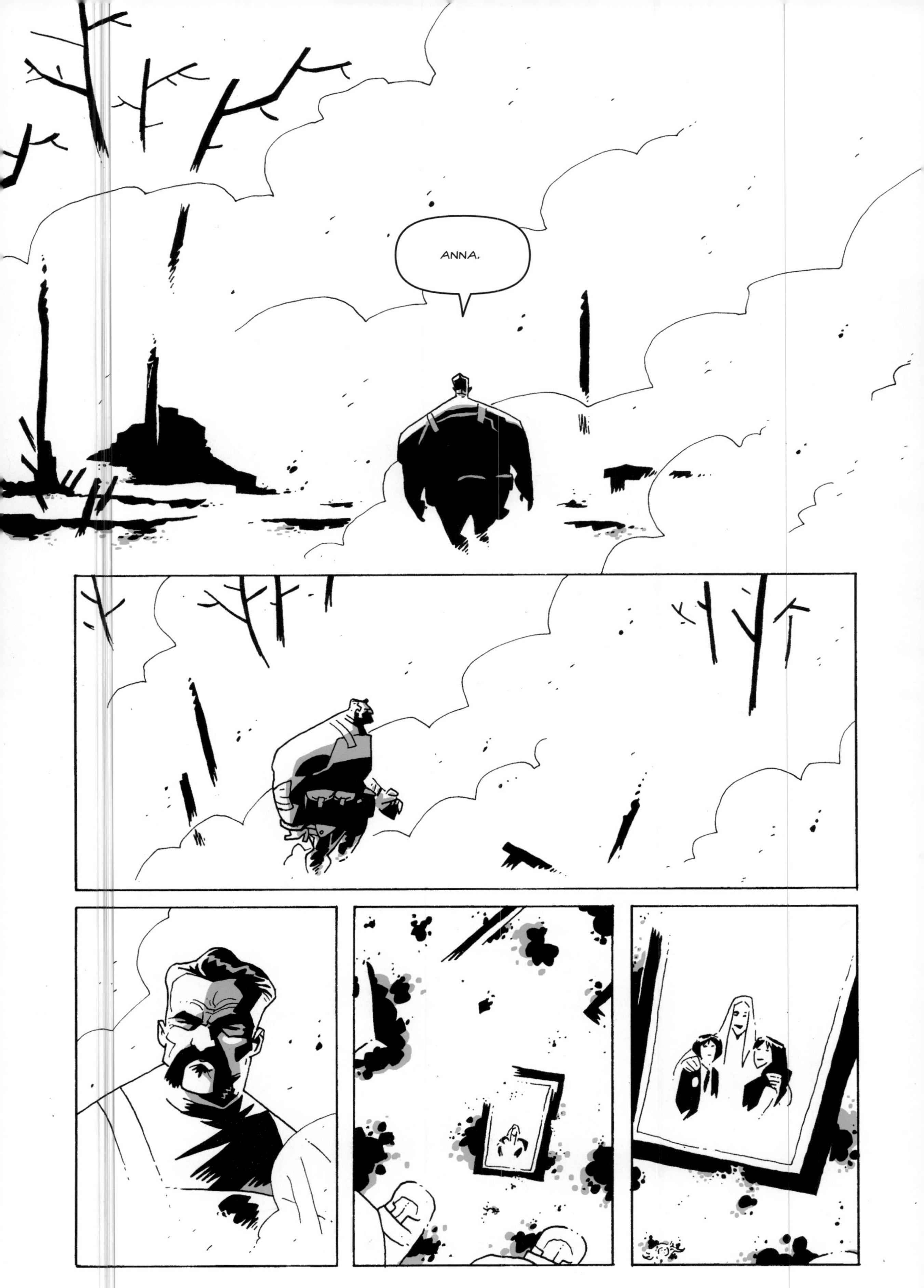
ANNA.

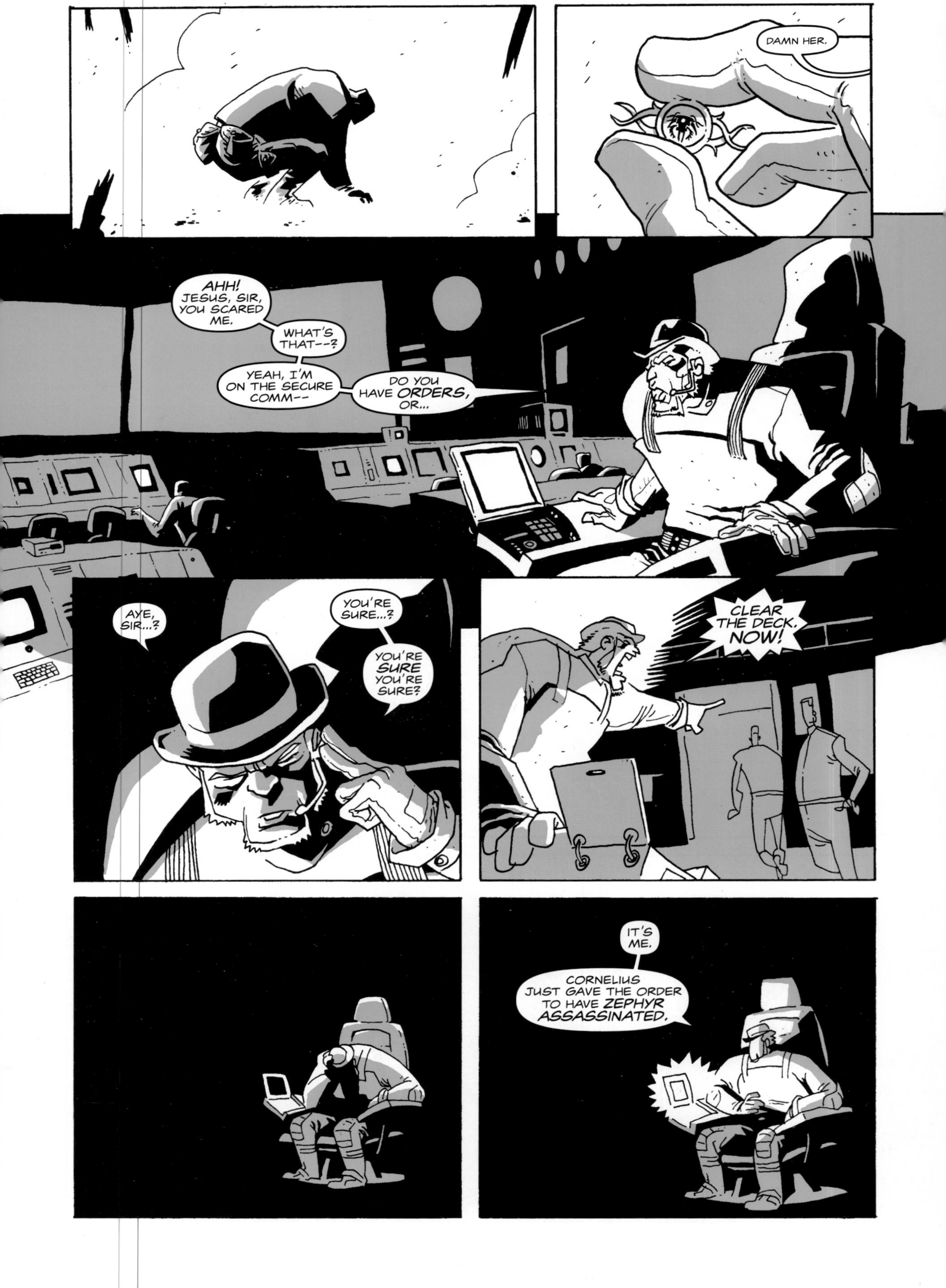
DAMN HER.
AHH! JESUS, SIR, YOU SCARED ME.
WHAT'S THAT--?
YEAH, I'M ON THE SECURE COMM--
DO YOU HAVE ORDERS, OR...
AYE, SIR...?
YOU'RE SURE...?
YOU'RE SURE YOU'RE SURE?
CLEAR THE DECK. NOW!
IT'S ME.
CORNELIUS JUST GAVE THE ORDER TO HAVE ZEPHYR ASSASSINATED.

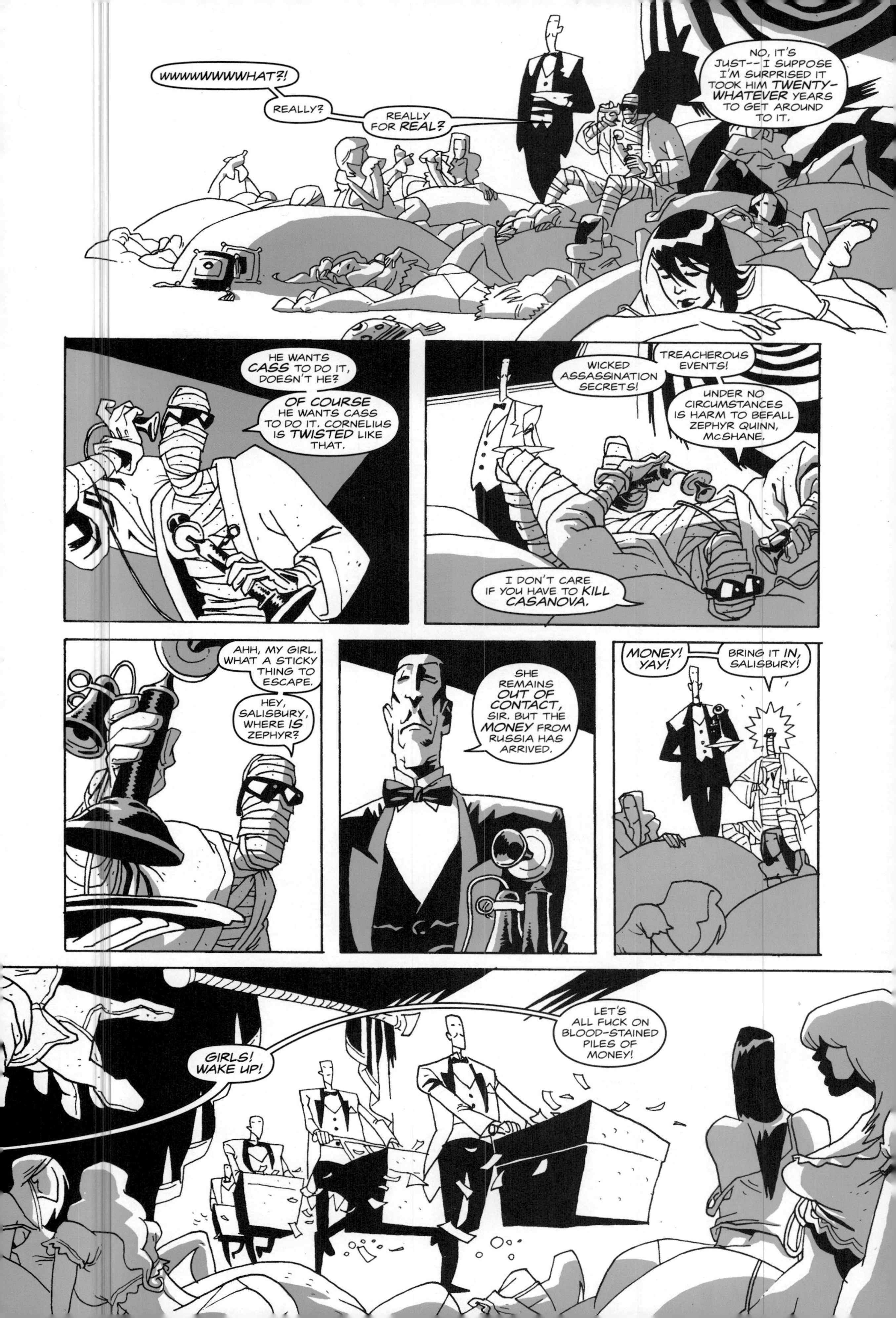
WWWWWWWWHAT?!
REALLY?
REALLY FOR REAL?
NO, IT'S JUST-- I SUPPOSE I'M SURPRISED IT TOOK HIM TWENTY-WHATEVER YEARS TO GET AROUND TO IT.
HE WANTS CASS TO DO IT, DOESN'T HE?
OF COURSE HE WANTS CASS TO DO IT. CORNELIUS IS TWISTED LIKE THAT.
WICKED ASSASSINATION SECRETS!
TREACHEROUS EVENTS!
UNDER NO CIRCUMSTANCES IS HARM TO BEFALL ZEPHYR QUINN, McSHANE.
I DON'T CARE IF YOU HAVE TO KILL CASANOVA.
AHH, MY GIRL. WHAT A STICKY THING TO ESCAPE.
HEY, SALISBURY, WHERE IS ZEPHYR?
SHE REMAINS OUT OF CONTACT, SIR. BUT THE MONEY FROM RUSSIA HAS ARRIVED.
MONEY! YAY!
BRING IT IN, SALISBURY!
GIRLS! WAKE UP!
LET'S ALL FUCK ON BLOOD-STAINED PILES OF MONEY!

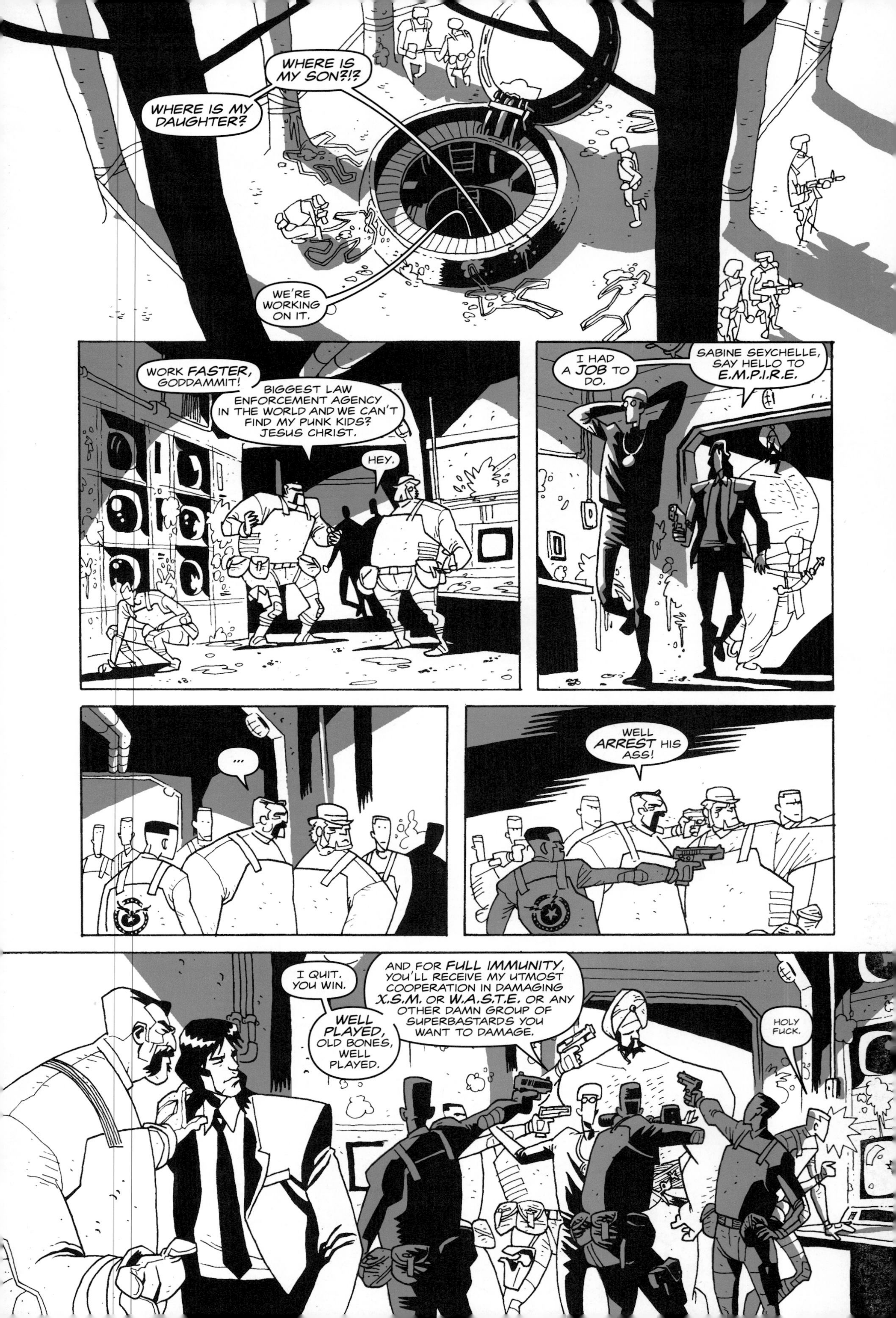
WHERE IS MY DAUGHTER?
WHERE IS MY SON?!?
WE'RE WORKING ON IT.
WORK FASTER, GODDAMMIT!
BIGGEST LAW ENFORCEMENT AGENCY IN THE WORLD AND WE CAN'T FIND MY PUNK KIDS? JESUS CHRIST.
HEY.
I HAD A JOB TO DO.
SABINE SEYCHELLE, SAY HELLO TO E.M.P.I.R.E.
...
WELL ARREST HIS ASS!
I QUIT. YOU WIN.
WELL PLAYED, OLD BONES, WELL PLAYED.
AND FOR FULL IMMUNITY, YOU'LL RECEIVE MY UTMOST COOPERATION IN DAMAGING X.S.M. OR W.A.S.T.E. OR ANY OTHER DAMN GROUP OF SUPERBASTARDS YOU WANT TO DAMAGE.
HOLY FUCK.

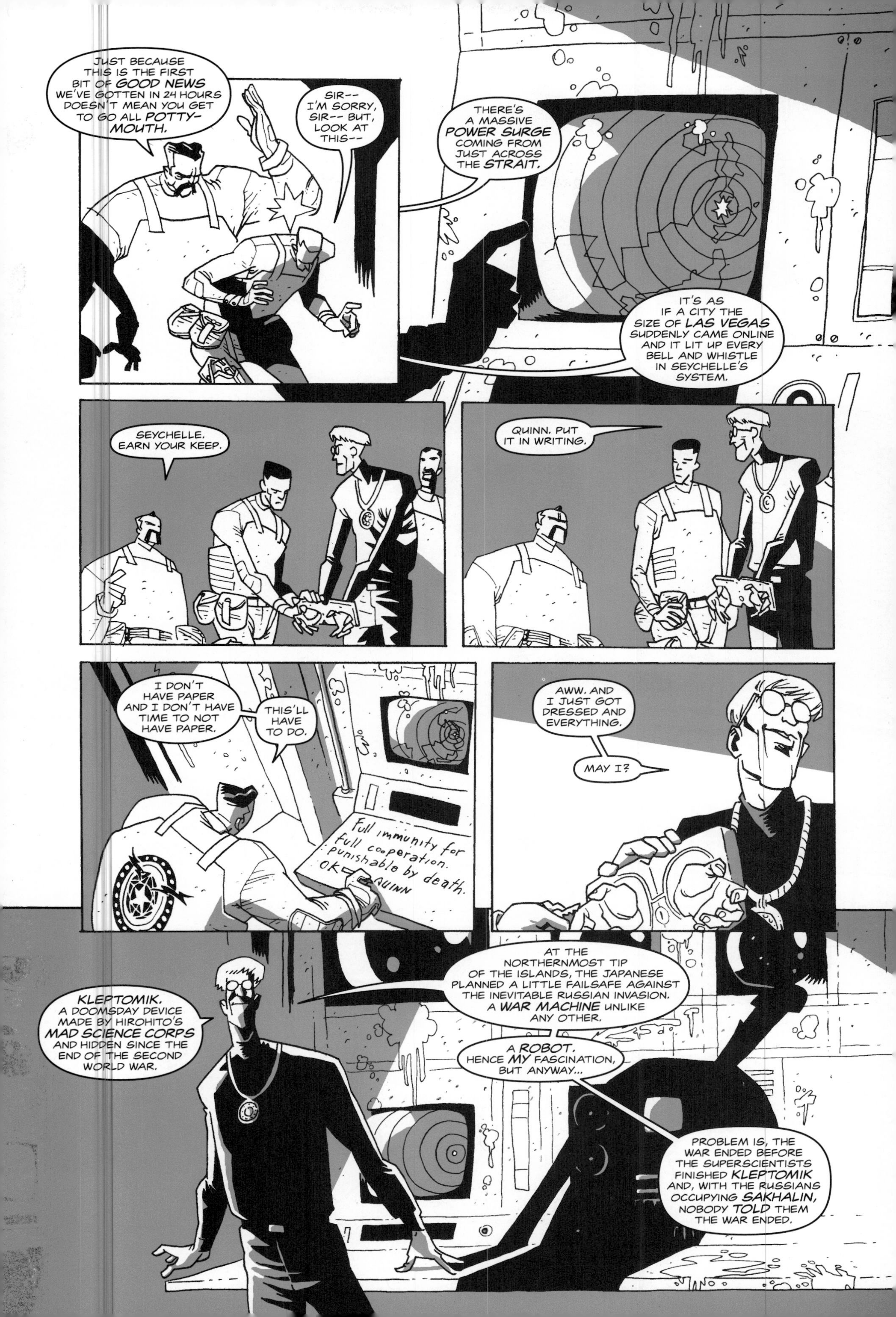

JUST BECAUSE THIS IS THE FIRST BIT OF GOOD NEWS WE'VE GOTTEN IN 24 HOURS DOESN'T MEAN YOU GET TO GO ALL POTTY-MOUTH.
SIR-- I'M SORRY, SIR-- BUT, LOOK AT THIS--
THERE'S A MASSIVE POWER SURGE COMING FROM JUST ACROSS THE STRAIT.
IT'S AS IF A CITY THE SIZE OF LAS VEGAS SUDDENLY CAME ONLINE AND IT LIT UP EVERY BELL AND WHISTLE IN SEYCHELLE'S SYSTEM.
SEYCHELLE. EARN YOUR KEEP.
QUINN. PUT IT IN WRITING.
I DON'T HAVE PAPER AND I DON'T HAVE TIME TO NOT HAVE PAPER.
THIS'LL HAVE TO DO.
Full immunity for full cooperation. punishable by death. OK-- QUINN
AWW. AND I JUST GOT DRESSED AND EVERYTHING.
MAY I?
KLEPTOMIK. A DOOMSDAY DEVICE MADE BY HIROHITO'S MAD SCIENCE CORPS AND HIDDEN SINCE THE END OF THE SECOND WORLD WAR.
AT THE NORTHERNMOST TIP OF THE ISLANDS, THE JAPANESE PLANNED A LITTLE FAILSAFE AGAINST THE INEVITABLE RUSSIAN INVASION. A WAR MACHINE UNLIKE ANY OTHER.
A ROBOT. HENCE MY FASCINATION, BUT ANYWAY...
PROBLEM IS, THE WAR ENDED BEFORE THE SUPERSCIENTISTS FINISHED KLEPTOMIK AND, WITH THE RUSSIANS OCCUPYING SAKHALIN, NOBODY TOLD THEM THE WAR ENDED.

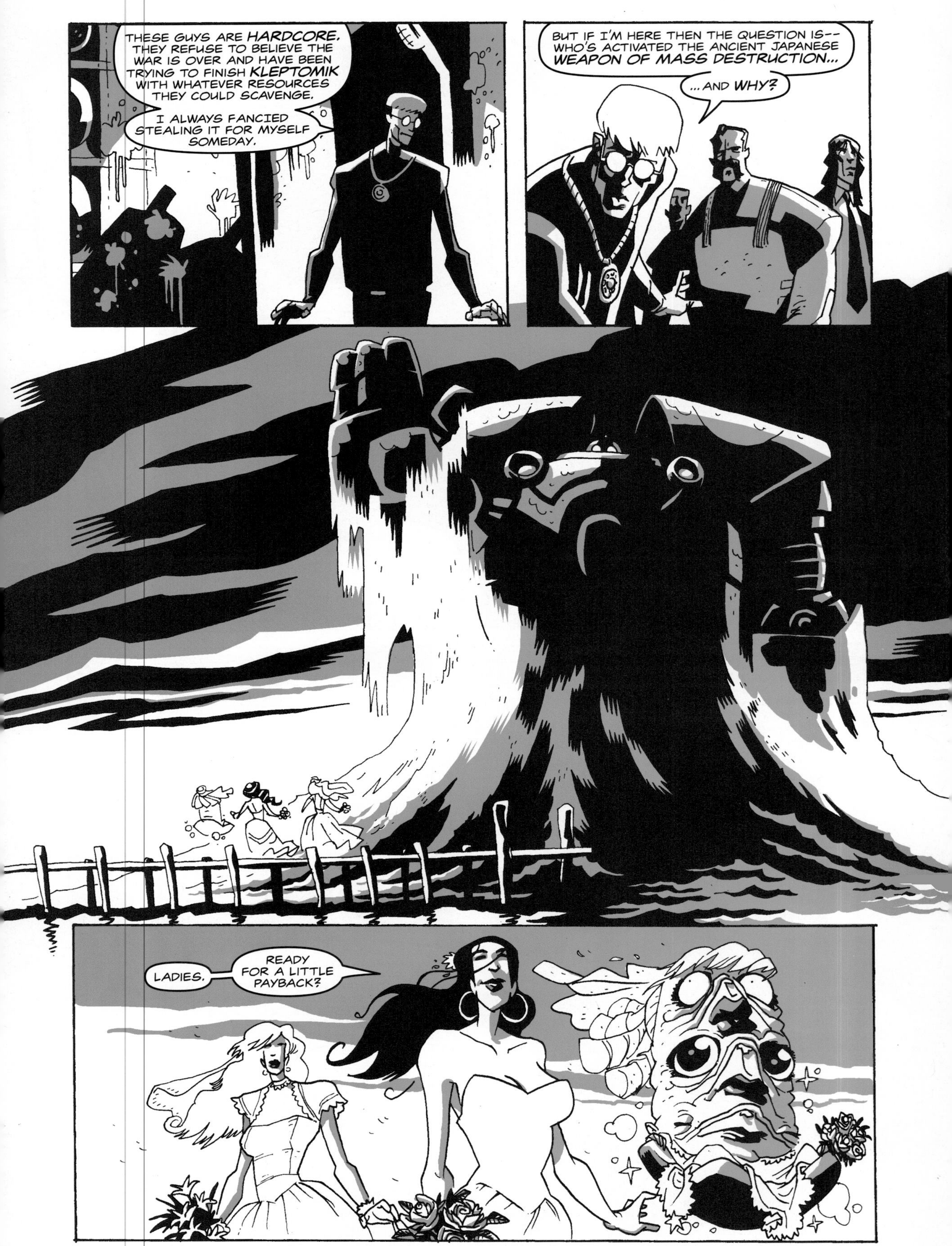
THESE GUYS ARE HARDCORE. THEY REFUSE TO BELIEVE THE WAR IS OVER AND HAVE BEEN TRYING TO FINISH KLEPTOMIK WITH WHATEVER RESOURCES THEY COULD SCAVENGE.
I ALWAYS FANCIED STEALING IT FOR MYSELF SOMEDAY.
BUT IF I'M HERE THEN THE QUESTION IS-- WHO'S ACTIVATED THE ANCIENT JAPANESE WEAPON OF MASS DESTRUCTION...
...AND WHY?
LADIES.
READY FOR A LITTLE PAYBACK?

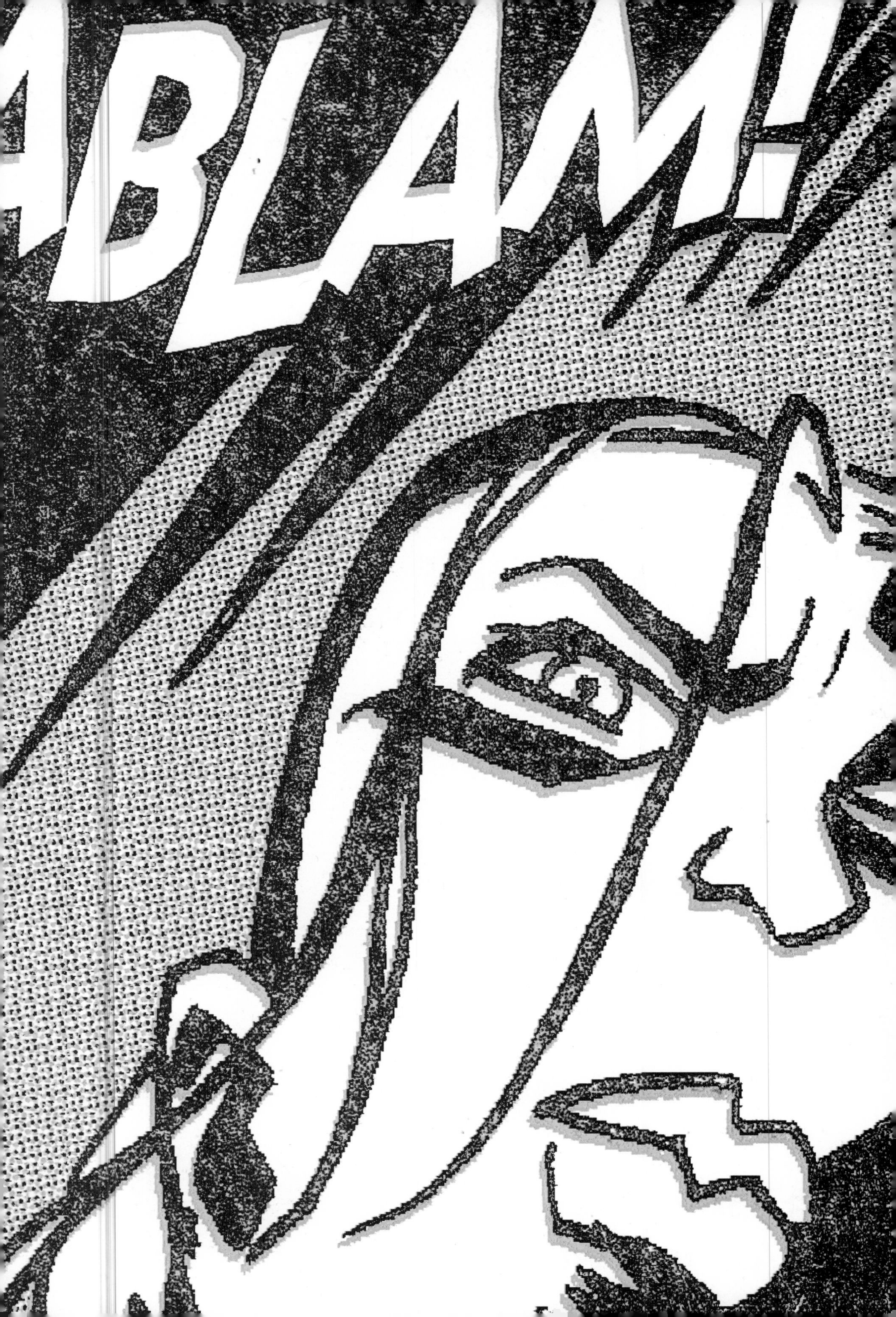
ABLAM!

Chapter Seven
Women and Men (Part Two)

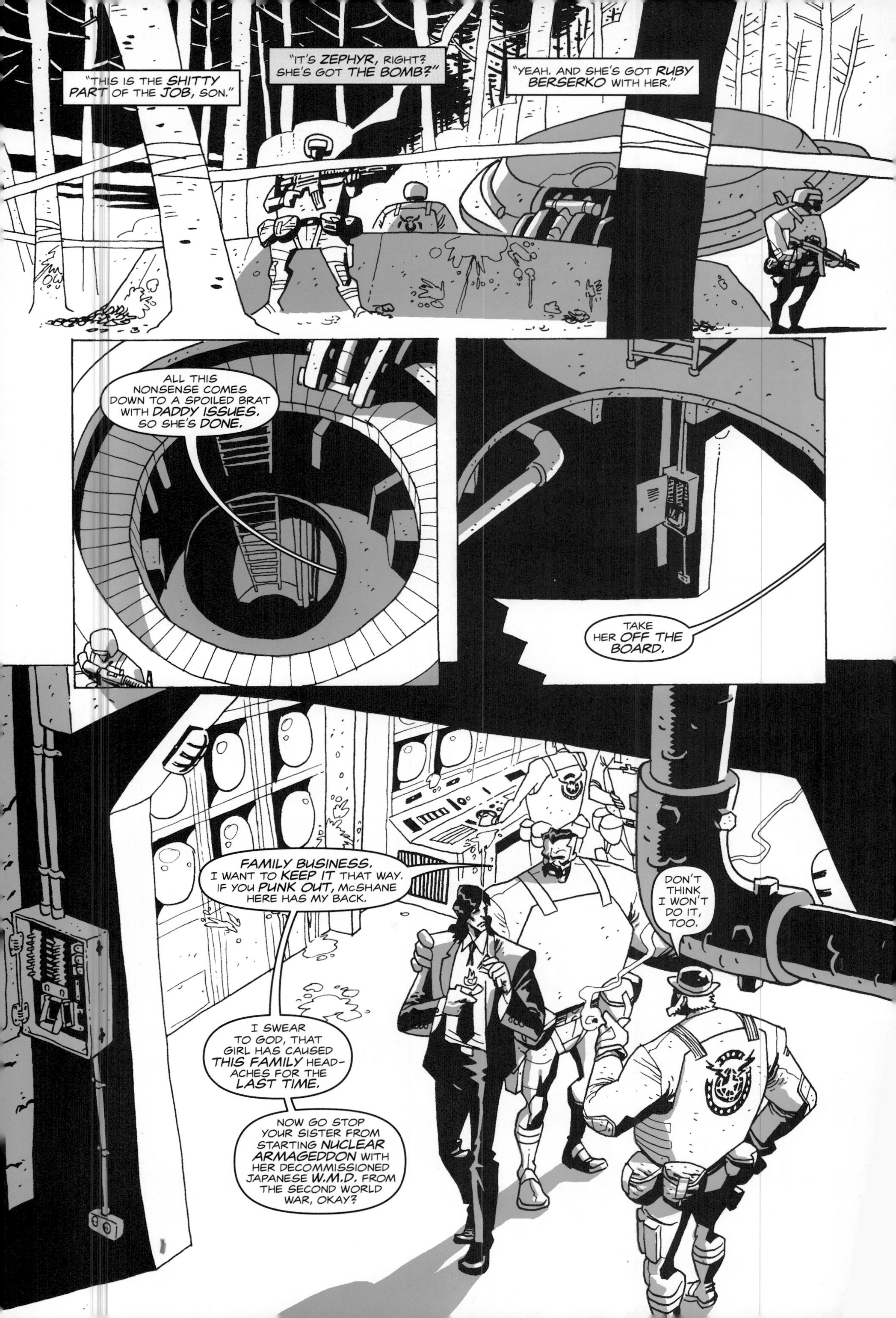
"THIS IS THE SHITTY PART OF THE JOB, SON."
"IT'S ZEPHYR, RIGHT? SHE'S GOT THE BOMB?"
"YEAH. AND SHE'S GOT RUBY BERSERKO WITH HER."
ALL THIS NONSENSE COMES DOWN TO A SPOILED BRAT WITH DADDY ISSUES. SO SHE'S DONE.
TAKE HER OFF THE BOARD.
FAMILY BUSINESS. I WANT TO KEEP IT THAT WAY. IF YOU PUNK OUT, McSHANE HERE HAS MY BACK.
DON'T THINK I WON'T DO IT, TOO.
I SWEAR TO GOD, THAT GIRL HAS CAUSED THIS FAMILY HEAD-ACHES FOR THE LAST TIME.
NOW GO STOP YOUR SISTER FROM STARTING NUCLEAR ARMAGEDDON WITH HER DECOMMISSIONED JAPANESE W.M.D. FROM THE SECOND WORLD WAR, OKAY?

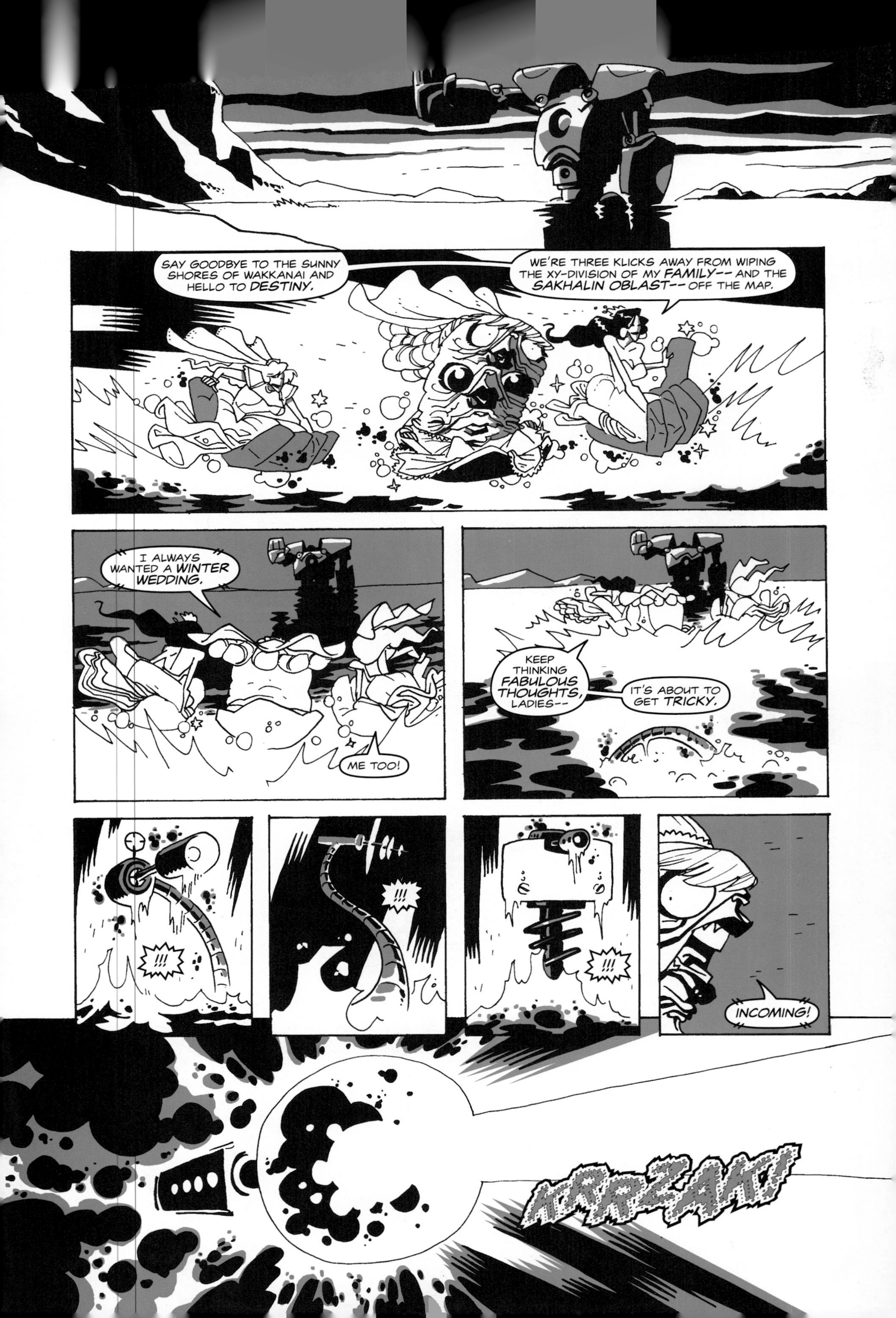
SAY GOODBYE TO THE SUNNY SHORES OF WAKKANAI AND HELLO TO DESTINY.
WE'RE THREE KLICKS AWAY FROM WIPING THE XY-DIVISION OF MY FAMILY-- AND THE SAKHALIN OBLAST-- OFF THE MAP.
I ALWAYS WANTED A WINTER WEDDING.
ME TOO!
KEEP THINKING FABULOUS THOUGHTS, LADIES--
IT'S ABOUT TO GET TRICKY.
!!!
!!!
!!!
INCOMING!
KRRZAK!!

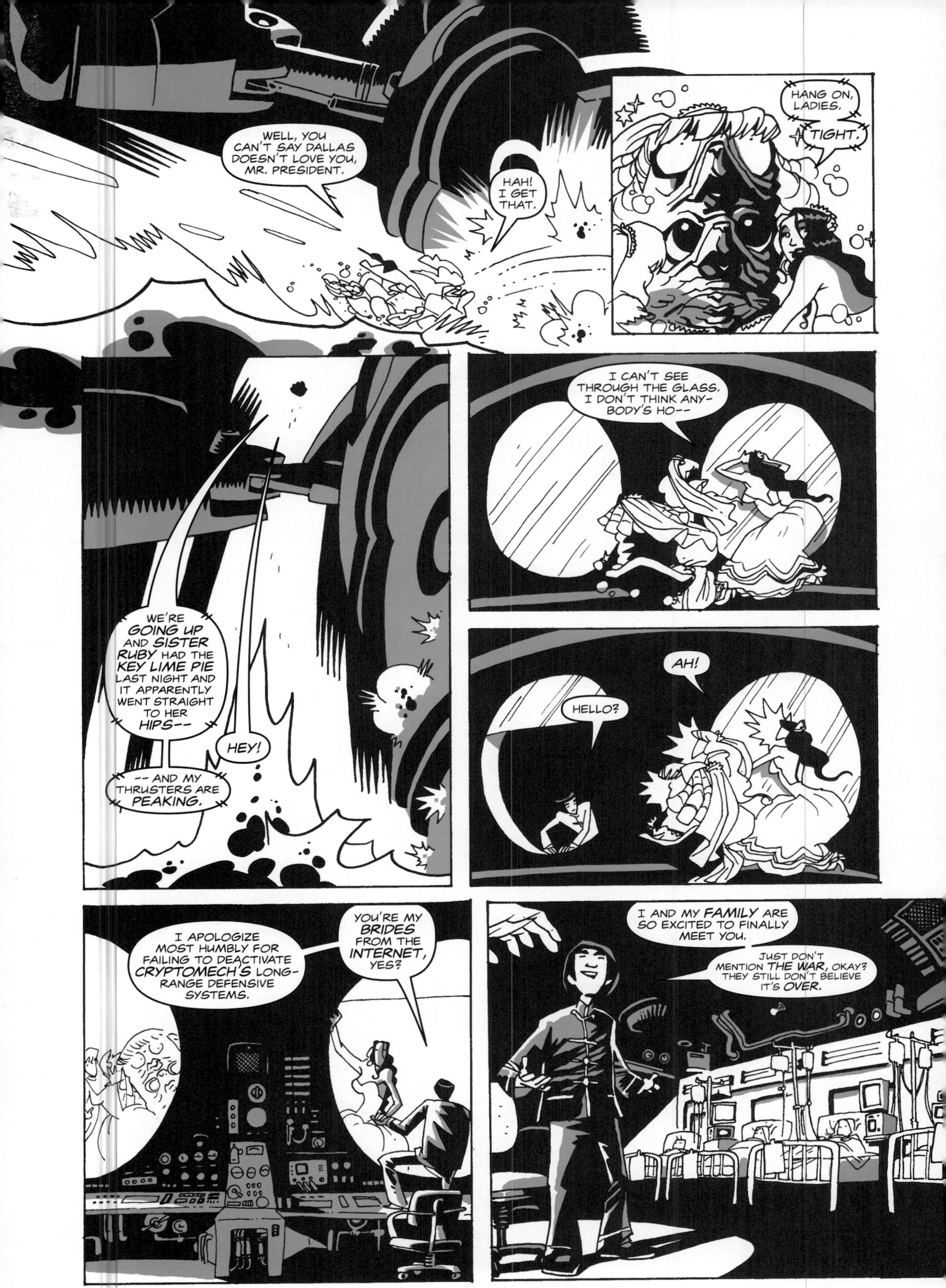
WELL, YOU CAN'T SAY DALLAS DOESN'T LOVE YOU, MR. PRESIDENT.
HAH! I GET THAT.
HANG ON, LADIES.
TIGHT.
WE'RE GOING UP AND SISTER RUBY HAD THE KEY LIME PIE LAST NIGHT AND IT APPARENTLY WENT STRAIGHT TO HER HIPS--
HEY!
-- AND MY THRUSTERS ARE PEAKING.
I CAN'T SEE THROUGH THE GLASS. I DON'T THINK ANY-BODY'S HO--
AH!
HELLO?
I APOLOGIZE MOST HUMBLY FOR FAILING TO DEACTIVATE CRYPTOMECH'S LONG-RANGE DEFENSIVE SYSTEMS.
YOU'RE MY BRIDES FROM THE INTERNET, YES?
I AND MY FAMILY ARE SO EXCITED TO FINALLY MEET YOU.
JUST DON'T MENTION THE WAR, OKAY? THEY STILL DON'T BELIEVE IT'S OVER.

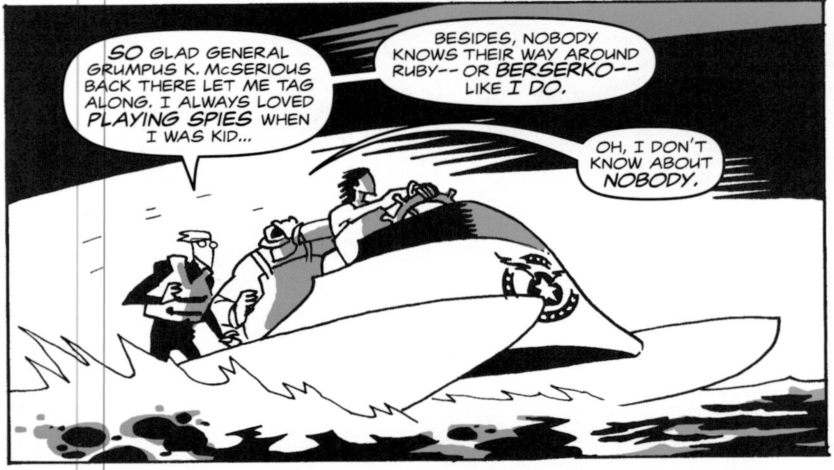
SO GLAD GENERAL GRUMPUS K. McSERIOUS BACK THERE LET ME TAG ALONG. I ALWAYS LOVED PLAYING SPIES WHEN I WAS KID...
BESIDES, NOBODY KNOWS THEIR WAY AROUND RUBY-- OR BERSERKO-- LIKE I DO.
OH, I DON'T KNOW ABOUT NOBODY.

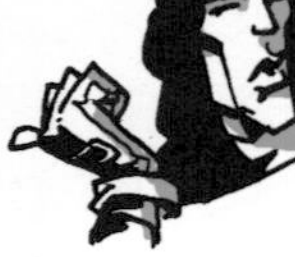

STUCK IN LA PEROUSE STRAIT ON A SILENT-RUNNING E.M.P.I.R.E. HYDROFOIL WITH RUBY'S TWO BICKERING EX-BOYFRIENDS?

YEAH, NO, THAT'S NOT AWKWARD FOR ME AT ALL, THANKS FOR ASKING.

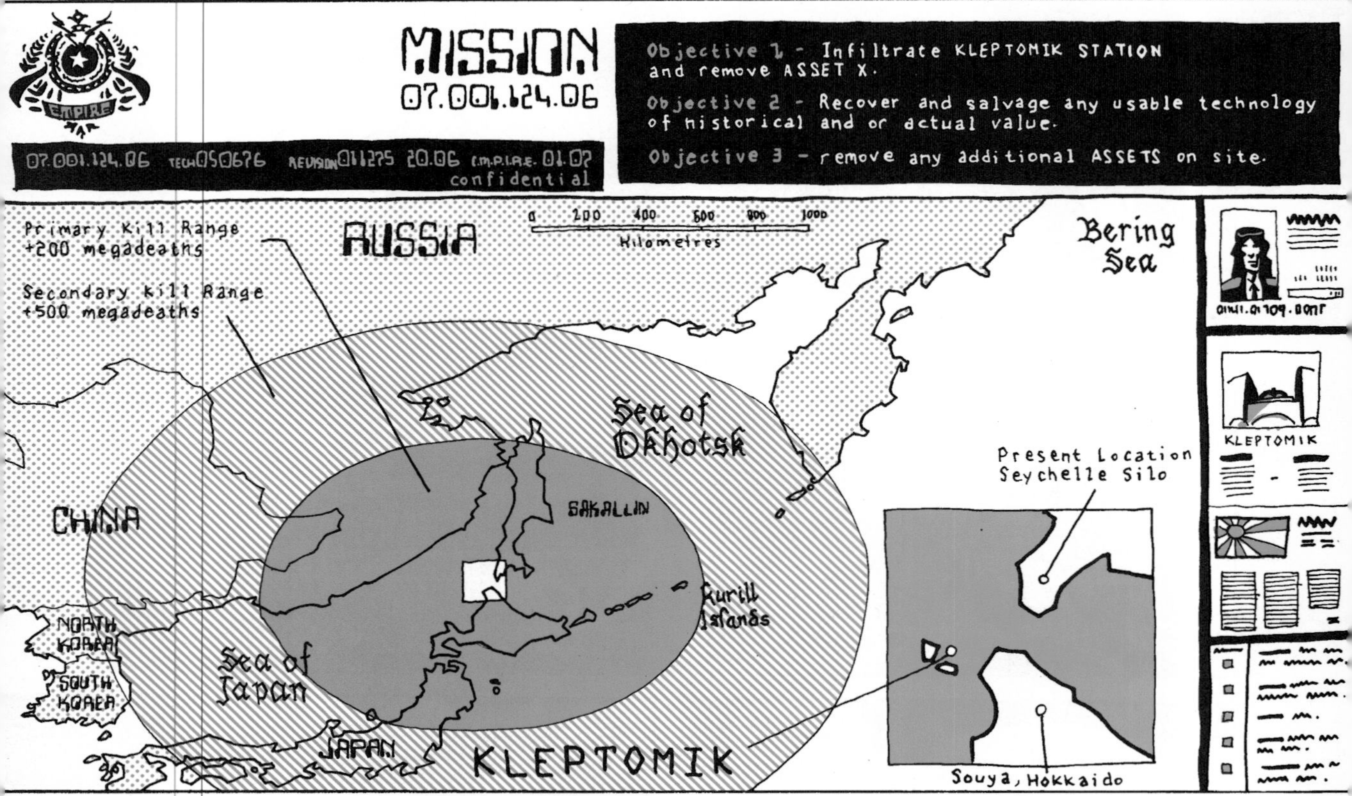
EMPIRE
MISSION
07.001.124.06
07.001.124.06 TECH 050676 REVISION 011275 20.06 E.M.P.I.R.E. 01.07
confidential
Objective 1 - Infiltrate KLEPTOMIK STATION and remove ASSET X.
Objective 2 - Recover and salvage any usable technology of historical and or actual value.
Objective 3 - remove any additional ASSETS on site.
Primary Kill Range +200 megadeaths
Secondary Kill Range +500 megadeaths
RUSSIA
0 200 400 600 800 1000
Kilometres
Bering Sea
Sea of Okhotsk
SAKALLIN
CHINA
Kurill Islands
NORTH KOREA
SOUTH KOREA
Sea of Japan
JAPAN
KLEPTOMIK
Present Location Seychelle Silo
Souya, Hokkaido
KLEPTOMIK

FOUR-HUNDRED SOME KLICKS OF THIS SHIT. WE'RE ROCKETING TOWARDS A DECADES-OLD WEAPON WITH A SEVEN-HUNDRED-PLUS MEGADEATH CAPABILITY AND I HAVE TO LISTEN TO McSHANE AND JOHNNY CRANK ARGUE DICK-SIZE.

I'M GONNA BEAT ST. PETER'S ASS WHEN I SEE HIM.

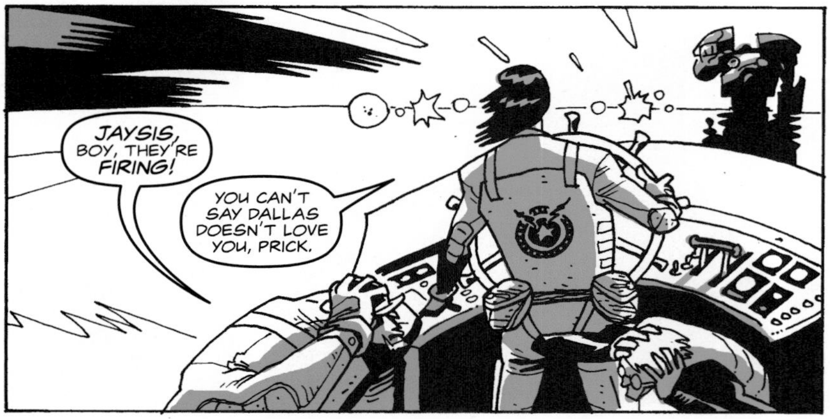
JAYSIS, BOY, THEY'RE FIRING!
YOU CAN'T SAY DALLAS DOESN'T LOVE YOU, PRICK.

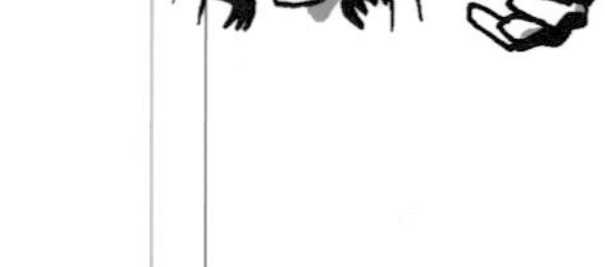

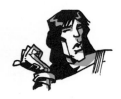

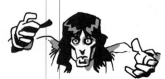

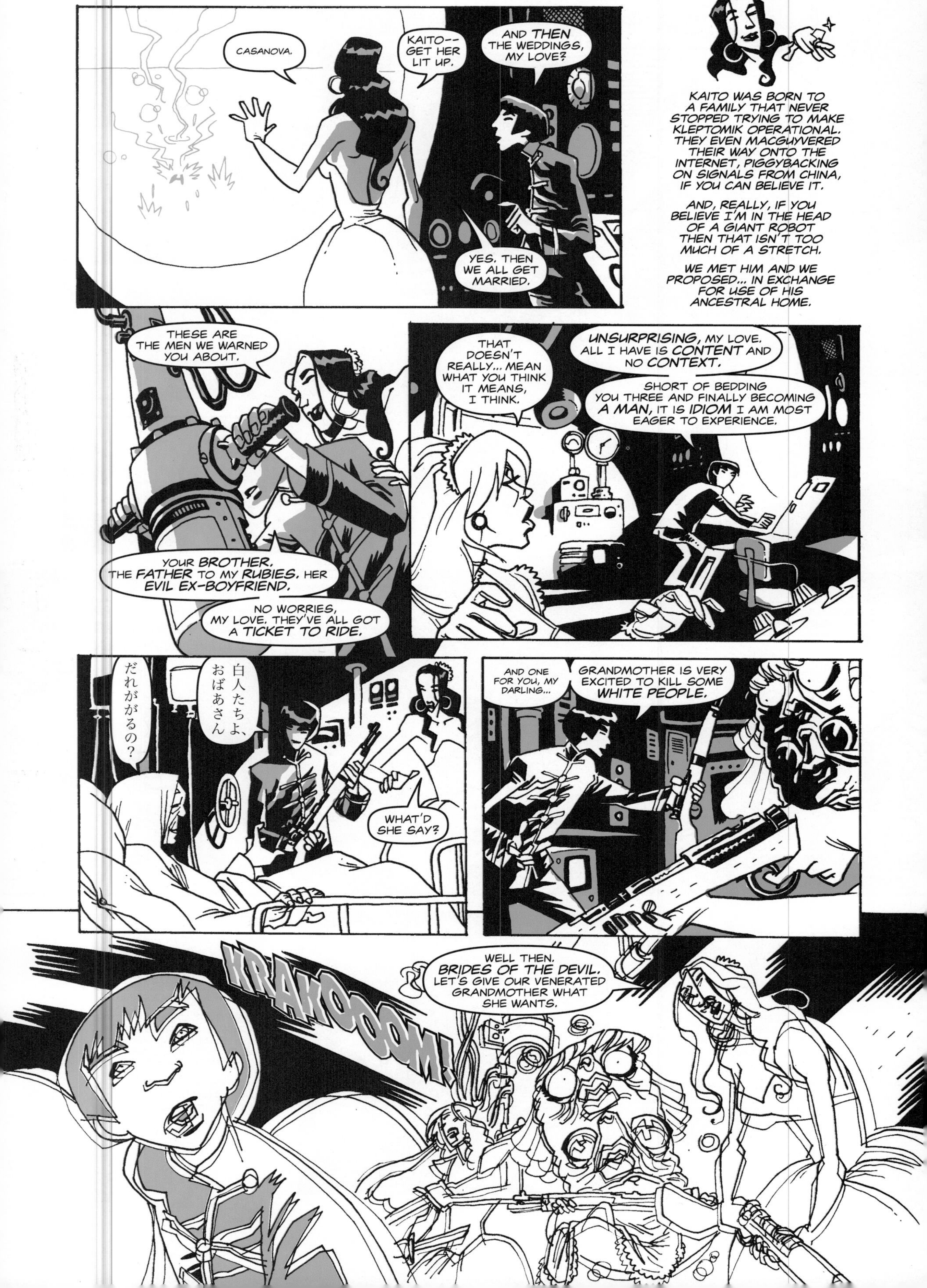
CASANOVA.
KAITO-- GET HER LIT UP.
AND THEN THE WEDDINGS, MY LOVE?
YES. THEN WE ALL GET MARRIED.
KAITO WAS BORN TO A FAMILY THAT NEVER STOPPED TRYING TO MAKE KLEPTOMIK OPERATIONAL. THEY EVEN MACGUYVERED THEIR WAY ONTO THE INTERNET, PIGGYBACKING ON SIGNALS FROM CHINA, IF YOU CAN BELIEVE IT.
AND, REALLY, IF YOU BELIEVE I'M IN THE HEAD OF A GIANT ROBOT THEN THAT ISN'T TOO MUCH OF A STRETCH.
WE MET HIM AND WE PROPOSED... IN EXCHANGE FOR USE OF HIS ANCESTRAL HOME.
THESE ARE THE MEN WE WARNED YOU ABOUT.
YOUR BROTHER. THE FATHER TO MY RUBIES. HER EVIL EX-BOYFRIEND.
NO WORRIES, MY LOVE. THEY'VE ALL GOT A TICKET TO RIDE.
THAT DOESN'T REALLY... MEAN WHAT YOU THINK IT MEANS, I THINK.
UNSURPRISING, MY LOVE. ALL I HAVE IS CONTENT AND NO CONTEXT.
SHORT OF BEDDING YOU THREE AND FINALLY BECOMING A MAN, IT IS IDIOM I AM MOST EAGER TO EXPERIENCE.
白人たちよ、おばあさん
だれががるの？
WHAT'D SHE SAY?
AND ONE FOR YOU, MY DARLING...
GRANDMOTHER IS VERY EXCITED TO KILL SOME WHITE PEOPLE.
KRAKOOOM!
WELL THEN, BRIDES OF THE DEVIL, LET'S GIVE OUR VENERATED GRANDMOTHER WHAT SHE WANTS.

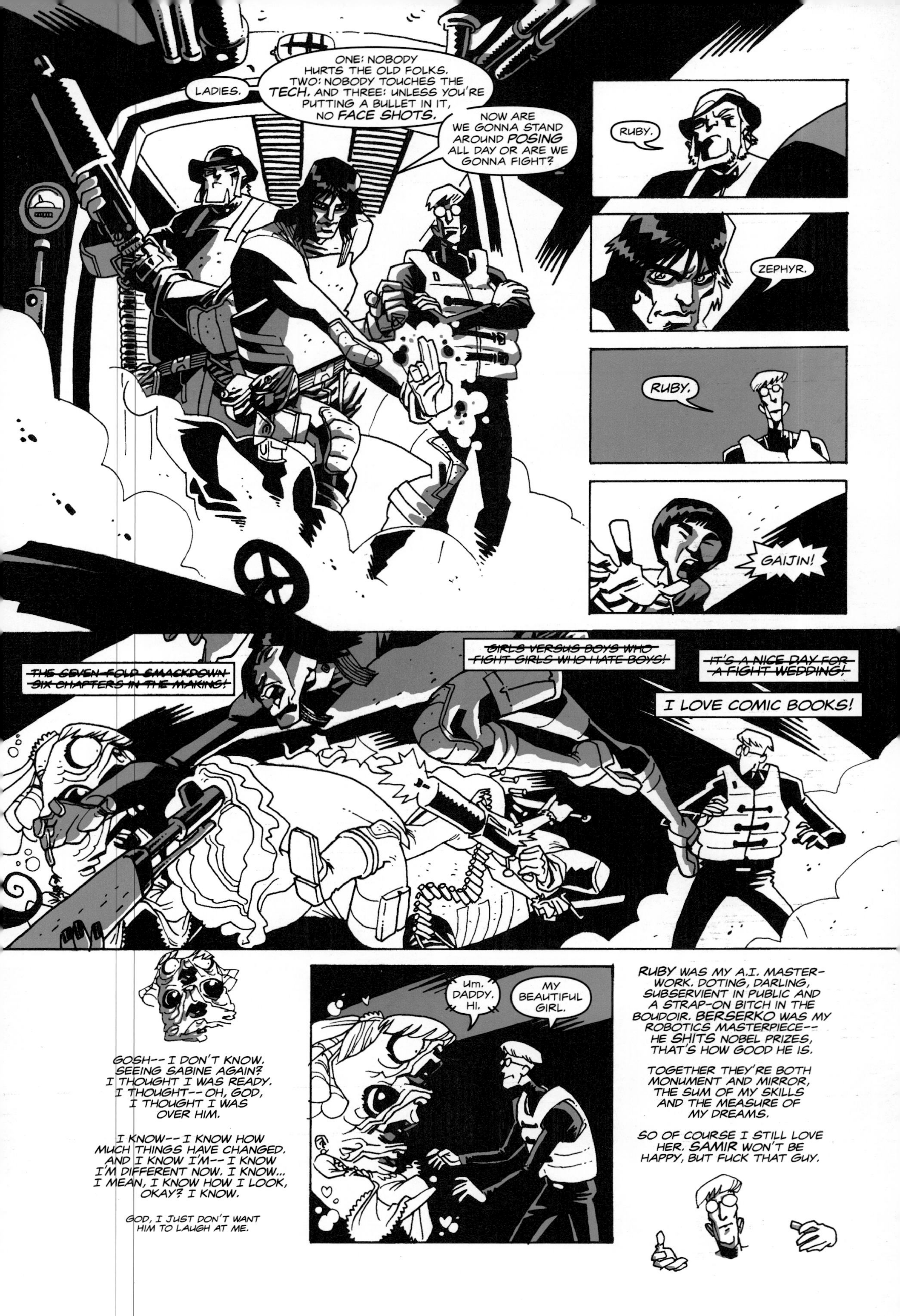

LADIES.
ONE: NOBODY HURTS THE OLD FOLKS. TWO: NOBODY TOUCHES THE TECH. AND THREE: UNLESS YOU'RE PUTTING A BULLET IN IT, NO FACE SHOTS.
NOW ARE WE GONNA STAND AROUND POSING ALL DAY OR ARE WE GONNA FIGHT?
RUBY.
ZEPHYR.
RUBY.
GAIJIN!
THE SEVEN-FOLD SMACKDOWN SIX CHAPTERS IN THE MAKING!
GIRLS VERSUS BOYS WHO FIGHT GIRLS WHO HATE BOYS!
IT'S A NICE DAY FOR A FIGHT WEDDING!
I LOVE COMIC BOOKS!
GOSH-- I DON'T KNOW. SEEING SABINE AGAIN? I THOUGHT I WAS READY. I THOUGHT--OH, GOD, I THOUGHT I WAS OVER HIM.
I KNOW-- I KNOW HOW MUCH THINGS HAVE CHANGED. AND I KNOW I'M-- I KNOW I'M DIFFERENT NOW. I KNOW... I MEAN, I KNOW HOW I LOOK, OKAY? I KNOW.
GOD, I JUST DON'T WANT HIM TO LAUGH AT ME.
UM. DADDY. HI.
MY BEAUTIFUL GIRL.
RUBY WAS MY A.I. MASTERWORK. DOTING, DARLING, SUBSERVIENT IN PUBLIC AND A STRAP-ON BITCH IN THE BOUDOIR. BERSERKO WAS MY ROBOTICS MASTERPIECE-- HE SHITS NOBEL PRIZES, THAT'S HOW GOOD HE IS.
TOGETHER THEY'RE BOTH MONUMENT AND MIRROR, THE SUM OF MY SKILLS AND THE MEASURE OF MY DREAMS.
SO OF COURSE I STILL LOVE HER. SAMIR WON'T BE HAPPY, BUT FUCK THAT GUY.

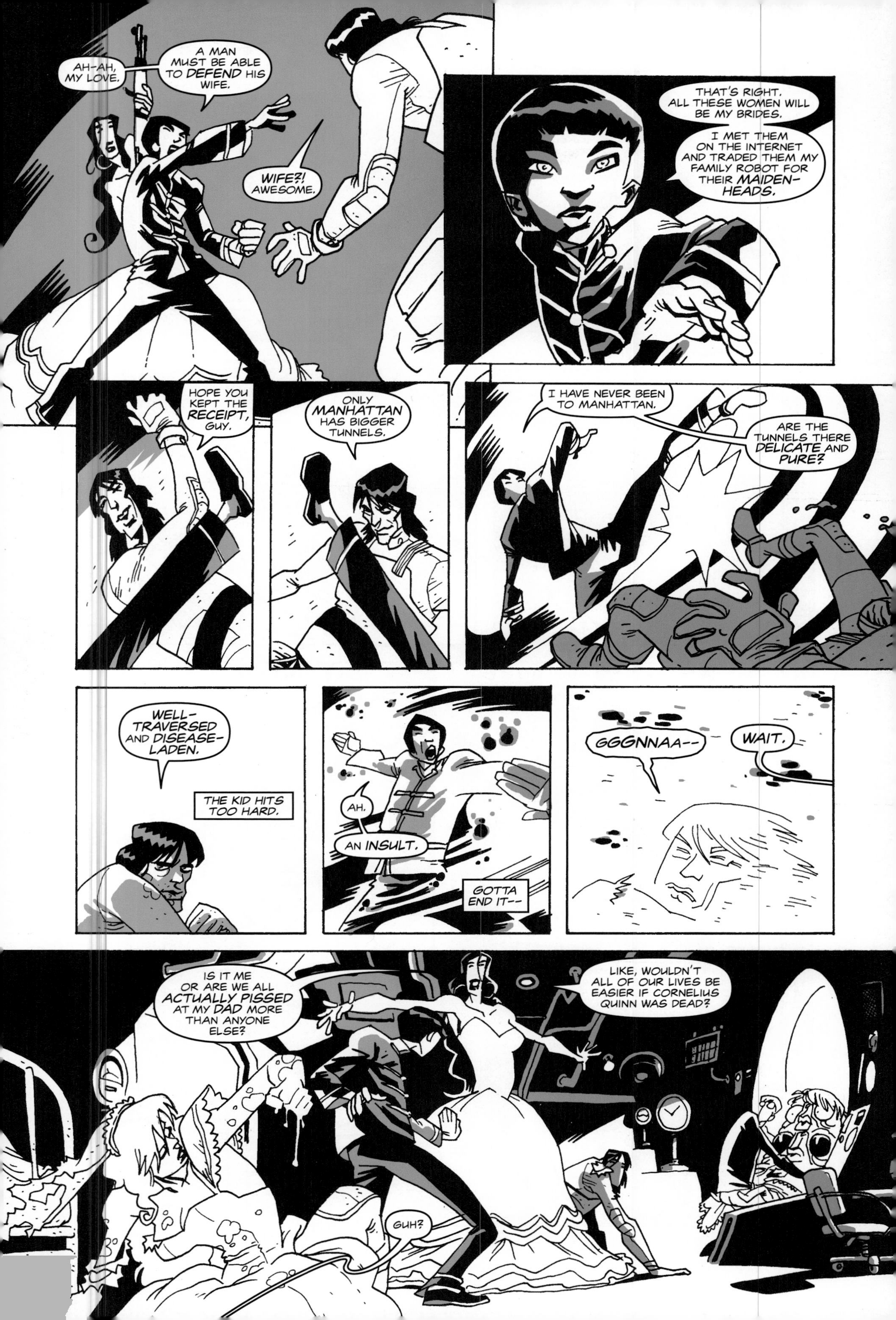
AH-AH, MY LOVE.
A MAN MUST BE ABLE TO DEFEND HIS WIFE.
WIFE?! AWESOME.
THAT'S RIGHT. ALL THESE WOMEN WILL BE MY BRIDES.
I MET THEM ON THE INTERNET AND TRADED THEM MY FAMILY ROBOT FOR THEIR MAIDEN-HEADS.
HOPE YOU KEPT THE RECEIPT, GUY.
ONLY MANHATTAN HAS BIGGER TUNNELS.
I HAVE NEVER BEEN TO MANHATTAN.
ARE THE TUNNELS THERE DELICATE AND PURE?
WELL-TRAVERSED AND DISEASE-LADEN.
THE KID HITS TOO HARD.
AH.
AN INSULT.
GOTTA END IT--
GGGNNAA--
WAIT.
IS IT ME OR ARE WE ALL ACTUALLY PISSED AT MY DAD MORE THAN ANYONE ELSE?
LIKE, WOULDN'T ALL OF OUR LIVES BE EASIER IF CORNELIUS QUINN WAS DEAD?
GUH?

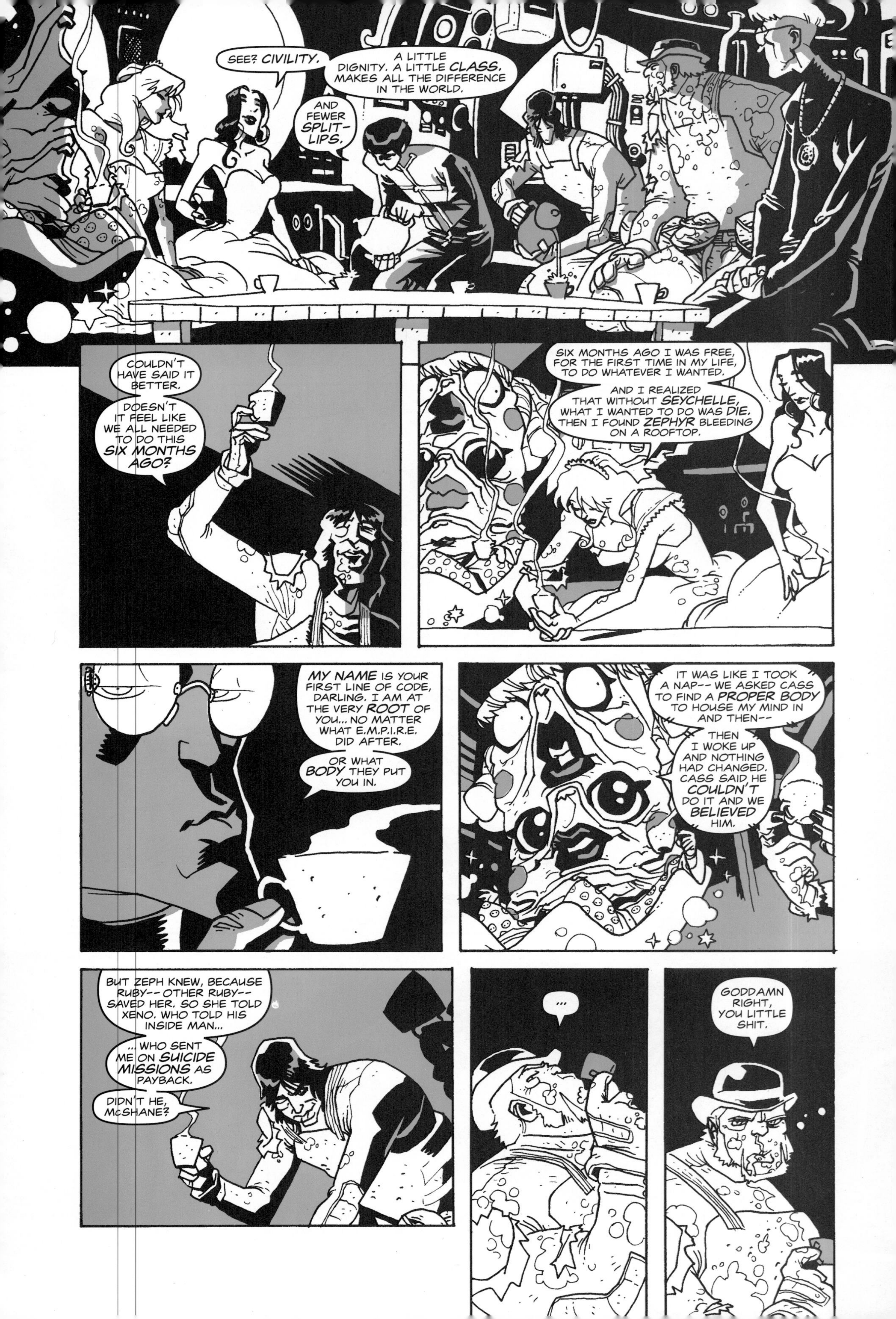
SEE? CIVILITY.
A LITTLE DIGNITY. A LITTLE CLASS. MAKES ALL THE DIFFERENCE IN THE WORLD.
AND FEWER SPLIT-LIPS.
COULDN'T HAVE SAID IT BETTER.
DOESN'T IT FEEL LIKE WE ALL NEEDED TO DO THIS SIX MONTHS AGO?
SIX MONTHS AGO I WAS FREE, FOR THE FIRST TIME IN MY LIFE, TO DO WHATEVER I WANTED.
AND I REALIZED THAT WITHOUT SEYCHELLE, WHAT I WANTED TO DO WAS DIE. THEN I FOUND ZEPHYR BLEEDING ON A ROOFTOP.
MY NAME IS YOUR FIRST LINE OF CODE, DARLING. I AM AT THE VERY ROOT OF YOU... NO MATTER WHAT E.M.P.I.R.E. DID AFTER.
OR WHAT BODY THEY PUT YOU IN.
IT WAS LIKE I TOOK A NAP-- WE ASKED CASS TO FIND A PROPER BODY TO HOUSE MY MIND IN AND THEN--
THEN I WOKE UP AND NOTHING HAD CHANGED. CASS SAID HE COULDN'T DO IT AND WE BELIEVED HIM.
BUT ZEPH KNEW, BECAUSE RUBY-- OTHER RUBY-- SAVED HER. SO SHE TOLD XENO. WHO TOLD HIS INSIDE MAN...
... WHO SENT ME ON SUICIDE MISSIONS AS PAYBACK.
DIDN'T HE, McSHANE?
...
GODDAMN RIGHT, YOU LITTLE SHIT.

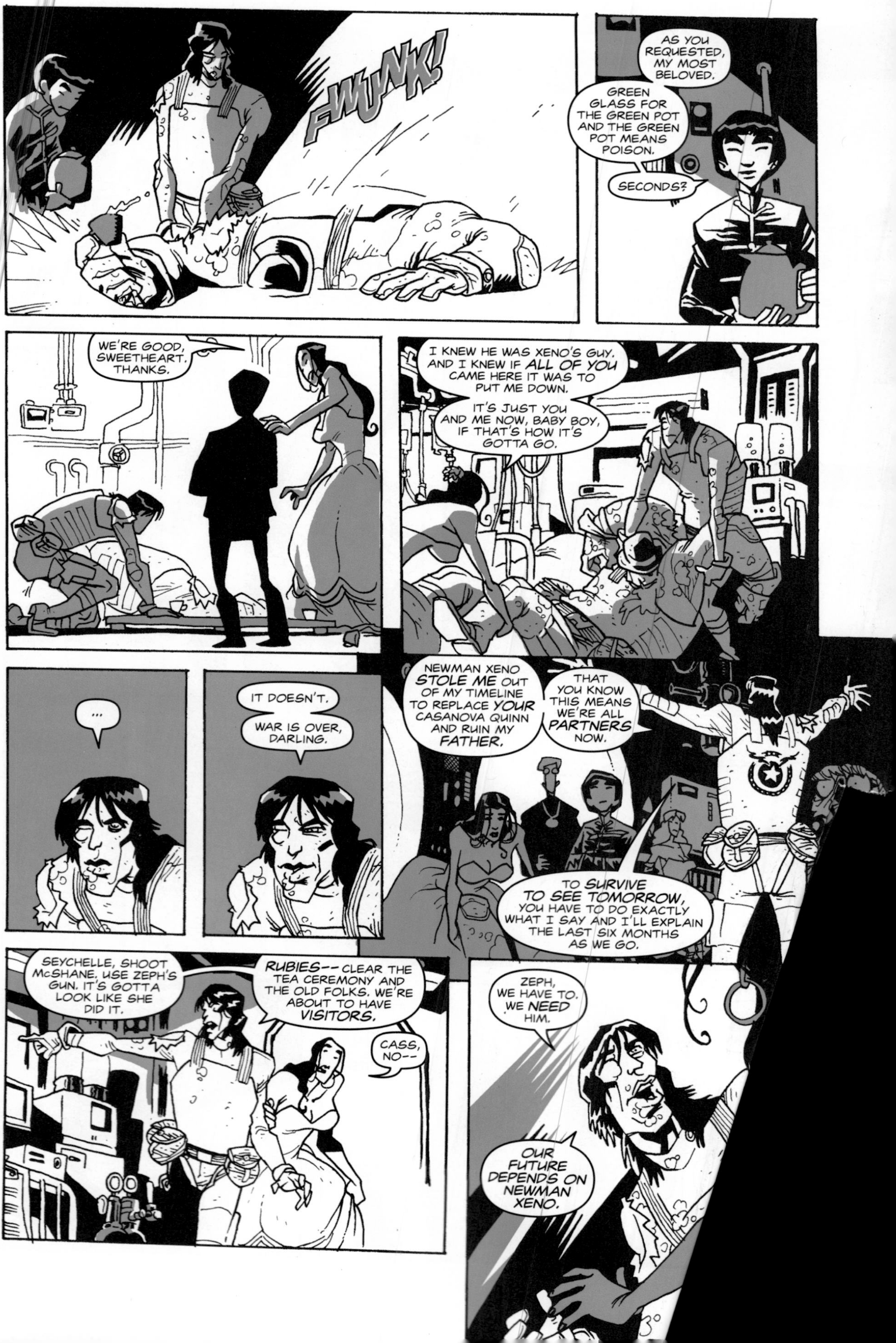
FWUNK!
AS YOU REQUESTED, MY MOST BELOVED.
GREEN GLASS FOR THE GREEN POT AND THE GREEN POT MEANS POISON.
SECONDS?
WE'RE GOOD, SWEETHEART. THANKS.
I KNEW HE WAS XENO'S GUY. AND I KNEW IF ALL OF YOU CAME HERE IT WAS TO PUT ME DOWN.
IT'S JUST YOU AND ME NOW, BABY BOY, IF THAT'S HOW IT'S GOTTA GO.
...
IT DOESN'T.
WAR IS OVER, DARLING.
NEWMAN XENO STOLE ME OUT OF MY TIMELINE TO REPLACE YOUR CASANOVA QUINN AND RUIN MY FATHER.
THAT YOU KNOW THIS MEANS WE'RE ALL PARTNERS NOW.
TO SURVIVE TO SEE TOMORROW, YOU HAVE TO DO EXACTLY WHAT I SAY AND I'LL EXPLAIN THE LAST SIX MONTHS AS WE GO.
SEYCHELLE, SHOOT McSHANE. USE ZEPH'S GUN. IT'S GOTTA LOOK LIKE SHE DID IT.
RUBIES-- CLEAR THE TEA CEREMONY AND THE OLD FOLKS. WE'RE ABOUT TO HAVE VISITORS.
CASS, NO--
ZEPH, WE HAVE TO. WE NEED HIM.
OUR FUTURE DEPENDS ON NEWMAN XENO.

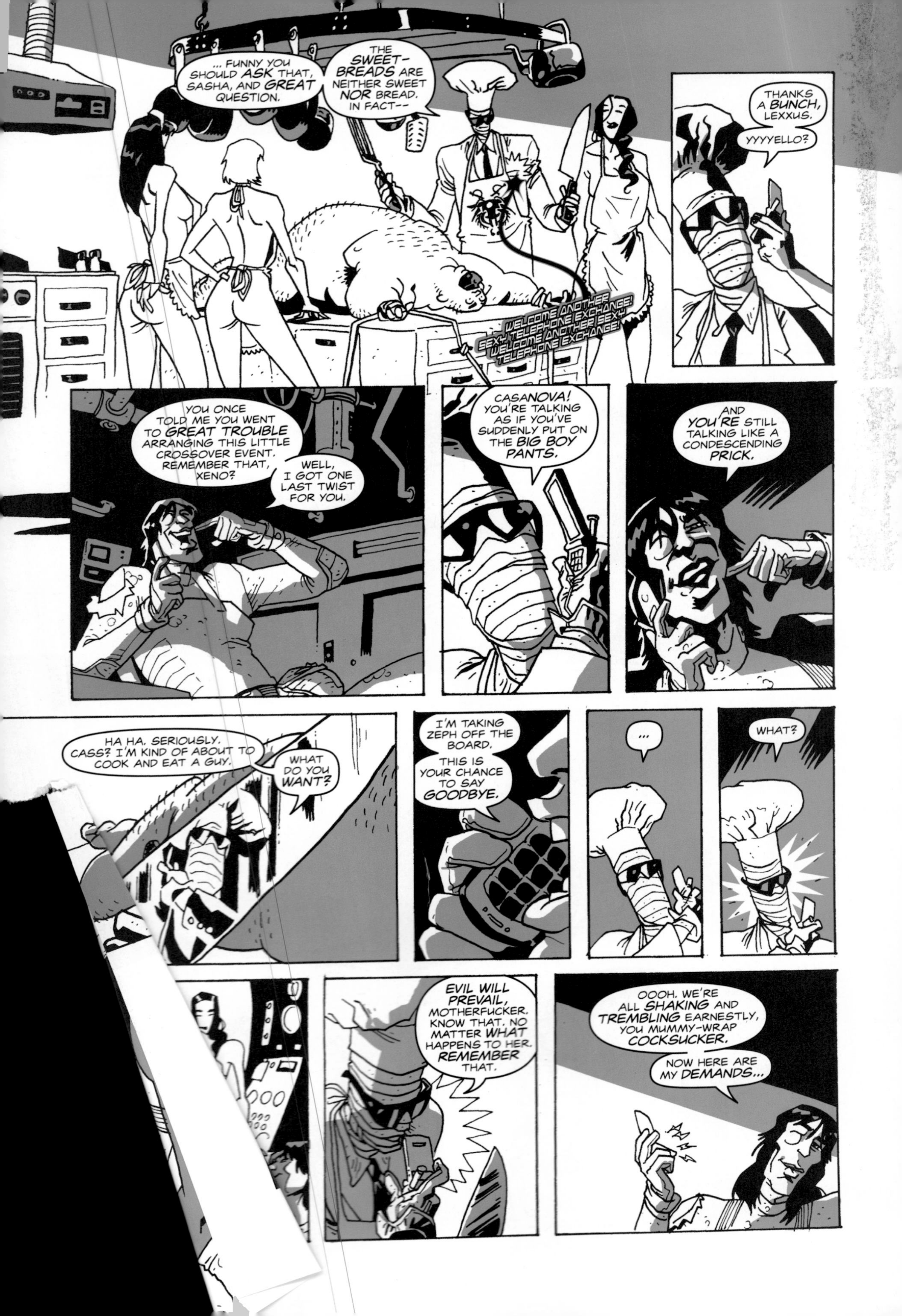

... FUNNY YOU SHOULD ASK THAT, SASHA, AND GREAT QUESTION.
THE SWEET-BREADS ARE NEITHER SWEET NOR BREAD. IN FACT--
WELCOME ANOTHER SEXY TELEPHONE EXCHANGE! WELCOME ANOTHER SEXY TELEPHONE EXCHANGE!
THANKS A BUNCH, LEXXUS.
YYYYELLO?
YOU ONCE TOLD ME YOU WENT TO GREAT TROUBLE ARRANGING THIS LITTLE CROSSOVER EVENT. REMEMBER THAT, XENO?
WELL, I GOT ONE LAST TWIST FOR YOU.
CASANOVA! YOU'RE TALKING AS IF YOU'VE SUDDENLY PUT ON THE BIG BOY PANTS.
AND YOU'RE STILL TALKING LIKE A CONDESCENDING PRICK.
HA HA. SERIOUSLY. CASS? I'M KIND OF ABOUT TO COOK AND EAT A GUY.
WHAT DO YOU WANT?
I'M TAKING ZEPH OFF THE BOARD.
THIS IS YOUR CHANCE TO SAY GOODBYE.
...
WHAT?
EVIL WILL PREVAIL, MOTHERFUCKER. KNOW THAT. NO MATTER WHAT HAPPENS TO HER. REMEMBER THAT.
OOOH. WE'RE ALL SHAKING AND TREMBLING EARNESTLY, YOU MUMMY-WRAP COCKSUCKER.
NOW HERE ARE MY DEMANDS...

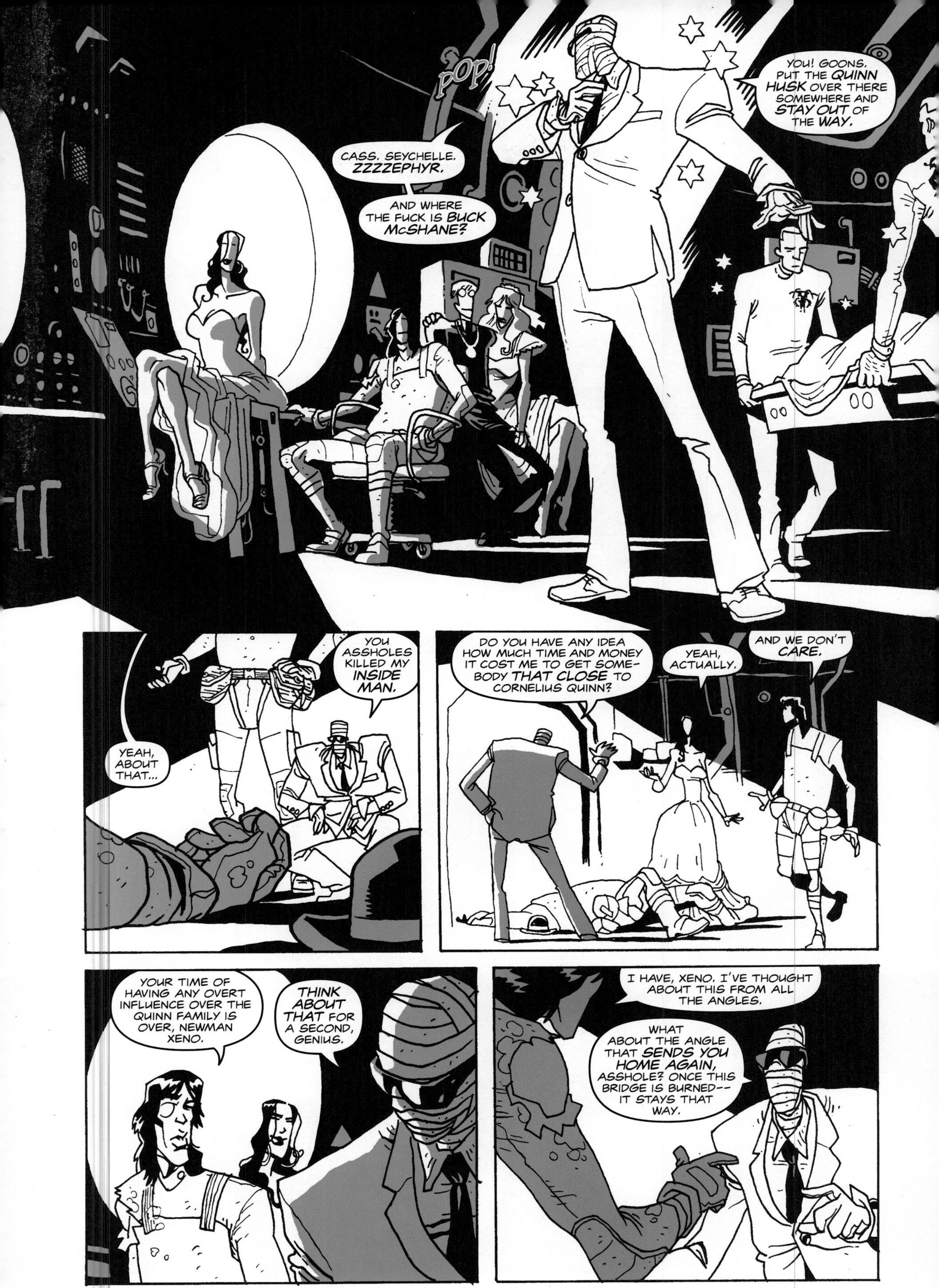

POP!
CASS. SEYCHELLE. ZZZZEPHYR.
AND WHERE THE FUCK IS BUCK McSHANE?
YOU! GOONS. PUT THE QUINN HUSK OVER THERE SOMEWHERE AND STAY OUT OF THE WAY.
YOU ASSHOLES KILLED MY INSIDE MAN.
YEAH, ABOUT THAT...
DO YOU HAVE ANY IDEA HOW MUCH TIME AND MONEY IT COST ME TO GET SOMEBODY THAT CLOSE TO CORNELIUS QUINN?
YEAH, ACTUALLY.
AND WE DON'T CARE.
YOUR TIME OF HAVING ANY OVERT INFLUENCE OVER THE QUINN FAMILY IS OVER, NEWMAN XENO.
THINK ABOUT THAT FOR A SECOND, GENIUS.
I HAVE, XENO. I'VE THOUGHT ABOUT THIS FROM ALL THE ANGLES.
WHAT ABOUT THE ANGLE THAT SENDS YOU HOME AGAIN, ASSHOLE? ONCE THIS BRIDGE IS BURNED-- IT STAYS THAT WAY.

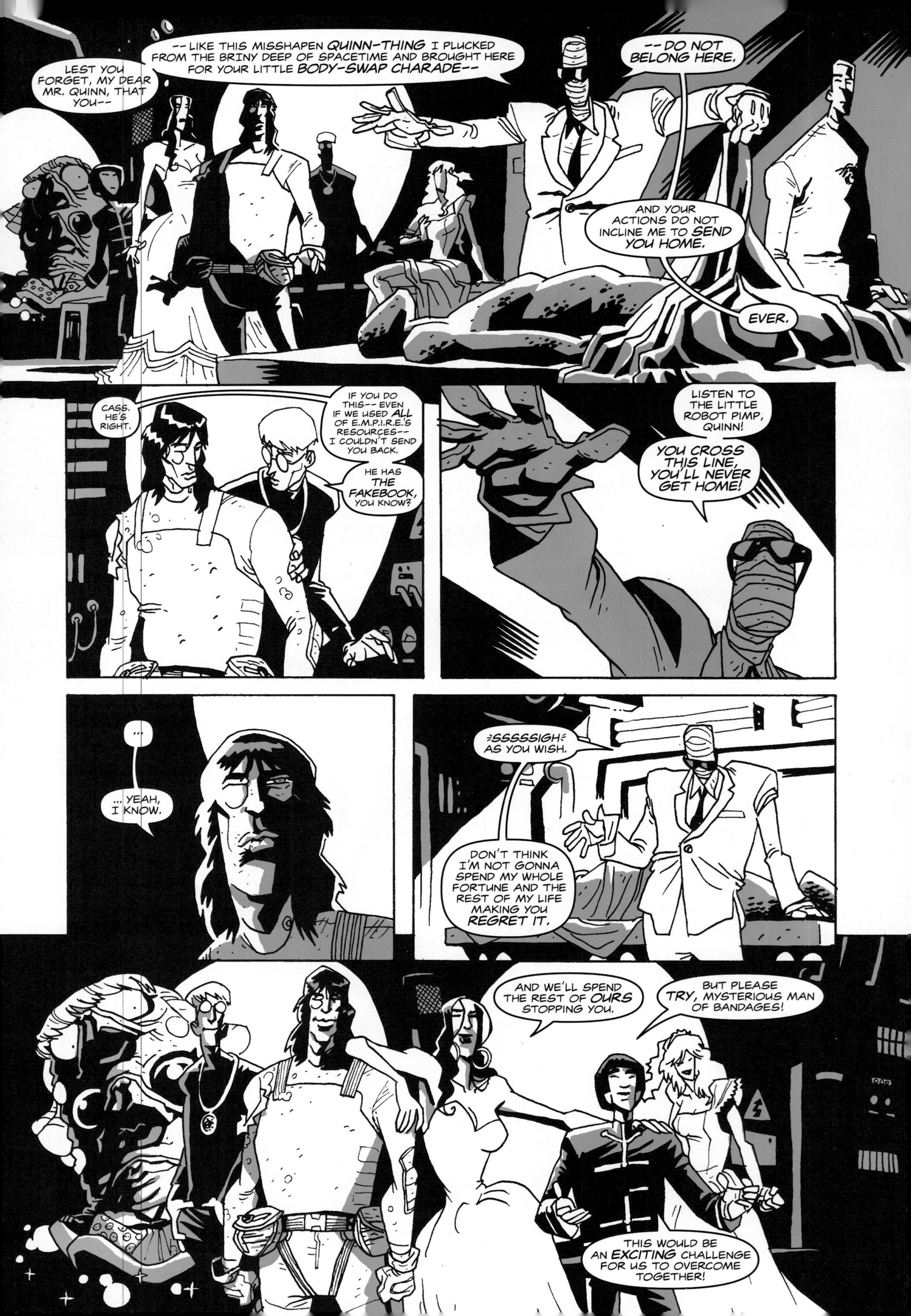
LEST YOU FORGET, MY DEAR MR. QUINN, THAT YOU--
--LIKE THIS MISSHAPEN QUINN-THING I PLUCKED FROM THE BRINY DEEP OF SPACETIME AND BROUGHT HERE FOR YOUR LITTLE BODY-SWAP CHARADE--
--DO NOT BELONG HERE.
AND YOUR ACTIONS DO NOT INCLINE ME TO SEND YOU HOME.
EVER.
CASS. HE'S RIGHT.
IF YOU DO THIS-- EVEN IF WE USED ALL OF E.M.P.I.R.E.'S RESOURCES-- I COULDN'T SEND YOU BACK.
HE HAS THE FAKEBOOK, YOU KNOW?
LISTEN TO THE LITTLE ROBOT PIMP, QUINN!
YOU CROSS THIS LINE, YOU'LL NEVER GET HOME!
...
... YEAH, I KNOW.
SSSSSIGH AS YOU WISH.
DON'T THINK I'M NOT GONNA SPEND MY WHOLE FORTUNE AND THE REST OF MY LIFE MAKING YOU REGRET IT.
AND WE'LL SPEND THE REST OF OURS STOPPING YOU.
BUT PLEASE TRY, MYSTERIOUS MAN OF BANDAGES!
THIS WOULD BE AN EXCITING CHALLENGE FOR US TO OVERCOME TOGETHER!

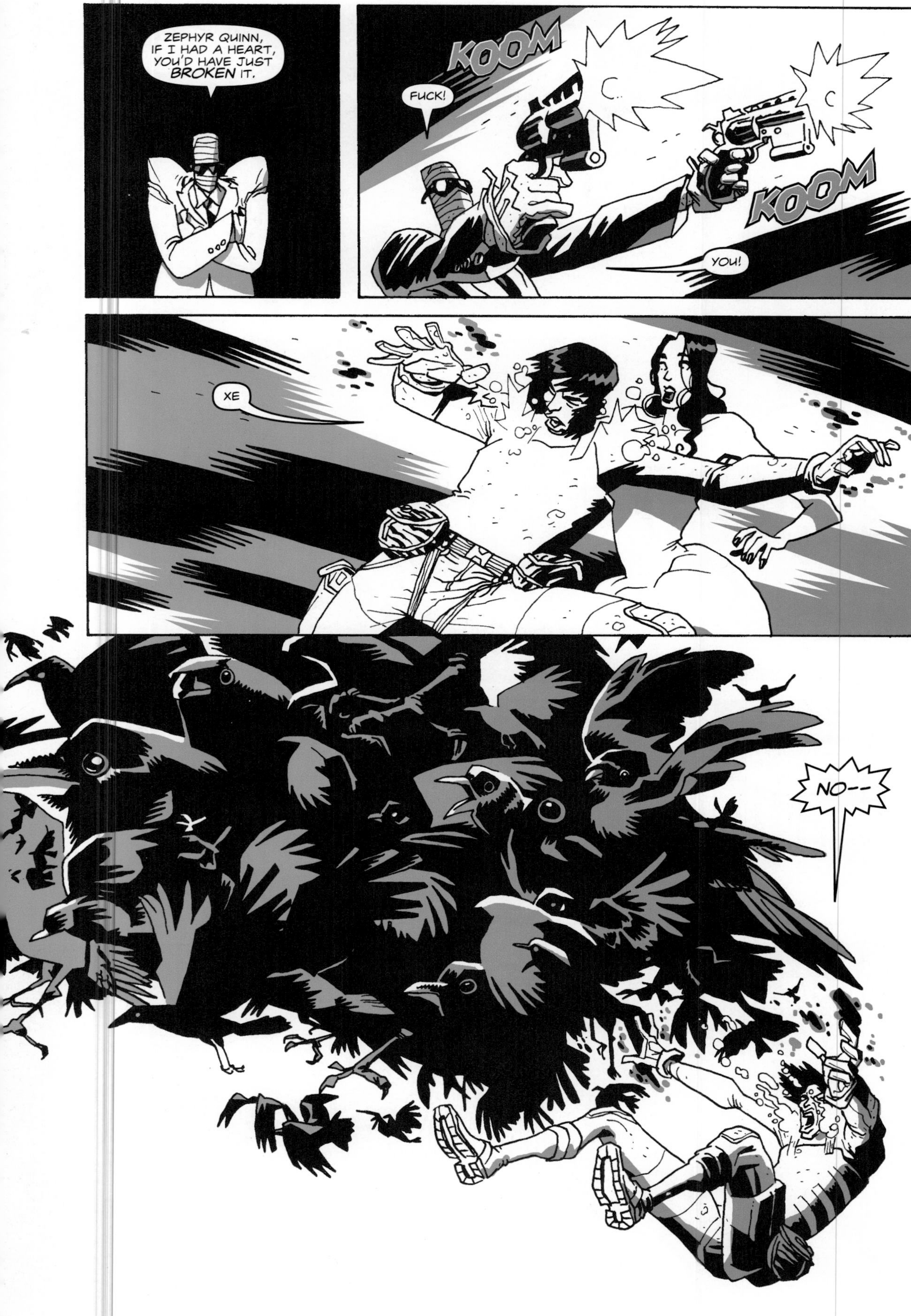
ZEPHYR QUINN, IF I HAD A HEART, YOU'D HAVE JUST BROKEN IT.
KOOM
FUCK!
KOOM
YOU!
XE
NO--

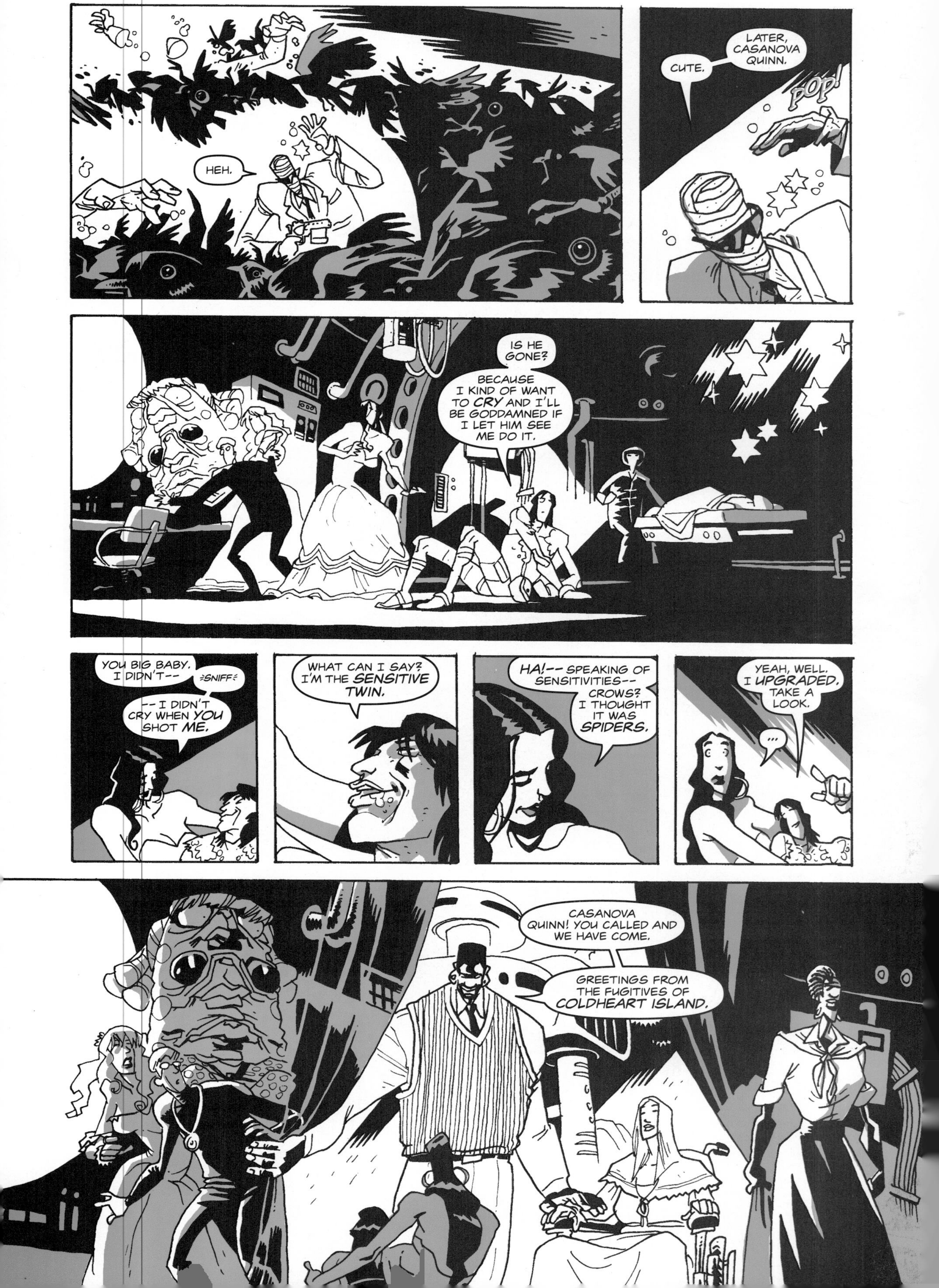
HEH.
LATER, CASANOVA QUINN.
CUTE.
POP!
IS HE GONE?
BECAUSE I KIND OF WANT TO CRY AND I'LL BE GODDAMNED IF I LET HIM SEE ME DO IT.
YOU BIG BABY. I DIDN'T--
SNIFF
-- I DIDN'T CRY WHEN YOU SHOT ME.
WHAT CAN I SAY? I'M THE SENSITIVE TWIN.
HA!-- SPEAKING OF SENSITIVITIES-- CROWS? I THOUGHT IT WAS SPIDERS.
YEAH, WELL. I UPGRADED. TAKE A LOOK.
...
CASANOVA QUINN! YOU CALLED AND WE HAVE COME.
GREETINGS FROM THE FUGITIVES OF COLDHEART ISLAND.

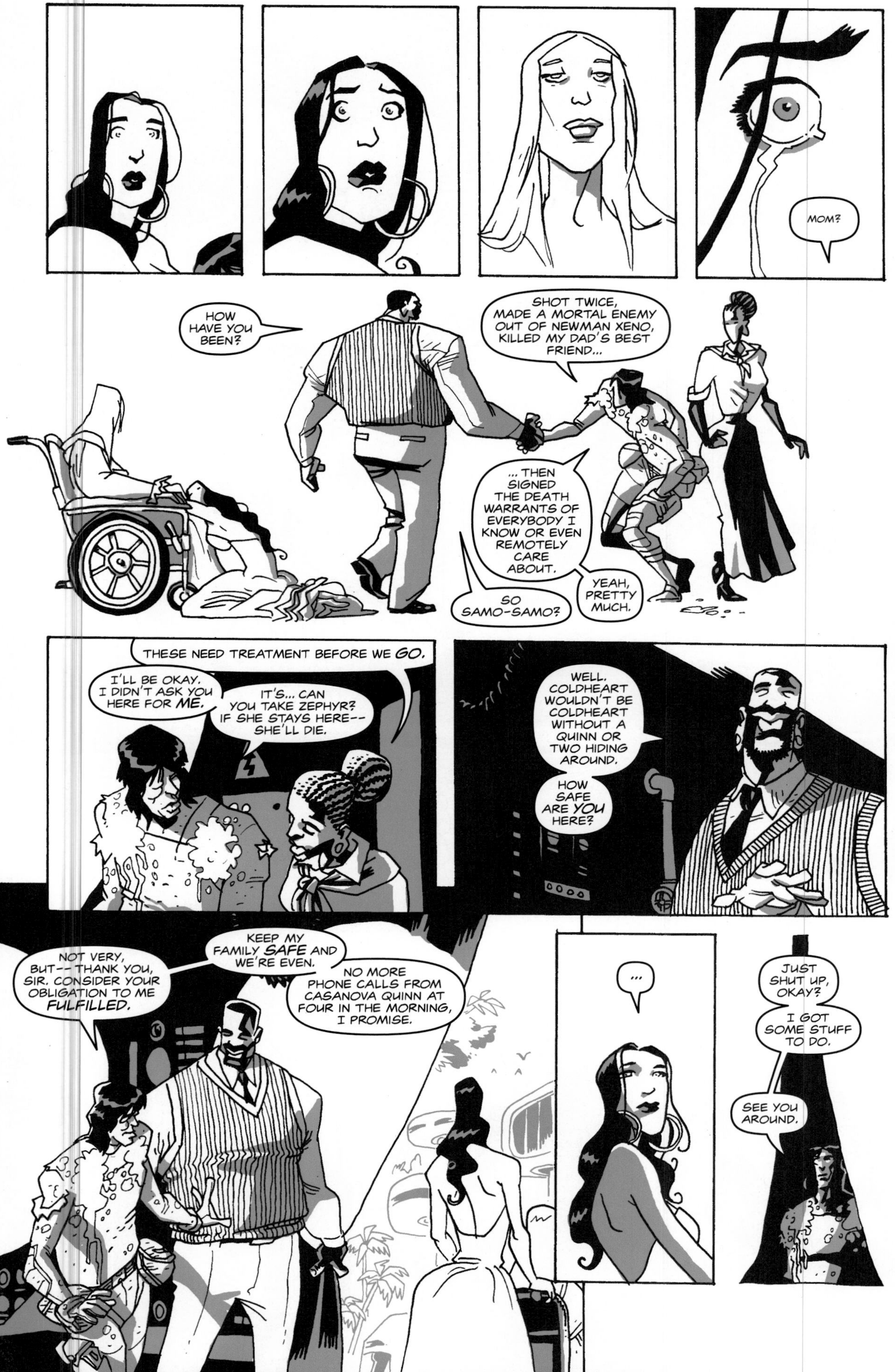
MOM?
HOW HAVE YOU BEEN?
SHOT TWICE, MADE A MORTAL ENEMY OUT OF NEWMAN XENO, KILLED MY DAD'S BEST FRIEND...
... THEN SIGNED THE DEATH WARRANTS OF EVERYBODY I KNOW OR EVEN REMOTELY CARE ABOUT.
SO SAMO-SAMO?
YEAH, PRETTY MUCH.
THESE NEED TREATMENT BEFORE WE GO.
I'LL BE OKAY. I DIDN'T ASK YOU HERE FOR ME.
IT'S... CAN YOU TAKE ZEPHYR? IF SHE STAYS HERE-- SHE'LL DIE.
WELL. COLDHEART WOULDN'T BE COLDHEART WITHOUT A QUINN OR TWO HIDING AROUND.
HOW SAFE ARE YOU HERE?
NOT VERY, BUT-- THANK YOU, SIR. CONSIDER YOUR OBLIGATION TO ME FULFILLED.
KEEP MY FAMILY SAFE AND WE'RE EVEN.
NO MORE PHONE CALLS FROM CASANOVA QUINN AT FOUR IN THE MORNING, I PROMISE.
...
JUST SHUT UP, OKAY?
I GOT SOME STUFF TO DO.
SEE YOU AROUND.

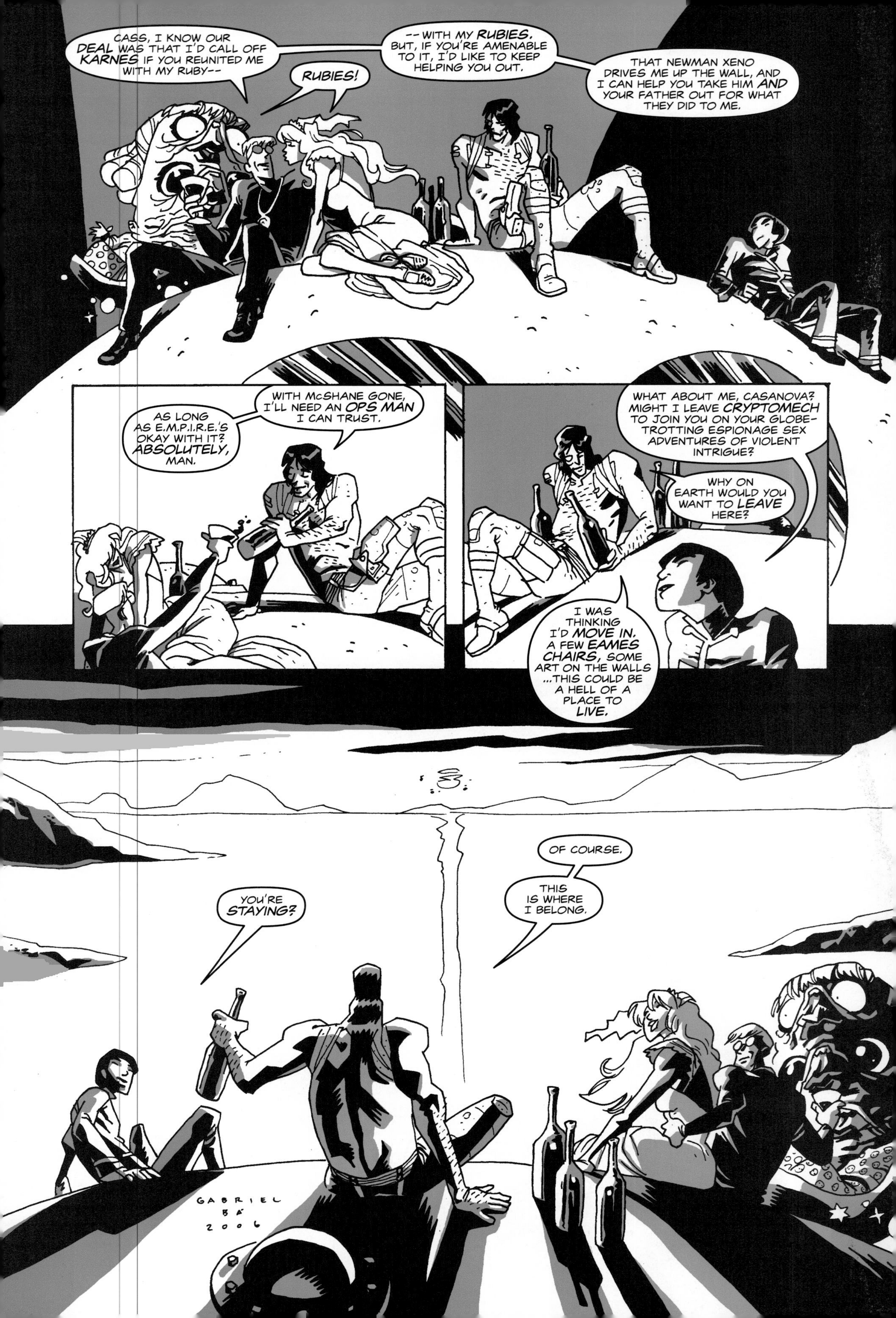
CASS, I KNOW OUR DEAL WAS THAT I'D CALL OFF KARNES IF YOU REUNITED ME WITH MY RUBY--
RUBIES!
--WITH MY RUBIES. BUT, IF YOU'RE AMENABLE TO IT, I'D LIKE TO KEEP HELPING YOU OUT.
THAT NEWMAN XENO DRIVES ME UP THE WALL, AND I CAN HELP YOU TAKE HIM AND YOUR FATHER OUT FOR WHAT THEY DID TO ME.
WITH McSHANE GONE, I'LL NEED AN OPS MAN I CAN TRUST.
AS LONG AS E.M.P.I.R.E.'S OKAY WITH IT? ABSOLUTELY, MAN.
WHAT ABOUT ME, CASANOVA? MIGHT I LEAVE CRYPTOMECH TO JOIN YOU ON YOUR GLOBE-TROTTING ESPIONAGE SEX ADVENTURES OF VIOLENT INTRIGUE?
WHY ON EARTH WOULD YOU WANT TO LEAVE HERE?
I WAS THINKING I'D MOVE IN. A FEW EAMES CHAIRS, SOME ART ON THE WALLS ...THIS COULD BE A HELL OF A PLACE TO LIVE.
YOU'RE STAYING?
OF COURSE.
THIS IS WHERE I BELONG.
GABRIEL BÁ 2006

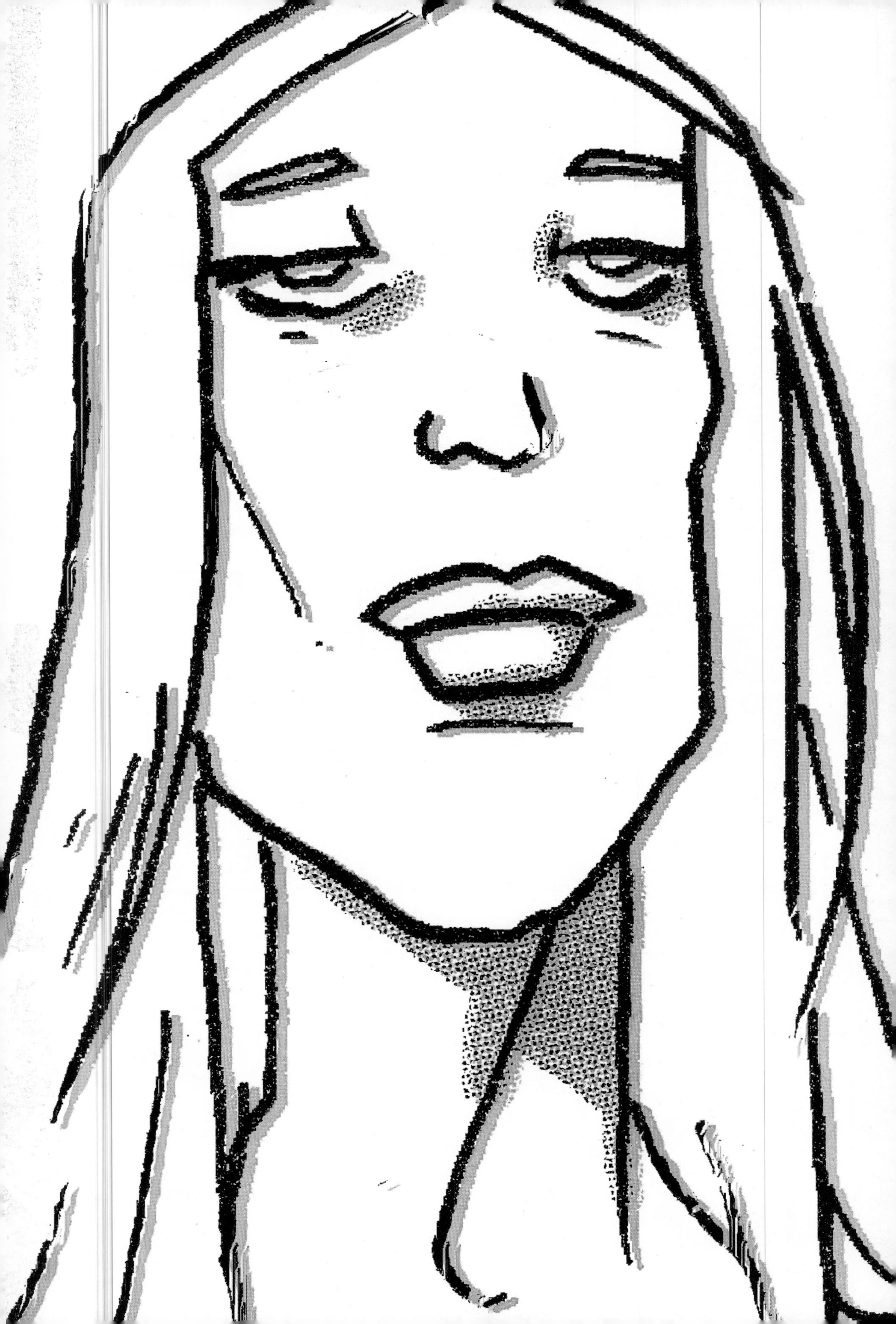

CASANOVA *sketchbook*

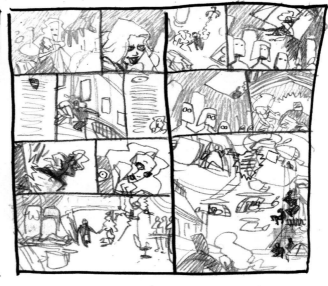

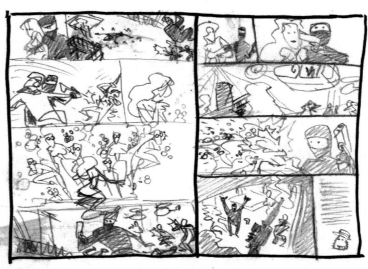

Gabriel Bá: *I love thumbnails, because I already know if the story will work when I make them.*

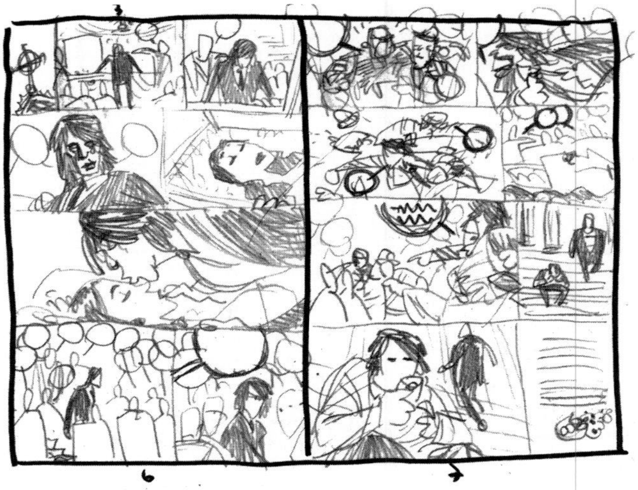
6
7

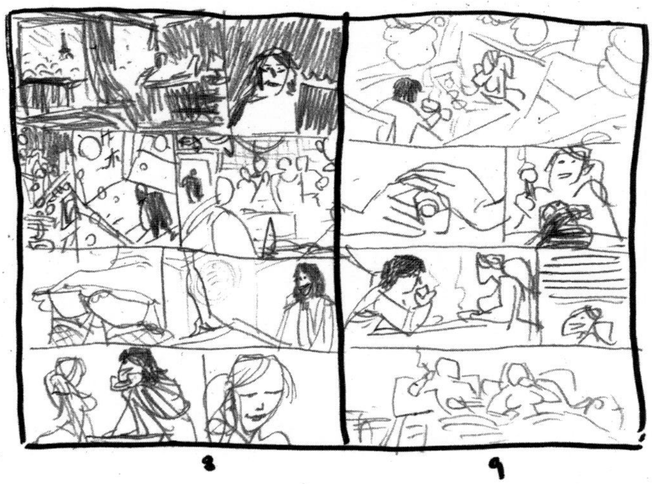
8
9

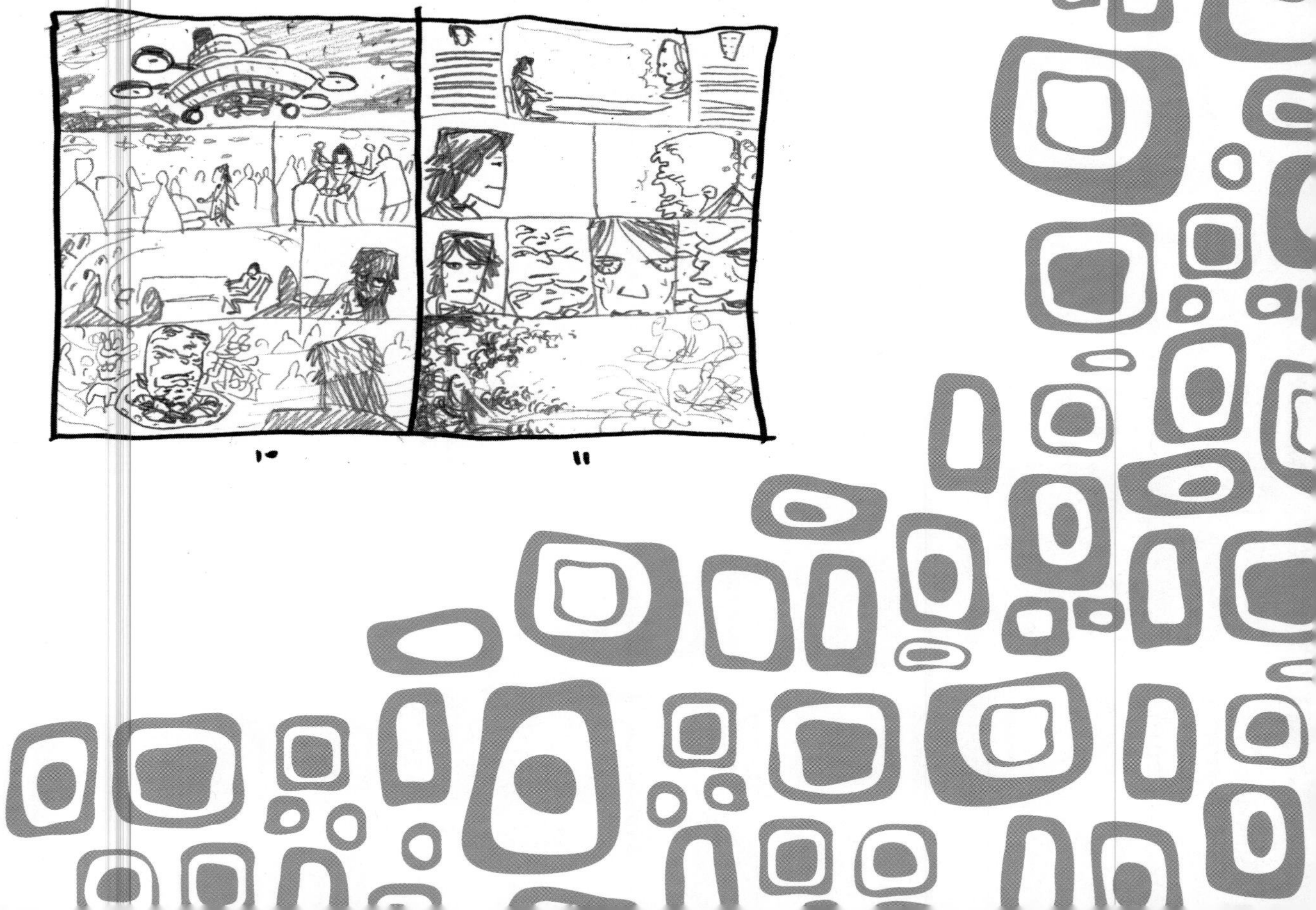
10
11

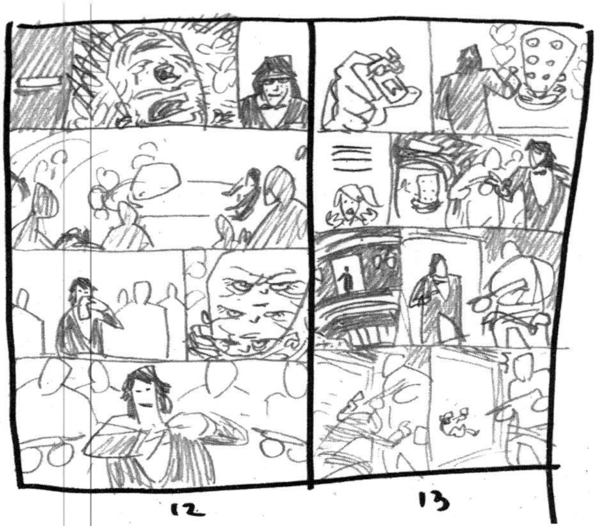

12 13

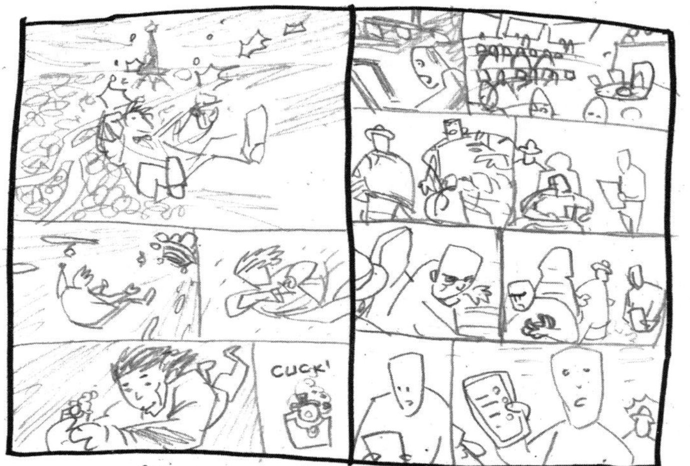
CLICK!

14 15

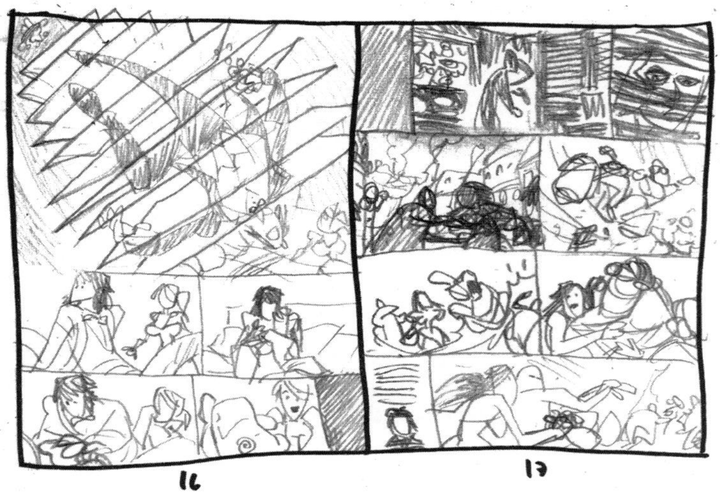

16 17

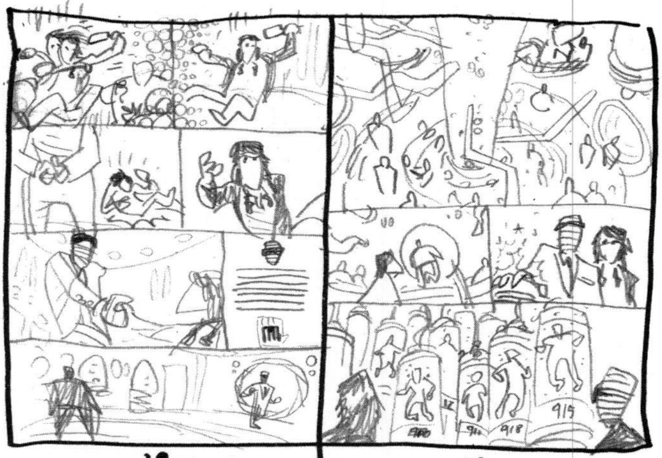

18 19

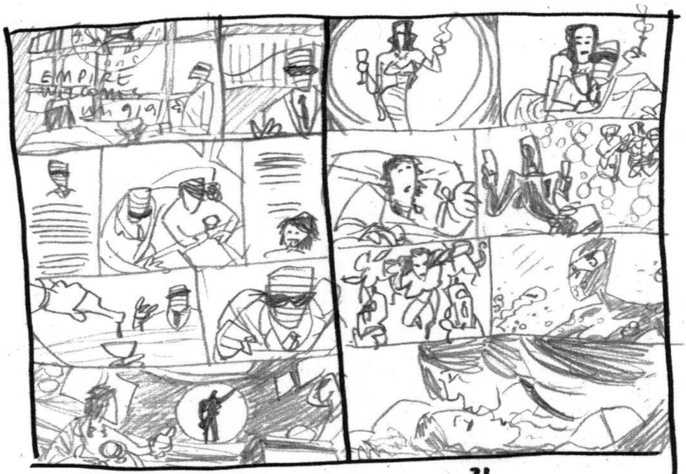
EMPIRE

20 21

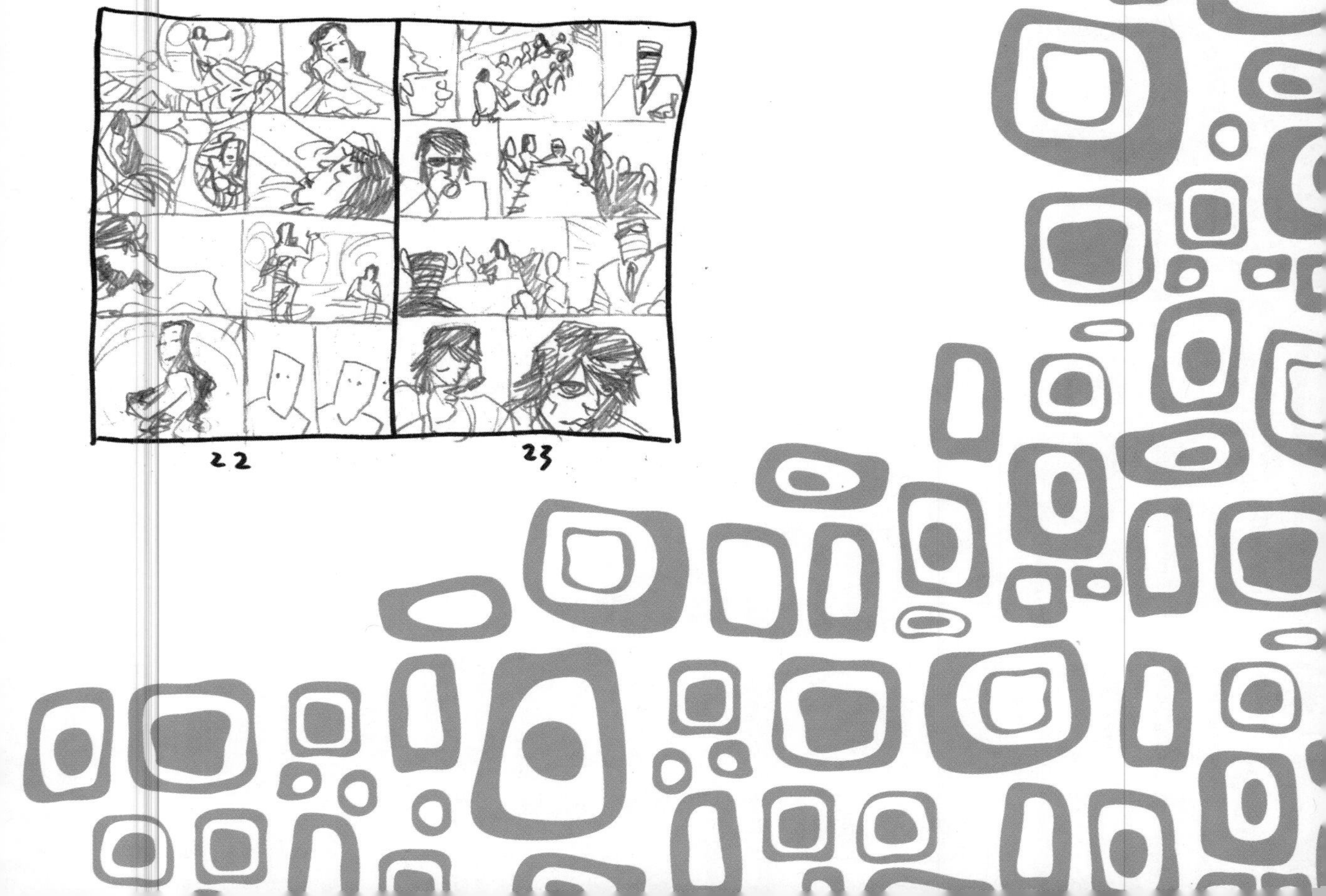

22 23

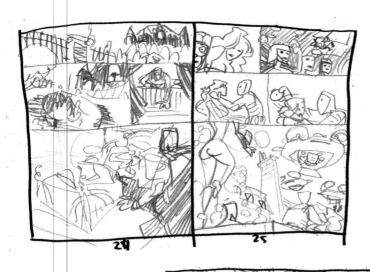

24

25

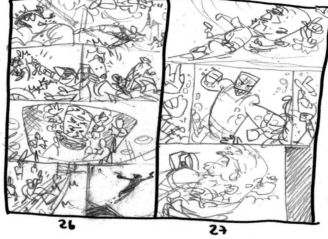

26

27

EXECUTION DAYS
MATT FR.
G. BA

28

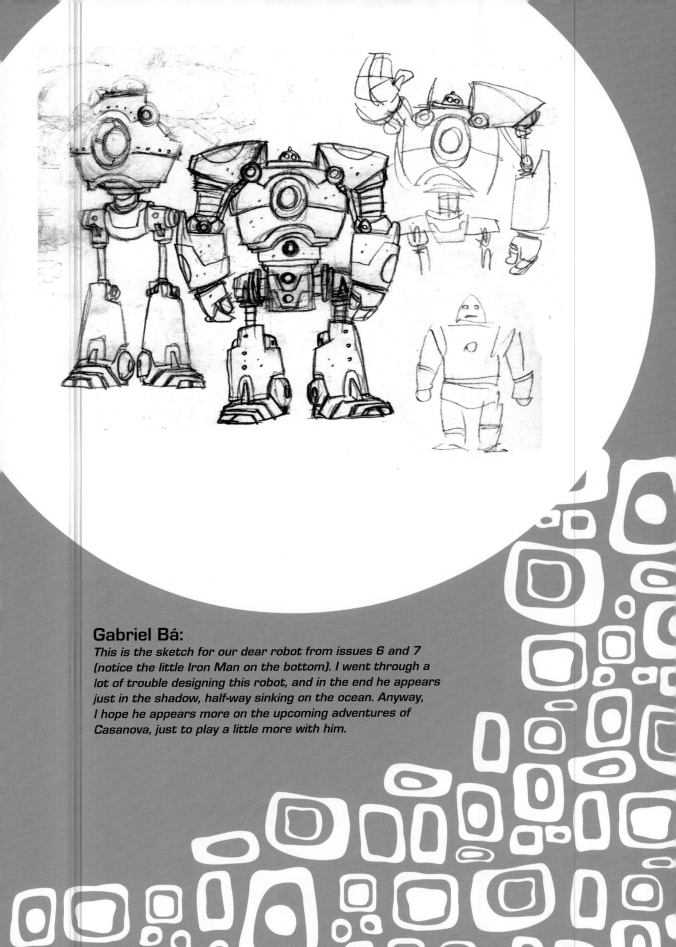

Gabriel Bá:

This is the sketch for our dear robot from issues 6 and 7 (notice the little Iron Man on the bottom). I went through a lot of trouble designing this robot, and in the end he appears just in the shadow, half-way sinking on the ocean. Anyway, I hope he appears more on the upcoming adventures of Casanova, just to play a little more with him.

CASANOVA

Cover Gallery

Gabriel Bá:
Fábio (Moon, Bá's twin brother) was the original CASANOVA cover artist, because he had always liked to do covers and it had never really been my thing. So these are the first studies he did for cover ideas or pinups.

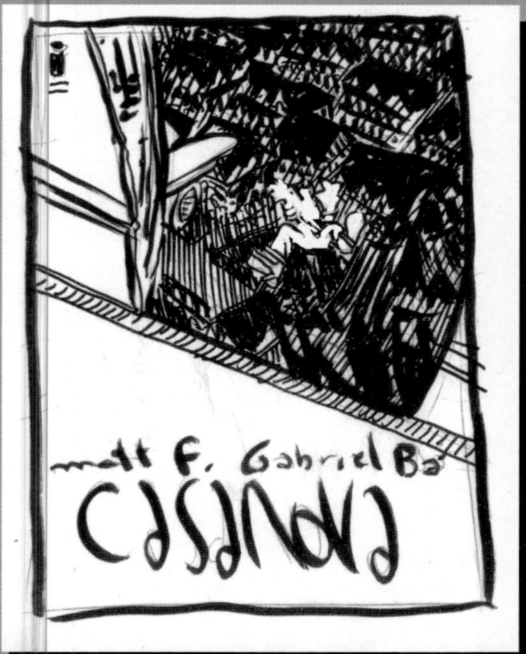
matt F. Gabriel Bá
CASANOVA

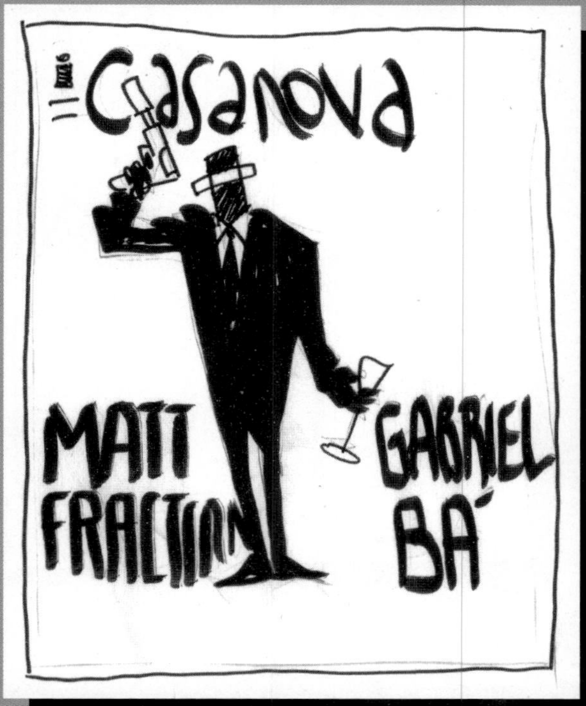
Casanova
MATT FRACTION
GABRIEL BÁ

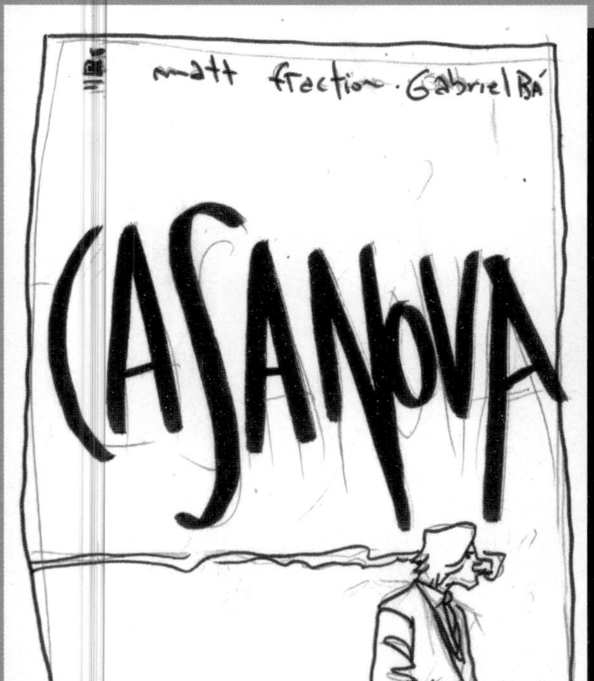
matt fraction. Gabriel Bá
CASANOVA

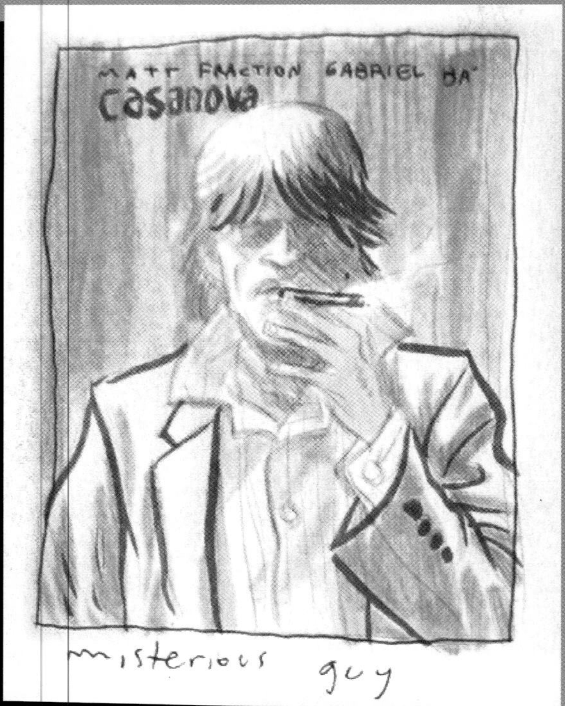
MATT FRACTION GABRIEL BÁ
CASANOVA
misterious guy

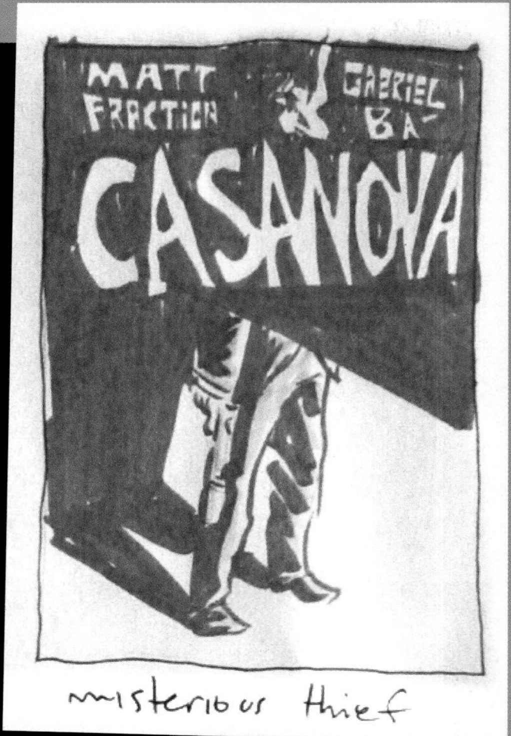
MATT FRACTION
GABRIEL BÁ
CASANOVA
misterious thief

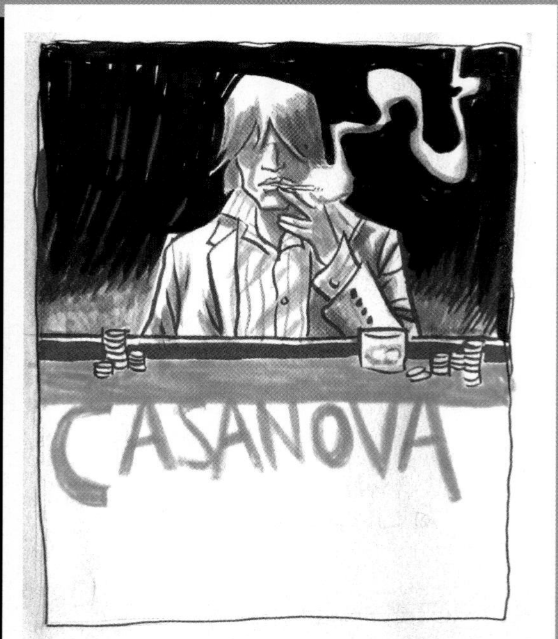
CASANOVA

Here it is, the sketch that finally sang the right song to Fábio. It has a good composition and nice color choices. All the elements from the story are there. The checkers board on the back represents gambling at Berserko's Casino. E.M.P.I.R.E. is written within those stars to give its governmental status. We have that hand with W.A.S.T.E. written on its fingers and the hands making kung-fu signs. They'll blend into the same thing on the final version. And we have Paris, just because we though it would appear more often throughout the story. Since the very first sketch, Fábio made the stylized red-outline white gun with silencer. That's the only thing that survived when I took over the covers.

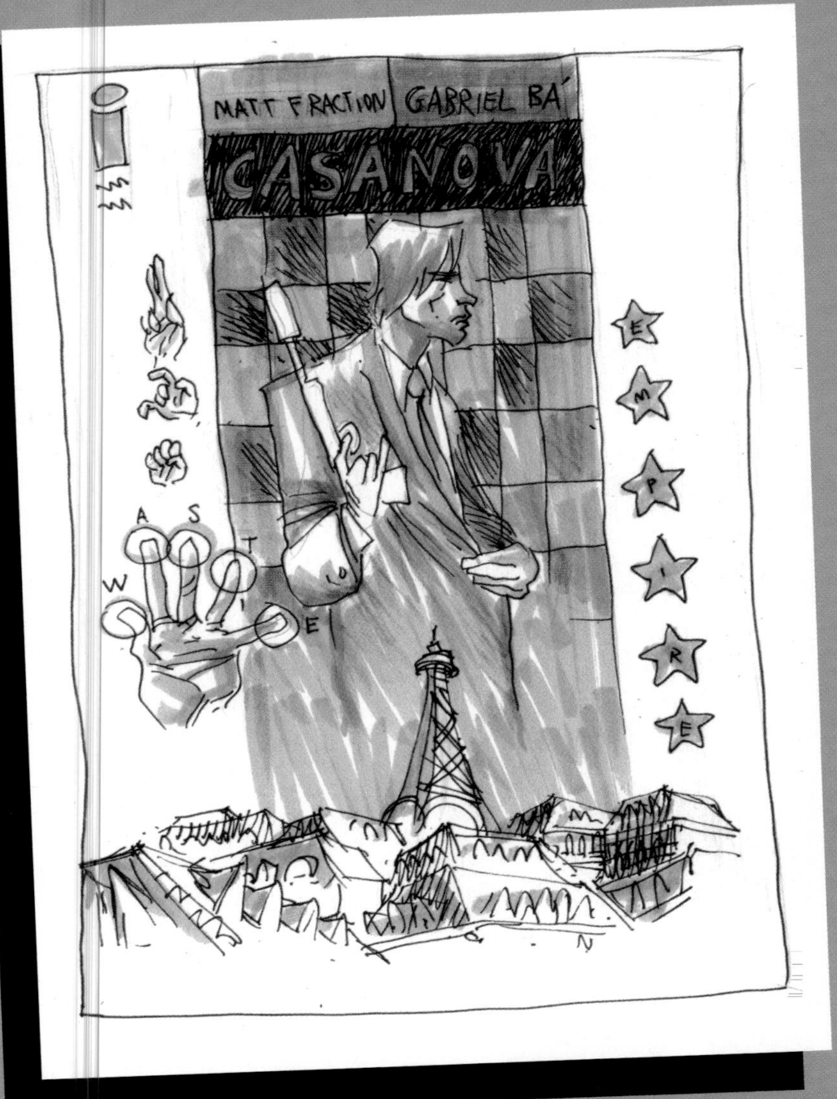
MATT FRACTION
GABRIEL BÁ
CASANOVA
E M P I R E
W A S T E

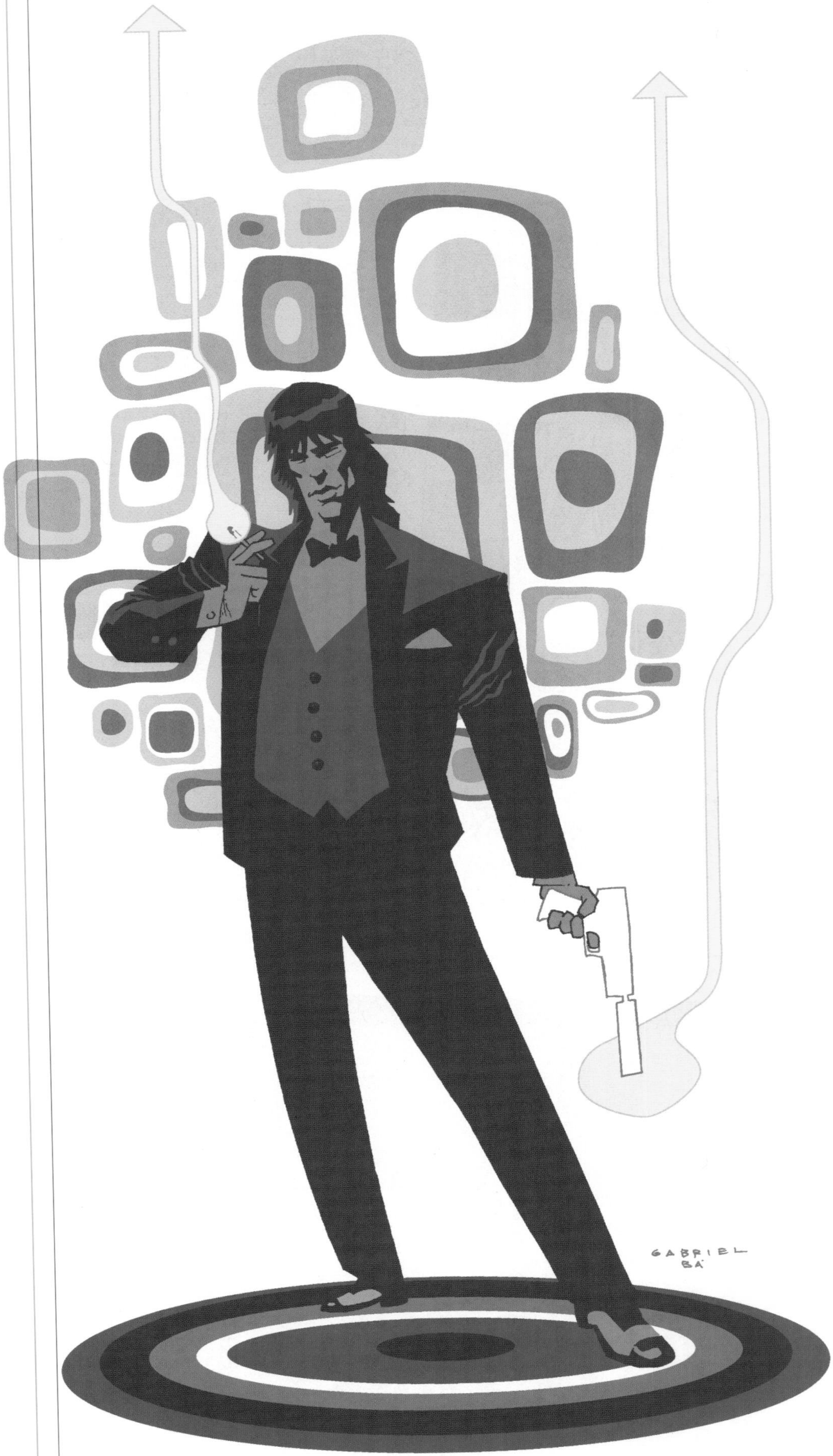
GABRIEL
BÁ

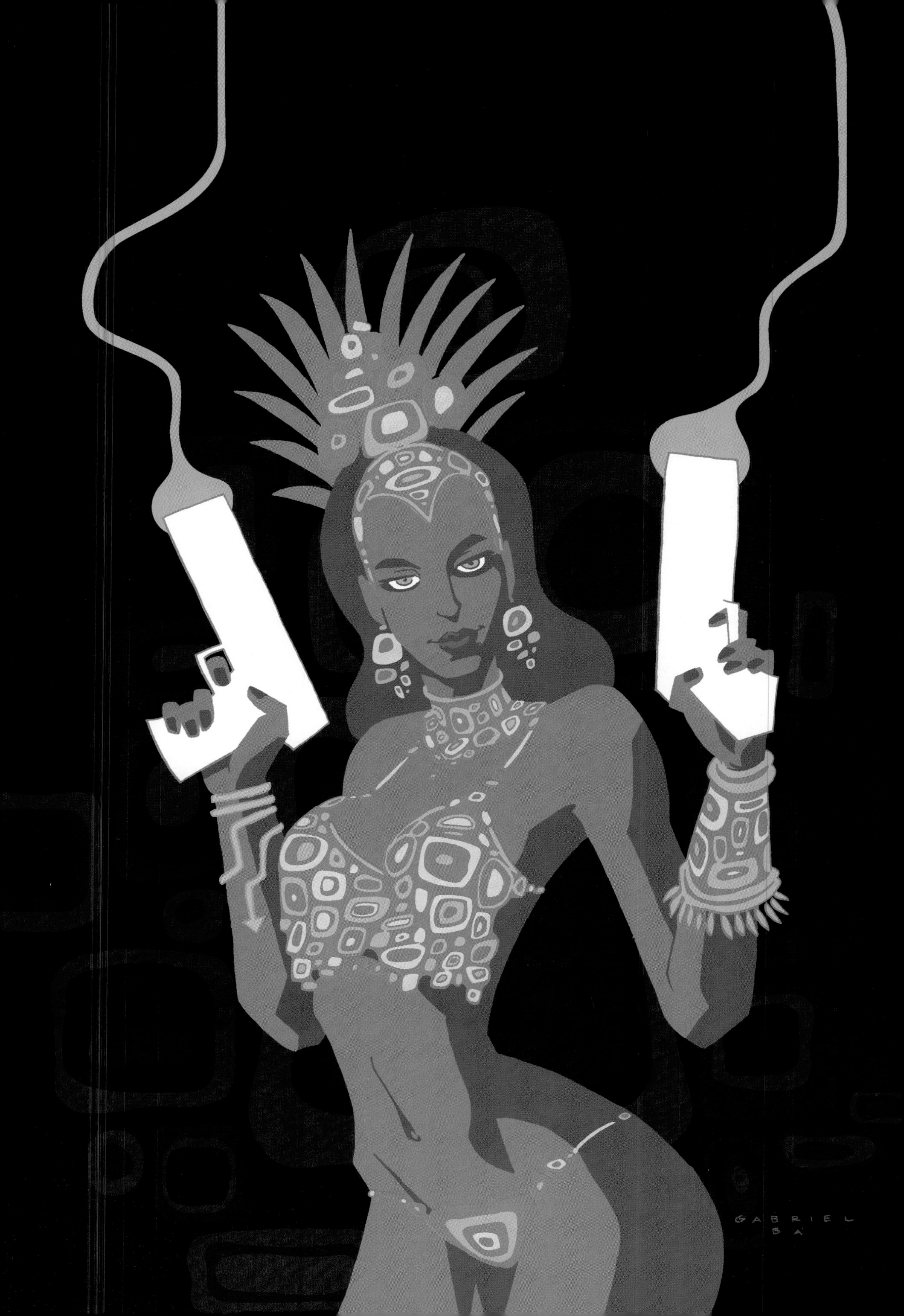
GABRIEL
BÁ

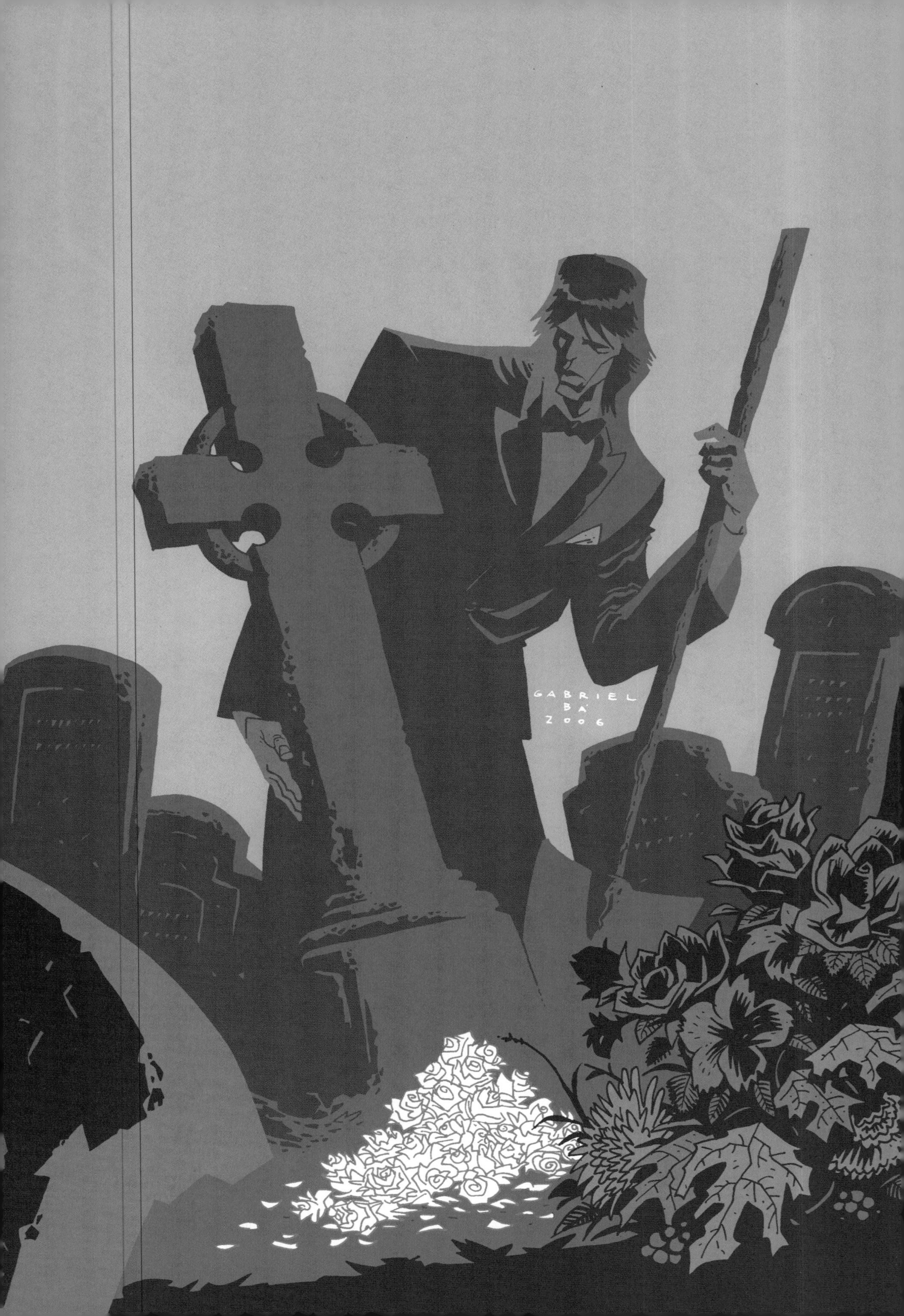
GABRIEL
BÁ
2006

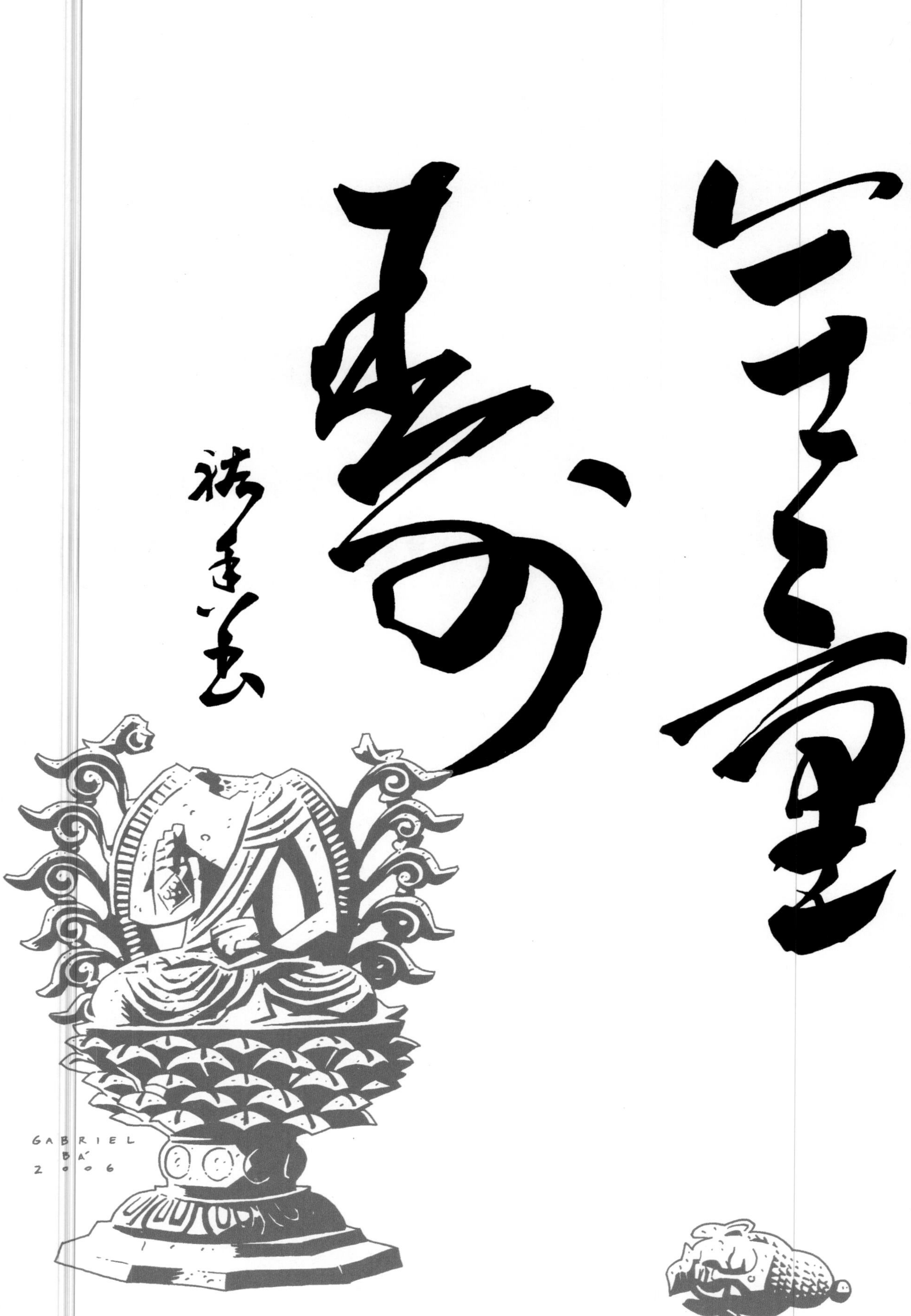
GABRIEL BÁ 2006

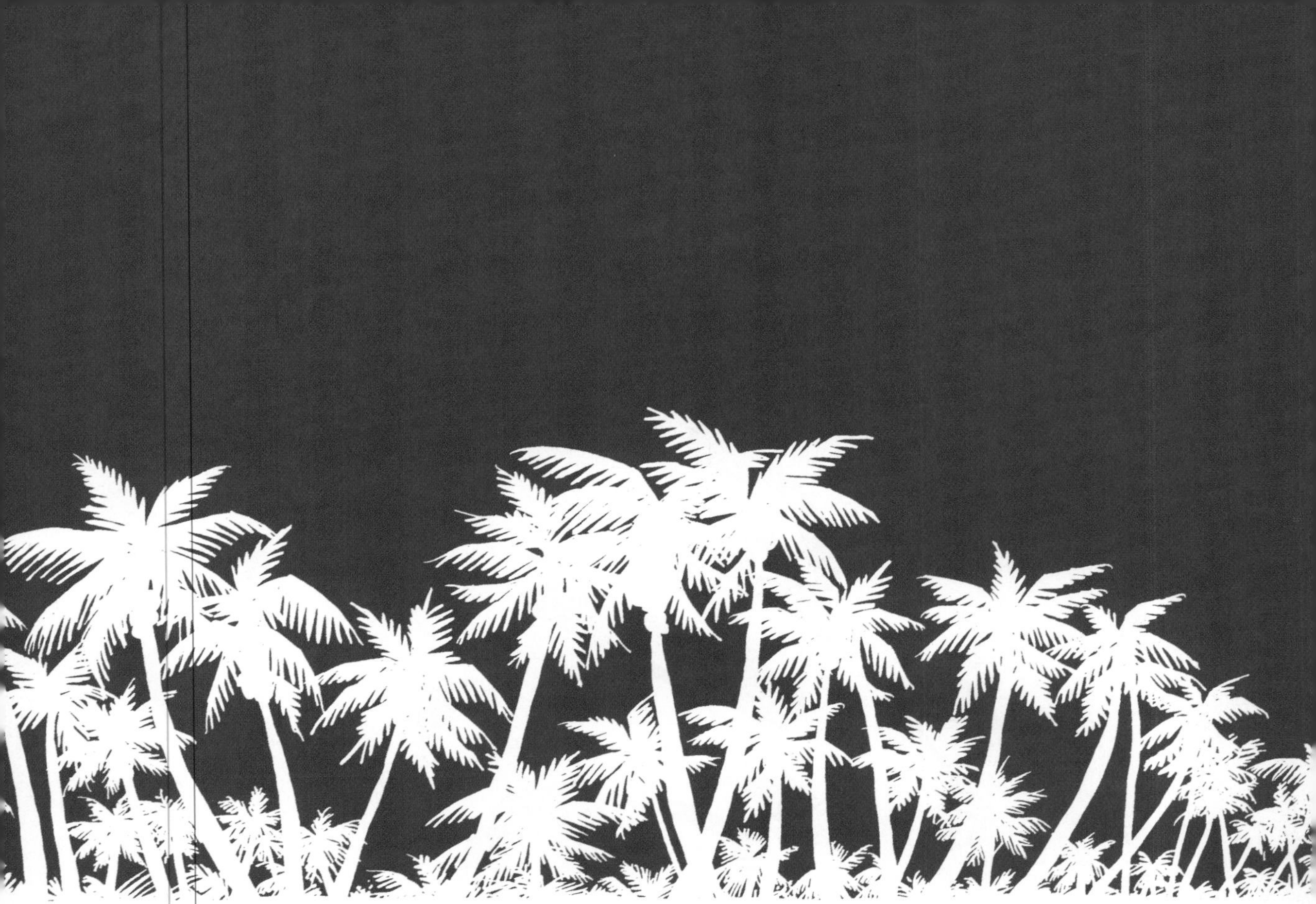

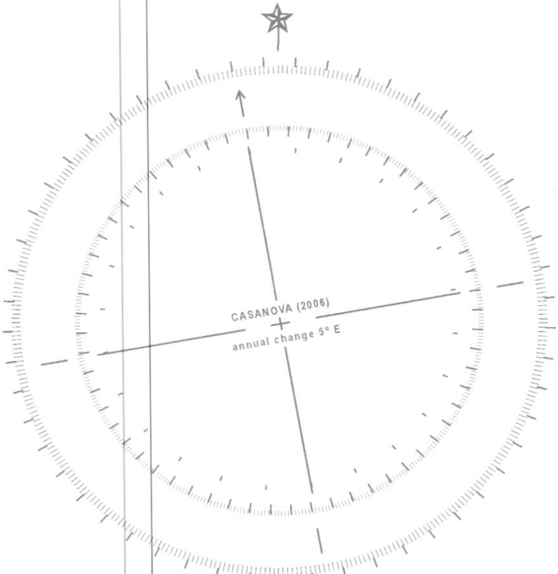
CASANOVA (2006)
annual change 5° E

0 1 2 3 4 5
0 1000 2000 3000 4000 5000 6000 7000 8000

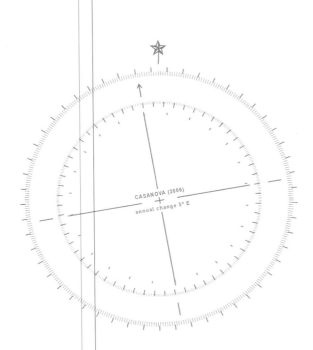

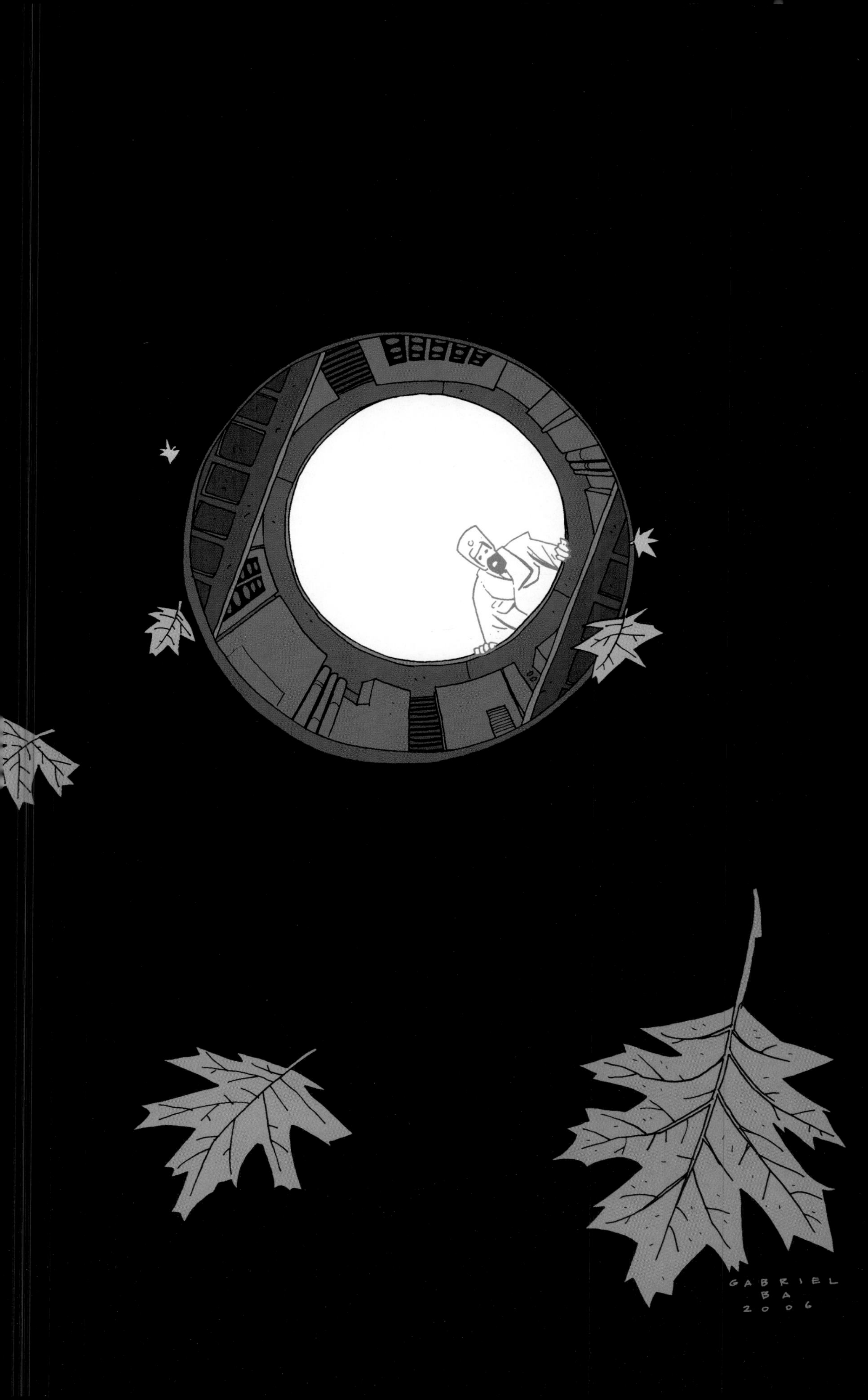
GABRIEL
BA
2006

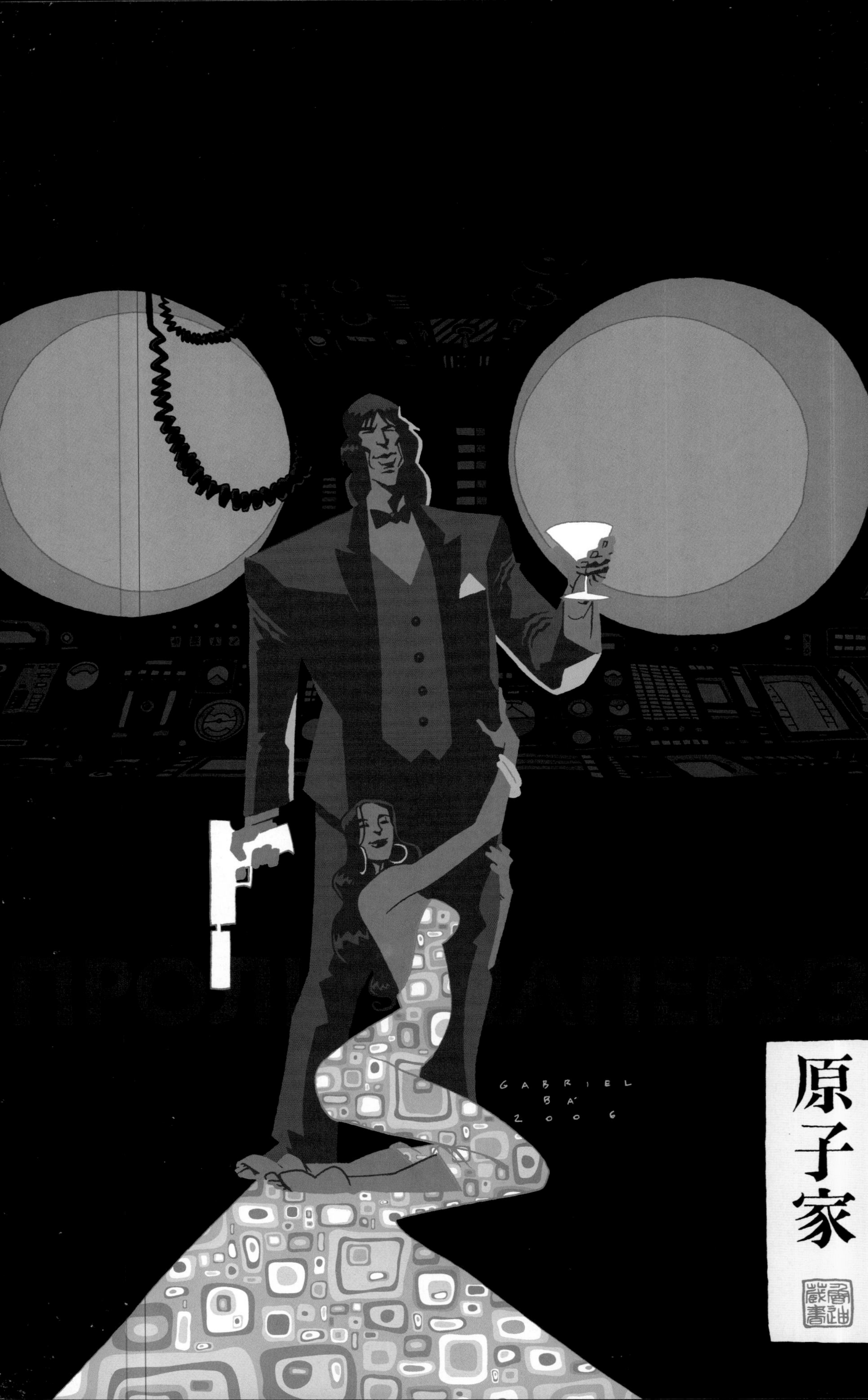
GABRIEL BÁ 2006
原子家